Mission Improbable

Richard Rosenthal

Mission Improbable
A PIECE OF THE SOUTH AFRICAN STORY

WITH A FOREWORD BY DEPUTY PRESIDENT THABO MBEKI

David Philip Publishers
Cape Town   Johannesburg

First published in Southern Africa by David Philip Publishers (Pty) Ltd, 208 Werdmuller Centre, Claremont, 7708 South Africa

ISBN 0-86486-390-X

Printed by ABC Press, 21 Kinghall Avenue, Epping, Cape Town

Contents

Foreword by Thabo Mbeki, Deputy President

This book, which is about the negotiated resolution of 'the apartheid problem', is published four years after our country held its first democratic elections.

As I read the manuscript, I was taken aback by the disturbing impact of the harsh truth it conveys, that the future which so many strove to bring about stands, still, cheek by jowl with the past, from which we all sought to distance ourselves.

The continuity from the past to the future is not only represented by the fact of a cast of dramatis personae who, despite their changing costumes, are as much part of the prologue as they are of the epilogue of the tale which Richard Rosenthal tells.

That intertwining of what was and will be, is conveyed also by the fact of the stubbornness and stability of the ideas and ideologies of the players on our national stage, which seems to give a lie to what all of us have believed we know, that a leap across the chasm occurred in April 1994.

The voices of the ghosts remain the voices of the living.

In addition to everything else it is, post-apartheid South Africa continues to be a battlefield of the old intellectual notions and rude passions, whose inevitable outcome of conflict, then, Richard Rosenthal sought to end, through his own 'creative, and seemingly eccentric struggle against the ongoing myths'.

If you listen carefully to the cacophony of the dialogue of 1998, through an ear attuned to listening and hearing, you will capture the living echo of the voices of 1988, which Richard Rosenthal records so faithfully.

What this must say to those who have ears to hear is that the conflict he sought to end, ten years ago, requires still in the 'new South Africa' its own Don Quixotes.

Richard Rosenthal arrived at our own doorstep an unknown traveller, so to speak, but to whom we could not say – traveller, pass by!

And so we detained him for a little while during his own life journey, so that we could hear what he had to say.

What he said, as recorded in this book, made sense because it gave hope that our country's political leaders and organisations, including our own, could, at last, speak to one another to end the agony.

At some point during the period of the end of the 1980s of which Richard Rosenthal speaks, Oliver Tambo told me that one of his nightmares was that one day our adversaries would communicate a message to us – which we would fail to understand – that they were ready to talk to us about a peaceful settlement.

We would not understand this message because of the gulf that separated the oppressed from the oppressor.

Thus would our country pay the ultimate price for the walls created by the apartheid system, when those walls made it impossible for us to hear one another, as the message was communicated that the walls must come down!

As we pondered the message of the traveller, we wondered whether his was the voice which Oliver Tambo had feared that he and we might, one day, not be able to hear and understand.

And so we stood still for a while so that we could listen!

And the message we heard was, indeed, the message that Oliver Tambo had known would come.

We had known that it might come in a jumbled and contradictory form. But that it came at all, even in such a form, meant that we had finally moved out of the years when a combination of the dementia of racial superiority and the deification of force had convinced the regime of apartheid that it could rule for a millennium.

A South African who dared to care had, by his daring, obliged the captains of apartheid to take another step forward towards the inevitable negotiated resolution of the conflict in our country.

Even as he despaired when Pretoria told him that he should end his initiative, we thought it important that Richard Rosenthal should nevertheless convey our views to our adversaries, to help them to extricate themselves from the quagmire of their confusion.

To read this short history now, recalling a particular episode, also has an impact very different from the somewhat depressing one I have written of, suggesting that we have not progressed very far from our past.

In the end, the tale that Richard Rosenthal tells speaks of the inspiring fact that we have heroes and heroines in our midst who, even now, will rise and make their own efforts to ensure that our country evolves into a society of happiness, peace and prosperity for all.

Thank God that Richard Rosenthal dared to try and that he lived to tell the story, so that each one of us may also know that to care is to dare!

Acknowledgments

I wish to record my deep gratitude for the friendship and encouragement of so many people who shared with me a part of this extraordinary journey. Many of them are mentioned by name in the text, but there are others who are not identified. I hope that they will all accept this modest token of my appreciation.

It is also appropriate that I once again formally record my appreciation to the Government of Switzerland and its representatives, including the State Secretary, Ambassadors, and officers of the Federal Department of Foreign Affairs, for their practical and moral support in this endeavour – but most importantly, for their personal friendship and empathy.

Grateful acknowledgments are made for the use of extracts quoted from *Tomorrow is Another Country* by Allister Sparks (Hill & Wang, New York, and Struik Book Distributors, Cape Town 1994); and from the other books specified in the text.

This book is dedicated to my wonderful family – Hilary, Caroline and Jonathan – who shared my anxieties, dreams and disappointments, and who kept the 'secret' all these many years.

Dear Mr Botha

It all began with a letter.

On the morning of 23 September 1987, I walked up The Avenue that marks the boundary between the old Kompaniej Gardens and the Houses of Parliament. Under the watchful gaze of armed guards, I approached the wrought-iron gates, recently raised and reinforced to further secure the offices of the President. Having explained my purpose, I was allowed through and rang the brass bell at the front door of Tuynhuys, where I delivered a letter marked 'Personal & Confidential' addressed to Mr P W Botha, State President.

Dear Mr Botha

I have decided to write to you in view of my wish to contribute in some constructive manner to the development of a process, which could lead to an end to the State of Emergency and a peaceful future for our country.

It has become increasingly apparent to me that the success or failure of our efforts to find a solution to the present impasse, will determine not only the quality of our personal lives in the future, but the course of history and the fate of millions of people on this sub-continent.

For some twenty-five years I have practised as an Attorney of the Supreme Court, and am currently a Senior Partner of one of the largest law firms in Cape Town. In this capacity I have acted for a large number of clients, both individual and corporate, and have been responsible for complex negotiations and litigation involving a broad-based clientele, which has included both the public and private sectors.

By way of background, may I state that I am a member of no political party or similar organisation, nor do I hold any pre-determined 'point of view', implying a prescriptive solution to these complex issues. However, I have come to believe :

1. That no 'independent' constitutional initiative can succeed in making a significant contribution, unless it is undertaken with your concurrence.

2. That the most impelling need at the present time, seems to be to find a means to facilitate an exploratory process, leading to meaningful negotiations, without foreign interference.

3. That one of the essential preconditions could be the facilitation of a few South Africans who stand outside the party political situation, but who are able and willing to offer their personal integrity and credibility to the success of a delicate exploratory process.

It would be most presumptuous to suggest that I am the possessor of all such necessary qualities. However, I believe that I may have certain attributes which could be of assistance. Thus, over a long period I have been involved in professionally representing a wide spectrum of persons and organisations concerned with political and social issues. Throughout my professional career, I have been at great pains to maintain my professional independence and neither to join nor to become identified with any such body as I may from time to time have represented. In the result, I believe that I am reasonably well known and trusted by a wide spectrum of individuals and organisations, whose involvement with such process is problematical but desirable.

I have no illusions that there are likely to be persons who will view any such offer of involvement on my part as incomprehensible, and even perhaps disloyal to their perceived best interests. However, this is a risk which, after much thought, I am willing to accept. I believe that there may also be others whom I could conceivably influence to participate in a serious negotiating process, and it is to this end that I am prepared to lend my efforts.

With deference to the great sensitivity of any such initiative, I have taken care to discuss this matter with no other person, and I will maintain such confidentiality. I anticipate that you might wish to know more about me and my background, and I would be entirely willing to make available any such further information as you may deem appropriate in this regard.

In brief, what I am suggesting, with all due deference, is that I could conceivably be of some assistance in the initial delicate stages of the preparatory work leading to the establishment of a successful negotiating process. May I state clearly, that I do not seek any official appointment or office, and consider that this would detract from my independence and efficacy at this stage.

However, I make this offer in the utmost good faith, and in the hope that it could prove to be of assistance. Should it be of interest, then I would value the opportunity to discuss the matter further, as you may deem appropriate.

Yours sincerely
Richard Rosenthal

It had taken all of five months and innumerable discarded drafts, before I had felt brave enough to sign the fateful letter. Earlier that morning, I had in fact telephoned the President's secretary to confirm once more how the

President should be addressed. 'Just Mr Botha,' she assured me. 'That's quite enough!' I was manifestly inexperienced in the niceties of communicating with Heads of State. Now that the die was cast, I awaited Mr Botha's response with some considerable trepidation.

I had little doubt that he might see my proposition as provocative and presumptuous. After all, I had neither a mandate nor a constituency, and was presuming to engage the State President in person – *die Groot Krokodil* (the Great Crocodile) – in the midst of a State of Emergency, on the issue that lay at the heart of the crisis which was tearing the country apart – the issue of negotiations.

Yet, however improbable the idea, and however daunting the President's fabled rage, I had concluded that the situation had become so desperate that I must risk his ridicule or his wrath. In fact, the wild idea of my initiating some discreet overture to the ANC had been germinating in my mind for a number of months. Despite the improbability of its acceptance, and the many compelling arguments against atttempting such an unlikely mission, it seemed to present the only faint glimmer of light in an otherwise dark situation. The country was sliding inexorably towards anarchy or civil war, and I decided that the concept needed to be tested, even if it offered little more than an extravagant hope.

One had no cause to doubt the views of Mr Botha on this issue. He had made his views on this, as on most other issues, abundantly clear. On six separate occasions during the nine years of his political tenure, P W Botha had offered Nelson Mandela his freedom, but subject in each instance to unacceptable conditions. Thus, in January 1985, he had made his most recent offer – provided that Mandela 'unconditionally rejects violence as a political instrument'. This offer, like all the others that had preceded it, was unambiguously rejected by Mandela, whose response on this occasion had been read by his daughter Zinzi to a mass rally in Soweto on Sunday 10 February . He had pointed out that the ANC turned to violence 'only when all other forms of resistance were no longer open to us'. He asserted that, in the circumstances prevailing in South Africa, it would be more appropriate if the undertaking to renounce violence came in the first instance from Mr Botha himself, adding, 'Only free men can negotiate. Prisoners cannot enter into contracts.' President Botha responded that it was no longer the Government which stood in the way of Mr Mandela's freedom. 'It is he himself!' he asserted.

Dr Frederick van Zyl Slabbert, Leader of the Official Opposition, commented on this ideological impasse in his political treatise, *The System and the Struggle*: 'In effect, the State President has said, not only to Mandela, but to the ANC, "If you give up violence, ie: the armed struggle, we can talk."

The response of Mandela as well as the ANC is an equally straightforward political one. In effect, they are saying to the State President, "If you give up apartheid, we will give up violence."'

My letter attempted to cut across this futile argument, and assumed that both parties, given a *bona fide* opportunity, would support the concept of negotiations, provided the proposal was genuine, and the agenda concerned the real issues of political power and democracy, and provided that neither the Government nor the ANC was called upon to make pre-emptive concessions, or compromise what each perceived as inviolable principles.

By September 1987, it was the view of many commentators that a strategic impasse had been reached in which neither party could achieve its objectives in the foreseeable future – the Botha Government could no more deliver peace, security, and prosperity, to its minority white constituency, than the ANC could deliver the dream of a just and democratic society to the black majority. As I thought about this ideological stalemate, I came to the conclusion that the capacity of both parties to frustrate the goals and objectives of the other might ironically create the very conditions that were necessary to release a deadlocked situation into one which might be transformed by negotiation. It was this sense of opportunity, born of frustration and despair, that finally impelled me to deliver my letter to the President.

In his authorised biography, *Stem uit die Wildernis*, Botha acknowledges that during this period he was being subjected to ever-increasing pressures, to unban the ANC and initiate negotiations. He states that such pressures came from many quarters, including the governments of the United States and Great Britain, and from foreign businesses, the media, civil rights organisations, the so-called Frontline States, and from a number of African leaders. However, it was Botha's view that the ANC and Mandela bore the primary responsibility for establishing the necessary preconditions for negotiations. This 'you first' attitude was exemplified by the President's address to the Transvaal National Party Congress in September 1985, when he stated that he was prepared to enter negotiations with any Party, provided it took place within a constitutional framework, and was not presaged by the threat of violence. Accordingly, the conditions set by Botha for a future dialogue were as follows: firstly, the ANC had to renounce its use of violence, without conditions or qualification, and give proof of having done so; secondly, it had to dissociate itself from the S A Communist Party and the Soviet Union; and thirdly, it had to commit itself to peaceful change through constitutional negotiations.

Soon afterwards at a public meeting in Springs on 24 October, the President had restated his terms. 'If the ANC wishes to talk with us, it must lay down its arms, put a stop to its terrorism, cease putting bombs in remote-controlled cars to explode in Pretoria and other urban areas, leading to the death of innocent people. It must stop its terrorism, its murder of innocent people in black suburbs, and free itself from international links with the Communist Party. Thereafter it should return, and engage in a constitutional debate.'

At the time of my letter to the President, a countrywide State of Emergency was in force, which had originated on 20 July 1985 and been reimposed on 12 June 1986. Unlike the previous Emergency, which had been applicable only to certain parts of the country (euphemistically named 'unrest areas'), the new Emergency would apply to the entire country, including what were termed the 'self-governing states', but excluding what were termed 'independent homelands'. In motivating a suspension of the ordinary civil law, Botha told Parliament that violence had assumed such proportions, that 'the ordinary laws of the country which are now on the statute book are insufficient to enable the Government to ensure the safety of the public and to maintain public order'. In familiar cadences, redolent with fascist logic, he claimed that the Government had at its disposal information 'concerning what is being planned for the coming days by radicals and revolutionary elements. This constitutes a real danger to all population groups in this country.' These were Mr Botha's views, and Mr Botha's views were essentially the views of the National Party, and of the Government.

The personal dominance of the President over the business of government had led me to conclude that no significant shift in Nationalist faith and doctrine was possible unless Botha, in the first instance, could be prevailed upon. In the near decade which had elapsed since his election as National Party leader, he had completely dominated the political topography, leading one of his biographers to describe his autocratic style as the 'Imperial Presidency'. Like some medieval potentate, Botha demanded virtual obeisance from friends and foes alike, and made short shrift of ideological deviance or independence of thought. He was not only titular Head of State, but also Executive head of Government, and Chairman of the all-important State Security Council (SSC).

This sinister cabal, ostensibly no more than an advisory body, in fact disposed of decisions and actions affecting every aspect of national life at its weekly meetings, which took place immediately prior to ordinary Cabinet meetings. In many respects, it superseded the role of Cabinet, and made nonsense of any pretence of accountability to Parliament. Through more than 500 'Joint Management Centres', the SSC exercised de facto hegemony at all levels of government, operating within a byzantine para-military bureaucracy known as the National Security Management System. Allister Sparks has observed in *Tomorrow is Another Country*, 'From the standpoint

of this militarized structure, white South Africa was engaged in a total war
for national survival against the forces of communism, spearheaded by the
ANC.' This was echoed by the apartheid government's head of Police,
General Johann van der Merwe, who in his evidence to the Truth and
Reconciliation Commission (TRC) said: 'There was an undeclared war ... It
was the responsibility of the authorities to defend the country.'

To understand my apprehensions upon delivering the letter, it is relevant
to recall some of the implications of this State of Emergency. The country
was effectively being governed at the will and whim of the President, who
in terms of the Public Safety Act was empowered to make such Regulations
'as appeared to him to be necessary or expedient'. Similar arbitrary and dra-
conian powers were vested in the Commissioner of Police, who was empowered to issue 'Orders' binding upon all members of the public and the
media. *Any* member of the Police, Prisons, or Defence Force, of whatever
rank, had the power summarily to detain *anyone* for a period of up to 14
days. The Emergency Regulations required only that the member of the
Force be of the opinion (right or wrong) that 'it was necessary for the main-
tenance of public order, or the safety of the public, or of that person, or for
the termination of the State of Emergency'. It is hardly surprising that these
powers vested in men of the character of Warrant Officer Jeffrey Benzien,
and his superior officers, ushered in a reign of torture and terror, that has
only gradually and grudgingly unfolded before the TRC.

To complete the trappings of the Police State, these arbitrary powers were
coupled with a right to interrogate, search, and give summary orders –
'without furnishing reasons, and without hearing any person'. If any order
was disobeyed, force could be used 'to prevent the suspected danger'. The
Emergency Regulations were meticulously drafted to prevent any judicial
interference, by stipulating that no court could hear proceedings against the
State or any person in the service of the State, if the issue related to an 'act
in good faith advised, commanded, ordered, directed or performed by any
person in carrying out his/her duties in terms of the Regulations...' The practical effect was to install a totalitarian regime in which people could be – and
were – detained, interrogated, tortured, and murdered – all on the basis of
untested opinion and suspicion, and frequently on the orders of the highest
authority in the land. The courts offered no protection, unless (impossible
task) *mala fides* could first be established and proved. Moreover, good faith
was to be presumed, unless the contrary could be proved.

By the time I delivered my letter to the State President, thousands had
been detained and were being held without trial, and without access to
lawyers, doctors, family or friends. Over a particular six-month period,
more than 25 000 people were reported as having been detained. The

Calvinist Government of President Botha saw itself as divinely appointed, and engaged in an apocalyptic 'total conflict' between Good and Evil. It propagated a 'holy war' psychosis. I realised that I was purporting to practise 'law', in a country where the fundamental principles of law, as it is generally understood, had been effectively negated. Increasingly, clients looked to lawyers to devise means of ameliorating the formidable wrath of the system. In reality, neither lawyers nor Courts had the ability, nor let it be said the courage or the will, to hold Government to account. I felt compromised by my own fears, by inertia, and a sense of paralysing impotence. Often one's best achievements amounted to little more than some trivial and temporary, albeit subjectively important, indulgence – like permission for a detainee to see a lawyer, have a visit from a spouse, or receive fresh clothing.

For many people, amongst them our own family, the turning point probably came that fateful night of 15 August 1985, when the nation gathered around its TV sets to listen to State President Botha make what had been promised as 'a major statement of policy'. Encouraged by government-supporting newspapers, there had been a general expectation of an historic announcement, which would serve as a watershed between the old and the new orders. *Die Burger* had predicted a few days earlier, 'Indications are growing daily stronger that a series of momentous announcements and policy adaptations are at hand.' Botha's speech was carried live from the venue of the annual Congress of the Natal Branch of the National Party meeting in Durban. I remember that evening vividly, as we sat together as a family, expectant and hopeful.

The 'Rubicon' speech would haunt Mr Botha to the end of his days. It was certainly, as promised, an epochal event, though not quite in the sense that had been anticipated or intended. With hindsight, it was probably the most self-destructive event of the eleven-year Botha regime. It led to the collapse of the currency on foreign exchange markets; the suspension of the Johannesburg Stock Exchange; a decision by foreign banks to call in existing credit, and to refuse new credit to either Government or the private sector. Inflation would rise to an historic 18,4 per cent, resulting in an unprecedented negative growth rate. Over the ensuing months, there would be an outflow of R10,46 billion on capital account. The economy had entered a state of siege.

It transpires that an alternative draft of this speech had been prepared, but was capriciously abandoned by Botha at the last moment. This alternative draft held out the prospect of Mandela's early release, it promised 'a process of negotiation', and announced the acceptance by Government of the principle 'that all our population groups must be jointly responsible for decision-making at all levels of government in matters of common concern, without domination by any one population group over another'. By contrast, Botha's chosen speech was truculent and bellicose. He pledged, 'I am not prepared to lead White South Africans and other minority groups on a road to abdication and suicide.' Ironically, the President retained the closing stanzas of the original version, which concluded portentously, 'I believe we are today crossing the Rubicon. There can be no turning back.' In one sense, of course, he was absolutely correct.

Helen Suzman MP has commented with reference to the undelivered version of the Rubicon speech: 'Had that speech been delivered, the course of history in South Africa over the ensuing five years may well have been very different. But Botha faltered on the banks of the Rubicon, deterred, it is said, by right-wingers within his Cabinet, and probably by his own basic sentiments.' Foreign Minister Pik Botha subsequently claimed the alternative draft as his own brainchild, but P W Botha's authorised biographer, Dr Daan Prinsloo, has been at pains to point out that the draftsperson was an official in Pik Botha's Department, one Carl von Hirschberg.

Shortly thereafter came the Commonwealth peace initiative calling itself rather grandiloquently, the 'Eminent Persons' Group' (EPG). Appointed at a Heads of State Conference in October 1985, the EPG mandate was to attempt to break the deadlock over the issue of Commonwealth economic sanctions against South Africa, to which Prime Minister Margaret Thatcher was the stoical solitary opponent. The EPG consulted widely, was given permission to meet Nelson Mandela in prison, and engaged in discussion with leaders of the Frontline States. Encouraged by these soundings, it formulated what was described as a 'Possible Negotiating Concept', having concluded that 'ground existed on the basis of which a negotiated solution to South Africa's problems could be attempted, if there was the necessary will among all concerned'. The EPG concept substantially mirrored and anticipated what F W de Klerk would announce four years later, on 2 February 1990. For a brief moment a spark of hope flickered, but was rapidly extinguished as the State Security Council launched simultaneous military raids into three Commonwealth countries – Botswana, Zambia and Zimbabwe. In fact Gaborone was hit on the very day, and just hours after, the Commonwealth mission departed the city. If their objective was to sabotage the Commonwealth initiative, the raids were an unqualified success. The EPG in its final report concluded that the imposition of economic sanctions was now unavoidable, and represented 'the last opportunity to avert what could be the worst bloodbath since the Second World War'.

A few months before my letter to the President, during May 1987, there had been a General Election. To our dismay, this whites-only affair resulted in a massive shift to the Right. The Progressive Federal Party ceased to be the Official Opposition, and was replaced by the Conservative Party, which instead of criticising the Government for being too oppressive, would now criticise the Government for being too lenient, and too liberal! In its election manifesto, the CP promised that, upon gaining power, it would reverse P W Botha's reforms; repossess black property rights which had been conceded only in urban areas; restore the ban on black trade unions; and reintroduce the despicable pass system of influx control. Oliver Tambo, President of the ANC, commented, 'These elections have blown the whistle for the ANC to intensify the armed struggle.'

In mid-February 1986, I met with Dr Frederick van Zyl Slabbert, shortly after his resignation as Leader of the Opposition. This meeting was for me another watershed encounter, contributing to a growing sense of the irrelevance of my work, and a looming premonition of disaster. Van Zyl had shocked his political colleagues and supporters by his precipitate departure from Parliament, and his dismissive judgment that Parliament could no longer contribute meaningfully to the changes that were desperately needed. A few months earlier he had travelled to Lusaka and held discussions with the ANC. Upon his return he met discreetly with President Botha and tried to share his perceptions; but faced with Botha's obduracy, he concluded that either the Government did not understand the basic principles of negotiation or the President chose not to pursue them. In the circumstances, he believed that Botha was set upon a course which would lead inexorably to the Masada of the Afrikaner nation. Van Zyl characterised the Government's much-vaunted reform initiatives as no more than 'rearranging the deck chairs on the Titanic'. He was convinced that the newly installed Tricameral Parliament was hopelessly flawed, having little or nothing to do with genuine power-sharing. Hence, he concluded, he could no longer 'act with integrity within the system'.

Shortly thereafter Van Zyl and his political colleague Alex Boraine established an extra-parliamentary advocacy organisation known as IDASA, which was to play a significant role in facilitating the change process. They were both my clients and my friends. During July 1987, just two months before my letter to the President, IDASA had initiated an historic encounter with the ANC in the West African city of Dakar. 61 invited delegates drawn from academic, professional, cultural, religious, and business sectors, met over a period of four days with a top-level delegation of 17 members from the ANC, led by Thabo Mbeki. This historic encounter, in Mbeki's words, opened the eyes of many of the delegates who had previously tended to demonise each other. 'The feeling of a common South African-ness', he concluded, 'was strong and got stronger as the days passed.' The Dakar

Conference ended with an historic declaration subscribed to by all but two of the delegates. It called for the release of political prisoners and the unbanning of the ANC and other proscribed organisations. Whilst acknowledging that not all the delegates supported the ANC's armed struggle, it declared that it had to be recognised as an historical reality. However, the delegates found broad agreement on the basis for a peaceful political solution; upon the need to end apartheid; and upon a shared vision of a future multiracial democratic society.

As in the case of the earlier EPG initiative, the Government now sought to undermine and stifle the possibility of negotiations. Acting in terms of the Emergency Regulations, it prevented the returning delegates from holding a press conference, and arrested 16 journalists at Johannesburg airport. The SABC, in its assigned role of 'His Master's Voice', described the Dakar delegates as 'political terrorists', and noted calls that they be prosecuted and charged with treason.

With the inevitability of a Greek tragedy, it seemed now as if nothing could deflect the country from the catastrophic course upon which it was set. After long and painful heart-searching, my wife Hilary and I came to the conclusion that, despite the heartbreak and loss it would involve, we had now to consider emigration. Over the years, as each new crisis had overtaken the country, increasing numbers of our friends and colleagues opted to leave, and start new lives in Britain, New Zealand, Australia, Canada, the United States, and elsewhere. On each of these occasions we had faced similar issues, but had always concluded that this was our home, our beloved country, the place where our lives had meaning and purpose. Now I was 48 years old. Our children were beginning their adult lives. To delay further might jeopardise their futures, and our ability to leave at all.

In the wake of these events, we finally decided to lodge an application for permission to emigrate to Canada. But then a strange thing happened – when the long-awaited permits arrived, we found ourselves unable to leave. Overwhelmed by the sense of impending loss and moral abdication, feeling ourselves inextricably involved in whatever might befall this country, and wishing by any means possible to play some role in turning the tide, we discovered, when the time came, that it was impossible to go. From then on, I began to wonder how a private citizen like myself, with no special claim to wisdom, knowledge, or status, might play some role in facilitating the essential dialogue that could lead to negotiations and a peaceful future for our children. It seemed that nothing less was needed, and that this desperate personal initiative, however improbable, was the best hope I could conceive of for helping the country to step back from the precipice of anarchy, mayhem, and civil war that now loomed. If finally, it transpired that the

Government was unwilling to countenance even this possibility, then without doubt the country was doomed, and it was time to leave. In the meanwhile, it was one's duty to exhaust every last hope.

And so finally, on that morning of 23 September 1987, with a considerable measure of fear, I handed my letter to the clerk on duty at the front desk of the Office of the State President.

2

Who is Richard Rosenthal?

Having returned to office from my foray as presidential postman, I tried with some difficulty to effect an air of calm and normality. My secretary, Barbara Puttick, the only person other than Hilary who had any idea of what was afoot, asked with a ghoulish chuckle whether I wanted to borrow a hard hat? I thanked her for her concern. I telephoned Hilary to let her know that the deed was done. She said, 'Well, now it's bread on the water.' We speculated what might happen next, and tried to imagine Mr Botha's likely reaction. There were a number of awesome possibilities. I am not sure whether I was more afraid of a 'Yes' or a 'No'.

That afternoon whenever the phone rang I would leap to it, expecting a summons or a warrant. In fact, nothing whatsoever happened, to my alternating relief and disappointment. In vain, I tried to concentrate on other work, but it felt trivial and irrelevant. I remember wondering, if I had been the State President, what might I have done on receipt of such a letter? Surely, I would have referred it to the security establishment for their comment? The President would want to know some basic information. Who is this Richard Rosenthal? Whom does he represent? Could there be some hidden agenda? A possibility which occurred to me belatedly, was that they might suspect me of being a 'hidden hand', some oblique emissary on behalf of the ANC. The very improbability of the proposal, and myself as the source, might be its principal strength or weakness. I wondered what the N I S and Security Police files might say about me.

I speculated that the President would be told that I was something of an enigma, a political conundrum. Though manifesting left-wing sentiments, my lifestyle was somewhat hedonistic and plutocratic. My background was replete with ambiguity. My father was a lapsed German Jew, and my mother a lapsed Irish Catholic. Both had somehow avoided a known political profile. They were good-hearted, decent, people. My father was a much-beloved semi-mythological character known for his prodigious memory, which he happily displayed on a popular weekly radio programme, known as 'The Three Wise Men'. He was reputed to know almost everything. As an author, he published more than 50 books, and had a prodigious output of company histories and newspaper articles.

If the security archivists had been meticulous, they might have discovered that before leaving school I joined the short-lived non-racial Liberal Party of Alan Paton, until it dissolved after the enactment of the Prohibition of Political Interference Act in 1968. My early 'political deviance' might be forgiven on grounds of youthful folly, but they might also know of my friendship with the late Patrick Duncan. I had been one of the last people to see Patrick before he broke his banning order, and escaped across the border into Basutoland, now Lesotho. The son of a wartime Governor General, Patrick was a gallant warrior for justice, though often a mystery to his friends and colleagues. In self-exile, he became the only white person admitted as a member of the Pan Africanist Congress (PAC). But the security gnomes might balance this left-wing tilt, against an equally improbable tilt in the other direction – my friendship with a certain Dr J F J (Hans) van Rensburg, a self-confessed fascist, who during the war years served as Kommandant-General of the Nazi-sympathising Ossewa Brandwag. He had later served, until his death in 1966, as Chairman of that most profane of all the bureaucracies, the Group Areas Board. One day he confided to me, 'I could never have done this job unless I was a fascist!'

During my student days I had been involved with the organisation known as Moral Rearmament, which campaigned with great zeal against Communism, Apartheid, and other totalitarian ideologies. I had also befriended many of the young radicals of the day, including one Adrian Leftwich, a tragic figure thrown up and discarded by the tide, like so much flotsam. It was Adrian who was described by Judge President Andries Beyers, at the end of a trial in which he had testified for the State against his friends and comrades, as 'a rat, were that not such an insult to the genus *rattus*'. Anticipating by a few years the formation of Umkhonto weSizwe (MK), Adrian was a founder member of the African Resistance Movement (ARM), into which he recruited some of the bravest and best of our generation. He persuaded them to commit acts of sabotage, for which they were tried and sentenced to long periods of imprisonment, whilst Adrian went free into exile – and lifelong shame.

Would the 'spooks' have known that in October 1960, the year I came of age, I had embarrassed my anglophile parents by voting 'Yes' in favour of South Africa becoming a Republic outside the Commonwealth? It was the first time I had voted. This rebellious act had particularly appalled my patriotic English mother, but she ultimately forgave me when I explained to her that I hoped a Republic might at last bring the Boer War to an end – if so, it would be a small price to pay. In later years, I identified closely with the Progressive Party, and was employed for a while as a fulltime member of its

Parliamentary Secretariat following the 1974 General Election. Later, I served as their legal adviser, and frequently assisted that most honourable of honourable members, Helen Suzman, MP. Curiously, I never joined the Party – nor any other – though I gave it moral, practical, and some modest financial, support.

What else might be known by these inscrutable faceless men who sur-reptitiously peered into our lives, listened to our phones, opened our mail, and invaded the sanctity of our homes? Socially, I was a member of no club, though on one memorable occasion my name had been abortively proposed for membership of an all-white, all-male, Afrikaans-speaking cabal known as Die Here Sewentien Klub in Cape Town. This improbable association resulted from a bibulous celebratory lunch at the end of a long trial. My grateful client was mortified when, to his huge embarrassment and my own commensurate relief, the application was 'blackballed'. I was never able to discover the identity of the true believers, who mercifully barred my way.

Perhaps, the President would be told that my legal practice had been an unusual synthesis of incompatibles – I was a rich man's lawyer, practising 'poor man's law'. (I had cultivated two very disparate clienteles, whom I would refer to as my left-hand and right-hand practices respectively.) Though I often acted in matters involving a challenge to the apartheid estab-lishment, I was a member of a law firm which had for a hundred years acted for a local authority – the Divisional Council of the Cape – which will be long remembered for its heartless decision, taken during the chairmanship of Hernus Kriel, until recently Premier of the Western Cape, to demolish thousands of squatter homes in mid-winter. At other times, I had acted as spokesperson and attorney for several beleaguered squatter communities at Modderdam, Unibell, and Crossroads, as they attempted to assert their sim-ple desire to subsist in what white South Africans regarded as its exclusive territory. My clients had also included large commercial undertakings, at least one State Corporation, and several business organisations such as the Cape Town Chamber of Commerce. In my 'left-hand' practice, I acted for such 'subversive' organisations as the Black Sash, the Dependents' Conference, and the Christian Institute. I was a Governor of the Urban Foundation, a Trustee of the Legal Resources Trust, and the founding Director of the Legal Resources Centre, Cape Town.

Of immediate concern to the President might have been my ongoing role in providing legal assistance to the organisation known as IDASA, which to the particular chagrin of Mr Botha had organised and sponsored the ground-breaking Dakar consultation with the ANC. In earlier years, I had served as legal adviser to the Urban Foundation, on whose behalf I helped to make representations aimed at securing land tenure for urban blacks, and a special interim dispensation for marginalised blacks in the Western Cape, thus circumventing the prevailing fiction that blacks were merely sojourners in 'white' South Africa, and that the apartheid doctrine of coloured labour preference prevailed in the Cape. I had registered the black housing company ULUNTU, and assisted in forming numerous NGOs, and non-profit organisations.

Against this background, it was hardly surprising that some of my work had incurred the wrath and displeasure of the Government, particularly in relation to Supreme Court actions which were successful in setting aside oppressive actions and decisions. In the words of an unlamented Minister, of what was incongruously described as 'Community Development', a certain Marais Steyn, MP, as recorded in *Hansard* (April 1977, pp. 6294–5), I was one of those lawyers who instigated court applications 'not because they had the law on their side, but merely on the grounds of technical points', and, 'to foment dissatisfaction and racial hatred, and discredit the Government and South Africa'. Introducing an amendment to the Illegal Squatting Act, Minister Steyn thundered that this 'obvious defiance of State authority' could not be tolerated. Accordingly, he introduced a law designed to prevent future access to the courts by 'illegal' squatter communities. As a result, the Government proceeded unchallenged to demolish more than 5 000 rudimentary squatter shacks in mid-winter at an infamous place called Modderdam. One supposedly honourable member of the National Party, Mr W J C Rossouw, explained to Parliament (*Hansard*, May 1976, p. 6879), 'There is an English saying: "Sometimes you must be cruel to be kind."'

My work had also contributed in some measure to the watershed litigation for the Legal Resources Centre, which under the able leadership of Arthur Chaskalson S.C., played an important role in sounding the death-knell for the infamous Pass Laws. During 1986, I acted as attorney for a group of conscience-stricken doctors who, at their own risk and expense, succeeded in challenging the SA Medical and Dental Council, with regard to its decision to exonerate Drs Lang, Tucker, and Keeley from medical culpability for the events leading to the death of Steve Biko in detention. Alongside many heartbreaking defeats, there were some memorable victories, including the setting aside of a gerrymandered 'general election' aimed at installing a puppet Community Council in a black town near Paarl, called Mbekweni; and landmark proceedings which compelled another jackboot Boland local authority, the Divisional Council of Stellenbosch, to reconstruct rudimentary squatter homes, which it had callously – and illegally – demolished, as always, in mid-winter.

These facts, if known to the President's men, might cause them to wonder whether I could be a trustworthy vehicle for so sensitive a mission as I was proposing. On the other hand, they might see me as naive and therefore useful, a convenient, available, and if necessary, dispensable, stalking-horse. Perhaps they would come to regard these wayward traits as evidence of political independence. This could give me some degree of credibility in the context of exploratory contacts.

As the weeks passed, and there was neither acknowledgment nor reply to my letter, my spirits rose and fell like a roller-coaster. After four weeks, I began to wonder whether no answer was in fact a 'NO' answer. The country was continuing to spiral out of control; a mood of siege and resignation had taken hold. Once more, as a family, we began to think about leaving South Africa. Having vacillated for several months, we now despatched to London – the South African Consulate having been closed by Canada as part of its diplomatic sanctions – the medical reports and X-rays which had been called for by the Canadian authorities. As Hilary wrote in our letter of application, 'Our decision to emigrate is arrived at with the greatest reluctance, and is motivated by our growing despair about the situation in this country, and our wish to provide our two children with some hopeful view of the future.'

Eventually, unable to contain my impatience any longer, I telephoned the State President's office, and asked whether my letter had in fact been received?

'Oh yes,' said his secretary cheerily. 'There's a reply to you in the post.' My heart missed a beat.

A few days later a portentous gold-embossed envelope arrived, bearing the State President's coat of arms. It comprised only two sentences, one of which contained a spelling error; but for all its deficiencies, it seemed astonishingly positive (see next page).

At least I was not about to join some of my friends in the Tower of London. That in itself was a relief. But what was implied by 'the necessary attention'? Could one read into that some indication of attitude? It was certainly not hostile, as I had feared. The 'thanks' and 'kind regards' also intrigued me. Were they just routine courtesies? I would have to wait to find out.

A week later, a second and more substantive response arrived.

I was hugely intrigued. Here was the Deputy Minister of Constitutional Affairs, Dr Stoffel van der Merwe, reputed to be one of the more enlightened members of Botha's Cabinet, proposing to engage me in discussion on this seminal issue, at the behest of the State President himself. The implications were breathtaking (see p. 18).

0869g

I.1

Tuynhuys
Cape Town

1987 -10-1 6

Mr R Rosenthal
P O Box 695
CAPE TOWN
8000

Dear Mr Rosenthal

The State Presdent has requested me to acknowledge with thanks,
receipt of your letter dated 23 September 1987.

Your letter is receiving the necessary attention.

With kind regards

ADMINISTRATIVE SECRETARY
/as

REPUBLIC OF SOUTH AFRICA

DEPUTY MINISTER OF INFORMATION
AND OF CONSTITUTIONAL PLANNING

Private Bag X745 Pretoria 0001
Telephone (012) 3236162

5/7/1 R   22 October 1987

Mr R Rosenthal
P O Box 695
CAPE TOWN
8000

Dear Mr Rosenthal

The State President has taken note with appreciation of
your letter to him dated 23 September 1987.

In view of the fact that he has charged me with the
task of investigating possible future constitutional
developments he has referred the letter to me for
further attention.

It seems to me that the appropriate action would be for
you and myself to get together to discuss possibilities
and I have therefore instructed my Private Secretary to
make contact with your office in order to arrange for a
meeting at a convenient time.

Yours faithfully

STOFFEL VAN DER MERWE

3

A Van der Merwe story

One week later I flew to Pretoria for a lunchtime meeting with Dr van der Merwe which took place in his plush seventh-floor offices in Midtown Building, located at the corner of Prinsloo and Vermeulen Streets, diagonally opposite the imposing new precinct of the Reserve Bank.

I had little time to prepare for this crucial encounter, and set about voraciously consuming as much background material as I could rapidly assemble and ingest; thinking deeply about the options which he would no doubt wish to discuss with me, concerning a future negotiation process. In fact, I had no idea what his attitude might be, and needed to be ready for various possibilities. As always, Hilary, in her quiet unassuming way, became my sounding-board, helping me to crystallise and formulate ideas. Despite the demands and strains of her own life, and work as Director of an NGO known as the Parent Centre, Hilary was entirely supportive of this risky venture and always ready to contribute her wisdom and important insights – on long walks over the mountains, and talks late into the night.

I wished to find out as much as I could about Stoffel van der Merwe. By all accounts, he was 'one of the better intellects in the party'. Like his Transvaal Leader F W de Klerk, he was a member of the small but influential 'Dopper' Kerk; and had only recently transposed from academic life to politics. It seemed that he had been the recipient of Mr Botha's unpredictable benediction, with the result that he had risen rapidly on the congested party ladder, causing more envy than affection. As newly appointed Deputy Minister of Constitutional Planning his office was now located within the office of the State President. It was rumoured that the Minister of Constitutional Planning, Chris Heunis, who had cross-cutting portfolio responsibilities, was particularly chagrined by this imposed appointment upon which his opinion had not even been sought.

Meanwhile I managed to obtain a booklet Van der Merwe had written for the National Party, entitled '... *and what about the Black People?*' I studied it closely, and found it quite revealing, and closely argued. Needless to say, it paid obeisance to orthodox faith and doctrine, but there were glimmerings of independent thought, which I chose to regard as reassuring. Thus, it acknowledged that the Verwoerdian vision of 'separate development' had proved impracticable and unachievable, and it posed the question of a new dispensation 'in which every nation and population group – including the Whites – will have a place in the sun; in which all the groups brought together in this land by Providence will achieve fulfilment without any one of them being able to disadvantage, dominate or destroy any of the others.' Were these not the dialectical rumblings of a reflective Dopper at work?

In this booklet, Van der Merwe characterised the issue of political rights for blacks as 'South Africa's vital problem', and acknowledged that, 'The new constitutional dispensation for Whites, Coloureds and Indians (the 1983 Tricameral Parliament) did not address this problem in any way'. It went so far as to envisage an inclusive negotiating process, which should include 'a wider group of people than those leaders already elected'. It seemed to recognise that the Nationalist speciality of conducting make-believe negotiations with docile black leaders would not suffice, and that real negotiations had to draw in the UDF, and ultimately the ANC, and other extra-parliamentary groups. However, its opening litany of constitutional guidelines was depressingly familiar; and in a closing paragraph it sought to reassure the party faithful that they would not be required to surrender their racist prerogatives:

> Because these guidelines will be adhered to in all future negotiations and constitutional developments, people may rest assured that their interests will be safeguarded ... in two ways: firstly the National Party will, at all times, be committed to protecting the interests of its own people, and secondly, to ensuring that this does not take place at the expense of other groups and individuals. In this way, it will ensure that other people and groups will not be tempted to promote their sectional interests by trying to disadvantage or suppress the Whites.

Here once more was the fatal propensity of National Party ideologists to blow hot and cold at the same time, to approbate and reprobate simultaneously, and finally to contradict even the positive things by stoical adherence to the negative things. They acknowledged the need for things to be different, but promised that things would remain the same.

This equivocation was illustrated a few days later, when 77-year-old Govan Mbeki was released on 5 November, having served 23 years of a life sentence imposed upon him, Mandela, and five others at the end of the Rivonia Trial. To mark the occasion of his release, the Government organised a press conference, attended by a large contingent of the media. Mr Mbeki promptly dismayed his captors by announcing, 'The ideas for which I went to gaol, and for which the ANC stands, I still embrace.' The Government then appeared to lose its nerve, and banned his homecoming rally three weeks later in Soweto. This was followed by further punitive restriction orders, which confined him to the magisterial district of Port Elizabeth, and banned him from either being quoted or giving further press interviews. In due course, his passport would also be withdrawn, thereby (as they presumed) preventing him from consulting the ANC in exile, or from being reunited with his two exiled sons whom he had not seen for a quarter of a century. In due course he would also be prohibited, as I was to discover, from meeting more than one person at a time.

On Thursday 12 November, I flew to Johannesburg for my lunch meeting with Dr Stoffel van der Merwe. A newspaper handed to me on the aircraft headlined a belated admission by the Chief of the SADF, General Johan Geldenhuys, that as previously suspected but routinely denied, South African forces were providing logistical support to UNITA, and were also involved in conventional warfare using heavy ordnance against Cuban and MPLA forces defending the Angolan town of Mavinga. This battle was to result in unprecedented losses for the SADF, for which the misinformed public was quite unprepared. The battle was followed by the struggle for the key town of Cuito Cuanavale, which was again misrepresented to the South African public as a great victory, and not as a defeat. These military humiliations were to become the turning-point of the war, and would lead in due time to the withdrawal of South African troops, and to the eventual signing of a US-brokered peace treaty. Events were now moving rapidly towards an international crisis, involving South Africa's military adventurism.

Like most government buildings at that time, Midtown Building was replete with entry obstacles, scanners, video cameras, and grim unsmiling guards who fingered very impressive-looking weapons. Pretoria had begun to resemble the fortress that it really was, and not without reason. A few months earlier, Umkonto weSizwe (MK), the ANC's armed wing, had bombed and severely damaged the SADF Witwatersrand Command headquarters in Johannesburg. The capital city itself was still reeling from the audacity of an earlier bomb which had been planted opposite the headquarters of the South African Air Force, causing considerable damage, killing 19 people, and injuring more than 200 others. 'Never again', promised Oliver Tambo, 'are our people going to do all the bleeding.'

At the entrance to Midtown Building, my bag and I were X-rayed. My name was checked against a list of anticipated arrivals, and I was escorted to the sixth floor, where the Deputy Minister was ensconced in a luxurious suite. I had no idea what to expect, and felt both nervous and excited.

Not long after I had been seated in the ante-room, Van der Merwe appeared, with outstretched hand, and his trademark puckish smile. I was immediately struck by the warmth of his manner, and the almost comic likeness he bore to a nefarious TV character with whom Dallas fans would be familiar, one Cliff Barnes. I half-expected to be offered bourbon, and for JR or Sue-Ellen suddenly to appear. We sat down at a corner table in his private sanctum, a large office with a fine view of the city, a formidable safe, the inevitable flag, and the prescribed Presidential portrait. His secretary served pre-prandial drinks – not bourbon!

The meeting would last just over three hours, and in due course we adjourned to a next-door dining-room, where lunch was served. The atmosphere was cordial and relaxed, with only the two of us present.

We started by exchanging pleasantries and inanities. He asked about my flight, and I asked about his busy life. He hoped I would not 'take it amiss' that the President had been unable to see me personally, but had asked him to meet me on his behalf. I said if I had been the President, I probably would have done the same. Eventually, he came to the point.

'What brings you to do something like this?' he asked. In other words, what on earth are you about, and who are you really?

Having embarked upon this improbable journey, I realised that one of my persistent problems was going to be how to persuade people that I was not more than I appeared to be – and certainly not some 'hidden hand' bearing someone else's imprint and message. But how was he to believe that this was in fact the case; that this was no more than a personal initiative, and that I wasn't completely crazy? To protest, often has precisely the inverse effect. So I decided to start off ingenuously sketching my personal background, in the hope that he would come to see me as an ordinary human being, deeply concerned about the situation, but without a hidden agenda. He remarked that he had not met my father but of course knew of him. We talked about his famous memory. No; alas, I did not share this remarkable faculty, but rather what my father characterised as his 'forgettery'. He hadn't realised that my father was dead, and apologised for this mistake.

I then came to my political background, and made no secret of my long-standing involvement with the Progressive and Liberal Parties. I said I was basically not a 'joiner', or 'political animal'. I wondered whether he believed me. I spoke about my work, and how I spent a considerable portion of my professional time acting for people and organisations diametrically opposed to his Government. 'I don't think I am held in very high regard by some of your colleagues,' I ventured, to which he replied, 'Well, nor am I!' We laughed. Hopefully, he had a sense of humour.

I told him I was reasonably well known, in circles where his Government enjoyed little credibility. He said this could be an advantage. I said that my political sentiments were opposed to his government, but that my preferred role was professional rather than political. As the conversation progressed, I began to feel that he needed to understand that I was not willing to be 'used', or to allow my goodwill to be prostituted in the service of his cause. However, it was still early days, and the first base was to establish some personal rapport.

He seemed interested to know which of the better-known political leaders I had been in touch with. I assured him that many were personally known to me, but that I had not discussed this concept with anyone. I emphasised that complete confidentiality was the touchstone of any role I might play. What I tried to convey was that my low profile and personal credibility could qualify me to play some discreet intermediary role at an initial stage.

As I had expected, he wished to know what my own ideas were as to a future negotiating process? I didn't want to be drawn into specifics, and responded by saying that although I had ideas and opinions, I did not want to try and persuade him of the rightness of these beliefs. Rather I sought to serve an honourable process. I was particularly interested in the pre-process – those first tentative steps that someone needed to take to establish the willingness of both parties, and the feasibility of the concept. Again he wished to know what was my relationship with the UDF or the ANC? Again, I assured him that the only relationship I had was at a personal level. His difficulty was how to believe me. To some extent, I was in a 'Catch-22' situation. If I regaled him with my views as to the profanity of his ideology, I would lose the man. On the other hand, if I withheld my views, then he might have reason to believe I had been less than frank.

What was most urgently needed, I suggested, was some way to break the silence between the antagonists. Perhaps we would one day find that the true divide was not as we had always assumed between those who held differing views, but rather between those who held the same views – some of whom wanted a peaceful outcome, and others of whom were ready to embrace conflict. Such a line might cut through the middle of his party as well as others.

He was a good listener, asking relevant questions, but not interrupting. Finally, he said that although the Government was committed to a policy of constitutional dialogue, it did not know how to begin. He said his own function was to engage in dialogue with a broad spectrum of parties. In this sense, he had more latitude than Constitutional Affairs Minister Chris Heunis. I sensed there was not too much affection and empathy between them. When I expressed scepticism about the proposed National Statutory Council as the proposed forum for a future constitutional process, he nodded in seeming agreement. He said the State President had now charged him with exploring alternative strategies. He would be keen to develop personal relationships across the political spectrum. He asked whether I could help by introducing him to some of my friends? Again, I had to explain that I was not offering to help him implement his goals, but rather to serve all parties and ultimately the process itself.

I explained that in my view there were certain factors which suggested the existence of a unique and historic opportunity. It was not only Government that did not know how to proceed, but also, I believed, the ANC. On both sides, the leadership was getting older, and the prospect of arriving at 'the Promised Land' was becoming dimmer. Not even P W Botha was immortal. Surely any leader wished to be remembered as having delivered reform rather than repression? The political careers of the older men were drawing to a close. Perhaps the old men could still see visions and dream dreams? Perhaps Mandela and Botha would wish to go down in history as the first of a new generation. That, at least, was my hope.

Several times he tried to engage me in debate or argument, but I was keen to resist this temptation, and to limit myself to the offer on the table. Already I had gone beyond my original intention of discussing outlines only, but he too had the right to determine the agenda.

People could not be expected to negotiate under duress, I said. The State of Emergency had immobilised particular leaders, but it could never deliver a climate for negotiations. The ANC had largely succeeded in making the country 'ungovernable', but it also could not deliver on its political goals. In this sense, the parties were co-dependent, and had succeeded in frustrating each other, but no more. This was surely a window of opportunity?

I did not doubt the Government would be able to contain the limits of challenge for a long time yet; particularly if it was sufficiently ruthless with its adversaries; but this might mean an indefinite State of Emergency, the detention of increasing numbers of leaders, and the suppression of protest by force. Such a policy would exact a terrible price, and could never deliver peace. I quoted Bismarck, who said that one could do almost anything with bayonets, except sit on them!

Referring to that morning's headline news, I argued that the escalating conflict in Angola would sap morale and resources, and increase South Africa's international isolation. In a worst case, it could resuscitate the abandoned option of military intervention, with the eventual involvement of the super-powers. Russia would not stand by and watch Cuba suffer humiliation or defeat; nor would Ronald Reagan's administration or a British Government under Margaret Thatcher stand by and watch a Cuban–Russian axis establish a firm foothold in Southern Africa. On the other hand, the latest developments in Angola might serve to demonstrate South Africa's capacity and willingness to resist. Past efforts to pressurise the Government into reform and contrition through quiet diplomacy had failed. Zimbabwe, Mozambique, and Zambia, were all experiencing huge economic and social problems, no doubt aggravated by South Africa's policy of regional destabilisation. There were all the ingredients of a major international crisis in this region.

Dr van der Merwe looked as though I was talking about the moon. He was concerned with our domestic political situation, not the war in Angola. That was not his brief, he pointed out. It was Magnus Malan's affair. How would one commence such a process, he wanted to know. I didn't have the answer, but suggested that the first priority would be to establish some basis for trust and good faith. What was desperately needed was a quality of leadership and statesmanship. I didn't know P W Botha, but hoped he might have the capacity to become a statesman. Dr van der Merwe looked inscrutable.

Whilst trying not to be prescriptive, I suggested a possible five-stage process, commencing with discreet 'soundings' about the principle of some kind of exploratory dialogue. If initial signals were positive, then a next stage might be to engage in discreet low-level contacts between the Government and the ANC, leading eventually to a more substantive encounter at a senior political level. I could not foresee a leader-to-leader meeting until much later. I also mooted the possible need for third-party mediation, and suggested that some other African country such as Kenya or Nigeria, or the OAU itself, might play such a role. In due course, one would have to consider the need for task groups, and for some independent Secretariat. A formal negotiation process would probably need to be hosted by one or more of the major powers. Such a conference would have to define its own process to arrive at a new constitutional model for South Africa.

At this stage, Dr van der Merwe shifted gear, and began to talk about himself and his own career. He said there were similarities and differences in our backgrounds. He too was now 48 years old, and had initially embarked upon a legal career. 'So you are in fact a "reformed" lawyer?' I suggested. He rather liked this description of himself. He had a BA.LLB degree from Pretoria University, and entered politics almost by chance with very similar motivation to that which I had just been describing. After ten years in the Department of Foreign Affairs, including a stint as Vice-Consul in Milan, he had returned to the academic world and studied Political Science at Rand Afrikaans University (RAU). I asked the subject of his thesis, and he said it had been concerned with the Theory of Revolution. 'An appropriate topic,' I ventured. He grinned. Thereafter, he had become a lecturer at RAU until 1981, when P W had persuaded him to enter politics.

He believed the National Party had moved radically away from its origi-

nal adherence to white domination, and that it had undergone its own internal process of reform. This had occurred 'sometimes hesitantly, but by now
irrevocably'. He acknowledged that the National Party had moved only a few
steps, but said that even this had exacted 'a high political cost' in terms of
Afrikaner unity. He was convinced of the State President's sincerity in wanting to bring about a genuine inclusive negotiation process. He saw this as
the only alternative to revolutionary violence. The problem was that the
Government was unsure how to begin, and did not see the necessary flexibility in the ANC. He volunteered that Chris Heunis's National Council
would not be the solution, although he didn't wish to be perceived as disloyal. Real negotiations could not be treated as a public relations exercise,
for domestic or overseas consumption. A process that was just appearance
and not substance would be futile and even dangerous.

He drew the analogy of people being so far apart that the only way they
could communicate was by shouting at each other. 'We have to lessen the
distance,' he said, 'and start building trust and getting closer.' One of the
concerns with incremental steps from the Government side only was that
these could be interpreted by the ANC and others as showing flexibility and
weakness. This gave rise to a certain nervousness and hesitation in
Government about making further moves.

In his view, it was just a matter of time before a split came within the
ranks of the ANC – between what he called, the Africanists and the
Communists. The Government would like to encourage such a split 'but any
attempt on our part to bring this about would naturally be counter-productive'. He believed that a split would happen in any event as a consequence
of a future negotiating process. At this stage, there was need to do business
with both factions. His studies had taught him that Communists viewed
negotiations as just a stage in a process leading inevitably to revolution, and
the dictatorship of the proletariat. History had shown that no violent revolution ever yielded a democratic society. 'Those who live by the sword per-
ish by the sword.'

The meeting had gone on for most of the afternoon. Already there were
indications of that familiar Pretoria stampede – the homeward flight of tens
of thousands of civil servants who migrate from their offices at about 3.30
or 4 p.m. From time to time, Van der Merwe's secretary came in bearing
messages, but he waved her away. Now he suggested that she go home, as
he would not be requiring her again that afternoon.

He concluded our meeting by saying that he was extremely interested in
the proposal. However, I must understand, that he was not the only person
involved in such a decision. He also had 'a number of ideas', but they were
still too tentative to share. He hoped that we might be able to resume our

discussion at a later date. In the meanwhile, little could be accomplished until the end of the year. 'Things are already closing down for Christmas,' he said. I marvelled at the Government's majestic lack of urgency. 'The New Year could yield important new possibilities,' he added. In the meanwhile, he would report to the State President, but could give me no promises at this stage.

As I was preparing to leave, he riveted me by asking another question, 'When might you be available?' Taking my cue from his own lack of urgency, I suggested perhaps the end of February? To my surprise, he said, 'That could be a bit late.' I said if the need was there, I would be available any time when required. There was nothing more important. However, I had a practice to look after, and would need to consider some other implications. Did my partners know about this, he asked. I assured him that no one had been consulted – other than my wife.

If this thing went ahead, he said, we would need 'some kind of structure', adding with a sort of stammer, 'a kind of front'. I did not like the term or undertone of deceit, but said we would need to talk about such matters in due course, and how it could be funded. That should be no problem, he assured me. I said this was not as straightforward as it might appear. Whatever the source of funding, it would need to be discussed and approved by both the Government and the ANC. I did not think one could accept support from the business community, as my role needed to be demonstrably independent of any interest group, such as business.

It was late afternoon by the time I departed for the airport. The meeting had gone on far longer than I had anticipated. Although no approval had been given, and no decisions taken, there was an atmosphere of anticipation. Van der Merwe promised to be in contact shortly, and said that he would welcome any further communication from me in the interim.

'How about a Political Consultancy?' he suggested as I departed.

4

A slightly crazy idea

It was not long before Hilary and I were confronted with a new crisis of decision. With diabolical timing, an envelope lay on my desk when I returned from meeting Stoffel van der Merwe, which contained our long-awaited visas to emigrate to Canada. It was no longer simply a theoretical option. We were now free to go, but the permanent resident visas were of limited duration. We would have to make up our minds soon, or forfeit the right to this valuable escape route. The decision still hung in the balance. If the President's answer was 'Yes' we would stay; if it was 'No' we would leave. Hopefully, we wouldn't have too long to wait.

The ambiguities and contradictions in our lives created other tensions and strains. The prospect of emigration was patently incompatible with the offer made to the President, which implied a commitment to stay and to work for the future of the country. Moreover, my politically sensitive legal work might now be seen by Government as incompatible with an implicit undertaking of neutrality. At the same time, I could not simply abdicate the professional responsibility owed to my clients, and which imposed other obligations and constraints. One of the most difficult conundrums involved a duty of transparency owed as a legal obligation to one's partners, but this too was incompatible with my fundamental commitment to secrecy in this matter. I felt morally conflicted, as though silence implied some level of deceit. Integrity doesn't absolve one from ethical complexity. In the midst of this maelstrom, we were forced to find ways to maintain some semblance of a normal family and personal life. Though in dire need of friendship and support, I could not share these realities with family or friends, and experienced a growing sense of isolation.

Whether or not I had previously been the subject of police surveillance, I had no doubt that the security establishment would henceforth be watching and listening, if only to find out with whom I might be in contact? For years we had assumed that our phones were routinely tapped and our mail opened – no doubt, part reality and part paranoia – and we had become inured to the use of metaphor and circumlocution. Sometimes one would hear strange clicks on the phone, which could as easily have been monitoring as the notorious malfunctioning of our Stone-Age telephone system. Whatever the reality, one experienced the corrosive effect of simply not knowing. I found myself looking more diligently in the rear-view mirror. I was also burdened with the responsibility as a lawyer of being the repository of other people's confidences. In the small hours of one morning, I got up from my bed to bury a plastic bag containing sensitive papers under a tree in the garden – just in case!

One domain that I was not prepared to compromise was my right to choose the clients I acted for. I realised this could create problems of perception, but on the other hand, it would be strange if I ceased to be available in politically sensitive matters. There were many such matters that I was handling at the time, apart from continuing work on behalf of IDASA.

Thus, one day I was consulted by Rashied Seria, at the time editor of the community newspaper *South*, which was threatened with closure under the prevailing Emergency Media Regulations. In due course I would visit Rashied in detention at Victor Verster Prison near Paarl, the penitentiary from which Nelson Mandela would walk free some three years later.

I was also proud to be acting for another courageous editor, Tony Heard of the *Cape Times*, in the aftermath of his decision to publish, without permission, a full-page verbatim interview with Oliver Tambo, President of the ANC. Tony was rewarded by Times Media Limited, owners of the *Cape Times*, for this flagrant act of defiance of the Emergency Regulations, the Suppression of Communism Act, and half a dozen other 'security' laws, by a contrived case for dismissal from his post as Editor. In due course this intrepid act of journalism would earn Tony international recognition through the award of the Golden Pen of Freedom by the International Federation of Newspaper Publishers.

One day Dr Stuart Saunders, Vice-Chancellor of the University of Cape Town, asked me if I would act for one of his students, Jennifer Schreiner, who had been arrested and detained in the most dramatic circumstances. Jenny was the daughter of Professor Deneys Schreiner, Deputy Vice-Chancellor of Natal University, and she came from a most remarkable family, which included a former Premier of the Cape, and one of South Africa's most distinguished authors and early feminists, Olive Schreiner. As a clandestine member of an MK unit, Jenny had been arrested during a midnight raid by the fearsome Terrorist Detection Unit, commanded by one Captain Willem Rudolph Liebenberg, who with the aid of his in-house torturer, Warrant Officer Jeffrey Benzien, would later testify and apply for amnesty from the Truth and Reconciliation Commission (TRC).

During this period of waiting, another of my clients Van Zyl Slabbert had a different sort of contretemps with the guardians of public morals, the

Directorate of Publications. His offence involved the discovery in a raincoat
pocket of a copy of Nelson Mandela's book, *No Easy Walk to Freedom*. This
apparently heinous transgression sent the police on the Swazi border into
paroxysms of indignation, and a prosecution was only averted as a result of
my representations to the Transvaal Attorney General – on the basis that he
would only make a fool of himself, and a laughing-stock of his masters, the
National Party. It was required that I admonish the erstwhile leader of the
Official Opposition, and urge him henceforth to lead an exemplary and
virtuous life!

What would the President's security advisers make of all this? Time
passed, and there was still no word from Van der Merwe nor the President's
office. The situation in the country was becoming increasingly tumultuous,
and seemed poised on the brink of mayhem and anarchy. Once again, I
wondered how to interpret the hiatus – although some delay had been fore-
shadowed by Van der Merwe's comment about the system 'winding down'
for the Christmas holidays.

An unforeseen aspect that began to trouble me increasingly was the fact
that I was acting entirely on my own judgment, without the benefit of
others' objectivity or sharing of responsibility. This seemed inherently
unwise. There was no way I could consider myself competent to make
unilateral decisions about such momentous and complex matters. Even
taking informal soundings could have political and strategic consequences.
I realised that if my initiative went ahead, I would need to share my
dilemmas with a few trusted confidants. The problem was how best to structure this without risking and compromising the essential confidentiality of
the project.

Ultimately, I decided to talk – albeit in strictest confidence – with a few
carefully chosen individuals whom I regarded as wise and trustworthy. I
needed objective judgment, and an ability to maintain confidence. There
was another aspect on which I needed guidance and assistance, namely how
to contact the ANC at an appropriate level, in the event that the initiative
was given a green light by the Government. One could not ask or assume
that particular persons were in fact members of a banned and illegal organisation. In due course, the ANC would also need reassurance as to my
credentials and integrity. After giving the matter a lot of careful thought, I
decided to speak off the record with three persons, without letting them
know that in fact the first moves had already been taken. As far as they
would be aware, we were discussing only a hypothetical possibility.

The first of these discussions involved Advocate Dullah Omar, who
would later become Minister of Justice in the new democratic South Africa.
At the time, he was an influential and outspoken leader of the United

Democratic Front (UDF) and the Mass Democratic Movement (MDM). I guessed, but had no certainty, as to his formal membership of the liberation movement. One day I simply rang him up and asked if I could come round and see him. There was 'something' I wanted to discuss. As professional colleagues, we'd known each other for a number of years. On a few occasions whilst he was practising at the side bar, he'd sought my assistance. We had also liaised on several matters – including the establishment of the Cape Town Legal Resources Centre. More recently we'd been in touch regarding litigation that was pending as a result of the demolition of the KTC squatter camp, in which Dullah would act as Junior Counsel. He would also later become involved in the trial of Jenny Schreiner and other members of her cadre.

Inured to the nuances of obscure phone calls, Dullah acquiesced and agreed to our meeting at his Chambers on the afternoon of 26 November. I recalled that when we had last met, he'd been recovering from a heart attack. Now he looked fit and confident, which was the prevailing mood of many who were then involved in 'the struggle'. No doubt they sensed that at last they had the tiger by the tail. International pressures on South Africa were increasing exponentially. The UN Security Council had just met in emergency session, to demand the withdrawal of South Africa's forces from Angola.

Realising the pressures on his time, I came straight to the point. 'I have been wondering whether the time may have arrived to attempt some kind of exploratory process with a view to initiating negotiations between the Government and the ANC'.

I studied Dullah's reaction. His customary equable affability gave way to a look of inscrutability. Whatever he had thought I might be coming to discuss, he certainly hadn't anticipated this. I realised I would be dropping a bombshell, but there seemed no merit in beating about the bush. I did not assume, or expect him to share confidences or to divulge his political affiliations. I told him that my own career as *gewone prokureur* (normal attorney) seemed to be drawing to a close, and I was now keen to identify a new role in which I would hope to be a bit more 'relevant and useful'. I said that I had thought deeply about the situation, and had come to the conclusion that there might be some value in my trying to act as some kind of confidential intermediary.

Dullah looked amazed. I said that I had wanted to talk to him in particular because he was politically involved, and I needed some independent views whether this proposition was appropriate, strategically and otherwise, or whether it was totally 'off the wall' – or indeed, whether perhaps there was some other role I could usefully play.

'You take my breath away,' was his initial response.

He looked at me with a degree of bafflement, if not suspicion, wondering perhaps, whether I was quite as innocent and apolitical as I had always claimed. Maybe he was also wondering, as no doubt others had and would, whether I was the bearer of some oblique message from some unidentified constituency – Government, organised Business, the Urban Foundation, or some other interest group. It is very difficult, I discovered, to prove one's innocence. Part of the cost of this role was that I too could become the subject of doubts.

Dullah was far too much of a professional to give any knee-jerk response, and he started off characteristically by disavowing his knowledge and influence. He said that he had not really had occasion to apply his mind to such 'macro issues', having been more concerned with local political issues and community affairs. He also professed no direct contact with the ANC outside the country, in part because he had been denied a passport. For these reasons, he was reliant upon information given him by others. However, he didn't wish to prejudge the issue, which he described as 'a remarkable idea'. He would like time to think about it.

He said he had always perceived me in the context of professional practice, and passed some complimentary comments about some of the work I was doing. He particularly appreciated the fact that as part of an establishment practice I remained willing 'to do some things that were politically useful'. It was important, he said, to have this kind of assistance from people in my position. Like Van der Merwe, Dullah asked whether I had any particular ideas how the concept might be implemented. Once again, I recited the mantra that although I had some ideas, I believed it would be a mistake to canvass or promote them. The process needed to define itself, a sentiment with which he seemed to agree.

He asked pertinently whether the concept of dialogue was not already receiving the attention of other entities, such as the Afrikaner Churches, and certain academics. I agreed, but said these were often 'media events', and those involved were not always 'disinterested'. The business community, for example, and certain political figures, had recently been putting out feelers, but they had their own particular agenda of self-interest. What I was proposing was something qualitatively different. The essence of this initiative would be its independence and secrecy.

Warming to the subject, Dullah speculated as to the possible reactions of the ANC and SACP, and of individuals within the UDF and MDM. He thought there would probably be a range of opinions. However, most people would oppose negotiations at this stage, 'at least until the political process had been normalised, and our leaders released'. The Government might imagine that it had succeeded in 'robbing the people of their leaders', but momentum was in fact increasing.

Concerning the current political context, Dullah spoke of his particular concern about the youth in the townships – the breakdown of education, the loss of parental authority, and the 'de-humanising' effect of endemic violence and repression. Symptoms such as necklacing and gang criminality were a deep concern. He saw his role as trying to encourage greater unity within the community, and drawing black youth into the political structures so that discipline could be established. There had been some success, but it was no easy task.

We also discussed the recent release of Govan Mbeki, and what signal the Government might intend by this step. He asked whether I thought it indicated a shift in attitude? I guessed it did, and imagined Government now hoped for some reciprocal gesture from its political adversaries.

Dullah said he did not know what my financial position was, but that the source of finance for any such initiative would be most important. It would be self-defeating, for example, to accept any money from the Government. He also warned of the Government's propensity for co-opting people into the system by offering them positions with attractive remuneration! I laughed, and said that, although I was not financially independent, I was not open to such inducements!

In conclusion, Dullah said that the idea could have merit, and the timing might be favourable, but he needed to give it more thought. As I left, he said it would be nice to get together one of these days for a drink under a tree in my garden. I hoped I had not been too forthcoming, realising that Dullah's Chambers were almost certainly 'bugged' by the Security Police.

As events transpired, we were to meet again early in the new year, on the afternoon of 5 January. Dullah said he had been wanting to talk again after giving these matters considerable thought. There were certain observations he felt he should make. I had assured him that I was talking to him on a personal level, as one friend seeking advice from another. Now he said that, although he appreciated this, it created some problems for him. He empathised with my wish to be involved but not politically affiliated. In different circumstances he might have had a similar preference, as he also didn't like 'joining things'. 'But', he said with a great guffaw, 'I have been less successful than you. In fact, I have been very unsuccessful! I'm no longer a "personal" person.' His responsibilities included the Chairmanship of the Western Cape Region of the UDF, and he also headed up NADEL, the National Association of Democratic Lawyers.

Although he might wish to respond more openly to my theoretical ideas, he was obviously subject to the constraints of his office. One had to be careful about making 'individualistic statements', which could cause division and disunity within organisations. He was on record as emphasising the importance of shared decision-making, and of organisations conducting their affairs in a participative and democratic manner. This was an important principle, and involved democratic accountability. These were values we would have to establish in a new society. For these reasons, he had decided it would not be appropriate to engage in 'secret' discussions with me about such an important matter. If we were to pursue this topic, our discussion could quickly progress beyond the point where we were just talking theoretically as friends, and he would then need to involve other people. Accordingly, the condition of our continuing to discuss this topic would be that he was free to involve the organisations and people with whom he was associated.

He pointed out that present conditions were hardly conducive to a genuine dialogue about such issues – inter alia, because of the large numbers of people in detention and the intimidation and harassment of the Police. It would be virtually impossible for substantive discussions to take place whilst many of their colleagues – people like Trevor Manuel and Christmas Tinto – were in detention. Personally, he doubted there was a genuine wish on the part of Botha's Government to engage in a serious dialogue about real issues with real leaders. Heunis's National Statutory Council was simply a non-starter. It was for the Government to come forward with its own proposals.

He said he was sorry if he sounded discouraging, but he didn't wish to become the repository of 'dangerous confidences'. He would therefore propose that we refrain from discussing these matters further, unless he was at liberty to canvass them with his colleagues and the organisations they belonged to. But he would leave the door open, and I could revert to him if this seemed appropriate.

After this inconclusive discussion, I decided to approach another important personage, Archbishop Desmond Tutu, whose credentials included considerable international influence and a deep spirituality. He seemed to have that rare combination of political independence and practical wisdom. As leader of the Anglican Community, and Nobel Prize winner, Tutu was becoming increasingly influential. He had been at the forefront of the campaign to isolate South Africa through economic and other sanctions, which he believed represented the last and best hope for bringing peaceful change to this country, and avoiding those consequences which he described as 'too ghastly to contemplate'. He was a client of my firm, and we had dealt with each other on several occasions, including efforts to resolve the fratricide and leadership conflicts within the Crossroads squatter camp.

My initial meeting with Archbishop Tutu took place at his official seat, 'Bishopscourt', on the morning of 3 December 1987. I arrived early for my appointment, and found myself waiting amongst a number of others who wished to see him. It had been several years since I had last visited Bishopscourt. Previously, it had seemed to me to have a somewhat intimidating aura of sanctimonious privilege. 'The Arch', as he enjoyed being called, had wrought a great transformation. People were now known by their first names, and there was none of that erstwhile bowing and scraping, and 'Your Grace'-ing. Even the waters of the ecclesiastical swimming-pool had recently been consecrated by township children. There was a tangible atmosphere of playfulness, and the richly carpeted corridors resounded with his characteristic cackles. Despite the demise of protocol, the office buzzed with efficient activity. Phones rang, the telex rattled, and people rushed hither and thither, bearing portentous piles of files. I watched the spectacle with enjoyment but impatience.

In arranging this appointment, my initial difficulty had been to satisfy the protective inquisitiveness of his staff. Precisely what did I wish to discuss, they wished to know. Unfortunately, I explained, I was not able to divulge the nature of my agenda. The Archbishop's secretary, Lavinia Brown, eventually tired of my imperviousness, and put the call through to the Reverend Matt Esau, whose job it was to protect Tutu from people just like me. In vain he tried to persuade me to tell him what it was all about, or to defer the meeting until next year. Finally, he promised me 'just a few minutes', sandwiched between other more important commitments. When I arrived, Matt came and shook my hand, and explained once again the difficulty of arranging appointments at this time of the year. He told me there was an important meeting in progress, and that it was altogether doubtful whether I would be able to see the Archbishop at all that morning! 'Why don't you go away and come back another day,' he pleaded, but I decided to stay. 'Well, you can wait if you wish, but I can't promise anything,' he warned.

About an hour later the Archbishop came out of his office and discovered me waiting like the importunate widow. Apologising profusely for having kept me waiting, he now kept me waiting some more. Eventually I was invited into his sanctum, and he indicated that he had only a few minutes to spare. He suggested that Matt should join us 'because he has more time than I have', but I demurred. I said I needed to speak to him on his own. Despite the obvious time pressure, the Archbishop still conveyed genuine concern, and was able to indulge his particular brand of humour and playfulness.

Coming directly to the point, I told him that I had decided to resign my law practice, and was considering the possibility of exploring some intermediary role between the Government and the ANC. He asked a number of questions, which I answered as best I could – but once again, I didn't disclose to him that some steps had already been taken. Was there any reason to think the Government would be interested in such a dialogue, he asked. I replied that this was precisely what I was trying to find out. He expressed himself as totally disillusioned with the obduracy of P W Botha, whom he had met on several occasions. As a pastor, he said, he couldn't exclude the possibility of a man changing, but he doubted whether my efforts would be any more successful than his own. 'But one never knows what might happen,' he said with a laugh, adding that each of us must follow his own intuition. 'But don't be surprised if you seem to have failed.' Sometimes, there was value in the ordinary things we did. However, he was worried about my intention to resign my practice. 'That seems a rather risky thing to do,' he suggested, 'unless of course you have other sources of income?' I assured him that I had not.

I explained that my decision was as much the product of desperation as from any sense of mission. For this reason, I needed the objective opinion of someone like himself. 'D'you think it's crazy?' I asked. He was thoughtful for a few moments, then replied with a great cackle, 'Yes, I think it's crazy! But it's the kind of crazy thing religious people are meant to do;' adding, 'I don't know; are you a religious sort of person?' I decided to spare him my religious ambiguities.

'There are of course tremendous difficulties in the way of what you are proposing', he continued, 'but many good things have come out of ideas that seemed a bit crazy!' He cackled again. 'Besides, you'll never know unless you try it. In fact, you're bound to try. If one doesn't follow through on such impulses, one can just disintegrate as a person. So go ahead. You have my blessing!' He thought for a moment, then added, 'And if it doesn't work out, some good may have come of it. Maybe you'll have moved the pieces a little bit. And, if it fails, well ... *so what!* Once again he laughed uproariously. More seriously, he said if I wanted his opinion on specifics, he would need more time to think and pray about it. Perhaps I could arrange another meeting at a later date.

Following up this invitation, I telephoned Bishopscourt again just before Christmas, to the unruffled dismay of his secretary. Once again the long-suffering Matt Esau found himself at the receiving end of my dogged persistence. With hindsight, 23 December must be one of the most dreadful days of the year for an Archbishop. However, two weeks of unrestful holiday at Nature's Valley had left me desperate for decisions and greater clarity.

My appointment was for 10.30 a.m., but it was not until 1.30 p.m. that the Archbishop finally saw me. I was allotted half an hour. Matt once more made vain but valiant efforts to defer the meeting, but I insisted that the matter was of great importance. He said there was a meeting of bishops that morning, and such meetings generally took at least two hours. Then it would be lunchtime. I might have to wait all afternoon. I replied, 'Well, so be it,' adding, 'I believe what I need to discuss is of sufficient urgency and importance.' Matt responded, 'Yes, of importance to you; but other things are of importance to other people!' 'No,' I insisted, 'this is of importance to many people.' Matt was forgivably sceptical.

Eventually an obviously tired Archbishop saw me at 1.30 p.m., and (I suspect) it cost him his lunch. I felt only moderately penitent. Once again I was struck by his warmth and gentleness. He insisted upon saying a prayer before we began talking. Despite the pressures, he seemed unhurried, and showed me a card he had received from a child in his parish.

'I feel like I have a fire in my belly about this thing,' I said. Tutu said, 'Good. Then you must do it.' He referred me to the Prophet Jeremiah who apparently also had a fire – though in his breast, rather than his belly. I asked again, 'Was this totally crazy?' and he replied, 'Not totally crazy, just slightly crazy!' adding, 'But a good many things have come out of ideas that were a little crazy.' He asked that I let him know what happened. Although he could not officially endorse my initiative, I was at liberty to mention that I had discussed it with him in general terms. He explained that he needed to preserve his independence from specific actions. However, there was no problem in my saying we had discussed it, and he was generally supportive of the idea.

Before leaving, I asked his advice on the issue of financing the initiative – if it were in fact to be launched. He agreed there were a number of possibilities – including the Government itself – but the Government would not be the appropriate source. However, sometimes too much fuss was made about where the money came from. I asked what he thought about my approaching a foreign Embassy, such as Germany or Japan. He thought there might be some merit in that, but it would need to be sensitively handled.

He then gave me his blessing, and asked that I let him know what happened. He also urged that, before I leave, I should give Matt Esau some explanation of what we had discussed, because this would make it easier for me to arrange future meetings with him. So Matt and I sat down on a bench beneath a large oak tree, and I tried over the ensuing hour to sketch for him the nature of my proposal, apologising once again for gate-crashing the ecclesiastical diary.

Two weeks later I sought out my friend, Arthur Chaskalson, who had just returned for a short visit from an academic sojourn in the United States. He was back to consult in connection with the forthcoming Bethel trial, which involved the prosecution of leading members of the UDF on capital charges of treason. Arthur is someone for whom I have the greatest admiration and affection. Ten years earlier, he had aborted a flourishing career at the Johannesburg Bar to commit his fulltime efforts to establishing that most remarkable institution, the Legal Resources Centre. Under his leadership, the LRC conducted some of the most important human-rights litigation of the apartheid era. Arthur is a man of unassuming manner and great modesty, whose qualities as a human being and as a lawyer have been recognised by his appointment as President of the Constitutional Court. A few years earlier he had invited me to help establish the Legal Resources Centre in Cape Town.

In my discussion with Arthur, I went further than I had with either Dullah Omar or the Archbishop. I gave him a detailed account of the steps already taken, including my meeting with Stoffel van der Merwe. I had come to feel that I needed at least one person who knew everything. I also had in mind that if something untoward happened, Hilary would need the support and guidance of someone like Arthur. Without his seeking or accepting this thankless role, Arthur became 'my brother and my father confessor'. I could not have asked for more, or received better.

Like Omar and Tutu, Arthur was obviously amazed. He said that if I had asked him to predict P W's likely response, he would have expected my proposal to have been rejected out of hand. The fact that this had not happened showed how difficult it was to make predictions in such matters. One would now have to see how the situation developed. Perhaps it had real potential? He would be returning to Columbia University within a few days, and would not be back in South Africa until May; but when he returned – if it was viable – he would like to become involved. In the meanwhile, he offered whatever assistance he could give whilst overseas.

We went on to discuss how best one might manage and structure the initiative – if it finally received the 'go ahead'. I said I would have felt much more comfortable if I could operate under the aegis of an institutional structure such as the LRC or Urban Foundation, with both of which I was involved. However, it didn't seem that either of these bodies – nor any other I could think of – would represent an appropriate institutional 'home' for this orphan.

I asked whether my involvement in such a venture, and my anticipated resignation from law practice might affect my suitability as a Trustee of the Legal Resources Trust. Arthur said that he didn't see this as a problem at this stage, but one might have to keep it in mind as the situation evolved. With regard to my suggestion of creating some kind of informal 'steering group', Arthur felt one would need to be extremely circumspect in handpicking the individuals involved.

As to the costs issue, he felt it would be impracticable to request assistance until the project had at least received the informal sanction of both the Government and the ANC. In the meanwhile, there was probably no alternative but to carry these costs myself. Looking ahead, I asked his view about how one might seek to structure future contacts in a way that afforded the participants some degree of protection in the event of a breach of confidentiality. Arthur felt that initially one would probably have to deal only with the ANC outside the country. There were ways in which they could communicate with those inside the country. One possibility might be for each party to appoint another tier of intermediaries – perhaps lawyers – who could serve as the initial communication channel, thereby providing a layer of protection. But the more people involved, the greater the risk of disclosure and indiscretion. Especially at the initial stages, both parties would probably want to retain their ability to 'disown' the process.

Though sceptical as to the likelihood of success, Arthur was nonetheless supportive of the concept and indulgent of my wish to attempt it. If it proved practicable, he would like to consider the possibility of becoming involved. In the meantime, his friendship and moral support were assured.

5

Building a bridge

As the year 1987 drew to an end, it became necessary, despite the uncertainties which persisted regarding the fate of my initiative – and the related issue of our emigration – to let my law firm know that I would be departing in the reasonably near future. This was a particularly traumatic decision, representing the end of a quarter century of practice. I would have much preferred to leave matters in abeyance until the situation had clarified. However, the firm was then embarking upon a strategic planning exercise, and it would have been invidious to allow them to proceed on the assumption that I was part of the equation. Although I still didn't know whether I would remain in South Africa or emigrate to Canada, at least my departure from the firm seemed assured.

So with a heavy heart, I convened a meeting of my colleagues in early December, and told them that I was 'considering various possibilities', which would involve my retiring from the practice in the not too distant future. I asked that for the time being they keep this information to themselves, and undertook to let them know as soon as my plans had clarified. They expressed regret, and were curious as to my future plans. I had no option but to remain irritatingly vague.

Naively perhaps, I assumed that my partners would tolerate my need for obfuscation, and indulge my wish to consider other options at this stage in my life. However, my intention to leave seemed to evoke a degree of alienation, and I began to feel isolated and almost disloyal. Once the announcement had been made, they seemed anxious to hasten my departure and get on with the task of building the practice. Clearly they felt entitled to know what I had in mind, and when, and why I was leaving. I could give them no simple answers. It was not a very happy situation.

Within a few weeks, there was a further partners' meeting. Again I was asked about my future plans; and again I replied, that they would have to wait a little longer. Their response was blunt: 'If you're intending to leave, then the sooner the better.' I was not a little surprised, and felt as though I was being shown the door. I couldn't explain what was really afoot, but obviously had ceased to be part of 'the family'. After discussing the matter with Hilary, I told them they could assume I would leave at the end of August.

However, a long wait ensued before my next meeting with Stoffel van der Merwe, which finally took place towards the end of January. This two-month hiatus, though extremely worrying, had the signal benefit of providing me with time to study background documents, and to start exploring alternative strategies.

On the international terrain, several factors seemed to confirm my instinct as to the existence of a unique climate for negotiations. There had come a thaw in the 40-year Cold War, resulting in unprecedented coopera-tion between the United States and Russia in the business of peacemaking. The Angolan peace negotiations were amongst the first beneficiaries. By the end of the year, this new spirit of détente was illustrated when Presidents Reagan and Gorbachev delivered reciprocal uncensored New Year messages. International pressures for negotiation were also beginning to bear upon the Government of P W Botha and the ANC in exile. Botha faced international isolation and sanctions; whilst the ANC had to contend with growing concerns regarding the willingness and ability of the Soviet Union to main-tain its former financial and logistical support. There were also rumours of some kind of low-key dialogue taking place between the South African and Soviet Governments. Several of South Africa's important trading partners, including Switzerland, Germany and Japan, remained largely impervious to the ANC's pleas for more effective economic and diplomatic sanctions. Switzerland, in particular, relying upon its unique history of neutrality, continued to handle South Africa's gold sales, and acted as this country's principal clearing bank.

The ANC was also facing other diplomatic pressures. In the US, President Ronald Reagan declined to meet the ANC's Oliver Tambo, but agreed to bestow this ceremonial benediction upon Chief Gatsha Buthelezi of Inkatha. By contrast, Mr Tambo was accorded some gratuitous diplomatic instruction by Secretary of State, George Schultz, concerning the ANC's armed struggle and its perceived susceptibility to Communist influence. UK Prime Minister, Margaret Thatcher, also pronounced reproof upon the ANC, which she described at the Vancouver Commonwealth Summit as 'just another typical terrorist organisation'.

The year 1987 had been named by the ANC at its 75th anniversary cele-brations in Lusaka, as 'The Year of Advance to People's Power'. The organi-sation committed itself to an intensification of the armed struggle, until the South African Government was willing 'to negotiate the abolition of apartheid'. In August 1987, the ANC issued a statement indicating five 'minimal conditions' to be satisfied before negotiations could be considered.

These were:

- The release of all political prisoners and detainees;
- The lifting of the State of Emergency and withdrawal of all SADF personnel from the townships;
- The repeal of 'politically repressive laws';
- An end to the Bantustan system, and reintegration of the 'independent homelands';
- An unconditional right of return for all exiles and political refugees.

Meanwhile, the Nationalist Party clung like a drowning man to the raft of Chris Heunis's brainchild, the so-called National Council. Its impervious belief in the immaculate conception of this never-to-be-born structure, which was to be chaired by the President himself, resulted in a dearth of meaningful dialogue. The Council was perceived as the forum through which Government would 'negotiate in a peaceful manner with leaders of other communities'. Another 'dead-duck' concept was Botha's 'Council of State', conceived as some kind of 'super-cabinet', in which African leaders would have some kind of unspecified representation. These concepts were supported by F W de Klerk, then Minister of National Education, in a speech delivered during a visit to Switzerland, when he explained that the Government envisaged 'own legislative assemblies for urban blacks and executive ministerial councils, of which the final outcome would be a number of high-level authorities with full decision-making powers'. In another masterpiece of dialectical obfuscation, De Klerk had also said that the Nationalist Party envisaged:

- A policy of power-sharing in which no group could dominate another;
- The establishment of legislative and executive structures for blacks outside the national states;
- Joint decision-making on the basis of consensus within a Council of State; and
- Effective protection of minorities and group rights.

Frustrated by his inability to govern and lead, Botha in desperation resorted to newspaper advertisements. In one such media campaign, in May 1987, the President declared: 'I am now extending my hand of friendship to all South Africans of goodwill. Join me in talks and negotiations. We will find the answers to our questions together.' Needless to say there was no great clamour to grasp the President's extended hand.

But as though to head off premature proposals for constitutional dialogue with the ANC – official or otherwise – the President continued to intone that negotiation with the ANC was 'a far-fetched idea'. He explained that organisations like the ANC only entered negotiations 'to force others into capitulation'. In Parliament, he poured scorn on IDASA's Dakar Conference, and said, 'The ANC is laughing up its sleeves at the naiveté of these "useful idiots", who as Lenin puts it can be used to further the aims of the first phase of the revolution.' In the President's view, the Dakar delegates had not held 'penetrating discussions', as they claimed, but had merely attempted 'to coordinate strategies and find out what the ANC expects of "democratic patriots".' The President saw such talks as 'a means to an end, namely, the revolutionary takeover of power'.

After ten weeks of delay, my second meeting with Stoffel van der Merwe finally took place at his Ministerial office in Stalplein House, Cape Town on Thursday 24 January. We started in the late afternoon, and continued for some two and a half hours.

It was now his view that the climate for negotiations had become problematical. However he remained committed to the concept, and wished to be assured that I too was willing to carry forward the proposal? I confirmed that I was absolutely willing, but couldn't allow the matter to be deferred indefinitely, if only because of my personal circumstances. I told him that following his cue as to the likelihood of some early action, I had already informed my partners that I would be leaving at the end of August. It was therefore urgent that I now clarify the situation.

With surprising frankness, Stoffel then told me that he was feeling terribly disheartened after his recent meeting with the State President. They had discussed possible themes for the Opening of Parliament speech. The discussion had left him feeling less hopeful than ever about the immediate prospects for 'serious political reform'. The ongoing polemic between the Revd Alan Hendrikse and the State President 'though just a side show' was distracting attention from the more important issues. Ironically, it had served to confirm some people's belief that power-sharing with Coloureds and Indians was doomed to fail, and that this formula should not be followed with Blacks. The President's current preoccupation was the economy, and the need to restore business confidence. Stoffel anticipated that the President's speech would focus on social stability and a strong economy, as the essential preconditions for any further reform initiatives. I pointed out that we might not have 'the luxury' of managing the 'reform process' under ideal conditions of stability and a growing economy.

Always ready to engage in theoretical digression, Stoffel argued that there were now two mutually opposed dangers in the reform process – proceeding either too fast or too slow. He said that in a recent article in the *Financial Mail* he had been described as one of those urging a faster pace. Warming to his thesis, he said reform could be likened to an animal with four legs – not all the legs moved at any one time. Though some legs might not be seen to be moving at a particular moment, the whole animal was still in motion. He seemed very enamoured with this metaphor. Taking my cue from his biological analogy, I reminded him about Hilaire Belloc's Water Beetle, which 'moved upon the water's face with ease, celerity, and grace', until it stopped and 'thinkt, "How is this done?"– and then of course, it sinkt!'

Stoffel admitted that reform had slowed, and attributed this in part to electoral gains made by the right wing. There was a fear in some circles that the National Party might be getting too far ahead of its own constituency. I warned him that Belloc's Water Beetle had drowned as a result of too much introspection!

Returning to the subject of my proposal, Stoffel said he was really disappointed at being unable to respond more positively. As he had mentioned in our previous discussion, there were 'certain ideas and projects' which he would like to discuss with me at an appropriate time. However these were still 'on the table', and he had not been able to establish their formal acceptability. For the next three to four weeks the focus would be on the No Confidence Debate, and no real progress could be expected. He suggested we get together again a month hence.

With my impending 'retirement', I was becoming increasingly anxious about his sanguine attitude to the passing of time. I began to wonder whether I should not in fact follow my own instincts, and proceed, if necessary without their blessing. This could have a side benefit of reducing the risks for both parties, as I would then be taking personal responsibility for making the initial overtures. So I asked Van der Merwe what his reaction might be if, hypothetically of course, I decided – without anyone's approval – to make contact with the ANC in much the same manner as I had approached the State President? For a few moments he looked thoughtful, and then said he would be interested to hear how this developed. However, he obviously could not give me any encouragement. The disadvantage of such an interventionist strategy would be that the initiative could then be seen as no different from others which had preceded it – and failed. The Government would resist being pre-empted or co-opted into some third-party initiative over which it had no control.

As though to reassure himself, Stoffel recalled that the President had mandated him to become 'the eyes and ears' of the Government. For this reason he was keen to develop contacts with black leaders, so that he could be exposed to their views, and they to his. His junior status in the Cabinet gave him greater latitude, and limited the political risks for the Government.

'Happily or unhappily,' he said with a grin, 'I will be dispensable.'

I asked him about the contradictory versions of 'the adventures' of one Cobus Jordaan, an official in the Department of Constitutional Development and Planning, about whom there had been some controversy. It was rumoured – though subsequently denied – that in September 1987 Jordaan had tried to make contact with the ANC through Zambian President, Kenneth Kaunda. The ANC declared that 'such attempts at contact' should be seen as an effort by the Government to sow confusion, and to drive a wedge between those in exile and those within the country. I wondered whether this might be an indication of its possible response to my own proposals?

Shifting course, Stoffel said he was keen to start meeting with lower-echelon community leaders, and wondered whether I could not assist him in making initial introductions. There were people with whom he could readily make contact, but others who were largely inaccessible to him. He was open to suggestions, and ready to take some political risks. 'Obviously, I can't ask you to go and talk to the Broederbond for me, but perhaps there are people whom you could communicate with better than I.'

I was concerned that his preoccupation with making 'lower-level' contacts and establishing personal relationships might involve a different agenda from my own. The ANC suspected the Government of pursuing a deliberate strategy of promoting ideological differences and confusion. I therefore reminded him that I was concerned with the possibility of a 'high-level' dialogue about constitutional issues. I did not see that I could be helpful in setting up dialogue with other parties about other issues. He assured me we were both talking about the same agenda.

I also asked whether he had formed any view as to my suitability to serve as an intermediary? He parried for a while, and then said he felt cautiously positive. He believed my background as 'an English-speaking liberal' could be useful. I knew it was important that I be not too inquisitive, but could not resist asking him another leading question: Could he give me any idea what the Government's reaction might be, if the ANC said that it was interested in the kind of dialogue we had been discussing?

He replied that he was not yet in a position to answer that question. It would have to be considered in the light of circumstances prevailing at the time. Then, as though reciting some kind of rehearsed liturgy, he added, 'There would need to be an initial suspension of violence.' I replied that the parties had to be careful not to disable a dialogue before it began by setting impossible conditions. 'It is most unlikely the ANC would be prepared to play its strongest card first,' I pointed out. He said it would be far too risky for the Government to initiate any overtures, but he didn't think 'it would be unreceptive to overtures from the other side. As far as we are concerned, the ball is in their court. We've made a number of moves and taken some flak, but we've yet to see any movement from their side. If they want negotiations they're going to have to make it clear.'

Stoffel said that he personally favoured an incremental process commencing with initial contacts at a relatively low level. It would not be practical to consider leader-to-leader meetings at the outset. 'It would be like trying to build a bridge across a chasm without providing supports.' He talked about the need first to create 'the right climate for negotiations'. Recalling another project with which he had been involved, he said things had been 'quite far advanced', when the Pretoria car bomb exploded. This had caused everything to be summarily aborted.

I then raised the issue of costs and logistics of my initiative. He reiterated his view that my role should be independent of any organisation. He would understand that I might need some kind of reference group, and said at a later stage he 'might introduce me to certain persons'. The pivotal concern at this stage should be to preserve complete confidentiality. With regard to the need for some financial subventing of expenses, he said it might be possible to arrange 'something like a directorship'. I said that, although starvation was not imminent, I would not be able to finance these activities personally over the long term.

We talked about a number of possible funding sources, including the Urban Foundation, or perhaps a corporate sponsor such as the Anglo American Corporation or even the Rembrandt Group. For different reasons, each seemed inappropriate. What were his own views? He said I might have to 'compromise a little' on my sensibilities. He saw the real problem of third-party funding as creating the need for 'accountability or reporting'. This would create the suspicion of some kind of influence or control. I reaffirmed my belief in the importance of complete independence, and made it clear that, whatever arrangements might be decided upon, they would have to be known and approved by both sides. I didn't wish to find myself behoven, financially or otherwise, to either the Government or the ANC. He said he was confident this problem could be resolved, if there was 'some flexibility' on my part.

We had begun in the late afternoon, and it was now growing dark. He led me out of his office, and we agreed to meet again three or four weeks hence.

During the weeks that followed, I resumed my legal work, and tried as best I could – though not very successfully – to generate an income and maintain the appearance of normality. I began to hand over work to my partners, in anticipation of my retirement. One matter with which I decided to remain personally involved was that involving Jennifer Schreiner. By this time she was formally accused of various acts of 'terrorism', including the planting of bombs at Cape Town Airport, and at the Police barracks. She was being held in solitary confinement and, as the Regulations required, denied access to lawyers, doctors, family, and friends. She had been continuously interrogated, threatened, abused, and assaulted over many months, until finally during January, she reluctantly agreed to make a statement. Shortly thereafter she attempted suicide. Her interrogators had included the notorious 'official' police torturer, Warrant Officer Jeffrey Benzien.

In acting for people like Jenny, I felt an enormous sense of responsibility – though we had never met. I tried to provide some reassurance to her parents, and to her friends, comrades and family, who would come to see me periodically. At this stage I could do no more than maintain a barrage of telephone calls, faxes, letters, enquiries, and requests, to the Ministers of Police and of Law and Order, to the Commissioner, to the Commanding Officer of the Prison, to the Head of the Security Branch, and to other individual warders and policemen.

After Jenny's forced confession and suicide attempt, the need to gain access to her became ever more urgent. This could only be achieved by way of 'special concession', as no consultation was permitted in terms of the Emergency Regulations. In spite of these restrictions, Jenny smuggled out two brave and moving letters, in which she spoke of her continuing ordeal. It subsequently transpired that she had been given assistance by a member of the prison staff at great personal risk.

The family sought my advice when this warder was identified, and the Police tried by bluster and threat to induce Jenny's father to give them an incriminating statement. Eventually I was granted a consultation with Jenny in the cells at Pollsmoor. Although we were strangers, I felt it my privilege and duty to give her a discreet (illegal) hug, to the obvious consternation of the vigilant warders! For some time my fortnightly visits were her only link with the outside world, and I felt awed by such a responsibility. Sometimes when I visited her in the single-storey block known as the Women's Prison, I would look across at the huge square bulk of the adjacent Men's Prison, and imagine one day visiting another prisoner incarcerated there – Nelson Mandela.

In the world beyond Pollsmoor and my office, the country was moving inexorably towards ever-greater crisis. 1988 was to become the most violent year in South Africa's history. Minister of Law and Order, Adriaan Vlok, told Parliament that during the year there had been 291 'terrorist incidents', and 64 'acts of terrorism'. The Government in its passion for statistics reported 5 028 'incidents of unrest and violence' – 'or 14.3 per day'. Since P W Botha's accession as President under the Tricameral constitution, there had been over 4 000 fatalities attributable to political violence.

But the Government remained obdurate. It took comfort from events such as the visit of Bavarian Prime Minister, Franz-Josef Strauss – whom Botha described as 'a true friend of South Africa'. During his ten-day visit at the beginning of February, Dr Strauss denounced sanctions and hailed what he termed 'changes for the better'. He visited Chief Mangosuthu Buthelezi at Ulundi, and caused much consternation in both South Africa and Germany by appearing to give recognition to the puppet regime of 'independent' Bophuthatswana – whose President Lucas Mangope was in rapid order ousted, rescued, and reinstated by a small company of SADF troops, all in the course of a single day, 10 February. (President Botha announced revealingly: 'We are back in control'; which he quickly corrected by saying: 'The President of Bophuthatswana is back in control!'

It was becoming evident that Canada, our country of possible adoption, had chosen a more assertive line against South Africa. The South African Ambassador, Hennie de Klerk, thought it necessary to warn 'well-meaning Canadians' that they 'should not fool themselves or be misled into thinking they can take out some form of moral insurance by supporting sanctions against South Africa'.

President Botha told Parliament on 5 February that constitutional development and renewal had to take place in an evolutionary manner. Mysteriously, he promised: 'During this session and thereafter we shall accordingly proceed with the measures which have already been announced, and which are under consideration.' Nobody knew precisely what this meant. Professor Lawrie Schlemmer drew an interesting comparison between Botha and Gorbachev, both of whom he described as 'trying to share power, without losing control'.

At about this time, Nelson Mandela's Ministerial jailer, Kobie Coetsee, who would later anoint himself as Mandela's liberator, speaking in the No-Confidence debate, speculated that the ANC's demand for the release of Nelson Mandela was 'just a huge bluff'. He said Mandela and his fellow prisoners were worth far more to the ANC in jail than out of it!

Then came the events of 24 February. At the very moment when one hoped for some enlightened restraint and initiatives, it seemed that the Government had taken a great leap backwards. In a massive crackdown, restriction orders were placed upon 17 organisations, including the United Democratic Front (UDF), the Congress of South African Trade Unions (COSATU), and the Azanian People's Organisation (AZAPO). Minister of Law and Order, Adriaan Vlok, in a 'lame duck' speech to Parliament, said the Government did not wish to prohibit all the activities of the organisations concerned, but 'only those which endangered law and order'.

Within forty-eight hours, a deluge of international criticism descended. The European Community issued a statement in which it condemned these measures as a 'new manifestation of political suppression'. Countries such as the United States, Great Britain, France, Japan, and Israel summoned South Africa's Ambassadors to receive messages of censure. UN Secretary General Dr Perez de Cuellar predicted that these measures 'could aggravate existing tensions and lead to new violence'. Inside the country there were massive protests, which involved leaders of most religious denominations. Anglican Archbishop Desmond Tutu and Roman Catholic Archbishop Stephen Naidoo were amongst those arrested during a march through downtown Cape Town which was eventually stopped by water cannon. They had been on their way to deliver a petition to the State President protesting the bannings, which Tutu described as 'an unmitigated disaster'. Speaking shortly thereafter at the All Africa Conference of Churches in Nairobi, Tutu called on Western nations to impose full economic sanctions and break diplomatic relations with South Africa. It seemed that only the Conservative Party thought otherwise. It condemned the Government's actions on the grounds that they were 'inadequate' and 'too late'.

I wondered how Dr van der Merwe would reconcile such decisions with what we had been discussing. On 27 February, a few days before our scheduled third meeting, he was quoted as saying at a press conference: 'There is no doubt that the restrictions placed this week ... will negatively affect the Government's negotiations with black leaders in the short term ... but because restrictions had been placed on some individuals, this did not mean the Government would not talk to them.' The report continued: 'As the Government's chief negotiator with black leaders, he was asked if he had agreed to these restrictions, Dr van der Merwe replied: "I can't dissociate myself from them. I don't even want to try. I'm part of the Government, and I accept what the Government does."'

When we met again on the morning of Monday 7 March, I asked the meaning of these events. In the Security Council, two days earlier, Les Manley, South Africa's representative, told the international community 'to do its damnedest' – a bombastic style, which no doubt accurately reflected His Master's Voice. Foreign Minister Pik Botha added that the world was now hearing 'the authentic voice of a regional power asserting itself, its position and its role'. I said to Van der Merwe that I didn't know how one could extend the hand of friendship and simultaneously proffer an iron fist. How did he reconcile these events with the Government's declared commitment to reform and peace?

Stoffel didn't hesitate to acknowledge that these steps would have an immediate negative impact, but he remained optimistic. 'These questions will be receiving our specific attention during the next few weeks,' he assured me. He saw these measures as an 'unfortunate short-term necessity'. In the longer term he believed they would help to create a more favourable atmosphere for negotiations. The Government had become convinced that organisations like the UDF were engaged in activities that were destructive to its reform initiatives. It had therefore become necessary to take these actions. They should not be seen in isolation, but rather as the precursor to later 'concessions'. I listened in dismay, wondering how the Government could imagine that it could negotiate with those it had silenced.

By this time, six months had passed since my initial approach to the State President. I still had no more than the vaguest idea whether there was any compatibility between our respective 'ideas'. I was eager to identify a role that I could play, but my availability was neither unconditional nor indefinite. In response to my question, Stoffel said that the 'ideas' he had referred to a few times related to a managed sequence of events – 'a process' – the details of which were still under discussion. There was a growing consensus, he said, that the point of departure needed to be some Statement of Intent by the Government. This would set the guiding principles for which a broad-based consensus would then be sought. He foresaw that I might have some role in securing that agreement. What was undecided, and still under discussion, were the precise steps to be followed in the wake of such a Statement of Intent.

He apologised for the continuing ambiguity in my situation, but said he was unfortunately not a free agent. He reaffirmed that the Government was committed to pursuing a course involving substantial reform, and that it was no longer feasible to backtrack on their commitment. Despite periodic delays as at present, the long-term objectives remained intact. However, the Conservative Party gains in the recent by-elections at Standerton and Schweizer-Reneke had once more emphasised the political risks that the Government's reform initiatives involved. As an *Argus* editorial intoned: 'The CP advance bodes ill for the politics of negotiation and realism.'

Our allotted half hour was up. Before departing, I expressed concern about the repetitive pattern of delays and deferments. In my view, the most dangerous course would be one of vacillation. Already there had been a long period of stasis which was very damaging to the prospect of success. What was now needed, I argued, was a new momentum, a sense of anticipation and expectation – 'the chemistry of vision' was a phrase I used. Once again, he invited me to set down my ideas in writing, and once again I declined. I ventured that the National Party might be surprised one day to discover the support it received if it was able to take bold initiatives. Dr van der Merwe agreed, 'Perhaps you are an early example of this?' I decided his interpretation didn't warrant my reply.

Van der Merwe indicated a wish for us to meet again within a fortnight. He apologised for the difficulty in arranging our latest meeting, and said he was endeavouring to find 'a solution' to his diary. He had decided to 'put the whole thing on a computer', in the belief that this might make more time available. I refrained from pointing out that even a computer could not extend the duration of the 24-hour day.

Two weeks later, the President announced the appointment of Dr Stoffel van der Merwe as a full member of the Cabinet. Henceforth he would be Minister of Information, strategically located in the office of the President. Brian Pottinger in *The Imperial Presidency* describes Van der Merwe as 'one of the new technocrats', whom he characterised as 'figures whose loyalty, ultimately, lay with the President, not the Party'. He commented: 'Only Botha's complete control of the Party, brought about by a mixture of author-itarianism, gerrymandering, and real inspiration, made this leap-frogging of younger appointees possible, without creating a serious revolt within party ranks.'

I wrote the new Minister of Information a somewhat overly indulgent letter of congratulations.

6

A basis of deniability

In early March, the Nationalist-supporting media reported portentously that the Cabinet had gathered '*op 'n onbekende plek*' ('at an unknown place') to consider '*diep sake*' ('profound affairs'). Apparently, this early *bosberaad* (bush conference) was focused on the future political dispensation for urban blacks. Various pontifical pronouncements followed, which appeared to give belated recognition to the self-evident need for a new constitutional framework. Chris Heunis, the Minister with responsibility for Constitutional Development and Planning, chose the auspicious occasion of the opening of a new fire station at a place called KwaNobuhle, near Port Elizabeth, as the occasion to vent his sage thoughts on the matter: 'Time is running out for a choice to be made between violence and negotiations.' At a Transvaal gathering of National Party youth, the President called upon black leaders to come forward and communicate with each other. He also warned ominously: 'Let us be on our guard at all times to ensure that one population group cannot dominate another.'

On the other hand, Chief Mangosuthu Buthelezi set his face against a future dialogue which included the ANC. Speaking in the KwaZulu Legislative Assembly, he said that, in the light of what he characterised as the ANC's attempts to destroy Inkatha, 'I see no earthly use any longer in hoping for constructive discussions with the ANC mission in exile.'

Internationally, the campaign to coerce and isolate South Africa continued to gather momentum. In the UN Security Council a call for mandatory sanctions was only narrowly defeated – as a result of vetoes cast by Great Britain and the United States, with West Germany abstaining. The sanctions issue, like the armed struggle, divided the anti-apartheid forces, both inside and outside the country. Predictably, the South African business sector adamantly opposed economic sanctions, as did the Progressive Federal Party and the Urban Foundation. In a joint written submission to the US Congressional Committee, PFP members Colin Eglin and Helen Suzman commented: 'While the pace of change is painfully slow, we cannot believe that such change will be accelerated by externally induced impoverishment of millions of black South Africans.' Jan Steyn speaking on behalf of the Urban Foundation described sanctions as an 'over-spontaneous, superficial, and poorly considered reaction'.

In response, Archbishop Tutu asserted that it was not for others to concern themselves with the suffering of South Africa's oppressed peoples. They were already suffering and were prepared to suffer more. They didn't need advice from foreign governments, or from the South African business community, regarding their willingness to make further sacrifices.

Increasingly restive about lack of progress, the US Congress scheduled two days of public hearings during March on the sanctions issue, which prompted President Botha to warn: 'Total sanctions by the US will merely mean you will lose what little influence you still have.' In the wake of the failure of the Commonwealth mission (the Eminent Persons' Group), Sir Shridath Ramphal, Commonwealth Secretary General, called for an intensification of the sanctions campaign against South Africa, proposing consumer boycotts, and a cutback in trade and investments. West Germany also became unusually voluble. Its President, Richard von Weizsaecker, in an unprecedented – and highly controversial – venture into foreign policy, announced during his State visit to Zimbabwe, that recent developments in South Africa had necessitated a reappraisal by Bonn of measures needed to bring apartheid to an end. 'It is the Government in South Africa itself that makes it more and more difficult for other countries in the world to go on asking for peaceful dialogue to end the country's racial conflict,' he said.

Meanwhile the pattern of violence and counter-violence continued inexorably, with bombings, sabotage, assassinations, and raids into neighbouring countries. On 29 March, two days before my next scheduled meeting with Stoffel van der Merwe, Dulcie September, the ANC's representative for France, Switzerland and Luxembourg, was gunned down in a Paris street by unidentified assassins. There was strong suspicion that this too was the work of South African agents – supposedly, in retaliation for a car-bomb explosion outside the Krugersdorp Magistrates Court on 17 March, when 3 persons had been killed and 22 injured.

On 31 March, just prior to the Easter weekend, my fourth meeting with Stoffel van der Merwe took place at his Cape Town offices. It had become routine for him to commence these encounters with ritual apologies for unforeseen circumstances and difficulties which had occasioned further delays. This meeting was no exception. He said that once again adverse political developments, coupled with his own pressure of work, and the demands of his new portfolio, had prevented more rapid progress being made. His formal induction and swearing in as a full member of the Cabinet had taken place earlier that day. I congratulated him, and he noted with pride the speed of his elevation, first to the rank of Deputy-Minister a year

ago, and now to the rank of full Minister. He said it was particularly grati-
fying because his appointment involved enlarging the size of the Cabinet, at
a time when the President was committed to reducing it. I asked whether
his new appointment meant the end of his involvement with negotiations,
but he assured me this was not so. He would remain very much involved –
though 'perhaps unofficially'.

Following months of delay, I had decided prior to this meeting that I had
to bring matters to a head. Having placed my career on the line, I could no
longer sustain interminable delays, and feared an ongoing hiatus. Six
months had elapsed since my letter to State President Botha. I now needed
specific answers to a number of questions. Firstly, what timescale did they
have in mind? Secondly, was the Government in fact ready for such a significant move? And then, what were these 'ideas' to which Van der Merwe had
repeatedly referred? I said if I understood better, perhaps I could serve the
process better. For the time being, everything was too vague and tentative to
enable me to plan or make personal commitments. In fact, it was not even
clear at this stage that the essential preconditions were present.

Stoffel responded by acknowledging the difficulty of my position, and
said he too was embarrassed by the situation of uncertainty. However, he
was also the victim of circumstances. He attributed his prediction that the
commencement of the process was imminent to his own innate optimism.
However, he could not have anticipated some of the difficulties that had
occurred. Things were taking far longer to crystallise than he ever imagined.

However, he was now in a position to inform me that certain encouraging
developments had in fact taken place. Significant progress was being made.
'There is already an amber light,' he said, 'and I hope this will soon become
a green light.' I had to understand that a matter of such importance needed
to be very carefully weighed. Such decisions involved more than one person.
He had to be completely certain that he had the necessary approval for what
was envisaged. Ongoing discussions were taking place, and he hoped that
within a relatively short time, he would be able to clarify the position. At this
stage, he was 'reasonably confident' of the outcome.

Stoffel thought it might be a good idea if he were to clarify certain matters
which I needed to understand. Firstly, the Government was not at this stage
considering formal negotiations with the ANC. However, this didn't mean
that discussions involving individuals could not take place 'on an unofficial
basis', provided there was no grandstanding or media publicity. Official
contacts would have to wait for a later stage – until the ANC had abandoned
violence.

The second point he wished to make clear was that the Government did
not have in mind one single dramatic step. Rather, it foresaw a series of small

incremental steps, leading to 'a point of equilibrium' midway between mutually unacceptable White or Black domination. Although the Government was willing to negotiate about the issue of White domination, it was not willing to see it simply superseded by Black domination. The process was likely to take some time, and one had to realise that as the point of equilibrium was approached, the steps might appear to become smaller and more tentative.

At this stage, the primary concern was to reduce the dangerous 'talking distance' that existed between the Government and the ANC. He believed there was a role for an intermediary like myself, to facilitate such proximity, and to help narrow the talking distance 'if not with the ANC as an organisation, then at least with individuals with whom the Government may be willing to talk'.

He emphasised the Government's sincerity about its commitment to reform. It had already taken 'the irreversible decision to abandon "baasskap", and Strijdom-style white domination'. The task now was to create the opportunity for ongoing dialogue. The Government was not just posturing or foot-dragging, he assured me. I emphasised that the process had to be in good faith, and there had to be a reciprocal commitment to a realistic time frame. I didn't want to find myself co-opted into some dishonest or simulated process. The essence of the role I wished to play was integrity, and genuine independence.

It was approaching 4.30 p.m. when we parted. Stoffel said that with a long weekend ahead, he still had certain urgent matters that needed attention. However, he wanted us to set aside uninterrupted time in the very near future to deal with 'the next most important part of our discussion'. In fact, we were to meet just ten days later, on the afternoon of 7 April. It was a lengthy meeting extending over several hours, and was in effect, a continuation of our discussions just prior to the Easter weekend. Despite his reference to 'the most important part of our discussion', I had not anticipated anything of particular moment. I was wrong.

We began by discussing once again how best the costs associated with the initiative could be underwritten. He proposed that such costs might be covered by some 'nominally independent' source, such as a Government company or corporate surrogate. I replied that I would be entirely opposed to any obfuscation in that matter. The source had to be genuinely independent, and known and approved by both parties.

I questioned him about a Bill then being debated in Parliament, the Promotion of Orderly Internal Politics Bill, which would empower Government to prohibit and control foreign funding of political activities and organisations. It was clearly aimed not only at restricting the financial subventing of political parties, but also at organisations like IDASA which had organised the Dakar consultation. I asked Stoffel whether this legislation could not also have the unintended effect of preventing me seeking foreign funding for this initiative? He replied that this was certainly not the intention, and that the Bill was likely to emerge from the Select Committee 'somewhat nuanced'.

He saw no difficulty in the principle of my seeking foreign funding, provided it did not imply interference or control over the process. He suggested I consider Great Britain or the United States as the source. I was doubtful that the ANC would be receptive to either proposal which would imply the patronage of Margaret Thatcher or Ronald Reagan. 'Then how about the German Government?' he ventured, pointing out that they seemed to want to become more directly involved in Southern Africa. I raised the possibility of a co-sponsorship – such, for example, as might involve two countries, say Germany and Japan – not for the reason of quantum, but to overcome any perception of 'foreign ownership', and to secure authentication by South Africa's major trading partners.

I had begun to think that Switzerland might provide the solution. It had a centuries-old tradition of neutrality and non-alignment, and a reputation for discretion and secrecy. The Swiss were neither members of the United Nations nor of the European Community. Swiss financial institutions had become increasingly important to the beleaguered South African economy. After some discussion, Van der Merwe agreed. 'Yes, Switzerland could be the ideal solution.'

At our last meeting he had used the phrase an 'amber light', hoping that it might soon become a 'green light'. I asked what this implied? Did an amber light not mean that I might now begin to move slowly and cautiously? Or, had I still to await some event before commencing the first exploratory steps? He replied, rather obliquely, 'This need not be the case!' He said I need no longer defer opening up a communication channel with the ANC!

I was absolutely stunned. This sounded like the 'green light'. Could I assume the approval of State President Botha? It was always implicit that Stoffel was reporting to the President. It was surely inconceivable that a project of such momentous importance could be launched without the President's nod? Officially and publicly, the President continued to pour ridicule and abuse upon those, like IDASA, who tried to encourage and promote dialogue with the ANC. Terms like 'traitors', 'idiots', 'fraternising with the enemy' were commonplace. Yet, here I was receiving approval for a project that involved precisely that which was officially disavowed. Such a contradiction bore tremendous political risks. How could they know I was trustworthy? Or, was it simply that I would be 'dispensable', to use Stoffel's own chilling phrase? This scared me. I knew that Van der Merwe was a member of the State Security Council, which was chaired by the President. Could it be involved?

To add to the conundrum, Van der Merwe made it clear that it would not be possible – nor would it be correct – to indicate that the proposal had been placed before 'the full Cabinet'. However, he insisted, he was acting within the terms of his authority and mandate. He was fully aware of the risks. He had assessed these risks, and had come to terms with them. 'As a Junior Minister, I am obviously dispensable,' he insisted. I understood him also to be saying that I too would be dispensable. The matter was to proceed, he said, on a basis of 'deniability'. If it became public, he would have to take the rap. If he was 'the hand', who was 'the voice'? The implications were quite astounding.

After some further discussion, it was agreed that an approach would now be made to the Swiss Government. But how were the sceptical Swiss going to believe me? They would need to authenticate the genuineness of my request. I asked Van der Merwe whether in the circumstances he would be willing to confirm that the Government was supportive of this initiative? He replied that he would not be able to say so formally or in writing, but he saw no difficulty in giving certain assurances verbally. A conversation of this sort, rather than a letter, would be preferred. He would not like to initiate the contact, but would respond if he was contacted by the Swiss Ambassador. He would have to give further thought to the message he could convey, but it would be along the lines that he was aware of the initiative; that it had the general support of the Government; and that it was regarded as 'potentially constructive'.

I pointed out that as yet there had been no approach to the ANC along similar lines. What would I do, he asked, if the ANC was unreceptive to these proposals or objected to the concept of Swiss financing? I replied that we would have to cross that bridge if and when we came to it. Would it not be wiser, he suggested, to go ahead and assume the ANC's approval, rather than risk a problem at the outset? I said it was essential that I deal with both sides on an exactly equivalent basis.

This conversation marked the end of four months of obfuscation. I was astonished at his apparent readiness to give unofficial backing to the initiative – albeit verbally, and on a person-to-person basis. Testing his limits, I suggested that I might also need a message to be conveyed to the ANC – who would no doubt be similarly concerned to establish the genuineness of my version. He said he could not give any formal assurances of the Government's knowledge or backing for this initiative 'at this stage', but this might change later on.

We discussed some of the implications of foreign funding. If there was to be third-party financial sponsorship, one of the consequences would be the need to provide enough information to satisfy reasonable concerns that the project was 'on track'. He said it was recognised that some measure of reporting would be unavoidable. 'It will be necessary to lift the veil a little.' But this need not include all the details. They were entitled to be assured only that their money was not being wasted.

I asked how much confidentiality was appropriate in relation to his personal involvement, and he replied that there was obviously a degree of trust in our discussions. He did not wish his role or the detailed content of our discussions to be divulged for the time being. However, he had a certain amount of latitude, and the location of his office at Stalplein House, away from the main Government offices in Hendrik Verwoerd Building, was deliberate.

I also asked his views on the question of my own public profile. How was I to fend off questions as to my 'retirement' activities? Thus far, I had maintained a high degree of obscurity that verged on the paranoid, but paradoxically this sometimes provoked rather than dispelled curiosity. Van der Merwe saw a few possibilities. Might it not be possible for me to remain associated with my existing firm and call myself a Consultant? This was not an uncommon relationship with retired senior partners. It would have certain practical advantages, and I could continue to use the description of myself as an attorney. Alternatively, 'How about describing yourself as a Political Consultant,' he suggested. These days there were all sorts of consultants. In fact, it wouldn't be too far from the facts. After some discussion, we agreed upon the term 'Legal Consultant'. I would need to arrive at some understanding in this regard with my erstwhile partners.

Concerning my future access to his office, Stoffel said that he would instruct his private secretary, Riaan Smit, that I was to have privileged access to him, whenever required. We should keep in close contact. He concluded by wishing me good luck. 'You have quite a lot of work to do!' he beamed.

7

Dear Mr Ambassador

I'll never forget opening the newspaper on the morning following that meeting with Stoffel van der Merwe. On the front page, in gory detail, was a picture of my friend and erstwhile legal colleague, Albie Sachs, whom I had last seen 20 years ago just before he escaped into exile. I stared with horror at the heart-rending picture of this most gentle of men leaning on the stump of a shattered arm, calling for help, his face bloodied with shrapnel, bystanders looking on helplessly. This attempted assassination was part of the Government's widening campaign of State-sponsored terrorism. I was stunned. It was stark evidence of the reality of the kind of war now being waged. Like nothing else, this event in Maputo convinced me of the urgency and compelling need for negotiations, if we were to avoid the nightmarish alternative of mutual carnage. Some years later, when he returned from exile, Albie and I would meet again at the offices of the Cape Town LRC. He greeted me with a broad smile, and a one-armed hug. I felt like weeping.

Until now my proposal had seemed little more than a remote possibility. Our family plans for emigration were far advanced. I had been prepared for Botha's rebuff, but found myself unprepared for his acceptance. That night Hilary and I talked into the small hours. We felt awed and afraid. Naively or otherwise, I had assumed an enormous responsibility. There was no doubt about the risks – political and personal – should things go awry. Ultimately, I would be 'dispensable'. What made my situation specially perilous, was the link to the President. If I was seen as too great a liability, or my actions were to threaten or embarrass the President, or the State Security Council, it would be a simple matter to disown or discredit me – or worse. The stakes were high, and I could expect no forgiveness for indiscretions or errors of judgment. The Government had the resources available, men like Eugene de Kock and the hit squads of Vlakplaas, to 'neutralise' people like me, if I became troublesome. There were certainly greater threats than my being called a liar.

In the final analysis, it would be my word against that of Dr Stoffel van der Merwe. The only insurance I had lay in the circumstantial detail, and the meticulous minutes, letters and records which I kept and copied in various safe places. From now on, I would be operating on my own. This had been a conscious choice, to lower the risks for the participants, but it left me substantially without protection or corroboration.

I had no alternative but to accept Stoffel's deliberate unclarity as to how he had confirmed his mandate, and precisely who had sanctioned his actions. It was implicit that the State President was either the author or the editor. I had also to assume that certain key persons on the State Security Council, such as Dr Niel Barnard, were aware of my mandate. However, I had no idea whether the NI S was involved, or perhaps Military Intelligence? And if either of these entities, then one had to assume it would be at a very high level. If 'they' were only half-awake, my actions must surely become known to them. They would be watching and listening. I did not trust my telephone or my mail, and had no way of knowing whether my home, office, or car were 'secure'. This sense of being watched takes a terrible toll on one's quality of life and relationships. My secret fear was that at some lower level, an agent not privy to high State policy, might stumble upon my activities, draw his own conclusions, and take independent action against me. There was always the danger of rogue elements – men like Clive Derby-Lewis, MP – who would not seek authority for their entrepreneurial initiatives in opposing any suggestion of negotiations.

There was need for immediate decision and action. A weekend followed, and on the Monday morning I took the next big step. I wrote and delivered a personal letter to the Swiss Ambassador, H E Mr J O Quinche:

Dear Mr Ambassador

After very careful consideration, I write to you with reference to a possible role for the Swiss Government in facilitating the commencement of a negotiation process in South Africa.

My personal involvement in this matter arises from an approach which I have made to the South African Government, indicating my willingness to participate, if required, in the delicate initial stages which must inevitably precede a negotiating process in this country. This approach has resulted in a series of confidential meetings with a Member of the Cabinet, deputed for this purpose by the State President, which has culminated in a positive decision with reference to the proposal which I have initiated.

The letter went on to give some details of my personal and professional background, as a result of which,

I believe it may be said that I am reasonably well-known and trusted by a large

number of persons concerned with opposing the racial policies of the present
Government, and bringing about a new and just society.'

The letter concluded:

*... it has become apparent to me that unless certain initiatives are taken in the
immediate future to bring about genuine and substantial negotiations, this country
– and with it, most of the sub-continent – is likely to be caught in a spiral of
violence and repression, with the inevitable tragedy enveloping millions of people
of all colours. I believe that the situation is so serious and ominous that it demands
extraordinary initiatives from those, particularly within the situation, who may be
able to contribute to an alternative scenario.*

*Accordingly, I have decided to resign my present position in order to make
myself available as an intermediary, and in whatever capacity may seem appropriate, to attempt to facilitate the commencement of a meaningful negotiation
process. Hence, my approach to the State President, my discussions with a senior
Cabinet member, other confidential discussions already held with certain leaders
in the Black community, and now this letter to yourself.*

*It will be self-evident that the confidentiality of this initiative is absolutely
crucial to the possibility of its success. Accordingly, I respectfully request the privilege of a personal meeting with your Excellency as soon as may be convenient, in
order that I may explain the nature of this proposal and the consequent basis of
my approach to your Government.*

Yours faithfully
Richard Rosenthal

A reply was not long in coming. Within twenty-four hours I had a phone
call from someone who introduced himself simply as 'Quinche'. He referred
to my 'very important letter', and said that he had referred the matter to
Berne and was awaiting their instructions. It was being dealt with on a most
urgent basis, and he would revert to me as soon as possible.

A few days later he telephoned again, to inform me that he had been
requested to arrange a meeting. I suggested that we should meet at the
Embassy, but he said it would be 'more convenient' to meet at my own
office. I imagined he also wished to find out something about my work environment. A little later in the day, our receptionist advised, 'There's a
gentleman here to see you. He says he doesn't want to give his name, but
you'll know who he is!'

Jean Quinche is quintessential Swiss, a man of few words and little visible
emotion, somewhat formal, precise, and efficient. I thanked him for coming

to my office, and he replied that it was 'really nothing'. He said his Government viewed my letter as 'very important'. He had been instructed to discuss the issue with me in greater detail. It was understood that the matter was most urgent and confidential. He would deal with it on that basis. I must understand that a request of this nature was something 'rather unusual'. The Swiss Government would naturally wish to be helpful, but required more details. He pointed out that my letter was a bit vague as to precisely what assistance was required, and over what period. This sounded like practical Swiss veneration for the sanctity of money. Unfortunately, I could give only the vaguest of answers. Did I detect a note of excitement in him, despite his studied diplomatic inscrutability?

He asked some questions about the process I had in mind, and once again I could do little more than sketch a rough outline of some tentative ideas. His problem was how to be a conscientious rapporteur without being inappropriately inquisitive. He said he understood the need for discretion particularly with reference to the State President's involvement. However, he believed it would be essential for his Government to obtain some independent corroboration of my request. How could they confirm the State President's backing for the initiative? I had of course anticipated this request, and was able to tell him that there could be no formal written confirmation, but that he could contact the Minister of Information who would be able to give him certain assurances. Mr Quinche said he would act on this immediately.

He had made careful notes of everything I said, and now assured me that he would be reporting the same day to his Government. Realising the importance of ensuring that any report to the Swiss Government was both factually accurate and comprehensive, I offered to prepare an *aide-mémoire*, which I could let him have later in the day.

Datelined 19 April, it gave a resumé of the evolution of the initiative, and an analysis of the current political impasse, describing the basis of my proposal in these terms:

> ... if acceptable at least to the South African Government and the ANC [I will be willing to make myself available] as a confidential intermediary, with a view to facilitating the initial stages of a communication process, which hopefully will contribute towards the establishment of a genuine and substantive negotiation process. The objective of the initiative is directed to establishing a "process", and not to the advocacy of any particular product or outcome to such negotiation. Accordingly, the modus operandi, including the details, structure and financing of the initiative, are all matters requiring input from the principal parties concerned, whilst avoiding any predetermined or prescriptive formula.

The ten-page document concluded with the following motivation:

It is submitted that the provision of the requisite support as suggested, could represent a constructive contribution to the ultimate resolution of a regional problem, which will have a significant impact upon events throughout the sub-continent. It is further submitted that the facilitation of an initiative of this nature, would be consistent with Switzerland's independence and unique historic role in the mediation of conflict, and the promotion of world peace.

Two days later on 21 April, the President delivered what was vaunted as a keynote speech on what he termed 'the future of South Africa in the constitutional sphere'. Speaking in the Budget Debate on his Vote, he delivered a strange, rambling speech which covered the landscape of religion, philosophy, constitutional principle, and administrative exigencies. Bemoaning the fact that 'the office of the State President receives between 5 000 and 6 000 letters per week', he envisaged resuscitating the office of Prime Minister to deal with 'day to day administration'. He spoke of the prospect of black representation within a number of existing fora – the Regional Services Councils, the Provincial Executive Councils, the President's Council, and in future the proposed National Council. Defending orthodox separate development, he saw future black constitutional rights in terms of three demographic spheres: those living within the 'independent' states; those living within 'self-governing' territories; and those – millions of urbanised blacks – whom he termed, 'the black communities living outside the self-governing states'.

His speech contained a number of gratuitous pieties. Thus: 'It is the Christian standpoint that one must be prepared to grant to others what one claims for oneself' ... 'In each one of us, because we are human, there is sometimes a tendency to give way more to the hatred in ourselves than to our positive feelings. Hatred for, or prejudice against, others is not a prerequisite, however, for demonstrating love for what is ours' ... 'There is a vast difference between liberation theology, and what we as Christians believe in!' ... 'We as Christians know that Christ spent 33 years of his life on this earth of ours. Of those 33 years we know only about three. Of the rest we know nothing or very little.'

He went on to extol the virtues of his predecessors and their policies, noting that 'Our leaders who have led this country since 1910 as heads of government, were all honourable men' and that 'We believe that the Afrikaner and other white communities in South Africa are not, in the general sense of the word, a problem.'

The President dissembled at length about whether there was any instance during Christ's public life when he could be said to have 'led a demonstration against the State'! He rambled on about what he should or should not call the proposed National Council, relating how it had become clear to him from conversations he had with Black leaders that they did not like the term 'National Council'. He said that a well-known black leader shortly before his death had said to him, 'Call it the Great Indaba.' The President believed this deathbed suggestion deserved 'serious consideration'.

I waded through the trivia and ephemera in search of hopeful portents. There was precious little for my comfort. The best I could find were statements like, 'We ... must see to it that a meaningful debate on the future takes place. It is our duty to do so.' '... further structures will also have to be created and developed to effect deliberation and decision-making on the basis of consensus.' 'The Government is bound by the concept of a forum for consultation ... within the framework of which the Government wishes to pursue its politics of consultation.'

Having had no direct contact with the President for seven months, I seized on the opportunity of this speech to address him a further letter, anxious to confirm that he remained personally aware of what was happening, and that he could not later attempt to disavow my initiative. Accordingly, my letter of 27 April, expressed appreciation for the prospect of 'a process of consultation and negotiation involving the Black community, leading to significant constitutional changes in the future.' The letter continued: 'As you are no doubt aware, this central problem has been a matter of great concern to myself, leading to my having written to you on 23rd September 1987, and to a series of confidential discussions which I have had over the past six months with the Honourable the Minister of Information and Constitutional Planning, Dr S. van der Merwe, concerning the manner in which I might possibly be of assistance in facilitating an appropriate process.' The letter concludes, 'Hopefully I will be able to assist in some measure in bringing a successful process to fruition.'

Two days later, President Botha despatched me his enigmatic reply, which he personally signed (see page facing).

I sincerely hoped that his best wishes for the future related to the same future I had in mind, and chose to read the letter as an oblique but friendly nod of approval.

On the same day I also wrote Stoffel a letter, confirming my discussions with the Swiss Ambassador, and informing him that he could expect to be contacted shortly, as arranged. 'Needless to say, I am also concerned with the problem of initiating some early discussion with credible representatives of certain other Organisations, both here and abroad if necessary, and I shall likewise endeavour to keep you informed of progress in this regard. It goes without saying that I shall respect your confidence, and that I am fully

K.7

Tuynhuys
Cape Town

29 April 1988

Mr R Rosenthal
P O Box 695
CAPE TOWN
8000

Dear Mr Rosenthal

Thank you for your kind letter following my recent speech in Parliament.

Your interest shown as well as the kind words addressed to me are highly appreciated.

Please accept my best wishes for the future.

With kind regards

STATE PRESIDENT
/ss

appreciative of the delicacy of the matter and the necessity for absolute discretion and confidentiality.'

Dr van der Merwe's rather quaint reply followed shortly:

Dear Mr Rosenthal

The Minister of Information, Broadcasting Services and the Film Industry, Dr C J van der Merwe, requested me to acknowledge receipt of your letter dated April 27, 1988 with thanks.

Dr van der Merwe took with interest notice of the contents thereof and looks forward to be meeting with you at a later date.

Yours sincerely
(sgd) Adriaan Nortje
ADMINISTRATIVE SECRETARY

In due course I was informed by Ambassador Quinche that he had met privately with Dr van der Merwe in Cape Town, as proposed. They had initially had some difficulty in scheduling a meeting owing to Van der Merwe's very busy schedule. (That sounded familiar!) However, the Ambassador was pleased to confirm that he had been given verbally the assurances which the Swiss Government required, including 'in principle' support for my initiative, and support for the proposed involvement of his Government in providing financial and logistical assistance. These communications had already been conveyed to Berne, whose response was now awaited.

In the meanwhile, the Ambassador wished to know whether I had made any progress in initiating discussions with the ANC? He reminded me that in due course his Government would also require assurances of their agreement to these proposals. I confirmed that this next stage of making contact with the ANC at an appropriate leadership level was my top priority, but it was not a simple matter, and had to be handled with great sensitivity.

A walk in the woods

I was now faced once again with the practical dilemma of how a private citizen without status or mandate could attempt to engage the adversaries in a liberation struggle, without appearing presumptuous, eccentric, and possibly even subversive. The context was that of a society riven by conflict and polarisation. Bombs, 'dirty tricks', and assassinations, were becoming the order of the day. There was an ever-increasing toll of victims and casualties. To the best of my knowledge, there existed no trusted channel of communication between Government and the ANC; though there had been some discussions with certain businessmen, academics, politicians, and even the Chairman of the Broederbond, Professor Pieter de Lange, who met Thabo Mbeki informally at a Conference organised by the Ford Foundation on Long Island, New York. For each party, the ostensibly simple proposition of opening up a dialogue was likely to be viewed with scepticism and suspicion. In such circumstances, how were the parties going to trust me, a veritable outsider? Even the first step of attempting to make contact with the ANC would be fraught with difficulty.

Although I was known to many persons within the Mass Democratic Movement, I could do no more than guess at which individuals within the country occupied leadership positions in the banned organisation. It had operated underground for almost 30 years, and there was no simple or direct way of establishing a person's mandate or membership. This was a matter of huge importance and sensitivity. The issue I wished to discuss could only be raised with the top echelon. Who then was the appropriate channel for such confidences? In many ways, it had been far simpler to put the proposition to P W Botha.

It was immediately apparent that I could not simply write a 'Dear Mr Tambo' letter, along the lines of my initial approach to State President Botha. In any event, I had no idea how or where to address such a letter. As far as Nelson Mandela was concerned, he was held incommunicado in Pollsmoor prison, and one had to assume all his communications would be carefully monitored and controlled. If Stoffel van der Merwe could arrange access for me, this would necessitate some disclosure to the Department of Prisons, and the Security Police. Moreover, any such concession might imply the blessing of Government, which would be 'the kiss of death'. Indeed, as a prisoner, how was Mandela to communicate with his colleagues in the organisation? I had direct personal experience of prison consultations being illegally eavesdropped in breach of my client's professional privilege. The Appeal Court had sanctioned the legality of a prison regulation which forbade prisoners from receiving uncensored documents or communications – even from their own lawyers. The appellant in the leading case was Nelson Mandela himself!

One strongly suspected – and it has been subsequently confirmed – that some limited level of communication was maintained through the surreptitious assistance of 'friendly' lawyers like George Bizos and Ismail Ayob, and there was also some clandestine exchange of messages using the occasional permitted visits of Winnie Mandela. But at the time, all this was largely conjecture, and could not serve as an available or secure channel for me.

There were other problems affecting my contacting the ANC. Firstly, I needed to be trusted by people who were trusted. This was one reason for my discussions with people like Advocate Omar and Archbishop Tutu. But I could not safely increase this circle of confidants without simultaneously increasing the risks of premature disclosure. I realised that both parties would probably speculate whether I was not some kind of emissary from the other! No amount of denial or explanation would dispel such a doubt, and the only solution would be to satisfy them on a personal basis that I was a person of integrity. Apart from any third-party authentication, I assumed that the leadership, who did not know me, would wish to make their own assessment.

At the outset, I had seen the recalcitrance of the South African Government as the first obstacle to be overcome. There seemed little purpose in communicating with the ANC until that hurdle had been negotiated. In my view the first positive signal had to come from the President himself. I presumed the ANC's agreement would be more readily secured. Now I had to make good on this deliberate default, by contacting the ANC as soon as possible. I pondered the problem of perception. For example, if I were to ask someone known to me, such as Helen Suzman, it might create the impression – borne out by my earlier association – that despite any protestation of independence, I was in fact acting on behalf of the PFP. On the other hand, neither Archbishop Tutu nor Advocate Omar had offered their personal assistance, and a direct request of this kind might seem invidious. There were of course other possibilities, but each involved my making certain assumptions, and it would not be possible to ask too many questions. As lawyers acting for people involved in high-risk activity, one had learnt to restrict one's enquiries to the 'need to know'. Sensitive information should not be lightly sought or volunteered in a Police State.

Ultimately, I decided to confide in Dr Frederick Van Zyl Slabbert, a man for whom I have the greatest respect. Two years had passed since he made his watershed decision to resign as Leader of the Official Opposition, in the prophetic belief that the centre of political gravity had moved beyond the domain of Parliament, and mainstream white politics. It was a costly and widely misinterpreted decision, which led to painful incomprehension and woundedness amongst his political colleagues – and a predictable torrent of abuse from the President, who characterised Van Zyl and his ilk as 'traitors', 'well-meaning fools', and worse. I had met him shortly after his resignation, to share my concern and empathy with his decision and the feeling of disillusionment. My own actions arose from a similar perception. This sense of alienation had led Slabbert and Boraine to establish the organisation known as IDASA, and thereby promote dialogue with the ANC through events such as that which had taken place at Dakar. At one stage, I had wondered whether my own initiative should be subsumed into IDASA, but decided otherwise. I believed what we had in mind was different, and that any identification of my initiative with a high-profile, politically contentious, advocacy organisation such as IDASA would be counter-productive to its acceptance by the President. To P W Botha at least, IDASA was the devil incarnate.

Thus, one day I called Van Zyl, and invited him to come with me for 'a walk in the woods'. It was 17 April, a beautiful Sunday morning. We walked the circular path of Orange Kloof overlooking Hout Bay. I explained that I wished to consult him in absolute confidence, knowing that he was one of those rare politicians able to differentiate between public and private information. Van Zyl looked puzzled and quizzical, and said something about a reversal of our usual roles of client and consultant. Without beating about the fynbos, I put to him my improbable proposition. He looked astonished, but immediately grasped what I was talking about. 'You realise of course', he said, 'that you're talking about the central political issue? In fact, it is the issue that brought me into politics in the first place. It's the issue I've concerned myself with most of my political life.'

He had profound doubts about the feasibility of my venture, believing that P W had set his face firmly against any such process. The National Party and the President were on record as opposing any negotiation process involving the ANC. It would be diametrically opposed to official Nat policy. 'With the threat posed by the Conservative Party and their right wing, it would be hugely risky for the National Party,' he said. In fact, his inability to persuade P W of the need for such a dialogue had been the 'straw' that finally precipitated his resignation. 'It would be incredible if you now succeeded where everyone else has failed,' he mused. I had to confess that I had no special ideas, no special genius, and no special quality, which would equip me for this particular role! 'Perhaps that's what makes you different.' He said the attitude of Stoffel was intriguing. At present, he was 'the President's blue-eyed boy' – 'but the President's infatuations are transitory'. One thing was clear – there was no love lost between P W and his Minister of Constitutional Development, Chris Heunis.

Would he be willing, I asked, to help by putting me in touch with the ANC? He thought for a while and then said he felt it his duty to warn me as a friend that I was getting into very deep water. 'This is the big game,' he said ominously. 'People can get hurt. I don't want to scare you, but that's the reality.' He then spoke about the hawks within the coterie closest to the President. They were ruthless people, he said. They could be expected to oppose any pre-emptive effort to establish a dialogue with the ANC. It was their turf. Who was Richard Rosenthal anyway? I would be placing myself in their line of fire, he warned, but he was fascinated by my exchange of letters with the President, and the dialogue with Van der Merwe. He raised the intriguing possibility that in sanctioning this initiative, the President might be moving without the knowledge or approval of the State Security Council. In Van Zyl's opinion this would not be 'out of character'. Nothing would give P W greater pleasure than to show up his security advisers as flat-footed and incompetent!

However, this did not reduce the risks for me, he said, and in fact probably increased them. The assassinations in Gaborone, Paris, and Maputo should leave no doubt about their capabilities. They believed quite simply that the ANC had to be wiped out. The 'securocrats' were opposed to engaging the ANC until it had been defeated. They believed they could stem the revolutionary tide by a judicious mixture of reform and repression. Equally there was no way the ANC was going to abandon its armed struggle. They too believed in the inevitability of eventual victory. There were 'wild men' on both sides, who would adopt a principled objection to negotiations – on strategic as well as ideological grounds. Men like Niel Barnard and Jannie Roux saw Communism as 'the anti-Christ'. If at any stage there was to be dialogue, they wanted to initiate and control it. 'Why would they want an outsider like you to get involved,' he asked pertinently, 'except perhaps as a "stalking-horse", but then later on they will probably dispense with you.' Van Zyl said that personally he had come to terms with the risks of getting involved, but he didn't want me to get hurt through being naive. With this one reservation, he said he would like to encourage me to go ahead. 'Who knows, it might work out? In fact, you've already advanced further than I would have predicted!'

Van Zyl recalled how, a few years earlier, he had made a similar offer to P W – suggesting that he might be able to serve as an intermediary – but this offer had been rejected out of hand. Perhaps, he speculated, the situation was now more fluid. Recently, he had learnt of a planned meeting between Govan Mbeki and Stoffel van der Merwe. It had been virtually agreed in principle, when the preparations were summarily aborted, because of another bomb blast. He was given this information by Braam Viljoen, brother of General Constand Viljoen. There were various different role players. What was particularly significant in this instance was the State President's personal involvement. But P W was notoriously unpredictable, even capricious. In Van's view, it was most unlikely a junior Minister like Van der Merwe would dare to pursue such an initiative without the President's approval. But it was quite possible that P W had not discussed it in Cabinet, or even with the State Security Council.

He found the Government's seeming acceptance of my proposal very surprising. He doubted they had the imagination or ability to undertake such a process successfully. However, one could never prejudge these things. He would be surprised if P W and Stoffel were capable of such imaginative initiatives. Stoffel could have an important role, but it was still too early to know. One needed to accept the inevitability of a stop/start process – with accompanying 'theatricals', including the slamming of doors, and a fair amount of posturing. But one would have to persist and be patient. When I referred to myself as a 'political virgin', he laughed, and said 'Well, hardly a virgin, though you do have the useful appearance of innocence!'

He proposed Thabo Mbeki, son of elder statesman Govan Mbeki, as my point of entry to the ANC. He was the organisation's Director of Information, and a rising star. In his own right, he was already an influential member of the National Executive. He was also highly respected by the diplomatic community, and would probably 'go down well with the Swiss'. Van suggested that before meeting Thabo, I should try to contact his father, who was restricted to his home in Port Elizabeth. The old man could serve as a bridge not only with his son and others outside the country, but also with Nelson Mandela and those still in prison. It would also be a useful way of communicating indirectly with both the external and internal ANC.

Van Zyl spoke of a number of confidential IDASA initiatives then underway – in particular, a consultation being planned in Germany towards the end of April. This was intended as a follow-up to the Dakar conference. Though still early days, he hoped Thabo Mbeki would be part of the ANC delegation. Would I not also like to attend, he asked. I considered it, but decided that I needed to distance myself from other organisations, and in particular from IDASA, which was anathema to the Government. However, I much appreciated his offer. One advantage to my being present, he suggested, would be that it would not attract particular interest of the media, or the intelligence community. He volunteered to speak to Thabo Mbeki on my behalf, and urge him to meet me, without saying more than that it concerned 'something of great importance'. He would absent himself from any meeting.

One of the purposes of the proposed IDASA consultation was to explore ideas about bringing together various groupings in a new political constellation. Van Zyl believed this could eventually lead to a new alignment involving a potential membership as high as 2 million. There had already been some initial contacts, which were encouraging. I asked what he saw as his own political future. He said he would be reluctant to become involved again in mainstream political life, having withdrawn with difficulty and relief. He anticipated that a proposal to form a new political party might be one of the topics to be discussed at Frankfurt. These events were not simple to arrange. One of the concerns was the safety of senior ANC members, particularly following the killing of Dulcie September and the bombing of Albie Sachs. They were both SACP members, as was Thabo himself. A perception was gaining ground of a concerted campaign to eliminate key SACP members. Far from undermining Communist Party influence in the ANC, or causing division in the ranks, these events caused ranks to be closed and encouraged solidarity. He said with a chuckle that if the Government and the ANC really wanted to cause each other division, they should promote a negotiation process!

The suggested role for the Swiss intrigued him. He reckoned that it might prove difficult to persuade conservative Switzerland to back such an improbable venture. For a long time their relationship with the South African Government had been rather ambiguous, but things could be changing. Recently they had offered IDASA a grant of three hundred thousand Rand, which was unprecedented. It suggested the possibility of a new trend in their policy towards this country, which could make them more receptive to my request. If required, he would also be willing to respond to any approach by the Swiss Ambassador. People like Tutu and Omar might also be useful in authenticating me. If the process really got moving, he assured me, there would be no shortage of would-be funders, and the Swiss would know this.

After three hours we returned home, and agreed to remain in contact. Van Zyl said he would be fascinated to know how things evolved. In the meanwhile, he would explore the possibility of my meeting discreetly with Thabo Mbeki during the planned Frankfurt consultation. 'Don't forget,' he said,

'I've been in this business a long time!'

But the Government continued giving out conflicting signals on the issue of talking to the ANC. The MP for Innesdal, Albert Nothnagel, who had once before been slapped down for having the temerity to suggest that Government would eventually have to talk to the ANC, now caused new political turbulence by restating what might have seemed obvious to others – that all 'black political groupings', including the ANC, AZAPO, and the 17 recently restricted organisations, were important to the political future of South Africa. 'As far as radical black politics is concerned we must not bluff ourselves that we can wish them away with rifles and violence.' The *Cape Times* hailed this rather unspectacular insight as 'a sign of hope'. But such limited hopes were soon dashed by a phalanx of more orthodox Nationalist luminaries, who came to the defence of traditional Party thinking, and provided a depressing exegesis on Nothnagel's heresies. Such oracular utterances included one by F W de Klerk, who reassured the faithful that it was not NP policy that the ANC should be included in South Africa's future. Con Botha, Nat MP for Umlazi, said Mr Nothnagel was not talking about the ANC as an organisation, but only about its ideas. 'He said these ideas could not be imprisoned and discounted, and I agree with him.' It would be some years before Mr de Klerk could be similarly persuaded.

Commenting on the debate, the *Cape Times* provided its readers with a gloomy prognosis. In an editorial it concluded, 'The climate is not ripe for negotiations, although the participation debate has shown signs at times of gaining ground, only to be set back by such actions as the recent restrictions on organisations. The essential preconditions for negotiation do not exist, and they will remain beyond reach while the country is in a State of Emergency ... Failing some dramatic action to transform the climate, there can be little hope of any breakthrough.'

I was wagering on the possibility of such 'dramatic action'. Meanwhile from Switzerland came word that State Secretary Edouard Brunner would like to meet me. They had studied my Memorandum, and although still awaiting word of the ANC's attitude, they would welcome an opportunity to discuss these ideas in principle. I bought an air ticket; postponed several appointments; took a few days' leave; and one Friday morning 6 May found myself on the train from Basel to Berne.

A view from the Alps

I arrived in the Swiss capital of Berne one hour early for my scheduled meeting with State Secretary Brunner, having heeded the dire warnings of well-meaning friends regarding the Swiss obsession with time-keeping. We were to meet for lunch at the Restaurant Schultheissenstube, on the first floor of the Hotel Schweizerhof, which is located just opposite the main railway station.

I had spent the previous evening with my old friend Professor Markus Barth, son of the famous existentialist theologian Karl Barth. We had talked late into the night about apartheid, liberation theology, and the role of the churches in a situation of gross injustice. He quoted Mahatma Gandhi: 'Those who think religion and politics are not connected, know little about politics, and less about religion.'

As my father confessor of many years, I shared with him the reason for my latest visit to Switzerland, and he was greatly intrigued. But he saw fit to warn me: 'Don't try to teach the Swiss how to conduct their foreign policy!' He didn't know State Secretary Edouard Brunner, but had a high regard for the newly appointed Swiss Foreign Minister, René Felber. Over the years, I had shared with Markus our recurring uncertainty about staying or leaving South Africa. For him there had never been any question. 'There is no question,' he had written. 'You must stay, and work for change.' Now he relished telling me, 'You see, I was right!'

Ever the pragmatist, he suggested that in my discussion with the State Secretary, I should emphasise the possible commercial advantages to Switzerland if it were to become associated with a successful negotiation process. He hoped the Swiss Government would see its investment in peace-making as a feasible alternative to its refusal to participate in trade sanctions.

Mr Brunner arrived at the restaurant, as arranged, like the proverbial Swiss Post Bus, at precisely 12.30 p.m., accompanied by Christian Blickenstorfer, a senior adviser to the Federal Department of Foreign Affairs. They had secured a discreet table in a corner of the restaurant. After formal introductions and aperitifs, Mr Brunner commenced by stating that his Government had studied my *Aide-mémoire* with great interest. They regarded the initiative as potentially very important, and wished to be helpful. Through their Ambassador, they had received assurances from Information Minister Stoffel van der Merwe regarding the attitude of the South African Government. They had also taken some informal soundings from a number of parties, and had discussed the matter confidentially with a few people. Generally, the reactions had been positive.

It was evident that I was an object of some curiosity, and I did my best to allay their understandable concerns. Our discussion ranged across the broad unfolding political drama in South Africa. It was immediately apparent that they were well informed and perceptive. Mr Brunner said that if they became involved, it would not be the first such occasion, and that his country had been able to play a peacemaking role in a number of world conflict situations. This was what they hoped might also happen in South Africa.

At their invitation, I explained once again the genesis of my initiative, and why Switzerland had been suggested as the most appropriate sponsoring government. Would it not for example have been more logical, they asked, for me to have approached sources within South Africa? They were intrigued that I had thus far borne all expenses myself, and that I had not been receptive to Dr van der Merwe's offer of South African Government assistance. I explained my reasons, which they appeared to understand. Had I thought about a funding organisation such as the Ford Foundation? I said this had been considered, but such international agencies came with their own particular baggage, and might not be found acceptable to all the parties. It had seemed that Switzerland was the country most likely to be the least offensive to the majority of those concerned.

We agreed that no such initiative was likely to succeed without personal support from the State President. His personal dominance meant that it would be impossible to proceed in any other way. Mr Brunner asked to what extent it could be assumed that the President was personally involved? I told them that I had also wondered about this, but there seemed to be a deliberate strategy to distance him from the actual discussions and decisions. This was hardly surprising given the extreme sensitivity of the issue, and his past negative pronouncements on this matter.

Apart from my initial exchange of letters with President Botha, I had since been forced to rely upon Dr van der Merwe's innuendos from which I deduced that Mr Botha remained informed and involved. Dr van der Merwe had made it clear that part of his function was to provide the President with some protection. It was my clear understanding that the President had approved the initiative. In fact, it seemed that it was precisely the need for his approval that had so long delayed the launch. But in reality I still did not know precisely who was involved. It could be the State Security Council, the so-called 'inner Cabinet,' which included a coterie of senior Cabinet members (including Stoffel van der Merwe) and leading Military, Information and Security office-bearers. Alternatively, it might involve a group brought together specifically for this purpose by the President.

They were at pains to explain to me the special situation of Switzerland in relation to international efforts to isolate and bring pressure upon the South African regime. Because of its long-standing neutrality, Switzerland was not able to support UN-sponsored sanctions. In fact, Switzerland was not a member of the United Nations. It was, however, committed to the proactive and constructive use of its neutrality. In recent times, it had ventured beyond the traditional parameters of neutrality and non-involvement, and had for example played a role in helping to finance IDASA's Dakar Conference. It had also adopted a self-imposed constraint upon the export of arms to South Africa. However, it had been unable to support trade, diplomatic, and financial sanctions. This had inevitably drawn criticism from the ANC, but the issue was one of constitutional principle. In any event, Mr Brunner was of the opinion that trade sanctions were unlikely to work in practice. There were too many loopholes, and ways to evade sanctions. Even American 'divestment' was little more than a restructuring of commercial relationships. Few benefits had accrued to blacks as a result of the withdrawal of American interests. The flow of dividends continued unabated, under the guise of 'royalties'.

The Swiss were clearly well briefed on the current situation, and raised several pertinent issues for comment. These included anticipated changes to the Group Areas Act, and whether the Government was contemplating its total repeal or merely certain adjustments, like the notion of 'open' areas. I made it clear that I had no inside information, but doubted that the Government was yet ready to make radical changes to the essential fabric of apartheid. What Botha and Heunis evidently had in mind were some largely cosmetic changes, which might create the appearance of reform, without sacrificing any principles. The four pillars of apartheid would still be firmly in place. This gave rise to anomalies. Thus, one had the contradictory situation that although the Mixed Marriages and Immorality Acts had been repealed, it was still forbidden for 'mixed' couples to cohabit in the same Group Area.

Insofar as inducements to change were concerned, Mr Brunner speculated that it might one day be helpful to say to South Africa, 'We will readmit you to the community of nations, provided you implement a process of substantial reform.' Although this might be a good negotiating strategy, it was probably not politically feasible. The present frustration and impotence of the world community were due in part to the fact that sanctions had been tried, and had been seen to fail. This meant that the threat of sanctions no longer had the same impact. One could not threaten and recall the 'bomb' after it had been dropped.

One aspect of my initiative which obviously aroused particular concern was that Governments ordinarily communicate through their Foreign Affairs Departments, using diplomatic channels. In this instance, they were not even sure whether Foreign Minister Pik Botha had been consulted. It would be surprising if he had not, but I could give them no assurance. President Botha had been known to act on occasion without consulting his Cabinet. On the other hand, Pik Botha was himself a member of the State Security Council. Maybe he too wished to be at a distance from something which could go awry. Because of the sensitivity of this matter, no formal communications would be possible, and one therefore had no alternative but to rely upon verbal assurances and inference.

Mr Brunner explained that there were certain special internal administrative arrangements that would be necessary to enable them to grant assistance of this nature, on a basis of secrecy. This was due to constitutional principle, and the need to ensure public accountability and transparency. Some years before there had been a similar problem involving an Algerian initiative. Although the financial reporting aspect was rather delicate, he was sure that a mechanism could be found. Once there was approval from the ANC, they would be open to suggestions as to the precise nature of the assistance that would be needed. At an appropriate stage they would, for example, be ready to provide a venue and accommodation, to guarantee security, and to give such other practical assistance as might be required. He mentioned that there had been occasions when it had been necessary to accommodate negotiating delegates in separate chalets, and to take 'practical measures' to ensure their reciprocal safety. This had been successfully managed in the past without media attention.

I had expected a fairly non-committal response, but towards the end of lunch, Mr Brunner said he was prepared to confirm in principle the availability of Swiss Government assistance, subject to one important condition – they would need to obtain independent confirmation that the initiative – and the principle of Swiss involvement – was equally acceptable to the ANC. As with their Ambassador's discussions with Dr van der Merwe, they would prefer some direct communication from the ANC.

We agreed to defer further detailed discussion of the specifics, such as a budget, until the ANC's attitude had been established. I said that in the nature of things I had no idea how much, or how long, such assistance might be required. I hoped an initial meeting with the ANC could be

arranged within the next few weeks, but I volunteered no further details. I
also undertook to be in touch again once this contact had been made. They
confirmed that they would be available to meet again as soon as might be
necessary. I could contact them either directly or through their Ambassador
in South Africa.

Mr Brunner emphasised their awareness of the need for sensitivity and
discretion. He wanted to know whether I had any idea how long this
exploratory stage might last? Naturally, I could no more predict a timescale
than a likely sequence of events. I foresaw the possibility of an incremental
process involving initial exploratory contacts at a fairly low level. Perhaps I
was being too optimistic, but I hoped there might be something to show
within a period of say three to six months.

Mr Brunner said it had been an interesting and useful meeting. As we
shook hands, he said, 'I hope we shall be able to do something helpful for
your country.' I walked out into bright sunshine. The mists and clouds of
the early morning had cleared. A huge weight had seemingly lifted, and I
had the sense of being at the beginning of an extraordinary journey. Perhaps
a way could yet be found to avoid the disaster which had for so long seemed
unavoidable. In a few days I would fly home, and discover whether Van Zyl
Slabbert had made any progress in arranging my meeting with Thabo
Mbeki. I caught a train to Geneva, and spent that afternoon deep in thought,
walking along the beautiful shoreline of the lake. I felt apprehensive and
excited. Over dinner that evening, I ordered the best bottle of Swiss Dole
wine, and slept like a babe.

Next day I flew to Toronto, concerned to secure our right to emigrate – if
it should become necessary – and to obtain advice as to what to do if things
went awry. I explained that I was committed to staying in South Africa as
long as there was some prospect of a negotiated outcome. I met with lawyers
and a senior member of the Cabinet, and secured for my family some important alternatives, in the event that our safety became threatened.

Within a few days I was home again, sharing my adventures with Hilary,
returning inscrutably to the office, and catching up on the events of the past
two weeks. Two issues seemed to have dominated the news during my
absence – the imminent prospect of the US Congress adopting tough new
sanctions measures against South Africa, and a high-level surprise
Ministerial meeting which had taken place in Brazzaville between Angola
and South Africa. There were reports that this meeting had 'stunned' diplomatic circles, and had served to pre-empt American-sponsored efforts,
orchestrated by US Assistant Secretary of State Chester Crocker, to convene
four-nation exploratory talks in London. This propensity for producing
rabbits from hats bore the unmistakable hallmarks of the two Bothas – Pik

and P W – who were intent upon avoiding 'foreign interference' in South Africa's internal affairs. It was seen as an attempt to produce an 'African solution' to the war in Angola, and the stand-off with the UN in Namibia.

The proposed new US Sanctions Bill would halt all exports and imports between South Africa and the United States, with the exception only of certain 'strategically important minerals', and would impose a ban on loans and business dealings between the two countries. Pretoria's bellicose response was to threaten counter sanctions, thereby seeking to exploit the demographic irony that a number of minerals vital to US defence technology were available from two sources only – South Africa and the Soviet Union. It was arguable who was the devil, and who the deep blue sea.

Immediately following my return, I went to see Van Zyl Slabbert again, and gave him an account of my visit to Switzerland. He was fascinated. At his suggestion, we went into the garden to talk, because he regarded his lounge as not the safest place for such a discussion. He said that the arrangements for my meeting with the ANC were still in place, but he had decided that it would be more prudent not to discuss my mission with them either by letter or by phone. We would have to rely upon last-minute arrangements which could only be confirmed after the delegates had arrived in Germany. He could not even be completely sure that Thabo Mbeki would be there as part of the ANC delegation. The travel arrangements of senior ANC members were particularly sensitive in view of the recent assassination attempts. If he got word that Thabo would not be present, he would let me know at once. In the meanwhile, he recommended I make my own travel arrangements, and he offered to assist with expenses through funding which IDASA had obtained for its conference. Once again – albeit reluctantly – I declined any financial assistance. Van Zyl assured me that no one apart from himself would know that I was present at the venue. He warned that many of the delegates would know me, and that I would have to be extremely careful to avoid being seen or recognised.

He urged once more that before meeting Thabo Mbeki I should first try to see his father, Govan Mbeki. He warned that, after the debacle surrounding Govan's release in November, he was being routinely watched and monitored. I would need to be careful in arranging any meeting with him. My ability to demonstrate that I could maintain secrecy in this matter would be important.

We also talked about the Brazzaville Peace talks, and whether they could be seen as an indication of a more conciliatory attitude on the part of the SA Government. Certainly it seemed to indicate a growing awareness of the need to involve African leaders in any future peace process. The composition of the South African delegation was illuminating – the Minister of

Foreign Affairs Pik Botha, the Minister of Defence Magnus Malan, and the ubiquitous and presumably omniscient Niel Barnard, head of the National Intelligence Service. The military situation in Angola was beginning to look increasingly ominous, with large formations of Cuban and SWAPO forces moving southwards towards the border with Ovamboland. Perhaps it was the reality of events on the battlefield that had induced a greater realism and willingness to negotiate. This was certainly the belief of Archbishop Tutu, who had earlier told members of Congress, 'I do not want sanctions just for the hell of it, but whatever has happened in South Africa has happened as a result of pressure.' He said that Blacks were willing to endure hardships to secure their liberation.

I speculated that South Africa's issues might eventually have to be resolved within a regional context, and suggested that one might have to involve other African governments in the process. Certainly they had a substantial interest in mediating and promoting a settlement, and perhaps they could exercise some moderating influence. Accordingly, despite all the rhetoric about foreign interference in South Africa's domestic problems, I imagined that international participation in the negotiation process might ultimately be a necessary mechanism.

When I left, Van Zyl warned darkly, 'Rosenthal, you're going to have only one chance at this. Please don't fuck it up!'

Just before leaving for Switzerland, I visited Jenny Schreiner once more in Pollsmoor Prison. She was her usual cheery self, making light of her own difficulties, and much more interested in what was happening to her friends and in the world at large. How amazed she would have been, had I then told her what I was really doing! We spoke about all manner of things, including her forthcoming trial, but no word about my initiative. Before leaving, I told her a story about Henry Thoreau, who went to prison for refusing to pay his taxes, as a protest against war. Whilst behind bars he had a visit from Ralph Waldo Emerson, who asked, 'What on earth are you doing in here, Henry?', to which Thoreau replied, 'The real question is, "What on earth are you doing out there?"' Jenny grinned.

A few days later, on Thursday 19 May, I was able to have another conversation with Arthur Chaskalson, who had returned once again from his sabbatical in the United States, to consult regarding the Bethel trial. Arthur told me that he had been giving a lot of thought to our earlier discussion in January, and he shared some ideas about how a future process might be initiated. He believed it might be advisable for there to be a fairly early meeting at leadership level, involving persons of the status of Thabo Mbeki and Stoffel van der Merwe. The purpose would be to set the scene and provide reciprocal assurances about good faith and seriousness of intent. This might be followed by a series of meetings at a lower level, involving representatives who could participate in what might be styled 'workshops' or 'study groups'. My own role might become that of a go-between, with special responsibility for maintaining momentum.

My concept was not dissimilar, although I believed that an early 'leader to leader' meeting was probably impracticable. Stoffel had expressed a preference for low-key contacts at the outset. Perhaps both parties would see this as less risky. The idea of focused workshops or study groups had obvious merit, and these could perhaps be hosted by the Swiss. However, such detailed speculation was premature. The initial steps had still to be accomplished, and there were many potential roadblocks ahead. I hoped that the ANC would not take exception to the fact that I had chosen to consult in the first instance with the Government. Later, I imagined, a similar issue could arise with reference to the participation of other parties – Azapo, the PAC, the UDF, Inkatha, et al. The difficulty was that, the wider one cast the net, the greater the risk of obstructionism and prevarication.

In the days that followed the Government used the Emergency Regulations to ban the weekly newspaper *South*, and I found myself acting for its editor, Rashied Seria, accused of promoting the cause of the ANC. On 8 May, the security forces claimed 'a great breakthrough' in capturing four 'white guerrillas' who were allegedly members of a 'terrorist cell' based on a farm near Broederstroom, outside Pretoria. The Minister of Law and Order, Adriaan Vlok, told Parliament that a huge arms cache had been seized, including SAM-7 missiles, limpet mines, hand grenades, AK-47s, assault rifles, pistols, machine guns, demolition charges, mortars and other explosives of Soviet origin. It was claimed that their capture had been the result of information leaked to the security forces by rival groups engaged in an internecine power struggle within the top echelons of the ANC. Similar disinformation was published by *Die Burger* to explain attacks in different parts of the world on a number of senior ANC members, including Dulcie September, Albie Sachs and others. Such fabrications were consumed and regurgitated by the British media, including such prestigious newspapers as the *Financial Times* ('ANC takes some hard knocks from Pretoria'), and the *Daily Telegraph* ('ANC's anti-South Africa campaign falters'). It was even rumoured that these internal struggles might lead to Thabo Mbeki taking over as leader from Oliver Tambo. The *Telegraph* quoted Thabo Mbeki as acknowledging that the ANC's morale was at a low ebb, and that things were looking worse for the ANC than a year earlier. He had been quoted as saying that the South African Government did not yet feel itself threatened by the ANC.

Sir Geoffrey Howe, British Foreign Secretary, speaking in London on 17

May at the Royal Commonwealth Society, had some advice for South Africans, black and white. He said to the whites: 'Change is coming, and the sooner the white community as a whole can face the fact, the better the chance of negotiating a settlement in which their concerns will be met, and in which the process will occur peacefully.' To Blacks he said: 'Violence is self-defeating. Violence is wrong. Bombing and burning are murder. The logical conclusion of those who advocate violence is civil war, leading to ruin, death and destruction ... turn away from prescriptions which would increase polarisation or leave the land an economic desert, reject violence and terrorism – they are a counsel of despair – and do not lose hope. Change must come. Change will come.' He advised both whites and blacks to 'avoid intellectual or political straitjackets. Negotiation, when it comes, will not take place to rigid preset formulas ...' All this imperial wisdom was preceded by the salutary insight – which he appeared himself to have overlooked – that 'No outsider has the key to unlock a settlement. Nobody can look to Britain to solve their problems as though they were a second Rhodesia.'

My Journal of Saturday 20 May records:

> I am finding it increasingly difficult to remain opaque in the face of persistent questioning from friends, partners, clients and colleagues. As my retirement approaches, they ask 'What are you going to do?' I answer facetiously – something about cultivating roses, or writing a novel. I do not like being evasive, as it generates suspicion and undermines intimacy.

> I worry whether I will have the staying power in the long term to see this through to its conclusion. I no longer fear rejection of the concept, but I do fear the cost in terms of my own isolation and alienation from those who are my friends. Already, I am so deeply involved that there is really no way back.

> Closing down my law practice, packing up files, saying farewells, resigning my position as Executor, Trustee, Director, whatever – it all feels irreversible.

> A whirlpool. Things are getting quite hectic. I feel somewhat out of control. Soon I will be on my way, and not without fear. There is also a sad feeling. My partners neither understand nor condone my unexplained resignation, nor is it possible for me to explain things to them. They now ask for 'a clean break', adding, 'It's what's best for the firm.' I am left feeling vulnerable and misunderstood.

> I remain troubled by the conflict between undertaking commitments which presuppose my staying, and preparing a 'last-ditch' option to leave – just in case. It is really trying to reconcile the irreconcilable. None of us wishes to go, but it seems irresponsible to

abandon the option. If this initiative does fail, I doubt that I will any longer have the heart to stay. The ambiguity of the situation is incredibly stressful. In a few months, I shall be without a job, without colleagues, without an income, and without security. That is really scary.

Jonathan is amazingly clear. He says, 'I want to stay, no matter what happens. I cannot run away from this country.' Cari is more like me. She says, 'I am afraid of the future, but I don't want to act on the basis of my fears. I love this country, but I really don't know what to do.'

Harry Oppenheimer, in a speech to the Commonwealth Society said, 'There is a whole generation of young [white] South Africans, who have never known what it means to be proud of their own country.' He's speaking about my children. There is an even more powerful statement that could be made about a whole generation of young (black) South Africans.

10

A tryst in Room 814

A week of relative normality followed, during which I visited Jenny Schreiner at Pollsmoor Prison, and dealt with various work commitments, including meetings with Counsel briefed by the Legal Resources Centre in the forthcoming KTC trial. This trial involved sensational allegations – vehemently denied by the Police Commissioner and Minister of Law and Order, but ultimately proved – that the security forces instigated and assisted in the burning down and demolition of an entire squatter camp comprising several thousand wood-and-iron houses, at a place called KTC on the outskirts of Cape Town. It was a strange irony to meet Jenny Schreiner and Advocate Dullah Omar, both deeply involved in the struggle, but to be unable to share with them what I was doing.

More than eight months had passed since my initial approach to President Botha, and at long last the time had come to make contact with the ANC leadership. On the night of Wednesday 25 May I flew Swissair to Zurich, and then on to Frankfurt, carefully avoiding the Lufthansa flight, which left Jan Smuts airport the same evening with the conference delegates aboard. A few days earlier Van Zyl had confirmed that Thabo Mbeki would in fact be present at the conference 'unless something unforeseen occurs'. It had been arranged that I would book into the same hotel as the other delegates – the Frankfurt Intercontinental – but my presence should not be known to any of the participants. As in a James Bond movie, Van Zyl and I would meet 'as though by chance' in the Prolog Bar at 6 p.m. that Thursday evening. He would then let me know what arrangements he had been able to make for a meeting with Mr Mbeki.

In the light of the Government's threat to withdraw passports and to inflict further recriminations upon delegates, their departure for the Frankfurt meeting had been a low-key affair. I assumed that, despite such precautions, the N I S must be aware of IDASA's plans, and that the intelligence services of other interested countries might have noted the coincidence of ANC and Afrikaner leaders converging from various parts of the world upon a venue in West Germany.

In fact, the news broke in the local media only the following day, when the *Cape Times* in its main front-page story reported: 'The leader of the National Democratic Movement, Mr Wynand Malan, and Dr Van Zyl Slabbert left for Frankfurt yesterday for sensitive high-level talks with the ANC, which could eventually change the face of South African politics.' It continued, 'The party flew out last night after denials by Dr Slabbert that he would be accompanying the NDM for talks with the ANC in Lusaka. According to reporters at Jan Smuts Airport, Dr Slabbert was not on the same flight, but he flew out of Cape Town yesterday morning. A spokesman at his home told Sapa last night, "He is in Europe."'

Anxious to remain unconnected with these media events, I had declined IDASA's offer of a free air ticket and hotel accommodation, my overriding concern being to ensure that my meeting with Mr Mbeki took place unnoticed, and that we were not observed and listened to. This created the obverse danger that my serendipitous appearance might accidentally become known to delegates who were in turn known to me – or to South Africa's intelligence community – and that my presence in such circumstances might arouse unwanted curiosity and suspicion. Paradoxically, I was equally concerned about the ANC's security corps. They would also be taking special precautions to protect their delegates, particularly after the recent events in Paris and Maputo. I had said nothing to Stoffel van der Merwe about my plans, as I didn't want him to know in advance, and alert the N I S. As country hosts, the German Police would probably be studying incoming flight and hotel registers. If they found an uninvited South African booked into the same hotel as that in which the event was taking place, would they not also become concerned and inquisitive?

I reached the hotel around noon on Thursday, and booked into a lofty 20th floor room, spending as little time as I could in the hotel lobby, and declining the bell-hops' help with my baggage. En route, I had changed airlines, switched flights, swopped seats, and moved around, in an effort to see whether I was being followed. The delegates were scheduled to arrive during the course of the day, and the conference was scheduled to begin that evening. I spent the ensuing hours closeted in my hotel room preparing for the crucial meeting with Mr Mbeki, awed by the responsibility, and concerned not to make silly mistakes. Though longing for a walk in the fresh air, I decided it would be more prudent to stay invisibly in my room, and look down on the city from a high window.

How was I to explain to Thabo Mbeki the role I had chosen? Indeed how did one approach a man who had spent the greater part of his life in exile, and whose father had languished almost 30 years in prison? How could one begin to understand such sacrifices? How was he to know he could trust me? I realised that I could do no more than speak as one human being to another; to let him know the kind of man I was; what had led me to attempt this thing; and the nature of my dreams and hopes. He would no doubt wonder, as others had and would, whether I was crazy; or whether I had some other covert agenda – in which case, he would speculate, whom did I really represent? And, why me? Ultimately, there was no way to prove integrity, and there was every reason to suspect and mistrust me. I was encroaching on the most fundamental question in our political life – whether in the present moment there existed a window of opportunity to facilitate the essential opening of a dialogue which could lead ultimately to fundamental change through negotiations.

The hours passed, slowly, but eventually it was time to go. I took a lift to the ground floor, found the Prolog Bar next to the foyer, sat down at a corner table as arranged, and ordered a drink. A few inscrutable characters were drinking morosely at the bar counter. I wondered who they might be. At exactly 6 p.m. a familiar voice greeted me, 'Hello! What a coincidence. Fancy meeting you here!' A slap on the back, and Van Zyl sat down at my table, and ordered a drink. He said that Thabo Mbeki had arrived, and had been persuaded to meet me. Van Zyl wrote down his room number on a paper coaster, which I put in my coat pocket. 'He is expecting you to contact him.' He grinned.

'Have you heard the news?' Van asked. There was a report that four people had been injured in a bomb blast in central Pretoria. Minister Adriaan Vlok had already been quoted as saying that it was 'incomprehensible' that people could be meeting with the ANC at the very time these 'abhorrent deeds were being perpetrated'. 'Unbelievable timing,' said Van Zyl. 'What is P W going to do about us now? What a background to this meeting between Afrikaners and the ANC! IDASA could well now be banned. The Government can't permit talks like these to go ahead when bombs are exploding in Pretoria. It's so stupid – the ANC's left hand doesn't know what its right hand is doing.' It was clear that those opposed to talks would be the only ones to benefit. He finished his drink, and stood up. 'Good luck,' he said. 'You're going to need it!'

I took a deep breath, and went in search of room 814. Emerging from the lift, I walked down a long corridor, and passed an open door. Someone came out casually and stared at me. ANC security men, I guessed. I found Mr Mbeki's door and knocked, my heart pounding. There was no answer. I couldn't believe it. I knocked again. Still no answer. I was now being attentively observed by two men standing in the corridor, and I began to feel distinctly uncomfortable. I didn't wish to ask or be asked any questions. So I turned on my heel, and went back to the lift. From my room I telephoned 814; and to my huge relief the phone was answered.

'Richard Rosenthal speaking,' I said.

'Hello, Rich.' A deep, resonant voice. 'Thabo speaking. I've been waiting for you.'

I suggested that I come down to his room, but he suggested rather coming up to mine. A few moments later he arrived. I had some mind-picture of this man who had come to play such an important role in recent years. But I was not prepared for his warmth and urbane gentility. He wanted to know whether I had a good flight? Did I mind his smoking in my room? This was an occasion when I was prepared to suspend all my neuroses. We agreed that it was a bad habit, but I didn't mind. Out came the trademark Mbeki pipe, plus a tin of the best Balkan Sobranie.

'Van Zyl has told me some nice things about you!' he commenced. I made some facetious reply about him not knowing me very well. He said he had heard a lot about me, and had looked forward to our meeting. He hoped I didn't mind this taking place in my room. 'The place is bristling with security people,' he explained, 'including our own!' He laughed.

After a couple of minutes of friendly chat, he said that before we had our discussion he would have to deal with a few practical matters. A cocktail party had been arranged to say goodbye to Wynand Malan and his group from the National Democratic Movement – including Esther Lategan, Pierre Cronje, Harald Pakendorf, and Dr Jannie Hofmeyr. He was afraid it might cause them offence if he didn't make some appearance there. So we agreed to postpone our meeting for another hour.

In fact, several hours passed before he returned, looking tired. He apologised for being late, and said that he had also had to take a call from Lusaka. We ordered double whiskies, and he made a few more calls from my phone – one of which seemed to involve making 'an excuse' to his own people for his unexplained absence. He said the American media had been trying to get hold of him all day, wanting him to make a statement. 'Americans don't seem to realise the rest of the world lives in a different time zone!'

He made himself comfortable, and fixed me with a piercing gaze. 'I believe you're a lawyer?' he said. I agreed, adding by way of mitigation – 'a reformed lawyer.' He laughed. 'What's that? Not a variety I've ever heard of.' He puffed away at his pipe, and sipped my Chivas Regal. A socialist, I thought, with plutocratic tastes! Though tired, he seemed confident and entirely at ease. From my coffee table he picked up Gorbachev's recently published *Perestroika*. 'Are you reading this?' he asked. 'What d'you think of it?' I said I was finding it fascinating. 'That man could change the world,' I ventured. 'I wish we had such a man in our own country.' He nodded.

'So where d'you come from; what's your family background?' he asked. I didn't know what he already knew about me, but told him about my life, my family, and my work. It was a rather long digression, but seemed appropriate. We also spoke about the meetings that had just taken place at the hotel. He seemed to regard the discussions with Wynand Malan and his group in the NDM with a certain measure of bemusement, experiencing them as rather wordy and pedantic. He said some of the delegates had expressed relief and surprise after meeting him. 'I wonder what they'd expected – that I would have horns?' He thought we were all the victims of disinformation. 'Afrikaners are funny people,' he mused, 'They make little speeches, sometimes for up to 20 minutes at a time. I listen carefully, but when they're finished, I'm not sure what they've been saying.'

One of our problems in communicating was that words had different meanings for different people, he said. He took the example of the term 'power-sharing'. It meant different things depending upon who was talking. 'That's one of the reasons why foreigners have difficulty helping and understanding us,' he said. Did he think this was one of the problems facing the Commonwealth 'Eminent Persons' Group', I asked. He looked noncommittal.

Reverting to the subject of the gathering that had just ended, I asked whether he felt people like Wynand Malan – or IDASA – could play a role in bringing the Government and the ANC to the table. He was doubtful, pointing out that they had a different role and context, which probably disqualified them from serving as intermediaries. However, he was warmly appreciative of the work done by IDASA, and particularly the roles played by Slabbert and Boraine. They were making an important contribution.

At one point, he stood up and walked to the window, looking down on the twinkling lights of Frankfurt. After a long silence, he said, 'This is really such a beautiful old city. We don't have cities like this in our country.' He then quoted Maxim Gorky: 'Old cities are like testaments of man's faith in the future.'

He had left South Africa in 1962. 'More than half your life?' I asked. He nodded ruefully. I could hardly imagine what that meant. He said it was something one had came to terms with. As a young student at Sussex University in the early '60s he had sometimes felt homesick. The University had then been in its infancy. There were only about 400 students. 'Those of us from Africa decided to stick together – partly for friendship, and partly because we realised one day we would go back to become the new generation of leaders. That is of course what has happened.' He recalled a young Afrikaner student at Sussex, who also seemed quite lonely. 'We felt sorry for him, and asked him to come and join our circle.' They had gone to parties and pubs together. 'But after eighteen months he told us he had decided to return home. He didn't even finish his studies. He thanked us for our friendship, but admitted he was just too much of an Afrikaner, and didn't really feel at home with us.'

'We have all been damaged and wounded,' I said. 'Yes,' he agreed, 'but one day when we solve our problems, won't we have something to teach the world?' We discussed the phenomenon of the world's preoccupation with South Africa's problems. He said the British prided themselves as high-minded liberals, but in his view the phenomenon of class prejudice was not very different from race. Germany was also anxious to distance itself from its fascist past; and America sought absolution from its history of slavery and racial discrimination. Not all our critics were as pure as driven snow.

Eventually, we came to the purpose of the meeting. He said that Van Zyl had told him that there was something important I wished to discuss, and had suggested that we meet alone. 'I have had to make all sorts of excuses of my own to meet you like this,' he said. Finally, I was able to tell him what had brought me to Germany, and how this idea had come about. I stressed the lengths to which I too had gone to protect the confidentiality of this discussion, and pledged that I would in all events maintain confidentiality, irrespective of the outcome. I then spoke about my initial letter to P W Botha and of his response, and the meetings which had followed with Stoffel van der Merwe. I told him that, after six months of delay, Van der Merwe had now advised me of the Government's qualified consent – but, on a basis of 'deniability'. Its approval for this initiative had since been independently confirmed by the Swiss Ambassador. I also spoke of my proposal that the Swiss be invited to play some supportive role, and referred to the pre-conditions they had mentioned for their involvement. Their decision would now depend upon the attitude of the ANC.

He seemed interested in the possibility of a role for the Swiss, and said that it was not the first time Switzerland had offered its assistance. 'But we really don't need help introducing us to people like Wynand Malan and Van Zyl Slabbert. It would be different if the Swiss could help us meet P W Botha!' With regard to their offers of financial assistance, the ANC position had been consistent: 'If you want to give us such assistance, then please hand us the funds, and let us control how they are spent.' He also spoke of other past attempts to set up some kind of communication channel with the South African Government. 'Even at Dakar there was someone interested in doing this. I think he was some relative of Constand Viljoen. He told us he was going back to talk to the Government – but we heard no more of it.'

He questioned me closely about the Government's attitude to my proposal. A future negotiation process was a very delicate and important matter, he pointed out. Obviously, he would not be able to respond imme-diately to the issue I was raising, but would need to report back on our discussion. Any response would have to involve others, including the President of the ANC, Oliver Tambo. I said I had expected this would be the position, but wished to stress the importance of maintaining confidentiality. I hoped it would not be necessary for him to involve too many people at this early stage. If secrecy was destroyed, the whole initiative might be in jeopardy. In such circumstances the initiative might simply be denied, and I would be called a liar. He understood this concern, and assured me that the issue would be handled very discreetly by a small group. Following Slabbert's advice he had met me alone on this occasion, and would not be discussing the matter with anyone else at the conference. 'But this is not a matter which can be decided by one or two people,' he warned.

He said that there were various matters that would need to be addressed at an early stage in any such process. In particular, they would insist on the release of political prisoners. This had been made clear in discussions they had with US Secretary of State, George Schultz. The release of prisoners would be seen as a token of the Government's seriousness of intent. Schultz had promised to convey this to the South African Government, but nothing seemed to have come of it. He said from time to time people came to talk with them on behalf of the Government 'using all sorts of pretexts'. 'We generally know who they are. So it is not as though we have no contact at all. However what you're suggesting, if I understand you correctly, is quite different. It is a very important question that we will need to discuss, and we will let you have our answer later on.' I asked how long this might take. 'It needn't take too long,' he replied.

As the hours passed, we called room service from time to time, and replenished our glasses. I erred on the side of neglect as a host, rather than allow my recall of the details of our conversation to become blurred by conviviality. Thabo Mbeki is a man of great charm, with a lovely sense of humour, and a great chuckle. Our conversation ranged easily over many topics, and he told some hilarious 'Van der Merwe' stories which I suspected were distinct to the ANC. The atmosphere was warm and relaxed.

I confirmed that I would be happy to come and meet him again at any time, when the ANC was ready. 'But please choose your venue carefully,' I warned. 'I have only a South African passport which is not universally welcome.' 'That's no problem,' he assured me. 'We'll warn the Immigration people in Zambia, and then your name will be on a list of people they will allow to come and see us.'

I raised a concern that had been troubling me for some time – namely, that I had been acting thus far entirely on my own initiative and judgment. This had advantages and disadvantages. If the initiative went ahead, would it not be appropriate for me to involve a few carefully selected people as my confidants and consultants? What were his views? Were there perhaps certain people he would like me to liaise with? He said he would think about that, and might come back to me at a later stage. 'Perhaps you will need some sort of lawyer's collective,' he suggested. It sounded dreadful. We talked about people like Arthur Chaskalson, Sidney Kentridge and George Bizos. 'Maybe we could put you in touch with one or two of our own lawyers,' he said. I pointed out that those we had mentioned were all white males. That was surely not a satisfactory prescription? He didn't see this as a problem at present. 'There are probably no black lawyers at this stage who have the same quality or experience.' He said one might also need to think about a few people 'who were good at being sceptical'. I asked what he thought about my trying to get permission to meet Nelson Mandela? He said it would probably be better at this stage if I dealt only with the external wing of the ANC, implying that they had ways and means of communicating with those inside the country.

He mentioned the role of George Bizos in exploring possibilities whilst Nelson Mandela was in hospital. It had seemed at the time as if the Government had seriously considered releasing him. Bizos was allowed an hour and a half to talk with Mr Mandela. This had led to some discussions involving Minister Kobie Coetsee, but his worry seemed to have been that Mr Mandela's release could trigger a situation that could get out of control. 'We agreed this was possible, but assured him that we would work to avoid it.' Minister Adriaan Vlok had also been involved in these talks. He said that there had been discussions about allowing the ANC to send a few people to talk with Nelson Mandela in prison, and about how his eventual release could best be handled. The ANC took some risk in conducting such secret talks. Minister Coetsee had been told that the ANC would insist on the right to hold meetings, so that Mandela could calm the people, and thank them for having remembered him through these long years. These discussions had progressed 'quite a long way', but eventually had just 'fizzled out'. I suggested that one of the reasons might have been the Pretoria car bomb, which I understood to have led to the shelving of certain possibilities. He thought for a moment, and said, 'Yes, that is possible.'

I mentioned that on my way to Europe I had tried to meet his father in Port Elizabeth, but that there had been some misunderstanding, and his father was not at home when I arrived. We hoped to meet soon after my return. I asked whether there was any small item he might like me to take him. He spoke of the family's initial joy and subsequent distress about the way their father's release had been handled by the Government. His father had been given virtually no warning of his impending release. He was now an old man, having spent long years in prison. One day they just came along and told him to pack his bags without warning. There had been virtually no chance to say goodbyes, or to consult with his comrades, or to prepare himself. He was put on a plane, and ten minutes before landing in Port Elizabeth they informed him that he would have to face a news conference on arrival. He was unprepared, and felt as though he had botched an important opportunity. It was ironic that in spite of his release he remained bound by restriction orders, which prevented him from meeting more than one person at a time, and from travelling outside Port Elizabeth. 'My father doesn't want to conform to these orders,' he said, 'but worries that if he ignores them, it could prejudice the chances of others to be considered for release.'

Like Slabbert, he also warned me of the personal risks of getting involved in this sort of thing. 'For myself,' he said, 'I have come to terms with those realities,' but he warned that I should not be naive about it. He saw risks coming from both the 'rogue element' on the right-wing, and also from the security forces. 'I don't want to frighten you, but you must be realistic,' he said. 'Even our own people get a bit jumpy about my safety!' he chuckled, as though that were some kind of joke. He had been warned by American and Belgian intelligence that his name was on a 'hit list'. 'I am not sure why I should be singled out,' he said. 'Maybe it's because when there are meetings like these, I am generally involved.' I asked what he did about protecting himself, and he said one took basic precautions, but there was really not very much one could do. 'You could put a whole platoon around you, but if people want to get you they can still do it.' I could see that there was steel beneath the velvet.

Twice during the evening, he spoke to someone on the phone, reassuring them that they were not to be concerned about him – but, no mention of where he was, or with whom he was meeting , or what we were talking about. Towards midnight, he said that he probably needed to go. It was getting late, and his friends might start to get worried. 'They will begin to imagine I am with a woman!' he laughed. He suggested that we could resume our discussion the following morning. 'How about an early breakfast, at say 7 a.m.?' I readily agreed. 'I have no other commitments.' He said he still had quite a lot to do before getting to bed; so we said goodnight, and I settled down to make detailed notes of our discussion.

In the small hours of the morning whilst I was still scribbling away in my notebook, Van Zyl appeared at my door. He wanted to know how it had gone, and what my impressions were of Thabo Mbeki. I gave him an outline of the evening's discussion. He felt the duration of the meeting had been encouraging, and that it was significant that a further meeting had been scheduled. It was clear that Thabo appreciated the significance of the proposal. Van said that one of the problems in dealing with Thabo Mbeki was that he was chronically overworked. Meanwhile, a splendid bottle of French champagne arrived miraculously in my bedroom. We agreed to polish it off at once. 'I wonder where this came from?' Van mused. 'You've no idea how much this stuff costs!'

I didn't get much sleep that night, but there were more important priorities than sleep. Two further meetings followed with Thabo – a breakfast which had to be postponed successively – from 7 to 8, and then from 8 to 9 a.m. He had been very apologetic, and explained that he was having to deal with several urgent matters. He looked distinctly jaded when finally he appeared, and had apparently been up for much of the night. Our third meeting took place over lunch. Each meeting started late, and extended beyond the time originally agreed.

At each of these meetings we traversed similar issues, but in greater detail. He made it clear that he attached great significance to what we were discussing. As far as my own role as intermediary was concerned, he was prepared to accept the assurances he had received. The principle of opening up a dialogue with the Government was a matter of fundamental importance, and would need full discussion before there was any response. Concerning the possibility of the Swiss Government's supporting the process, this too would require careful consideration. If the decision was to proceed, they would get in touch with the Secretary of State, as he had requested.

I asked whether he agreed with my sense that the time was ripe for such an initiative, and he replied simply 'Yes!' He gave the same reply in answer to my question whether my own involvement would be helpful at this stage. I told him that I did not envisage a role involving the formulation of substantive proposals, but rather as facilitating direct communication between the parties themselves. I understood the participants might wish to take some defensive measures as protection against the possibility of a breach of trust. Perhaps there might be value in using intermediaries initially? This would enable the process to be disavowed, if necessary; for example, if secrecy was breached. Another possibility would be for leaders to be present at meetings, but for others to do the talking?

I said that the Government was likely to call upon the ANC to suspend violence prior to any substantive talks taking place. Mbeki replied that it could not be expected of the ANC to play its strongest cards at the outset. I foresaw a future problem in reciprocity, in that the Government held a fairly large number of negotiating chips or 'trading options', but the ANC held relatively few. He agreed, but said there were some things they could do in the nature of reciprocity, such as suspending the cultural or sports boycott for particular events. I said that it seemed totally incongruous that something as secular as rugby, cricket, or tiddlywinks, could assume such symbolic importance in negotiating our future. I supposed it was just another of those incomprehensible things about South Africans.

Concerning the Government's anxiety that violence and anarchy could result from the release of political prisoners, Mbeki said one of the reasons they had argued for the right to hold country-wide meetings was to try to ensure that people's feelings could be expressed, without control being lost. He added, 'There will always be the possibility of things happening which no one intended. Whatever the truth, we will subsequently be blamed.' He gave the example of the 1985 Christmas bombing of a supermarket in Amanzimtoti. He said the man who planted the bomb was an ANC cadre, but had acted on that occasion on his own initiative, without orders. Six people had been killed, including three children. At his trial and before being sentenced to death, he had apologised to the ANC, and acknowledged that he had acted contrary to its policy of avoiding civilian targets. The man had explained that he had been angry because of the death of one of his comrades in an SADF raid into Lesotho. Mr Mbeki said, 'This sort of thing can happen when people are upset. They lose discipline, and that is one of the dangers.' He said it had never been ANC policy to hit white civilians. People should realise that South Africa is so structured that it would be relatively easy for the ANC to hit whites and be sure of not hitting blacks – segregated schools, separate Group Areas, and whites-only churches. 'But we don't want innocent people to die,' he said. This kind of thing could happen if there is no settlement.

We discussed how to make contact again. I suggested we might use the Swiss diplomatic bag, but he preferred no communications in writing. 'Let's rather use the telephone,' he said. So we agreed, and exchanged phone and telex numbers. (The fax revolution had not yet reached the outer reaches of Zambia.) 'We will need to use a pseudonym,' he said, 'What shall I call you?' After a moment's thought, he suggested, 'How about Richard Frankfurt?' I laughed, a bit nervously. 'One day I shall ring you up and identify myself by saying this is Richard Frankfurt speaking ... how about a meeting at such and such a place and time?' I would be willing to come to Lusaka, if that was preferred, on condition that he could deal with the problem of my little green passport.

At the end of our discussion we shook hands, and wished each other a safe journey. I packed my bags, settled my account, and slipped out of the hotel where I had arrived 36 hours earlier. I had spent the entire time closeted inside a hotel room, without even walking around the block. However, I left Frankfurt that Friday afternoon with a sense that something immensely important might have commenced.

Just before catching my return flight, I called Swiss Secretary of State, Mr Edouard Brunner, and informed him that I had made contact with the ANC, and our initial discussions had gone well. We would now have to await their response, which I was assured would not take too long. I told him that I had requested Mr Mbeki to contact him direct, as soon as the ANC's decision had been reached. Mr Brunner said he had read media reports about the IDASA conference in Frankfurt, and asked whether I had been part of it? I assured him that although I had been in the vicinity I had played no part in the conference. He commented that talks like these were encouraging, but seemed rather like a gathering of like-minded friends. Surely what was needed, he suggested, was a different kind of meeting – one between those who did not share similar opinions, but who represented the conflicting positions of the South African Government and the ANC? I could not but agree.

'Richard Frankfurt speaking'

I returned home over the weekend, and walked into my office on Monday morning, as though nothing out of the ordinary had happened. 'A good weekend?' asked my partner Joe. 'Yes,' I replied, adding mischievously, 'Just a bit busy.' He didn't enquire what or why. What an extraordinary feeling it was to have been involved in such high drama, and yet to be unable to share it. In fact no one but Hilary and my peerless secretary – not even close family members – had been aware of my absence. Barbara Puttick would one day be named Secretary of the Year, but her real unsung accomplishments include an astonishing ability to keep my secrets.

Local newspapers were dominated by the crowing of the National Party over the 40th anniversary celebrations of its accession to power in 1948. The State President summed up the feelings of the party faithful when he said: 'There is simply no alternative to the National Party. Our political opponents subsist on clichés, false perceptions, and a surfeit of self-appointed leaders. Some even travel overseas with foreign money in order to assail us.' He declared that the National Party was 'a miracle party'. Referring to the propaganda war against his Government, he said, 'We must not permit ourselves to be deflected by false propaganda from the path that leads towards freedom and a broadening of democracy, which we have for so long pursued, in the footsteps of our forebears.'

In the midst of this myopic self-eulogy, columnist Gerald Shaw discerned 'some faintly hopeful stirrings in the air', despite the fact, as he noted, that the National Party during its 40 years of power 'had alienated the majority of South Africans, and the country has never been more isolated'. He lauded Dr Slabbert for his bridge-building role, adding, 'The sad thing is that the Botha government has cut directly across this trend by imposing crippling restrictions on a wide range of extra-parliamentary organisations, and by threatening to take away the passports of anyone who might be so bold as to announce an intention to visit the ANC in Lusaka. Yet contact with the ANC is essential if there is to be a swing from confrontation to participation.'

I decided that Stoffel van der Merwe should be briefed regarding my latest moves, and called his secretary, Riaan Nel, to arrange an appointment for the following day. We met at 6 p.m. for only half an hour, because, as he explained, it was the week of his Parliamentary Vote, and he was extremely preoccupied. I gave him a brief account of my meetings in Berne and Frankfurt, and of the status of my opening discussions with the Swiss and the ANC. He seemed surprised, and possibly a little alarmed, at how far and fast I had progressed. He had the look of a man who has just rolled a small snowball down the slope, which he knows he can no longer recall. He asked that I keep him closely in touch with further developments. I reassured him that I was taking all possible measures to protect the confidentiality of the matter, but there were obviously some risks that I could not control. There was no way of exploring these possibilities without taking certain risks. He said he understood, and was ready to handle any fallout, if this became necessary. In the last resort, they would have to do some 'damage control'. We agreed once again that we were both 'dispensable'.

As soon as the debate on his Vote was finished, he would like us to get together, to discuss these matters in greater detail. It was important that I be properly briefed, he said. I asked that he consider taking me further into his confidence regarding the Government's concept of a future negotiation process. He said that up to the present time there were a great many ideas but very few decisions. He would convey what we had discussed today to those other (nameless) persons who were sharing with him the responsibility for this initiative. I inferred this would also include Mr Botha.

Three weeks passed without any word from Lusaka. It was another anxious period of waiting. The date of my 'retirement' was looming closer, but my future income and occupation remained uncertain. Moreover, the deadline on our Canadian immigration visas was also rapidly approaching, and I knew that we would soon have to make a decision or forfeit this option by default. There seemed little or nothing we could do to dispel our uncertainties. Thabo Mbeki had made it clear that he would need time for consultations, and I wondered whether this might also involve time to enable communication to take place with the leadership inside the country. I had no idea what this might involve.

One evening at around 6 p.m., as I was packing my briefcase and preparing to go home, the phone rang, and a familiar voice said: 'Richard Frankfurt speaking! How are you?' My heart missed several beats. I greeted him with unconcealed relief, and admitted that I had been anxiously awaiting his call. I could not help being amused by the schizophrenic transposition of *my* pseudonym – it transpired we were *both* 'Richard Frankfurt'!

Without further ado, he said they were now keen and ready to meet again. Could I come to Lusaka? We discussed possible dates. Each of us had certain commitments which made it awkward to get together for a few weeks. We agreed to be in touch again shortly to confirm dates and flights. In the meanwhile, I would make my travel arrangements. Our conversation was brief and businesslike. The scene was set for a pivotal meeting which would determine the feasibility of the initiative.

The ensuing weeks were spent taking final leave of clients, handing over my practice to colleagues, and making the practical arrangements to establish a separate and highly discreet office. I was also learning to come to terms with a kind of existential loneliness and a feeling of isolation, albeit self-imposed. It was becoming increasingly difficult to explain my 'retirement' plans, and deflect the natural curiosity of friends and clients.

My Journal tells the story:

Thursday 30 June 1988

What on earth am I going to tell people who keep asking me what I'm planning to do with my retirement? Every answer generates more questions. The best answer may in fact be no answer at all. But even inscrutability must be managed in such a way as to avoid further curiosity. For once, I feel grateful for people's lack of interest and concern. What a topsy-turvy life. The truth is that this could still turn out to be just a puff of smoke.

Why on earth did I undertake such an impossible task? Perhaps because of a little boy a long time ago, who thought he was more fearful than other kids, but desperately wanted to be brave?

A few days later, I began the arduous task of trying to make a telephone call to Zambia. Sometimes it seemed as if the whole country had dropped off the edge of the world. On other occasions, the ANC phone rang interminably but was unanswered; calls were misdirected; messages were left but never returned. I had decided to combine this next trip with a much-needed family holiday, and at the same time visit friends and relatives in Switzerland and Canada. Our bookings were made, but I needed to confirm dates with Mr Mbeki. Despite numerous heroic attempts to telephone him prior to our departure, I was unsuccessful. Richard Frankfurt left numerous cryptic messages with sundry telephonists, secretaries, and assistants, but all efforts were in vain. Ultimately, it became a concern that these repetitive calls would disturb the slumbers of our vigilant security police. It seemed best to resume these efforts only when we were overseas. Perhaps the problem also had to do with Mr Mbeki's difficulty in making return calls to South Africa?

Initially from a mountain top in Switzerland, and then later from various parts of Canada, I made dozens of calls, trying again and again to confirm the date and venue of our meeting. I was afraid to leave a substantive message as I didn't know who was privy to this matter. The ANC telephonists grew weary of Richard Frankfurt's evasiveness and reluctance to state the nature of his business. No one seemed to know, or they weren't telling me, when Mr Mbeki would be available. He was alternately 'away', 'in a meeting', 'busy', 'out of the country', 'unavailable' etc. etc. Finally, I left an exasperated message stating my real name and emphasising that the matter had now become extremely urgent.

In the early hours of one Canadian morning, as the sun was no doubt just rising in Lusaka, the long-awaited call finally came through. I was roused from a deep sleep, but my grogginess vanished like the morning mist when I realised it was the inaccessible Mr Mbeki. I was hugely relieved. He apologised profusely for my many unreturned messages, and explained that he had been 'travelling', and had been inaccessible by phone. He was friendly, and eager for us to meet as soon as possible, 'but this time with certain other people also present'.

A meeting was arranged to take place in Lusaka one week hence. On 10 July I celebrated my 49th birthday, but it was less of a celebration than a time of preparation for the journey from Toronto. I had never been to Zambia before. I would be travelling on my incriminating passport, and had no more than a verbal assurance that I would be met at Lusaka Airport when the flight touched down at 6.30 a.m. on a Sunday morning! I did not care to speculate what might happen if these arrangements went wrong. I would be travelling without visa, and without proof of the purpose of my journey. South Africans were not free to do business or to holiday in Zambia, and I didn't wish to invite an interrogation as to the true nature of my journey. The family holiday came to an abrupt end, and we all headed off in different directions. I calculated that at one moment we would all be airborne, – I would be on my way to Zurich, via London en route to Lusaka; Hilary would be on her way to Vancouver; and Jonathan and Caroline would be returning to school in South Africa. We needed the fulltime assistance of St Christopher!

Hilary said she was concerned to know what to do if her husband simply disappeared. By this time our children knew what I was doing, and felt very responsible to keep the secret. The truth was that I had no idea how the family could contact me, in case of need. I didn't even know where I would be staying, nor for how long. I was painfully aware of the vagaries of the Zambian telephone system. Finally, we arranged that if I was not in touch by a certain date, Hilary would call the Swiss Ambassador in South Africa or State Secretary Brunner in Berne. She also had the numbers of Stoffel van der Merwe in Pretoria, and Thabo Mbeki in Lusaka. Hopefully, someone somewhere would help her to find out what had happened to me. Neither South Africa nor Switzerland had diplomatic representation in Zambia.

Before leaving Canada, I telephoned State Secretary Brunner and we agreed to meet en route at Zurich Airport on the morning of 14 July. I wanted him to be aware of these arrangements, so that we might be in a position to request assistance should something go wrong! After a trans-atlantic flight, I was first off the plane when it landed at Zurich airport in the early morning. I was astonished to be met at the foot of the gangway by the State Secretary himself, accompanied by several aides. For the first time in my life (and no doubt the last) I was treated with the intoxicating courtesies extended to visiting dignitaries. My luggage was collected on my behalf, and I floated through Customs and Immigration in a most miraculous manner. We went directly to a private lounge in the airport building, which had been reserved for our meeting. I do admire Swiss administrative flawlessness. The meeting was attended by Mr Brunner, the State Secretary for Foreign Affairs; his assistant Mr C Blickenstorfer, and another aide Mr Jean-Jacques de Dardel, whom I had not met before.

I gave a fairly detailed account of the events since our last meeting, including my discussions with Thabo Mbeki in Frankfurt. I also explained the reasons for the delays which had occurred, and the difficulties experi-enced in communicating with Lusaka. The Swiss view with incomprehen-sion the inability of the rest of humanity to operate a telephone system that works, or a bus, train or plane that actually arrives on time! Mr Brunner confirmed his Government's wish to make available all necessary assistance that might be helpful. If it was a question of delivering documents or letters, I could approach their Ambassadors in South Africa or in Zimbabwe, to make the necessary arrangements. Both Ambassadors had been instructed to give me any assistance that might be needed. I was also given their official and private telephone numbers. We discussed my lack of a visa or suitable travel document, and Mr Brunner asked whether the ANC might not have some practical solution for this problem. What about a Zambian passport, he asked. Concerning my personal safety, if there was a problem, they would do what they could. It was enormously reassuring.

Regarding the future, I told them that I would be leaving my practice at the end of August. For the time being I would describe myself amorphously as a 'Consultant'. It was already clear that my continued presence in my law office would be inappropriate, as I was unable to give explanations of my activities, and there was far too much interest and curiosity. This left me with two alternatives – either to establish a separate office, or to operate out of my home. In view of these imminent changes, it was important to clarify our financial arrangements. Mr Brunner confirmed that this could be dealt with quite quickly once a satisfactory response had been received from the ANC. Later, they might be able to consider reimbursing me for some of the expenses which I was now incurring at an alarming rate.

It was suggested that our first objective should be to try to bring about a meeting between Mr Mbeki and Dr van der Merwe. Apparently they had invited Van der Merwe to pay an official visit to Switzerland, commencing 22 September. Could this visit perhaps also provide the opportunity to arrange an initial meeting? Mr Brunner said that, if both parties were in agreement, he would be willing to cooperate in creating some innocuous context, such as an 'accidental' meeting or a private dinner at which they would both be guests. Alternatively, they might wish to suggest other arrangements. He was flexible and willing to be present or not to be present, as they preferred. My own participation would likewise be a matter for the parties themselves to decide. Mr Brunner suggested that I establish the attitude of Mr Mbeki and Dr van der Merwe to his suggestion. It was important that he make the necessary arrangements in good time, and offered to telephone me on Thursday next, by which date I expected to have returned from Lusaka.

Mr Brunner said he had gained the impression that there might be a mutual willingness on the part of both the South African Government and the ANC to communicate on a variety of matters. Both parties could benefit from a dialogue on a range of issues, apart from the core political and constitutional debate. However, this was not possible at present because of mutual mistrust, political posturing, and the absence of a channel of communication. The objective should therefore be to try to establish such a channel, whilst at the same time being sensitive to the parties' need to contain their political risks. He anticipated that it might be necessary for early contacts to take place at a 'second tier' level, rather than at a leader-to-leader level. He was sure that a secure and discreet venue could be provided in Switzerland. If the concept was acceptable, I could assist in planning the necessary arrangements.

Looking further ahead, Mr Brunner said that following an initial discreet meeting, he hoped there would be willingness to accommodate the possibility of further meetings. If required, he would be willing to do some preparatory work on developing an agenda. However, he believed an initial meeting should take place without agenda. One could also anticipate that, if the process gathered momentum, there would have to be some mutual 'confidence-building measures', which would require reciprocation by both sides. He noted, with appreciation, that the execution of the Sharpeville Six had recently been deferred. He also noted good progress being made in the negotiations to end the war in Angola. These were encouraging portents.

At a theoretical level, I raised the possibility of establishing an independent research body, whose function might be to service the negotiation process by developing options and exploring issues. It could also assist the parties in authoring and initiating ideas, thereby removing the responsibility or risk of propagating particular models. In principle, Mr Brunner said his Government might be prepared to look at the possibility of underwriting the costs of such an undertaking.

He acknowledged that he was still wondering who in the South African Government was aware of this initiative. Their Ambassador had satisfied himself that there was Cabinet knowledge and approval, and it was implicit that the State President at least was involved. However he had gained the impression that his South African counterpart, Neil van Heerden, Director General for Foreign Affairs, had no knowledge of the matter. This was rather anomalous. In the meanwhile, he had received an invitation to visit South Africa during October. Although the principle and details of such a visit were still under discussion, he was personally in favour of undertaking the visit. However, the proposal raised sensitive issues for his Government, and it would have to be carefully considered. Should it take place, he would wish to meet the State President. He would also hope to meet leaders in the black community. It was inevitable that such a visit would provoke controversy in both countries.

Mr Brunner mentioned that the Swiss Government was keen to establish its own dialogue with the ANC, concerning a range of issues, including some misconceptions, which seemed to prevail. For example, he did not think that the ANC had sufficient appreciation for the unique situation of Switzerland, which of course had an influence on its relationship with South Africa. He would like to be able to discuss these matters with the ANC, adding, 'There have been some recent developments which I think will be satisfactory to their representatives.' Mr Brunner requested that I also indicate to Mr Mbeki his wish for a more substantive dialogue, quite apart from the arrangements involving Dr van der Merwe. He would appreciate my assistance in getting their reaction to the concept of such a meeting.

After some two hours, Mr Brunner said that he would have to leave shortly to catch a flight to Athens. In fact, he had been scheduled to visit Greece the previous day, but had deferred his visit so as to accommodate our meeting. He emphasised that the Swiss Government attached great importance to this initiative.

Later that morning I flew to London, where I spent a rather solitary few days waiting for an Air Zambia flight to Lusaka, which would depart on the evening of Saturday 16 July. I decided not to contact friends and relatives in England, to avoid once again having to explain myself. It seemed preferable to remain invisible, than to give contrived or opaque explanations. Even my sister Alison, who lives in England, was told that I was on a brief business trip, and would not be able to come and see her. On Saturday morning I went to Hyde Park, and saw workmen erecting a huge scaffold-stage for the celebrations of Nelson Mandela's 70th birthday. I would be in Zambia on Monday, and would wish him a happy birthday the best way I knew how.

At Heathrow, I stood in a queue of returning Zambians, and handed my ticket across the check-in counter to a bored-looking clerk. 'Could I see your passport, please?' It was the moment I feared. She studied it, and then asked, 'Could I see your visa, please?' I assured her that I didn't need a visa. She told me that all South Africans needed a visa. In fact, BA would not fly South Africans to Zambia unless they had proper visas. Those were her instructions. The queue behind me was becoming impatient. A supervisor was summoned. The problem was discussed in whispers, whilst I held my breath. Then speaking very slowly, as though to someone who did not understand English, the Cockney supervisor told me that I could not go to Zambia unless I had a visa. I had begun to imagine all my complicated arrangements going awry. How was I going to convince them? It took some dogged persuasion. Unable to advance any credible reason for my journey, I simply insisted that special arrangements had been made for my visit. I assured them that I had been assured that I would not need a visa. Did I have any proof? The answer was, No. They were highly sceptical. The last thing I wanted was to become involved in an altercation. To my huge relief, they eventually acquiesced. 'You will have to sign *this form*,' they said menacingly. By this stage, I was ready to sign anything. 'This form' turned out to be a document reminiscent of those daunting disclaimers one is required to sign upon being admitted to a hospital. I agreed to accept all consequences, civil or criminal, and would have no recourse against either British or Zambian Airways. I happily indemnified them for the cost of returning me to Britain, if necessary.

I celebrated my precious boarding-pass with a stiff drink, and boarded a plane abuzz with ebullient expatriates overjoyed at the prospect of going home. There was a festive atmosphere on board, with loud conversations taking place between people in widely separated parts of the cabin. The fiesta continued unabated after take-off, even when it was announced, to my alarm, that we were going to make an unscheduled landing in Portugal because of a doorlock next to me which had not sealed properly! Never at ease in the air, I uttered some ' 'asty orisons' as, dropping prodigious quantities of fuel into the ocean, we circled the Bay of Biscay before landing safely. Happily, the problem was quickly sorted out with a hammer, a spanner, and some potent Portuguese swear words. We then flew on into the night.

12

Fraternising with the enemy

Zambian Airways Flight QZ 001 landed right on schedule at Lusaka International Airport early on Sunday morning, and I followed a stream of bleary-eyed travellers into the Terminal buildings. Having been assured that someone would be there to meet and escort me through passport control, I now looked around anxiously, hoping to be accosted or recognised by someone. However, no one seemed in the slightest bit interested in me, and I realised belatedly that I had no idea whom I was to expect. For a few moments it seemed vaguely comic, until the queues of arriving passengers had all but disappeared, and I realised that, having no visa, the moment of truth was fast approaching. I kept reassuring myself with possible explanations. It was still quite early on a Sunday morning. Through a glass panel, I caught a glimpse of a few doleful and disreputable characters who appeared to be cocooned in a holding lounge, awaiting their fate. I wondered whether I would shortly be joining them.

Then, to my enormous relief, Thabo Mbeki himself appeared, puffing away at his pipe, up at the crack of dawn on a Sunday morning! It was a wonderful gesture. I had expected a chauffeur or some junior ANC official. We foraged through a soufflé of scrambled luggage, eventually locating my bags, and then simply walked through all the control points, exchanging friendly nods of recognition. I was taken to the new Pamodzi Hotel, where I booked into Room 535. With characteristic consideration, Mr Mbeki suggested that I might like a little time to freshen up after the night flight, and we agreed to meet at midday. In the meanwhile, I phoned Canada and reassured Hilary that I had arrived safely. She wept with relief.

The lunch party comprised Mr Thabo Mbeki; Mr Alfred Nzo, who at the time was Secretary General of the ANC and who now serves as South Africa's Foreign Minister; and Mr Anthony Mongalo, who was then personal assistant to Oliver Tambo, and who now serves as Deputy Director-General of Foreign Affairs. The meeting continued until about 3.30 p.m.

Thabo Mbeki assumed the role of spokesperson and confirmed that upon returning from Frankfurt he had conveyed the substance of our discussion to a small group including the ANC President, Oliver Tambo. They had given careful consideration to my proposal, and had now reached a decision, which they would convey to me. However, before doing so, and for the benefit of the others present, Mr Mbeki suggested that I restate once again what I had already told him about the background and evolution of this initiative.

They listened intently, and asked a number of key questions. Although they had no doubt heard most of it before, I imagined they wished now to hear it first-hand from me, in order to get a better idea of whom they were dealing with. There were high stakes, and they had to decide whether or not I could be trusted. When I had finished, Mr Nzo suggested they take a brief time to talk on their own, and I left the table for a few minutes. When we reassembled, Mr Mbeki once more spoke on behalf of the group.

He said that the ANC viewed with some scepticism the proposition that the Botha Government was now interested in a negotiation process. On the basis of past experience, they had no reason to trust the professed objectives of his Government. Indeed they had ample evidence of its deceit, and its propensity for breaching trust and good faith. As an example, he cited the talks on the future of Namibia, which had been going on for almost ten years. The ANC believed the Government wished these talks to continue indefinitely without result. Perhaps by going through the motions of nego-tiating with the ANC, they hoped to win approval and dissipate interna-tional pressures. In reality, it was believed they were really intent upon just 'wasting time'.

The ANC was unconvinced of the Government's professed reformist intentions. On the one hand, they were trying to promote broad participa-tion in the 'third tier' elections for new Local Authorities. On the other hand, they had banned the most important political formations including the United Democratic Front (UDF). This meant that meaningful participation in the electoral process would be impossible. Another example of a self-defeating agenda was their professed wish to facilitate an inclusive constitu-tional process. Instead of negotiating agreement on a mutually acceptable forum, they chose to prescribe their own invention, the National Statutory Council, which was unacceptable to most parties 'and even to Gatsha Buthelezi'. Whilst claiming to be committed to normalising society, they had once more extended the State of Emergency – and were holding in deten-tion the very leaders with whom they would have to negotiate.

The Government's lack of good faith was also evident from the manner in which they had handled the release of his father, Govan Mbeki. Initially, they had wondered whether his release might have been a sign of greater prag-matism. But any goodwill it might have generated was rapidly dissipated by the way in which the situation had been manipulated. Had there been a genuine wish to signal a new dispensation, they would surely have allowed him to address meetings around the country as had been his expressed intention. Instead, they chose to restrict him further despite his having served 26 years in prison. After the hastily convened press conference for which Mr Mbeki Snr had been completely unprepared, they now forbade him from making further statements or giving interviews to the press. In these circumstances, how was one to play a role in normalising the political process, or exercise a calming influence? They had effectively silenced his father, and had banished him to New Brighton. Had he not paid any debt he owed to society with 26 years' imprisonment? There were other examples of irreconcilable conflicts between reformist policies and repressive actions. New restrictions had been imposed upon Mrs Albertina Sisulu. He also cited the Government's vindictive attitude towards the people's wish to honour Nelson Mandela on his 70th birthday.

Mr Mbeki referred to a statement by Law and Order Minister, Adriaan Vlok, that the Government had not yet been given 'its pound of flesh' for having released Govan Mbeki. He asked: 'What on earth do they want from us? What do they expect?'

He referred also to the unofficial exchanges which had taken place during 1985, when Comrade Nelson Mandela had been hospitalised. Advocate George Bizos had been instrumental in conveying certain communications to them about the possibility of his release. The ANC had confirmed its willingness to discuss the matter, and how it could ensure that the event did not precipitate more violence. In order to perform this role, their leaders had to be able to meet their supporters around the country. However, the Government rejected this possibility, and as a result nothing had been achieved.

It was factors like these that impelled the ANC to require now some corroboration of the Government's seriousness of intent. On numerous occasions, the ANC had confirmed its willingness to participate in negotiations, but it could not allow itself to be manipulated or made to look naive or foolish. In any such process there were some unavoidable risks. Confidence could be broken, and the process could actually be set back – for example, by leaking private communications to the media. Both parties would probably have similar fears, but Mr Mbeki was categorical – the ANC would scrupulously keep its word. It would not seek to score cheap points or take short-term advantage. Both parties had much to gain by honouring the 'integrity' of the process. What the ANC was now conveying in response to my proposal was that only after it had received some genuine and convincing indication of the Government's good faith, would it be satisfied that this was not merely another exercise in wasting time.

I urged that this should perhaps be recognised as a unique opportunity, which might not recur in the foreseeable future. What was absolutely necessary was for both parties to contribute to the creation of an atmosphere of conciliation. At this early stage the 'atmospherics' might be almost as important as the substantive issues which would later constitute the real agenda. We went on to discuss 'confidence-building steps' which would be required of each party, and the need for reciprocal responses. At this early stage, and given the history of mutual mistrust, it would probably not be possible to reach prior agreement about such incremental steps. The parties would have to make their own assessment of the situation as it evolved.

Mr Mbeki emphasised that the ANC would be absolutely pragmatic, and would not make unrealistic demands. He recalled a discussion some years before with Gavin Relly, Chairman of Anglo American Corporation. Relly had asked Oliver Tambo whether the ANC was prepared to consider a phasing-in of the change process? Tambo had replied that the ANC understood the reality of white fears. They realised the need for some reassurance about the future.

The ANC had on many occasions expressed itself in support of the concept of negotiations, but only if it concerned 'the real agenda'. If the Government wanted to talk, the ANC would wish to know what the Government wished to talk about. I ventured a reply that the Government would say it was prepared to discuss sharing power but not abdicating power. Mr Mbeki pointed out that such terms could mean different things. The Government had been in the habit of quoting the ANC as saying that it was only interested in 'a transfer of power' – that is, to themselves. Mr Mbeki said that to his knowledge such a statement had never been made. They were committed to bringing about a genuinely democratic society.

By this time, our discussion had gone on for a number of hours. The afternoon had grown hot and humid. We decided to break, and meet again that evening after dinner. When they had departed, I sat down and made copious notes of our discussion. It seemed to me that their position was eminently reasonable. If the Government had the courage and the will, there was a genuine possibility of a process that might offer the prospect of peace and a negotiated outcome.

I took a brief nap, went for a walk, and discovered that Zambia had run out of Coca Cola. This was a drought indeed. We met again after dinner, and our discussion continued until 11 p.m.

Reverting once more to the theme of our earlier discussion, I asked precisely what indication of seriousness of intent did they have in mind? What would they regard as sufficient? Mbeki replied, 'I don't think we want to get trapped into prescribing formulae or a specific agenda. It is for the

Government itself to decide what it can do, and what it wishes to talk about. If it is genuine in its wish to engage in dialogue, and the agenda is serious, we will not be perverse and obstructive. We also want talks, but talks about real issues, not about trivialities.'

He recalled a discussion he had once had with a South American diplomat who had cautioned him, 'Remember, don't get trapped into agreeing to negotiations until you've established the agenda. If you don't insist on this, you can be easily outmanoeuvred.' It was a bit like taking a girl out on a date, he said. 'You must first agree on the principle of going out together. Only then can you discuss precisely what you're going to do together. Later still, you can talk about whether it is the theatre, the cinema, or whatever. At this stage, we're concerned with the principle of going out together. Later on we can talk about whether we go to the Circus, or listen to Beethoven's Fidelio!' I said I sincerely hoped it would not be a circus. Mbeki reiterated, 'We are not opposed to the principle of negotiations; but we have to know what they would like to negotiate about.'

The ANC was committed to a united, democratic, non-racial country. 'This is absolutely fundamental,' he said. 'We need a commitment to the underlying principles of a democracy. Then only can we talk about what kind of democracy; and how best it can be achieved.' He said the ANC's policies and goals were on record, and well-known. The early release of political prisoners was fundamental. 'Many of our leaders have been in prison for a long time. They have to be released – not only because it is right, but also because they must be part of the process. A negotiation in which they took no part would not have credibility. There would be no purpose in "baking a cake", unless it was going to be edible'.

Echoing the Swiss, I warned against the danger of setting demands as a condition for participation. The concern was that if for example the ANC insisted upon the prior release of all political prisoners, and the Government insisted upon the prior cessation of the armed struggle, as preconditions to talks, then quite possibly the process would never get started. It could become stalled before it had even begun. They replied that the ANC would always strive to be pragmatic. It would not set impossible preconditions. There were a number of possibilities. For example, it might be required that the opportunity be created for some consultation with those still held in prison, to seek their views regarding the principle of a negotiation process.

It had to be borne in mind that if there were no negotiations, there would be massive destruction of property and loss of life. Mbeki warned that one would need to be careful about the kind of language one used during the initial exploratory phase. As an example, he said P W had been quoted as saying, 'We have not yet used one-tenth of our available force.' Mr Mbeki retorted: 'What sort of statement is that? We could say the same thing; but that sort of comment serves no purpose.' The Government might be surprised how often their cadres had been restrained from taking action, because it could result in civilian casualties. 'We don't want to sow mayhem, but have no doubt that we have the capacity to do so. If we were to say, "Go ahead. No holds barred", there would be enormous casualties. There's no doubt about it.' There were at least two reasons for this self-imposed restraint. 'Firstly, random violence is inherently wrong. Secondly, once you start that sort of thing, there is often no way of stopping it. The conflict could become virtually unstoppable. We would eventually leave a wasteland for our children. This is a matter that is far too serious to play party politics.'

Concerning the possible involvement of the Swiss Government in a supportive capacity, they had no problem with the concept or principle. They undertook in due course to contact Mr Brunner, as suggested, to give this reassurance. They would also discuss with him the proposal for a general discussion around other issues affecting the relationship between the ANC and the Swiss Government. There could be mutual benefit in such a meeting.

However, Mr Brunner's suggestion of an early meeting with Dr van der Merwe needed more time and thought – and greater subtlety. A formal hosted dinner would be 'too upfront'. It would have to be a lot more casual – perhaps some kind of 'organised accident or collision'. If not a formal dinner, then perhaps something less substantial, such as a meeting over a drink, or a family supper from which the family might withdraw. They mentioned such a meeting arranged by a Zambian businessman with Cobus Jordaan, Chris Heunis's Director of Planning.

Times had changed. Mbeki remarked on the fact that these days all sorts of people wanted to come and talk with them. In the last month, there had been a visit by some Dutch Reformed Ministers. In fact, they wanted to return and arrange a larger meeting. They had also received correspondence from Dr Danie Craven, who wanted to come and discuss some kind of non-racial rugby union. It made Mr Mbeki wonder, 'With all these people wanting to come and talk to us, who is it that still wants old-style apartheid? Van Zyl Slabbert and Wynand Malan don't want it. The Afrikaans Churches assure us they don't want it. The Rugby Unions don't want it. So who does? Is it just P W and Magnus Malan perhaps? The N I S also says it doesn't want it, as do the Generals. It suggests that there may have been an important shift in South Africa.'

'If P W Botha would only recognise Black people as his allies, he would find that he had virtually the whole nation behind him. He wouldn't have to worry about people like Treurnicht and Terre'Blanche. If he really went for

a non-racial democracy, he would have virtually the whole nation behind
him. People may find this difficult to believe, but in those circumstances, we
might even put up a man like Slabbert to represent a constituency such as
Soweto.' That was the kind of non-racial vision they had in mind. He
predicted that eventually when a settlement had been achieved, it would be
a very emotional occasion for everyone, but especially for the beleaguered
Afrikaner people.

Mr Mbeki said that he wanted to reassure the Government that the ANC
would not play petty politics with such important issues. 'We will not try to
embarrass them, or seek minor short-term propaganda advantages. Our
concern is with the long term, to find a solution to this problem, not to win
a few cheap tricks. By the same token, we will not compromise our ideals
for the sake of some short-term advantage.' He repeated, 'If the Government
is serious about this matter, and if their response is genuine and substantive,
that will set the whole process in motion.'

For the time being, their strategy was to increase the pressures on the
Government, and to work for its international isolation – this meant trade
sanctions, divestment, cultural boycott, and economic as well as diplomatic
sanctions. The armed struggle would continue 'until finally Botha and his
clique find themselves so isolated they can no longer survive. Then
apartheid will simply collapse.'

I said, 'One hopes the country will not first have to experience its own
Masada.'

He replied, 'Yes, that is precisely what we are trying to avoid. We'll go on
trying, until there's no other possibility.'

I asked them once again whether it would not be desirable that I try to
meet Nelson Mandela, and perhaps other members of the ANC inside South
Africa. Mr Mbeki repeated that at this stage he did not see it would be necessary for me to try to make contact with Mr Mandela, although ultimately
there could be no substantive negotiations without his personal involvement, and whilst he was still in prison. With regard to my need for a reference group to work alongside, Mr Mbeki said that he saw no problem in my
liaising with people like Arthur Chaskalson, and at a later stage he might
suggest a few other names.

I was anxious to avoid a repetition of my difficulties in communicating
with them by phone. There was obviously a need to establish a safe channel
for confidential communications. Mr Mbeki said that he was quite agreeable
to my making use of the Swiss Ambassador in Harare, where the ANC also
had a permanent representative. He said that it would be wise to assume that
their telex and telephones in Lusaka were tapped. One therefore needed to
find other ways to communicate. Mbeki said he would be leaving within a

few days for a month's holiday in Russia. During his absence, I should if necessary communicate through Anthony Mongalo.

Next morning, an ANC car was sent to ferry me to the Airport. It was driven by a man who introduced himself simply as 'Cobus'. He told me that he had left South Africa in 1962, and talked nostalgically of what he still remembered. He was keen to find out how the country had changed. He had heard that all races could now mix at the Carlton Hotel, but he hadn't heard that other hotels and most public transport were already desegrated. He said that there were several thousand South African exiles in Zambia. They even had their own special school, where they taught a curriculum that included South African history. The ANC was concerned to preserve their children's ties with their home country. Many children had been born in Zambia, and some of them regarded themselves as Zambians rather than as South Africans. He wanted to return but he realised that he now had two home countries. 'If I came back to Johannesburg today,'he asked, 'would I recognise it?' He didn't have much hope it would happen soon.

When the plane took off for Johannesburg, I looked back at the clusters of little houses below, and thought of this community of thousands of exiles waiting to return, waiting for tomorrow. How long would it be before they could come home? And my thoughts that day were very much with a man called Nelson Mandela, whose 70th birthday was being celebrated around the world, including a rally of more than 200 000 people in Hyde Park, where I had seen the scaffolding erected and the preparations under way. We had not been permitted to see his face for more than 26 years. Like John Bunyan, he had said, 'I'll stay in jail if necessary to the end of my days, before I make a butchery of my conscience.'

It transpired that the Government, in its great compassion, had decided to give Nelson Mandela a 'birthday treat'. This was to have been a six-hour visit by members of his family. However, two days before his birthday, he had decided to reject this concession – in protest against his own continued imprisonment, and in sympathy with others to whom no such privilege was being granted. The newspaper handed to me on the flight back to Johannesburg reported: 'The Minister of Information, Dr Stoffel van der Merwe, said last night: "Arrangements were made for Mr Mandela's family to spend the day with him. Today, however, of his own accord, Mr Mandela has requested that the family's visit be cancelled ... Permission for the visit still applies should Mr Mandela change his mind." Van der Merwe should have known that his prisoner was a man who never changed his mind on matters of conscience.

On this day, Botha addressed the Natal National Party Congress in Durban, and said he did not 'think it wise for Mr Mandela at his age, and in his condition, to choose to go back to jail. I hope he will make it possible for me to act in a humane way, and in such a way that we can have peace in South Africa instead of violence ... This government will, in a responsible way, consider the whole position on its merits. If we get the cooperation we have so far got from Mr Mandela, I believe we will have positive results ... I am prepared to release Mr Mandela if he would say he rejects violence as a means to achieve a political end ... But I am not going to be told by individual pressmen what I should do; and I am not going to be told by Communists what I should do.' And be it noted, Mr Mandela in turn was not going to be told by Mr Botha what he should do.

13

An organised accident?

Looking back on my meetings in Lusaka, I felt that despite the predictable hedging, something quite significant had happened. It was difficult to define precisely, because much of what was said had been delicately nuanced. But once the verbal gauze had been lifted, there was a clear message that the ANC was ready to engage in a substantive dialogue with the South African Government, provided it concerned the real issues, and provided the Government did not attempt to use the occasion as an opportunity for winning delay, or deflecting the mounting international pressures.

This was more than sufficient to justify my ongoing commitment to the initiative. It would have been unrealistic to expect more at this early stage. However, the ANC had made the valid point that any negotiation process would have to be preceded by moves to build confidence and trust. Could I help in facilitating such predisposing conditions, as a catalyst to the commencement of such process? How could the downside risks be contained for the parties and the upside possibilities enhanced? These were questions that preoccupied me as I flew home from Zambia, bearing the hopes of return, of 'making Aliyah', of people like 'Cobus', who dreamed of starting a new life in their own country.

I remember my arrival at Jan Smuts airport, because of a small incident as I stood waiting to reschedule my flight bookings at the Passenger Services counter. Immediately behind me in the queue was an African man. We had both been there for about five minutes. Then I noticed that he had suddenly been shouldered into third place by a young white man who had seen a momentary gap between us. I was outraged, and busy debating with myself how best to intervene; but my assistance was unnecessary. The African man, politely but with complete assurance, pointed out that he had been ahead in the queue. The young man hesitated, snorted, made some inaudible comment, but yielded his place in the queue. I was deeply impressed – just a small thing, but almost unthinkable a few years back, and even now it might have ended in a very different way. I thought to myself, never mind all the bleating of white liberals, the oratory of politicians, this is what will finally bring down the temple of apartheid – when ordinary people, in everyday situations, decide to say 'NO!' I felt strangely hopeful.

It had been six months since I had last talked with Arthur Chaskalson, and decided it would be particularly valuable at this juncture to have his input. We talked for a couple of hours at his office in the Legal Resources Centre, about what had happened, and how one might proceed further. Arthur is one of the least excitable people I know, but he seemed genuinely amazed and enthused by the progress that had been made. I told him that his possible involvement as my confidant had been discussed with the ANC and approved by them. Arthur confirmed his willingness to play this role, though he admitted that it would be uncharted territory for both of us. However, he would be most interested to be kept in touch, and characterised the initial steps as 'very exciting'.

We discussed in particular what 'indication' the ANC might now require as proof of the Government's seriousness and good faith. Arthur wondered whether in fact the Government's agreement to meet the ANC might not in itself be evidence sufficient, but I doubted this. It seemed they were looking for something new and significant – perhaps the release of other long-serving political prisoners, like Walter Sisulu? The Swiss had also referred to the need for reciprocal 'confidence-building measures'. Obviously the release of political prisoners was of first importance to the ANC. However, the Government faced a difficult conundrum – how to 'let the genie out of the bottle', but at the same time retain control.

The position of Nelson Mandela himself was obviously crucial. We speculated whether the Government might be persuaded to release him initially on to a flight to a foreign destination such as Lusaka, for the purpose of engaging in consultations about a future negotiation process. There was no way of knowing how the Government would balance the risks and benefits in that situation. One knew they feared that his release could spark a tumultuous, and uncontrollable, response. Another possibility, which could satisfy the ANC's need, had in fact been tentatively suggested by Thabo Mbeki, namely, that the Government might permit Mandela to consult – if needs be, within the precincts of his prison – with some of the exiled leadership. The Government would have to realise that no credible process could be initiated without his personal participation.

On the flight home, I happened to meet Franklin Sonn, who now serves as South Africa's Ambassador to the United States. Franklin in his then capacity as President of the CPTA had been my client in an unsuccessful Supreme Court application brought on behalf of coloured teachers, to compel the Government to postpone school examinations as a result of the political disruptions of the school calendar at the end of 1985. We spoke about this profoundly disillusioning experience, and his response, which had been to adopt a far more proactive public role in opposing Botha's Government. Franklin berated me now for my low-profile professional involvement in the events of the day, pointing out that the time for sophisticated litigation and elegant protest was long passed. The issues had now to be taken on to the streets, he argued. 'Each of us must stand up and be counted.' I had to agree, but couldn't tell him that I too had decided to stand up and be counted – in a different way.

When the teachers' case had come to its dolorous conclusion, I had written in my Journal:

4th January 1986

Well, the case is lost, despite our best efforts. I feel devastated, and partly responsible. Perhaps if we had tried that little bit harder, or been a little more skilful? ... Now I'm afraid of the anger and disillusionment that losing the case may bring to those who trusted the legal process to deliver justice. The system has once again failed them, and I am an embarrassed part of that system. Yet, naively perhaps, I still nurture the expectation of justice. It's been a long time since I suffered such a defeat, in such a cause. To add insult to injury, the State will present us with a huge Bill of Costs that has to be paid by underpaid coloured teachers. It is really outrageous.

We took on the resources of the State. It was a moral argument. We gave the courts an opportunity to redress a substantial wrong, and once again the judiciary has failed us. What does one do in a situation like this? Franklin says one must no longer rely upon the courts and the legal system. But that is surely not the right conclusion. That will lead to anarchy and revolution. There are some battles that will have to be won in another forum. I think we have to go back to basics, to re-examine our premises, and review our strategies. This is at heart an evil system. No one ever said that bringing change would be easy? There will be some victories but many heartbreaking defeats. Ultimately, justice will prevail.

Upon returning to Cape Town, I immediately set about trying to arrange a further meeting with Van der Merwe. For various reasons, he was temporarily inaccessible – one reason for which was that he was handling a *broedertwis* (a family wrangle) between the Government and its usually pliant Transvaal newspaper, *Beeld*. Contrary to the National Party's authorised credo, *Beeld* had joined in the calls for Nelson Mandela's release. Responding to this deviance, Dr van der Merwe omnisciently declared: 'The public does not have all the information at its disposal why political prisoners cannot be summarily released in the present circumstances. The Government has to consider the possible consequences, and should be

trusted to reach a decision based on the fullest range of information.' *Beeld*
to its belated credit persisted in its view, and described Van der Merwe's
defence as 'unsatisfactory'. The *Cape Times* commented, 'In practice, the
release of Mr Mandela would be pointless, except in humanitarian terms,
unless it also signified a readiness to negotiate. The truth is that negotiation
is not in the Government's game plan, as it believes it can crush the ANC by
the use of force. So ANC violence continues and the stalemate persists.' It
was precisely this stalemate that I was hoping to crack.

One of the marvellous things about dealing with the Swiss, is their
complete reliability about time and money. At precisely 9.30 a.m. as
arranged, on Wednesday 20 July, my phone rang with a call from Mr
Brunner in Berne. He did not directly identify himself, but gave a few verbal
winks and nods. How had the meetings gone, he wished to know. I gave a
brief resumé, suitably edited because of the permeability of telephone calls.
He asked what had been the reaction of 'your friend in Pretoria'. I told him
that 'my friend in Pretoria' had been frustratingly inaccessible. After several
abortive attempts to speak to him, I had finally succeeded in arranging a
meeting with him on Friday afternoon. Brunner said he was particularly
anxious to have some early reaction to his suggestion of an initial
Government–ANC encounter during Van der Merwe's planned visit to
Switzerland in September. We agreed to be in contact again after the
weekend. He would ring me at 10 a.m. on Tuesday.

The meeting with Dr van der Merwe – our seventh – took place at his
Pretoria office in Midtown Building at 2.30 p.m. on Friday 22 July. He apologised for difficulties I had again experienced in making this appointment,
but hoped I would understand that his life was phenomenally busy. I said I
did understand, but at the same time recognised that we were talking about
something of huge importance to the country. I could hardly imagine
anything that deserved greater priority.

He listened carefully, making notes, as I described my latest discussions
in Lusaka. There were three matters on which I placed particular emphasis:
firstly, the invitation of the Swiss to initiate a discreet meeting between
himself and Mr Mbeki in Switzerland; secondly, the expressed willingness of
the ANC to accept my role as intermediary, and to approve financial assistance by the Swiss; and thirdly, the ANC's response to the concept of a negotiation process, and its insistence upon 'some indication of seriousness of
intent', and the need for reassurance about the substantive nature of the
agenda.

Van der Merwe responded that these were very important issues, and he
was not in a position to respond to them 'at this stage'. However, he could
not resist pointing out immediately, with reference to the ANC's professed

concern for avoiding civilian targets, that weapons like limpet mines were not discriminatory in their choice of victims. He failed to understand the subtle distinction which the ANC sought to draw between 'hard' and 'soft' targets.

I said that I would be speaking to State Secretary Brunner early the following week, and asked what I should convey about the attitude of the Government. Van der Merwe replied that I should inform Mr Brunner that they were giving these matters very careful consideration, and a formal response would be conveyed shortly. Concerning the possibility of a discreet meeting with Mr Mbeki, he said that although he would personally favour such a meeting, it had serious implications and would have first to be considered by himself and others. It was not something he could decide on his own, even if it was in the nature of 'an organised accident'. He was also concerned how genuine confidentiality could be assured. If it came to be known that he and Thabo Mbeki were both in Switzerland, and 'unaccounted for' at the same time, this could lead to speculation.

He apologised for having to abort our discussion, but said there was clearly insufficient time to debate the issues properly. Unfortunately, he had some other pressing commitment which demanded his immediate attention within the hour. We would obviously need further time to think about these issues. He suggested we arrange to meet again shortly. This would give him an opportunity to discuss the matter with the others involved. He called in his secretary, Jeremy Benze, and asked that he arrange an appointment before the mid-year parliamentary session commenced.

I came away concerned about the way in which Van der Merwe ordered his priorities. As the conveyor of messages, I had fulfilled my function, and it was not my right to insist upon deadlines or time limits. On the way home, I passed a wall that had become a favourite for graffiti wits. Today it had two new contributions to folk wisdom. The first read: 'This Nelson is not a seagull – he's a Jailbird!'; and beneath it was a scrawled rejoinder: 'He's an albatross around P W's neck.'

When I spoke to Mr Brunner on Tuesday 26 July, I could tell him no more than that I had reported to Dr van der Merwe, and was now awaiting his response. I had drawn his particular attention to the ANC's request for some 'positive indication of seriousness'; and the willingness of the Swiss Government to facilitate an informal and discreet meeting during his planned official visit in September. Dr van der Merwe had asked for time to consider the implications. Mr Brunner pointed out that the ANC had not yet made contact with him as promised, and I reminded him that Mr Mbeki was on holiday in Russia for a month.

During the week that followed, I had two meetings with Van Zyl Slabbert

– a lunch at a Pinelands restaurant on Monday, and a breakfast two days later at Maison Slabbert in Rondebosch. We talked at length about the delicate stage that had been reached, and how best these contacts could be progressed. Van Zyl felt that good progress had been made, and that the initiative was 'very much on course'. However, it was his feeling that more progress had in fact been made with the ANC than with the Government. He contrasted the fact that Thabo Mbeki had ensured that alternative contacts were available to me during his absence, whereas Stoffel was always careful to ensure that no one but himself was involved or available to deal with the matter. He also commented upon Stoffel's habitual propensity for taking on more than he could effectively handle. This could prove to be a serious obstacle in the future, as evidenced by the current hiatus. A further factor that concerned him was how to ensure that Van der Merwe remained within the scope of his mandate.

It remained unclear who, apart from Van der Merwe, was actually involved in this matter. It could be assumed that he was acting with the implicit approval of P W, who obviously wished to remain in the background. In Slabbert's view, it could be important to procure the involvement of at least one or two other persons within the establishment who also enjoyed the confidence of the President. He suggested a few names, including: Dr Das Herbst, Liaison Officer to the State Security Council; Dr Niel Barnard, Director of the National Intelligence Service; General Jannie Geldenhuys, Head of the SA Defence Force; Ters Ehlers, Private Secretary to the State President; and Professor Piet de Lange, Chairman of the Broederbond.

Van Zyl's knowledge of the political terrain and his personal acquaintance with many of the dramatis personae were valuable. He has an exceptional facility for political analysis, for thinking laterally, and for evaluating personalities and capabilities. On this occasion, we discussed several ideas including a suggestion about a possible meeting between Thabo Mbeki and General Geldenhuys; and whether it might be useful to involve certain third parties, such as the presidents of the front-line states, Kenneth Kaunda and Robert Mugabe. We also talked about the emerging role of the Swiss Government, and its recent announcement of a R6-million grant to assist human-rights organisations and promote dialogue in South Africa. He favoured my having a frank discussion at this stage with British Ambassador Sir Robin Renwick. However, he warned me against sharing too many confidences with the diplomatic corps, who in his view were somewhat 'leaky'. He foresaw that the present stage was going to be a stop/start process. One would have to learn patience, but not allow the essential momentum to be lost. This was part of the delicacy of my role. Van Zyl predicted that it could well be a year or more before anything substantial was achieved.

Despite the ANC's scepticism about South Africa's abuse of negotiations, significant progress was being made over these weeks in US-mediated talks on Angola. Following secret meetings on the Cape Verde Islands between representatives of South Africa, Angola, and Cuba, it became known towards the end of July that the parties had finally reached agreement on the principle of reciprocal withdrawal. They were now discussing details of a timetable. This was followed by a meeting in Geneva on 2 to 5 August, at which agreement was reached on an immediate ceasefire, with the signing of an historic agreement at Ruacana three weeks later. In terms of this accord, the parties agreed to a complete withdrawal of foreign troops from southern Angola, and the full implementation of UN Resolution 435, leading to independence for Namibia. Geneva was also the chosen venue for peace talks at this time, which succeeded in bringing to an end the protracted war between Iran and Iraq. Switzerland's credentials as a broker and venue for peace talks were once again being amply demonstrated.

Meanwhile, the situation in South Africa was under the spotlight in Toronto, where an eight-nation Commonwealth Committee met under the chairmanship of Foreign Minister ('Joe who?') Clark. It concluded that trade sanctions were having a 'discernible impact' on South Africa, and agreed upon an 'action plan of individual and concerted démarches' to bring pressure to bear on non-complying countries such as Japan, Taiwan and West Germany. Canada, my country of contingent adoption, was in the forefront of the sanctions and disinvestment campaigns. In commenting on these developments *Die Burger* editorialised: 'Such actions may satisfy the Canadian government, because it can advance its popularity amongst other members of the anti-South African choir, but it can give up hope of thereby influencing the course of events in South Africa. These latest moves indicate a sort of hysteria that has taken hold over rational decision-making.'

On Thursday 28 July I flew to Johannesburg for my next scheduled meeting with Stoffel van der Merwe, only to be told upon arrival – albeit with profuse apologies – that due to a secretarial error, my appointment had not been noted in the Minister's diary. He was committed to other urgent consultations throughout the day. Apart from the waste of my time and money in travelling from Cape Town to Pretoria and back, I was aghast that such a mistake was even possible. In the result, I met Stoffel for ten minutes!

He now conveyed to me his doubts as to whether even an 'accidental' meeting with the ANC at this point would be appropriate. However, he needed more time to consider the matter before making a decision. I emphasised the importance of establishing and maintaining some momentum, and of giving prompt replies – not only to the Swiss, but also to the ANC – with particular reference to its request for evidence of 'seriousness of intent'. If this initiative was to acquire any credibility, he would need to place me in a position to convey some response within a reasonable time.

I also used this opportunity to convey Slabbert's suggestion, that in the light of his other pressures and responsibilities, some other person should be identified to deal with me at times when he was unavailable. I said I was concerned about the implications of his perennial problem of over-commitment. Dr van der Merwe responded that unfortunately this would not be possible. The matter was of such a nature that he could not delegate it to anyone else, and would have to deal with it personally.

With abject apologies, he aborted the meeting, and promised to allocate substantial time for our meeting the following week.

14

A very secret document

We were to meet again some ten days later, on Monday 8 August. In the meanwhile, a great deal had to be done packing up my office, turning over my practice to my partners, and preparing to leave the firm after 25 years of practice. My son turned 18 on August 3, and we went away as a family for a peaceful weekend in the Cedarberg. As always, it was a time of solitude and wonder amidst the primal beauty of these ancient mountains. Uncertainties continued to plague our lives, and I was growing increasingly anxious about longterm financial security, with no assured income after the end of August. Although the Swiss had expressed willingness in principle to back the initiative, this was still subject to various conditions that had yet to be fulfilled. Moreover, at the rate I was incurring travel and other expenses, my resources would be exhausted within a relatively short period. I had already undertaken eight journeys at my own expense, including two involving foreign travel, and this was still early days. My resources could not fund the initiative over any length of time. To aggravate the famine, the value of our currency had depreciated substantially since P W Botha's Rubicon speech. Anticipating further delays, I decided to sell an investment property I had owned for a number of years.

I also decided to prepare for the Swiss Government an interim Status Report, in the hope that it might persuade them to make an early commitment. On Friday 5 August I despatched to State Secretary Edouard Brunner, through the diplomatic bag, a comprehensive document, incorporating a synopsis of the present status of the Initiative; a chronology of various salient dates; a schedule of expenses already incurred; and a projected twelve-month budget.

I reminded them that I would cease to be engaged in professional practice from 31 August, and that the costs of the initiative were beginning to look daunting. In the circumstances, I requested that they consider the feasibility of implementing their commitment at this stage, on the basis that their stated preconditions had been substantially if not completely fulfilled.

I proposed:

In brief, the stage has now been reached where both the South
African Government (represented by Minister Dr S van der Merwe)
and the African National Congress (represented by its Secretary for
Information Mr T Mbeki and Secretary General Mr A Nzo) have intimated their acceptance of the principle of this initiative, including
my personal involvement therewith, and the proposed source of
independent funding through your Government. In the circumstances, I trust that the pre-conditions envisaged by you in our original discussions have now been satisfied, notwithstanding the
inevitably qualified nature of these preliminary contacts.

In the accompanying documentation, I addressed the issue of the
approvals required as a condition of Swiss backing, stating with reference to
the position of the South African Government:

Ultimately, at the meeting on 7th April 1988, Dr van der Merwe
advised that he was now 'at last' able to convey his Government's unofficial approval of the initiative. No specific mandate or formality was
deemed appropriate. He also approved the concept of independent
funding by the Swiss Government, if available, and undertook, when
approached directly, to convey to the Swiss Ambassador on a personal
basis his knowledge of and approval for the proposal. He intimated
further that although he was not acting 'with formal authority of the
Cabinet', nevertheless he was fully mandated to pursue this initiative.
However, if confidence was broken and the initiative came to be
divulged at an inopportune time, it might be necessary to obfuscate
regarding his involvement or that of the Government.

With regard to the ANC's position, the report stated:

On 21st June 1988 advice was received that the African National
Congress was ready to convey its decision, and a further meeting was
requested. This meeting ultimately took place in Lusaka, Zambia, on
14th July 1988. The African National Congress was represented by
Secretary for Information Mr T Mbeki, and Secretary General Mr A
Nzo, in addition to Mr A Mongalo. In essence, the African National
Congress conveyed its acceptance of the proposals, on condition that
it received 'some indication of seriousness', with an assurance that
any such dialogue would concern·the central issues and not merely
trivial or peripheral matters.

The report confirmed that the ANC had undertaken to make contact with
the Swiss Government in order to convey directly to them, as requested,
approval of the principle of the initiative, and to communicate their formal
response to Mr Brunner's proposal regarding an early discreet meeting
between the parties, and a separate ANC–Swiss meeting to consider issues

affecting that country's relationship with the ANC and the South African Government.

In commenting on discussions held with my various consultants, the report stated:

> In essence, these Consultants regard an independent initiative as urgently needed to break the 'political logjam', but they are generally sceptical as to the willingness of the South African Government, in particular, to respond positively to any such initiative. The political risks and delicacy were repeatedly emphasised.

The Report concluded:

> ... the duration of this initiative and the continuation of your support will have to be reviewed on a regular basis, and will no doubt be subject to review in the light of experience gained, and the prospects of success. The initiative can only continue for as long as substantial and tangible results are being achieved. Should an impasse be reached which, in the view of either or both of us, implies that no further progress can be anticipated, then I fully accept that arrangements will have to be made to terminate your commitment. Having regard to the necessity in such circumstances for myself, and possibly other staff, to secure appropriate placements, I would propose that a period of say three months' notice be provided in these circumstances.

On Monday 8 August my ninth meeting with Van der Merwe took place in Pretoria, commencing at roughly 6.15 p.m. It was the end of the day, and there was an air of familiarity and informality. I could have done with a whisky, but Stoffel's hospitality seldom extended beyond a cup of coffee. By this stage, my visits to Midtown Building were almost routine, and I no longer needed to identify myself to the security personnel behind the entrance grid. The Ministerial staff were friendly and confiding, as though I too was part of the inner circle. We were solicitous about familiar frustrations, and agreed that 'the boss' was over-committed. His secretary, Jeremy Benze, confessed to me that he had almost had enough, and asked about the possibility of serving articles with my erstwhile firm. He was feeling demoralised, and wanted a more satisfying career outside the public service.

Stoffel was unusually expansive. He believed the time had come for us to have 'a broad-ranging discussion', no doubt intended for my political edification, but which he sought to justify on the basis that this perspective needed to be conveyed to the ANC. We had to place what we were doing in its true historical context. Stoffel then proceeded to deliver a fascinating but largely irrelevant academic lecture that might have been entitled 'History as viewed from the balcony of the Union Buildings'. It bore little relevance to the issues on which I was impatiently awaiting his response. But Stoffel was clearly more comfortable as a theoretical pedagogue than in grappling with the realpolitik of a tangible negotiation process.

His evolutionary survey encompassed the origins of white supremacy or 'baasskap' in the race policy of the old Boer Republics; the immorality of 'vertical separation' as propounded by successive Prime Ministers, Malan, Strijdom, and Vorster; and then the advent of Verwoerd's radical new vision – apartheid, or 'horizontal separation'. Warming to his subject, Stoffel argued that Verwoerd was the most maligned and misunderstood of all the National Party leaders. However, he was the first to have the courage to recognise that a policy of perpetual servitude was morally indefensible. Verwoerd's alternative of separate development would mean that there would no longer be any artificial barrier or ceiling on the level to which blacks could aspire. Tragically perhaps, the 'Verwoerdian dream' had become unattainable, owing to what Stoffel termed 'errors of forecasting'. The tide of population from the country to the cities could not be reversed, and therefore a new dispensation had become necessary.

This new dispensation had been the great achievement of President Botha's leadership. The National Party was now a completely different party from that of its forebears, having finally abandoned the Verwoerdian dream that 'eventually there would be no black South Africans'. It was proposed that Blacks should be given the opportunity to participate fully in all spheres of Government within a single country, perhaps organised on a federal model. In Stoffel's view, the ANC still didn't understand the significance of these changes, and failed to give credit for the watershed changes that had been achieved under President Botha.

'We have paid a high price for our convictions,' he insisted. The existence of the Conservative Party was proof of their courage and integrity. 'We have already changed a number of important laws – we have granted security of tenure; restored South African citizenship; abolished the Pass Laws; and still more changes are in prospect.' Even if each individual change was not fundamental, the impact of all these changes represented a paradigm shift. 'One accepts there is often a difference between rhetoric and reality, but at least we could have expected the ANC to say, "We don't believe you'll do all that you're promising but, if you do, that will make a real difference." But they don't even say that much.'

I interrupted Stoffel's flow to suggest that perhaps there were other reasons why they hadn't received recognition for having made a significant shift in policy – for example, there had been absolutely no expression of regret or remorse for past errors. The most they had admitted was some sort of unfortunate miscalculation or incorrect analysis. Meanwhile, millions had been forcibly uprooted and relocated; hundreds of thousands of decent law-abiding citizens had been criminalised by Pass Laws; generations had been impoverished and impaired by job reservation and so-called 'Bantu Education'. Despite all this, there was no murmur of regret or recognition of the enormity of the suffering caused in consequence of these 'errors'. It was hardly surprising that their sincerity remained in doubt.

Stoffel disagreed entirely. He contended that there had been some acknowledgement of past error but, he insisted, remorse and regret were not part of the political vocabulary; they were not 'realpolitik'. As though to prove his point, he said: 'Why should we be held accountable for mistakes and errors of previous administrations? Is Margaret Thatcher held accountable for the errors of previous Conservative Party Governments? Does anyone hold her responsible for Anthony Eden or Winston Churchill's mistakes? So why us?' 'Perhaps', he speculated, 'it is because in our case, there have been no intervening Governments. We are seen as the direct heirs to earlier National Party Governments. In reality, we are another generation. However, we are being forced to carry their baggage.'

'In what manner has the ANC changed its approach to our problems over the past 25 years?' he asked. 'They've not uttered a single word of appreciation for anything we've ever done. I know, because I am a regular reader of *Sechaba*. There's no suggestion or possibility of compromise.'

I was amazed and dismayed that the Government still hoped to convince the ANC – and the world at large – of the sincerity of its purposes, and the underlying morality of its policies. Stoffel needed to understand that I could not be used as an apologist for his party's ideological cause. I said that I saw my function as urging both sides to sit down and listen to the other. I would not be trying to convince them of the rightness or wrongness of either party. Mine was a belief in process, not the advocacy of a particular outcome.

Stoffel then stood up and went to the large combination safe which stood beside his desk. From it he extracted a document which he said was still 'very secret'. He said it represented an attempt by Government to gather together in a single document its vision of the future, and its goals for the transformation of society. He read some extracts, involving comments upon the political sphere, the economic sphere, and the structure of society. He said the document was a synthesis of various reform commitments, but it was still in draft and had not yet been adopted or settled. It had not even been decided how or when it should be issued. It might, for example, be embodied in a speech.

I asked whether the Government might not consider using me as a conduit to hand over such a document to the ANC, as a point of departure for a future dialogue? He seemed interested in this possibility. However, it was still much too early, he insisted. For the time being, he wanted me only to convey the fact of this document being in the course of preparation. They were not yet ready to divulge its contents.

I reminded Stoffel that I needed a response to Mr Brunner's proposal about an informal discreet meeting with Thabo Mbeki during his forthcoming visit to Switzerland. He shook his head, and replied that he had decided it would not be appropriate at this stage. Although personally he would be very interested to meet Mr Mbeki, such a meeting would be 'inopportune' in the light of recent bombings in which there had been a number of civilian casualties. In any event, he was not convinced that it would be possible to maintain confidentiality about such a meeting. However, he didn't want to rule out the possibility of some kind of meeting taking place at a non-Ministerial level. Even that would be a risky encounter, and he would need time to consider it. It might be a good test of the ability of both sides to maintain confidentiality.

He said he understood the ANC's expressed need for trust-building steps, and was prepared to consider delivering some kind of document such as that he had just shown me, 'even prior to its general publication'. He would like to discuss this possibility with others, and would let me have a decision by the end of the week. I said this seemed like an excellent idea, and there could surely be no great risk – particularly if it was in any event their intention to release the document into the public domain. I urged that he recognise the existence of 'a unique opportunity' which should not be lightly squandered. It was essential that a reply be conveyed soon, and some early momentum established.

It was almost 9 o'clock. We had been talking for three hours, and starvation threatened. Stoffel requested that I telephone him on Friday afternoon, when he hoped to be able to convey a decision.

15

Pursuing various other interests

I waited until 5 p.m. on Friday 12 August, as we had arranged, before tele-phoning Stoffel regarding the secret policy document we had earlier discussed. I succeeded only in speaking to his secretary who informed me that he was 'unfortunately not available'. On the Monday morning I tele-phoned him again, and we were able to have a few words, sandwiched between two meetings. He said that there had been further delays in final-ising the policy document. Discussions were continuing, and he was hopeful that it might be available early next week. He proposed another meeting in about ten days' time, and undertook to ensure that his secretary made the necessary arrangements. By then, he would be back in Cape Town for the start of the parliamentary session. In fact, his secretary telephoned me three days later, and we arranged a two-hour appointment on Thursday 25 August.

Yet again I found myself in the familiar but uncomfortable state of suspended animation, waiting for events to happen over which I seemed to have no control. I devoted most of my time to the business of packing up my office and saying goodbye. Cards were posted to our clients containing the elliptical statement: 'We regret to announce the decision of Mr Richard Rosenthal to retire from the practice with effect 31st August 1988, in order to enable him to pursue various other interests.'

People kept asking, What were these mysterious 'other interests'? And why was I being so obtuse? Are you going to write a novel? someone suggested. 'Nothing so ordinary,' was my stock reply, with a fair degree of accuracy. The truth was that although I appreciated their friendly interest, I was better off without it. Sometimes I would attempt some kind of lame joke, such as 'cultivating my roses' or 'studying my navel' – but people would eventually become impatient and irritated by my evasiveness. The truth was that I preferred evasion to deceit. But there was a resultant cost to be borne – of misunderstanding and alienation from people who had been my friends and colleagues.

One day my secretary asked whether I was to have a farewell party, as had been our custom on similar occasions. It transpired that no one had done

anything about it. I felt distressed and angry. No doubt it reflected my partners' feelings of ambiguity – I had been in the process of leaving for almost
six months, and they still didn't know whether to condole or congratulate
me. Eventually, I decided that I would arrange my own farewell party, and
be both guest and host. People said some nice things; they gave me a gift;
wished me well; and some even managed a few generous tears. I was
touched.

One 'client' with whom I remained in regular contact over this time was
Jenny Schreiner, whom I would visit at Pollsmoor Prison every few weeks.
Having established with difficulty a special right of access, and having
befriended her family and friends, I felt a commitment to her as a human
being and not just as a lawyer. How I wished I could tell her the reasons for
my 'retirement'. By this time, there had been several preliminary court hearings, and there were now 13 accused, facing charges, including treason, that
carried the death penalty. Preparations for the trial were well under way with
a team of lawyers led by Dawid de Villiers Q C. My own 'legal consultations'
were ostensibly about the conditions of Jenny's detention, and dealt with
such elevated matters as the scalding heat of the shower water; the absence
of salad and fruit in Jenny's diet; the need for more exercise time; the right
to access a computer (Refused: 'How do we know she won't use it as a
radio?'); the right to receive study materials (Refused: 'Anyway, what does
she want to study?'); and an abortive and failed attempt to persuade the vigilant prison authorities that a herb salad-sprouter could not be used for
subversive horticultural purposes. (Refused: 'We can't be sure what she's
growing in the sprouter – it might be dagga!') It was another signal defeat.

I brought Jenny books, and engaged her about anything under the sun,
in the belief that what she really needed at this time was 'soul and mind
food'; and hoping that our 'consultations' were not being bugged. There is a
strange intimacy that pervades relationships conducted within the precincts
of a prison. One day, I gave her a poem:

TO JENNY

And what can I say to her who is behind walls,
To the one who is a prisoner?

What can I say of the song that is unsung;
Of the thought that is unspoken;
Of the dance of the one without feet?

Yours is the wind, and the womb, and the water.
It is I who am behind the walls.

Meanwhile, international pressures on South Africa were increasing inexorably. After meeting in Toronto, the Commonwealth Foreign Ministers agreed to push for a 'global ban' on South Africa's trade credits; to urge banks to limit their rescheduling agreements to one year only; and to make available to anti-apartheid organisations data to assist them in campaigning against institutions which failed to cooperate with these measures. In Lambeth, the Anglican Bishops agreed to press governments to apply 'maximum pressure' on South Africa, including disinvestment, and to direct material and financial support to those involved in opposing apartheid. In the US, Ron Dellums' Anti-Apartheid Amendments Act was passed by Congress, with a substantial majority, heralding a total ban on imports, the compulsory withdrawal of US companies, and stringent sanctions against any foreign oil company doing business with South Africa. The Reagan administration had opposed the Bill, arguing that it would cause unemployment in both South Africa and the United States. Dr Chester Crocker, US Assistant Secretary of State for African Affairs, and National Security adviser General Colin Powell, both pleaded for a delay in the legislative process – on the basis that it could derail the delicately poised negotiations on Namibia and Angola. 'Sanctions hurt; but apartheid kills,' replied Mr Dellums.

In mid-August newspapers published carefully edited reports that Mandela, who was nearing the age of 70 years, had contracted tuberculosis. This evoked panic and anger. The Government was alarmed at the possibility of his death in prison, and the dire consequences this could provoke.

His admission to Tygerberg Hospital brought urgent calls for his release right across the political spectrum. *Beeld*, which had in the past accorded the National Party unquestioning support, now renewed its appeal for Mandela's release; and was joined by an unlikely ally, *Woord en Daad*, a publication of the Dutch Reformed Churches. This journal argued that Mandela's continued detention served no good purpose, and proposed that the ANC be given 'a second chance'. It pointed out that, 'In the view of the Government, there can be no negotiations until the ANC abandons violence. In the view of the ANC, there can be no negotiations until the Government releases its leaders.' It described this situation as one of stalemate. In the same vein, Tos Wentzel, Political Correspondent for the *Cape Argus*, wrote: 'President Botha and Mr Nelson Mandela are each the other's captive.' The *Cape Times* in an editorial on 19 August argued, 'If handled correctly, the release of Mandela could bring immense pressure to bear on the ANC to opt for negotiation; or else, in refusing to negotiate, to risk the loss of international support, particularly in the hard-pressed frontline states.'

My next meeting with Stoffel van der Merwe took place on the afternoon of Thursday 25 August. During the course of the day, our meeting was twice postponed to enable Van der Merwe to accommodate a meeting with visiting US Senator Paul Simon, Chairman of the Senate Africa Subcommittee, and a key proponent of the Dellums Bill. Eventually, we met at 7.15 p.m., and I observed the exodus of Senator Simon and his entourage, as Stoffel, ever courteous, saw them to the lift, where they continued talking volubly. He then collected me from the reception area, pulled a wry face, and slumped down into a chair. It had been a 'most unproductive' meeting, he confessed. Though recognising that the Government had delivered on some of its promised reform initiatives, Senator Simon had apparently insisted upon a specific timetable for further steps. Stoffel said he had told him that it was unrealistic to expect a fixed timetable. The United States had taken far longer to achieve desegregation than was now being demanded of South Africa.

Stoffel said it was high time the United States – and the ANC – gave credit to the Government for reforms it had already implemented. He referred to commitments made in official documents, and statements of the State President. I pointed out that it would not be sufficient to satisfy the ANC's call for a significant gesture, simply to refer to past achievements and utterances. This initiative existed precisely because the past record had been found inadequate. What was now needed was something of a totally different order. 'You can't expect to sell yesterday's bread today,' I said.

I said that I too was becoming very concerned about delays in the Government's formulation of a response to the ANC's message, and told him that if there was to be any progress, the Government needed to respond with the absolute minimum of delay. The ANC had required no more than 'an indication of seriousness of intent'. This was not an unreasonable request. If I was unable to take back anything of value in the near future, this would place in doubt my credibility as an interlocutor. The Government needed to decide whether they were going to empower or discredit me.

Stoffel replied that the Government was still working on the policy document, which he had hoped to be able to hand me for onward delivery to the ANC. It had already gone through several drafts, and was undergoing further study and review. Admittedly, the situation was frustrating, but I should remember that we were not dealing with 'something ordinary'. He felt embarrassed by the need for further time, but at this stage couldn't predict when the document would be available. He and the others involved had many commitments which required urgent attention.

I felt dismayed by this repetitive pattern of promise and deferment. He said it also embarrassed him, and he was keenly aware how many times he had conveyed this kind of message to me. I ventured that part of the problem seemed to be that he was simply overloaded. Surely, I pleaded, there is nothing more important or urgent than this? He didn't dispute that, but pointed to the files spread across his desk. Though it was past 8 p.m., he would still have to attend to several matters before he could go home to dinner. I suggested the solution might be for the State President to relieve him of other duties? It seemed absurd, I said, that other commitments could be allowed to interfere with the efficient handling of this most important matter. He queried whether the task itself would be sufficient, and whether he wouldn't end up with too little to do!

Coming to the subject of an initial discreet meeting with the ANC, as proposed by the Swiss, Stoffel said that after careful consideration, he had concluded that such a meeting would pose too great a risk in present circumstances. If it were to become known that such a meeting had taken place – even 'accidentally' – this could be catastrophic for the Government's prospects in the October Elections, and it could affect his own political future – adding as an afterthought, 'though this aspect is relatively unimportant'. In any event, he felt it was unrealistic to resort to subterfuge. It was unlikely that confidentiality could be maintained. The explanation that it had taken place 'accidentally' would simply not be believed. He felt what was feasible and appropriate at this stage was some kind of preparatory process, involving an initial exchange of information and views. In due course, this could lead to something more substantial. In his view, responsibility for starting the sequence belonged to the ANC, 'commencing with the suspension of its campaign of violence'.

I asked what steps the Government, for its part, could consider in order to create an atmosphere conducive to future talks? Did not the present illness of Nelson Mandela, for example, give the Government a wonderful pretext to take a first step 'even on humanitarian grounds'? This in itself could have a dramatic influence on the situation. I argued that, whatever risks might be involved in his release, they had to be weighed against the frightening prospect of Mandela dying in prison. This could unleash a reaction which would in fact be uncontrollable. I believed Mandela's release could be the single most powerful signal the Government could give to establish the preconditions for a negotiation process. Stoffel responded that such a step was impossible right now, particularly following recent ANC bomb blasts.

Pursuing the argument, I asked whether meeting with the ANC could not be seen in the context of the President's recent statement that he 'wished to be in a position' to release Mr Mandela? It could be presented as some kind of exploratory discussion to assess the viability of such release. Stoffel said although this argument appealed to him, I must accept that it was simply not possible at this moment. The Government was facing a serious challenge from the Conservative Party in the forthcoming local-authority elections. The release of Mandela at this time would be seized upon and exploited by the Conservative Party. If the Government was unwilling to accommodate a leader-to-leader meeting, I persisted, could it not permit a meeting to take place between Mandela and someone such as Thabo Mbeki – perhaps to discuss the possibility of future negotiations, and the suspension of the armed struggle? He said 'this was not entirely out of the question'. However, it was not as though the ANC had no communication with Mandela. The Government knew that some contact was maintained through the prison visits of his lawyers and Mrs Winnie Mandela.

Stoffel said that our society was now going through an 'extremely dangerous phase'. After the initial reforms there were now inflated expectations, and accordingly a high level of 'relative dissatisfaction and deprivation'. There was also a perception that the Government was indecisive and unclear about its own policy objectives. This was a core political problem. As an academic, he had studied revolutionary theory, and saw many historical parallels, including the Russian Revolution itself. 'We are almost a textbook case,' he said. 'Fortunately there are also some important differences, which should mean a different outcome!'

What did the President mean, I asked, when he referred to having received advice that the National Party should 'govern itself into a new dispensation'? Dr van der Merwe said it implied a step-by-step process of managed incremental change. It meant resisting the international clamour for dramatic or wholesale changes. Did this not create another danger, I asked, namely that the Government might be perceived as grudging in its reform programme? Surely, this strategy would lead inevitably to the very lack of credibility which he now bemoaned. In my opinion, the most self-destructive posture for Government to assume was one of indecision, and failure to deliver on its promises. If the Government had the courage to state its goals clearly, and to move resolutely towards their fulfilment, its electoral prospects in October might be vastly improved. I was momentarily struck by the incongruity of my giving the National Party advice on how best to improve its electoral prospects; but no matter!

It was approaching 9 p.m. I had no idea when dinner was served at Huis Van der Merwe, but I knew that at my own home I had already missed the main event. Stoffel suggested that we meet again the following week. We discovered we were both passing through Jan Smuts Airport at the same time on Friday 2 September, though in different directions. We agreed to meet between 4 and 4.30 p.m. at the airport VIP lounge.

I came home that evening deeply concerned. I had no option but to await the eventual delivery of Botha's policy document, but whether it would satisfy the ANC's request for something substantial remained to be seen. The Government was dealing with this matter as though it was master not only of the tides, but also of the passage of time. With one week to go before I was to depart my law office, the future remained baffling and opaque. Meanwhile, the Swiss awaited a communication from the ANC; the ANC awaited a communication from President Botha; and I remained out on a limb.

16

A frolic of his own?

Unbeknown to both Hannibal and Napoleon, the best time to cross the Alps surreptitiously is mid-summer rather than mid-winter. Virtually the entire population is on holiday during August, even State Secretaries and Ambassadors. Only a few hapless individuals are assigned to answer phones, and keep clearing the post-box. In August 1988, Peter Maurer was the lone Swiss watchkeeper at the Embassy in Pretoria. He called me early on the morning of Thursday 25 August, to make arrangements for me to meet his Ambassador as soon after his return from holiday as possible. I suggested Friday 2 September, when I would in any event be meeting Stoffel van der Merwe at Jan Smuts airport.

The Swiss are wondrously discreet. By this time, I had become a fairly regular visitor at the Embassy, but though recognised and greeted by name, there was never any question as to what was my business with the Ambassador. Arriving a few minutes early, I exchanged noncontroversial opinions with the reception staff about the weather. Their lack of curiosity was always reassuring, and consistent with the assurance given to me that this matter would be handled by the Ambassador only, and treated with utmost confidentiality. All exchanges of documents and letters were dealt with by cipher, and the escorted diplomatic bag.

Ambassador Quinche, looking sprightly and rejuvenated, came to fetch me from the reception area, and we went into his office which overlooked a lovely garden. The meeting commenced at 11.30 a.m. and continued through lunch until approximately 3 p.m. He told me that he had taken time out from his holiday in Switzerland to discuss the matter with the Foreign Office. They had studied my *Aide-mémoire*, and had been particularly interested in my discussions with the ANC in Lusaka. However, the attitude of the South African Government was still unclear and worrying. I had to agree, and brought him up to date about the latest developments. Later in the day I would be meeting Stoffel van der Merwe, and I told him that I hoped to receive further information about an important policy document which was in the course of preparation. We agreed, in the light of the delays now occurring, that it had become imperative to confirm the Government's continued commitment to this initiative. I assured him that I was no more willing to waste my own time than good Swiss money!

The Ambassador said he too would be meeting Dr van der Merwe the following day to discuss the itinerary for his official Swiss visit. He would not raise this particular matter, but asked whether I had received any further response to Mr Brunner's suggestion of a discreet meeting with the ANC during this visit. I told him that, despite my best efforts, Dr van der Merwe remained adamant that such a meeting posed too great a risk at this time. This was disappointing but not entirely surprising. I urged that if there was any likelihood of substantive talks taking place during Dr van der Merwe's visit, I would like, if possible, to be present. He assured me that there was no present intention to discuss this matter during the visit. They were very sensitive to the importance of not appearing to 'pressurise' him in any way.

Ambassador Quinche speculated once again to what extent this initiative had been discussed with and approved by the Cabinet. I reminded him of Dr van der Merwe's specific assurance to me, that although there was no formal Cabinet decision in this regard, he was acting within his mandate and authority, and with the approval of the State President. However, the possibility remained that the Cabinet as a whole might not be aware of the full implications of this matter.

We discussed the extraordinary irony of this initiative taking place against the background of the Government's categorical rejection of calls for the commencement of a dialogue with the ANC. This incongruity created a potentially volatile political situation. It was clear that the Government was eager to ensure that the existence of this initiative should not be publicly known during the run-up to the October elections. In public at least, the National Party remained categorically opposed to official and unofficial meetings with the ANC. The immediate peril lay in the possibility of unintended disclosure. Information about this initiative, and the involvement of the President and a Cabinet Minister, would be dynamite in the hands of the National Party's political adversaries, and notably the Conservative Party.

Our lunch was memorable for another reason unrelated to sober political analysis. The Ambassador had explained to me earlier that he was stoically managing the domestic arrangements of his home, in the absence of his wife who had not yet returned from holiday in Switzerland. It seemed that the Quinche's dog was forlorn in the absence of his mistress. Thus, my indulgence was sought for the presence of a hirsute Swiss dog of indeterminate variety, who followed us around with commendable devotion. All was well until we sat down to pre-prandial apéritifs, when the dog, no doubt stirred by the sound of iced water tinkling in my glass, relieved himself against magnificent red velvet curtains which draped the dining-room portico. The

Ambassador was engrossed in our discussion, and it therefore fell to my lot
to draw his attention to this canine *faux pas*. Help was summoned; there was
great consternation; the offender was reproved with some awful French
epithets, and banished to the nether regions; and several maids bearing
mops and pails administered counter measures.

Our discussion ranged across a number of issues upon which the
Ambassador's views were no doubt being sought in Berne. These included
geo-political developments on the sub-continent, and the ongoing
Angola/Namibia peace talks. It was anticipated that the SADF would depart
Angola before the end of the month – several months ahead of the Cubans'
withdrawal. The Ambassador asked my opinion as to the reasons for South
Africa's conciliatory attitude. What could have led to this change? I had no
inside information, but ventured the opinion that South Africa genuinely
needed peace, for a variety of reasons. Factors contributing to this shift
included military reverses on the battlefield, the ever-spiralling cost of an
extra-territorial war, and the unprecedented casualties which were being
incurred. Moreover, South Africa's internal security situation did not permit
of the simultaneous conduct of a foreign adventure; nor could its beleaguered economy sustain the massive drain on its shrinking reserves.

I sought the Ambassador's advice with regard to a number of logistical
and practical problems involving the initiative. I had responsibility to establish and maintain some momentum; but how was this to be achieved when
one party never answered phone messages; and the other was habitually
distracted and preoccupied? What was his view about my keeping detailed
records of my various meetings? The parties would no doubt be dismayed
that I was meticulously minuting all discussions. Did he feel this could be
viewed as a breach of my responsibility with reference to confidentiality?
The fact that the process was highly sensitive could be seen alternatively as
a reason for keeping records, or as a reason for not keeping records. I
assumed that some, if not all, my meetings were being secretly taped by
someone. It therefore seemed important that I too guarantee the integrity of
the process, by maintaining independent records. However, each party
wanted to be able to deny what was taking place. In these circumstances, my
own truthfulness might one day be in issue. In the circumstances, was this
permissible? Ambassador Quinche was quite forthright in his response: 'Of
course you must keep records,' he said. 'The parties would be completely
naive to imagine you didn't keep records. This is not a small matter.'

Of particular concern to me was the fact that I had still not received from
the Swiss Government a clear commitment regarding their financial
backing. With my withdrawal from practice this ambiguity was becoming
increasingly invidious. Ambassador Quinche explained that, apart from the

ANC's 'nod' which they still awaited, there was also concern in Berne about the ambiguity of the South African Government's stance, and the uncertain duration of the process. Van der Merwe's vacillation only aggravated these concerns. They had the impression that the Government might view this initiative as just one of several options. In fact, he was not yet convinced that the Government had fully committed itself. The Ambassador said that Mr Brunner was rather disappointed at the lack of progress to date. Personally, having been in the country for almost four years, he was not really surprised. 'We have been forced by hard experience to learn a more pragmatic time-scale,' he said wryly.

He said that his time in South Africa was drawing to a close, and it was likely that he would be leaving towards the end of the year. He had to admit that he was not feeling overly optimistic about the future of the country. He was particularly despondent about the Government's inability or unwillingness to grapple realistically with the demands of the situation. This initiative had been one of the most interesting things he had been involved with during his four-year tenure in South Africa. He believed the initiative had the potential to become very significant. He would be reporting on our discussions, and hoped to be able to confirm his Government's decision shortly.

An hour later I was sitting in the VIP Lounge at Jan Smuts Airport, awaiting Stoffel's arrival. When he finally appeared, he looked characteristically distracted and exhausted. It had been 'another torrid week', and he was feeling low in energy and morale. Once again, his schedule was impossible, and he could give me only half an hour.

Since our last meeting virtually no progress had been made on the policy document I was awaiting. He and other members of the Cabinet had been distracted by the events of the past week, involving a constitutional crisis over the refusal of the Coloured and Indian Houses of Parliament to deal with six Bills – including a Group Areas Amendment Bill – for which their concurrence was constitutionally necessary. As a result, the Government was having to use its overall majority to alter the rules of Parliament to categorise these Bills as 'Own Affairs' rather than 'General Affairs'.

The Government's over-riding priority was now the October municipal elections, which it was hoped might result in the emergence of a credible new black leadership. Future plans depended upon the elections being seen to have been inclusive, free and fair. Unfortunately a climate of resistance and confrontation had emerged. Several candidates had been murdered, and there was a threat to intimidate voters, and disrupt the electoral process. 'How can the ANC expect us to engage in negotiations when this sort of thing is happening?' he asked.

I said the ANC might well pose the same question in relation to the recent bombing of Khotso House, the home of the SACC, COSATU, and many UDF-aligned organisations. It was strongly suspected – and several years later, admitted and proved – that Government agents had been responsible for staging this event. Police Commissioner General Johann van der Merwe testified during his amnesty application before the Truth Commission that Mr Botha had given an instruction to Law and Order Minister, Adriaan Vlok, for Police to carry out this bombing. I said that one had to guard against allowing the peace momentum to be broken by each day's adverse events. The reality was that we were not to be blessed with propitious weather for peacemaking. It was not unlike a war situation. The Angolan talks were an example of how negotiations could take place in spite of ongoing hostilities.

Stoffel said that very little progress, if any, could now be expected before the October elections. Everyone was too preoccupied, and further decisions and actions would depend upon the election outcome. I asked what he suggested I should do during the intervening seven weeks. He replied, 'Keep your channels open. Maybe try to see the ANC again.' I said there could be little purpose in my seeing the ANC if I had nothing to offer. He admitted this was a problem, and suggested I contact him again before setting up a meeting, 'just in case there's something we could entrust you with'.

He reiterated that it was 'out of the question' for him to meet with the ANC in Switzerland at this stage. 'If it would have been wrong a few weeks ago, it is even more wrong today,' he said. In fact, it could be catastrophic for the elections. I asked once again whether it might be possible for me to meet with Nelson Mandela while he was recuperating in hospital? Stoffel replied that this would be 'very difficult'. He said there were other parties involved in decisions affecting Mr Mandela – notably Minister Kobie Coetsee, and Niel Barnard of the N I S. 'These people hold their cards very close to the chest,' he noted. I inferred that he too was not as fully informed as he would have wished.

Concerning the possibility of Mandela's release, he confirmed that some progress was being made. 'I am becoming cautiously hopeful,' he said, 'but the emphasis is on *cautiously*.' I urged that when the time came, the Government should take great care not to make the same mistake of trying to manipulate the event, as had occurred on the release of Govan Mbeki. This had caused much resentment, and had largely negated the possibility of any favourable impact. If properly handled, Mr Mandela's release could be the most significant step the Government could take in creating the necessary preconditions for a negotiation process.

Our meeting came to an abrupt end, when Van der Merwe had to depart for Pretoria. I returned to Cape Town, and used the intervening weeks to establish a separate office, do some essential background reading, and consult with my close confidants. It was largely a question of marking time, and waiting for the elections to happen. As the weeks passed my confidence in the future of the initiative waxed and waned. Although the necessary preconditions had been substantially established, the Government remained hesitant and unprepared. It was preoccupied with the need to confirm its mandate from an anxious white electorate, and to attempt to vindicate its Byzantine vision of the fast-failing tricameral constitution.

Amongst the more unlikely new converts to the need to talk to the ANC were the supremos of the rugby world, Drs Danie Craven and Louis Luyt. It was reported that two meetings had already taken place with the ANC in London, and a third was now planned. Stricken by chagrin at seeing his archrival Louis Luyt receive astonished acclamation for this unexpected manifestation of liberal enlightenment, Dr Craven explained that he had been ill at the time. He would certainly make sure that he attended future meetings. Stricken also by accusations of lack of patriotism and political naiveté, Dr Craven rounded on his critics, and said: 'If the Government can talk to Angola, why can't we do the same for sport? Our motives are unblemished and pure – if we speak to the ANC, it is because they are all around us, whether in underground organisations or as supporters belonging to organisations like SARU. We have to learn to live with them.' One had to be grateful for such sporting pragmatism.

By the end of September, I was discreetly ensconced in an unlikely office located in a two-roomed Higgovale apartment, looking down on the city of Cape Town. The office was equipped with the usual paraphernalia – telephones, fax, word-processor, photocopier, answering machine, and the like – but its location was known only to a few, and my telephone number was unlisted. However, what the office sorely lacked was other human beings, colleagues with whom I could discuss my decisions, friends with whom I could share doubts and dilemmas, staff who could assist in the various tasks to be undertaken. I was virtually self-sufficient, able to do almost anything; but extremely lonely and isolated.

One man always ready to meet and share with me his valuable insights was Van Zyl Slabbert. On Monday 5 September, we had lunch at a French restaurant in Pinelands. I sought his opinion about the ANC's unexplained failure to communicate with the Swiss Government, as requested and promised. I also wanted his views about the extraordinary dissonance between the Government's public rhetoric in opposing all meetings with the ANC, and its private flirtation with this initiative. Was this cowardice, duplicity, or did it indicate some deeper problem?

Van believed that the parties were squaring off for a major confrontation around the forthcoming elections. The Government needed a credible poll and a strong showing by its candidates to be able to pursue its envisaged constitutional strategy. Conversely, the ANC had targeted these elections as a test of its own ability to 'render the country ungovernable'. Accordingly, the parties were on a collision course, and this would inevitably lead to further confrontation and repression. He was surprised by Archbishop Tutu's call to Anglicans to refrain from voting in the forthcoming elections. Though couched in theological language, his intention was clear: 'We cannot say, do not participate, because this would be an offence ... so we say, consider prayerfully what God wants you to do on October 26!' The Police had seized a recording of his sermon. He had also said, 'We urge black people: do not participate in a process that is meant to perpetuate your own oppression.' A local newspaper had stated: 'The *Cape Times* is prevented for legal reasons from reporting fully on what the Archbishop said.' In Van Zyl's opinion, the Archbishop had now forfeited the possibility of himself serving as a mediator, and would henceforth be regarded as an apologist for the ANC. It was a new example of an old dichotomy between the things of God and those of Caesar.

Van Zyl was not unduly concerned about the present immobility of Government, and felt the ANC would expect a measure of paralysis during a pre-election period. In fact, he had discussed this with Thabo Mbeki at a recent lunch meeting in London. What was of concern however was the overall confusion and lack of direction in Government policy.

By this stage I had had thirteen separate meetings with Stoffel van der Merwe. I said to Van Zyl that it would seem inconceivable that he would devote such time to an initiative if it was not seriously intended and mandated. Van Zyl replied that it was clear that P W had approved the initial concept, but one did not know to what extent he remained in the picture. He felt there was a possibility that Stoffel was now acting beyond his mandate. He certainly would not have initially undertaken such a venture as 'a frolic of his own'. It was also extremely unlikely that the concept of an exploratory process would have originated with him. Van Zyl saw Stoffel as a rising star, but 'still a relative lightweight', though he enjoyed a close relationship with Botha.

Perhaps because he was inured to political paradox, Van Zyl said he was relatively undismayed by the stark inconsistencies between the Government's public avowals and its private actions. The President's formidable wrath was directed against all who advocated dialogue with the ANC – the most recent target having been the S A Rugby Board. He mentioned that it was in fact he that had arranged the first meeting between Louis Luyt and Mbeki. The Government was in disarray. Only the military establishment seemed to have a coherent strategy, albeit that it involved the suppression of protest and dissent; the detention and silencing of leaders; and the simultaneous promotion of social reforms to eliminate what were called 'points of friction'. In this manner they hoped that the 'revolutionary climate' would be dissipated, and a new cast of political leaders might emerge, more disposed to doing business with the Government.

We discussed whether there were any further steps I could take during this hiatus period. Van Zyl said he didn't favour my setting up another meeting with the ANC until I had something to offer them. He empathised with my difficulties in communicating with Lusaka, and said he had experienced a similar problem. He was less certain about whether I should try to establish some further contact with P W. It had been made clear that Stoffel's role was to provide protection for the President. On the other hand, one needed to confirm from time to time that the initiative still had the President's support. One possibility was that I might address another letter directly to the State President, to 'test the water'. In such letter, I might record the meetings held, and the general content of discussions that had taken place. Faced with this information, the State President would have to respond. He would have only two choices – either to authenticate or to repudiate the process. If Stoffel was acting without authority, this would be quickly flushed out. On the other hand, it might also provoke some 'fireworks', and lead to a formal disavowal of the initiative. That was a definite risk. I said I would think about it. My instinct was not to try to 'beard the crocodile' at this stage.

Botha had been remarkably expansive when he addressed the National Party's Free State Congress in Bloemfontein on 7 September. What prompted his emotion-charged speech was the prospect of competing celebrations taking place around the 150th anniversary of the Great Trek. Deploring disunity amongst Afrikaners, the President reached out what he called 'a hand of goodwill' to his arch-rival Dr Andries Treurnicht, the Conservative Party leader. The *Cape Times* reported, 'As he spoke, the State President's eyes brimmed with tears and his jaw quivered with emotion.' The President said he now waited for a response to his outstretched hand. Dr Treurnicht's response was not long in coming. He told the President bluntly: 'Return to the road of a sovereign white Parliament, where we cannot be vetoed by other nations. Turn around, away from mixed residential areas and mixed political structures, and you will find our hand right there.' Political commentators felt the President had been humiliated.

On Tuesday 13 September, I had a call from Thabo Mbeki in Lusaka. He confirmed that the ANC had now made contact with the Swiss, and that a meeting would be taking place that day in Switzerland between their representative Johnny Makatini and State Secretary Brunner. I told him that despite several meetings with Stoffel van der Merwe, I had still received no formal response from the Government, although I had been given to understand that further developments could be expected after the October elections. This would seem to apply not only to the ANC's request for 'an indication of seriousness', but also to the prospects for Nelson Mandela's release. Mbeki commented that they had received similar information from other sources. Concerning the possibility of our meeting again, he suggested this was really in my own hands. Although it could be useful to have a further discussion, he would not like to encourage me to come to Lusaka, until there was something tangible for us to discuss. We made a tentative arrangement for me to travel to Zambia for a meeting in early October.

On 10 September, President P W Botha and Pope John Paul ll both set out on their respective first tours of the African sub-continent. President Botha planned to visit Mozambique and Malawi. The Pontiff's itinerary would take him to Zimbabwe, Lesotho, Swaziland, Botswana and Mozambique. Foreign Minister Pik Botha described the Pope's decision to exclude apartheid South Africa as 'inexplicable', particularly in the light of the invitation he had personally extended to him in Rome during 1984. As events transpired – due to what might technically if not literally be described as 'an act of God' – the Pope was in fact constrained to visit South Africa on 14 September, despite his plans to the contrary.

For the first time in his worldwide travels, much to his own dismay and Pik Botha's delight, the Pontiff's plane had to make an unscheduled forced landing in Johannesburg, due to problems with the engines and navigation system aboard an Air Zimbabwe Boeing 737. It was however noted that the Pope did not kiss the tarmac, as was his custom on visiting a country for the first time. There were vivid descriptions of 'hair-raising moments', with the pilot 'gunning his engines and lifting the plane out of danger'. On board were a fair number of cardinals, archbishops, bishops, and clergy, and more than 70 members of the international press corps. The media solemnly reported that: 'The Pope, according to Vatican officials, kept calm during the crisis. He finished his morning prayer, and then read a book, while around him high priests of the church nervously clutched their seats, overcome with nausea.' Pik Botha's reaction was not on record.

The Rosenthal and Esterhuyse initiatives

Awaiting the local elections, I now devoted time to background reading, and familiarising myself with the negotiating positions of the Government and the ANC. I also used the opportunity to meet with various members of the academic and legal fraternities, whose knowledge and informed insights could be relevant to a future negotiation process. In most instances, it would have been inappropriate to divulge the particular reason for my interest. I simply said that I was concerned to identify ways and means in which I could become 'relevant and useful'.

One of those whom I met at this time was Attorney Essa Moosa of Athlone, with whom I had a long association going back to our days as law students at UCT. We had also had recent dealings as attorneys representing some of the accused in the pending Schreiner/Yengeni trial. Essa had played an important role representing individuals and organisations at the forefront of 'the struggle'. He acted for the UDF, and many of its affiliates. I knew that he had consulted with Nelson Mandela on the Island.

Essa came to dinner one evening in September, and we had an interesting and relevant discussion concerning the theoretical possibility of a negotiation process. It was his view that such a process was not even a theoretical possibility, until the exiled leadership was able to confer with Nelson Mandela and the other members of the internal leadership. He agreed that the forthcoming elections could provide a critical test between the Government and the ANC, and that the scope for negotiations at present was limited.

He had heard that the ANC had received some indication of the Government's possible interest in a future negotiation process. He had also heard of discussions between Ambassador Piet Koornhof and Senator Jesse Jackson in Washington. It was understood that Koornhof had urged Jackson to visit South Africa, and had gone as far as to suggest that he might be able to help in exploring contacts between the Government and the ANC. Jackson had expressed surprise at this suggestion, as he had been previously refused a visa. However, Koornhof was reported as saying that the Government saw him as a possible intermediary.

Concerning Nelson Mandela's release, Essa confirmed that although hypothetical discussions had taken place, there seemed to be no willingness on the part of either Botha or Mandela to concede the preconditions of the other. Like all who had been allowed to meet Mandela in prison, Essa spoke with near-veneration of his statesmanlike qualities, and his keen interest and detailed knowledge of current affairs. I asked whether there was any possibility that he could one day help me to meet Mr Mandela. Essa said it would be more appropriate if this were to be discussed with Attorney Ismail Ayob of Johannesburg.

Another of my contacts at this time was Professor H W van der Merwe (no relation!), who had established a Centre for Conflict Resolution on the campus of the University of Cape Town. 'H W' had tried to keep contact with all parties, and saw his role more as that of a 'communicator', rather than a mediator. He said that he tried to pass information between groups unable to speak to each other direct. His style was never to embarrass anyone, but to try to communicate 'the positive points' about each party to the other. In this manner, he had told the ANC about his discussions with Dr Andries Treurnicht. He evidently maintained contacts with the Security Police, Military Intelligence, and the National Intelligence Service. In fact, he had nice things to say about everyone – including General Johann van der Merwe, then Deputy-Commissioner of Police, whom he considered to be a man of intellect and integrity. 'H W' had gained the impression that the big issue was becoming, 'Who would *control* a future negotiation process?' He said that there was keen competition between various factions in the National Party, and even between different Ministers. Amongst those wishing to play the starring role were Niel Barnard's National Intelligence Service; Stoffel van der Merwe's Department of Information; Chris Heunis's Department of Constitutional Affairs; Pik Botha's Department of Foreign Affairs; and even Kobie Coetsee's Department of Prisons, which jealously guarded the right of access to Mr Mandela. This situation was causing incoherence and lack of cooperation.

I also met again with Arthur Chaskalson, who had dinner with us one Sunday evening at Hout Bay. We reviewed the stage that had been reached, and discussed future options for the initiative. I sought Arthur's view on a number of crucial issues, including my growing sense that the parties themselves were unlikely to come up with creative strategies to unlock the present impasse. As an intermediary I might have to be more proactive than I had originally envisaged. I asked what he thought about the time-scale that the Swiss were anxious to establish. In Arthur's view, the Swiss were being unrealistic in hoping for some tangible result within a period as short as three months. He believed one had to be prepared for 'quite a long haul', although one of the ways in which an intermediary might assist the process was to badger the parties, and try to accelerate the process.

I once again asked Arthur's view about my trying to meet Nelson Mandela. He said it was significant that both Thabo Mbeki and Stoffel van der Merwe were opposed to this. There were probably too many risks in pressing the issue. Apart from the political turf battles, any attempt by me to promote this could create concern about my impartiality, and might inadvertently lead to other persons becoming prematurely aware of the initiative. What did he think about the Government's hope to drive a wedge between the ANC and the SACP? Clearly, the Government hoped to be able to deal one day with an ANC purged of its communist members. Arthur's view was that these attempts were inept and futile. Although there were ideological differences, there was full agreement on critical objectives, and a close and mutually valued relationship of long standing. There was little likelihood that Government could succeed in its transparent attempt at promoting differences.

Arthur made two particularly interesting suggestions. Firstly, he wondered whether the ANC might not give thought to a means of acknowledging or rewarding the Government's 'good behaviour'. This could take various forms, but could demonstrate the ANC's ability to unlock South Africa's growing international isolation. For example, the ANC might choose to facilitate access to certain bank borrowing for an approved purpose, such as social housing. Another example might be that the ANC could give approval to specific international sporting events. The second suggestion he mooted was that each of the parties might at the outset depute trusted surrogates who could bypass the problem of leader-to-leader meetings. For example, Dr Anton Rupert might serve as an acceptable surrogate for the South African Government?

But it was my meeting with Professor Willie Esterhuyse, on Thursday 15 September, which was the greatest eye-opener. There were a number of reasons for my having decided to contact him. By this time he was a regular participant in the flurry of South Africa seminars being held in Europe and America over this period. *Die Burger* had reported his impressions of two such events which he had attended in England during March. I had known Willie at a distance for a number of years. To me he was an enigma, a grey eminence. As Professor of Political Philosophy at Stellenbosch University, he was certainly well placed to understand and interpret National Party thinking. I had also heard his spirited criticism of the establishment in relation to policy interventions of the Urban Foundation, which we had both served as Consultants. Willie was a man of intellect and insight, a member of the elite '*verligte*' community at Stellenbosch University, but – and there was a 'but' – he was also an influential, and presumably unrepentant, member of the Broederbond. This had been explained to me as the conscious choice of a man with basic liberal instincts, who wished to influence Afrikaner thinking from the inside out.

We sat down to lunch at Die Volkskombuis in Stellenbosch, a font of traditional Afrikaner gastronomy. We were amongst the first of the lunch patrons, and I chose a remote table, in the hope that we might avoid being overheard. In speaking to Willie, I had decided to take a conscious and deliberate risk. I needed better access to the Afrikaner intelligentsia than was being provided by Stoffel van der Merwe. I had judged Willie to be a powerful potential ally, although I realised the risks in enlarging my circle of confidants.

After we had patriotically ordered *tamatie bredie*, and a good bottle of local wine, I came straight to the point. I commenced by quoting Anton Rupert (of whom Willie was the commissioned biographer), who had observed sagely that crossing a precipice cannot be done in small steps! Willie allowed me to stumble on for a few moments in my lamentable Afrikaans, and then graciously put me out of my linguistic misery.

It was soon obvious that he was riveted. Willie is a good listener, and he stared intently at me as I recounted the story of the initiative thus far. He looked absolutely stunned, and his glass of wine remained completely neglected. When I had finished, there was a long pause, during which he seemed to reflect before responding. Finally, he asked whether I had been aware of his own activities? Now it was my turn to look puzzled. As I had earlier, Willie sought an assurance of confidentiality, to which I readily agreed.

He then said, 'I am completely amazed by what you have just told me.' Not only did my analysis of the current political situation correspond closely with his own, but, even more surprising, our personal response and reaction had been almost identical. He too had approached the State President, and had made him a similar offer to my own! Over roughly the same period of time, unbeknown to each other, Willie and I had both been engaged in conducting discreet meetings with the ANC, acting with the knowledge and approval of the State President.

Willie had been a delegate at the Intercontinental Hotel in Frankfurt on 26/27 May, though unaware of my presence. He explained that his meetings were intended to serve as a two-way conduit for an exchange of views and information. Unlike myself, he had direct access to Mr Botha, to whom he reported personally. In fact, he would be having the next such meeting the following week. I inferred that his expenses were covered directly or indirectly by the Broederbond. He clearly understood what was meant by the term 'deniability'.

The irony of our having serendipitously decided to confide in each other was extraordinary, and we enjoyed a good belly laugh and another glass of wine. I expect that P W and Stoffel might have been equally amazed at the spectacle of the two of us confiding in each other. In fact, I wondered whether Stoffel was actually aware of Willie's role? He was fascinated about my dealings with Stoffel, whom he knew well, and whom he described as 'Botha's eyes and ears'. He described him as a man of ability. 'He jolly well should be,' Willie laughed. 'He was one of my students!' In fact, Willie had been external examiner to his thesis. 'The thesis is now a bit out of date!'

He said that Stoffel van der Merwe did not have authority to take decisions in a matter of such crucial importance. It therefore didn't surprise him that our discussions had often proved inconclusive. There was no doubt in his mind that P W was behind it. Willie said that my account was the first indication of which he was aware, that serious consideration was being given by the State President to the possibility of a constitutional negotiation process involving the ANC. The concept of constitutional talks had been on the back-burner for some time, but the Government had been groping about in the dark.

He immediately tumbled to the risks posed to the Government by my initiative, and emphasised the importance of my preserving confidentiality in this pre-election period. I am sure he was also wondering why, of all people, Richard Rosenthal should be the repository of such politically volatile information. We agreed that neither of us should divulge our conversation, but we should remain discreetly in touch. It remained to be seen whether we could at some stage collaborate.

Willie agreed that little was possible until after the elections, and that the fate of both initiatives might be determined by the election outcome. It was uncertain how Government might respond to a major setback. It might prompt P W to proceed more resolutely with reform, but it could just as easily have the reverse effect. *Die Groot Krokodil* (Botha's nickname – the Great Crocodile) was notoriously unpredictable. A great deal would depend on the level of violence and intimidation in the pre-election period. After some two and a half hours, we shook hands like old comrades who by chance had met in the jungle, like Stanley and Livingstone.

Before the month was out, I had two further meetings with the Swiss Ambassador. The first of these took place at the Pretoria Embassy on 20 September, and was particularly important, because Ambassador Quinche was at last able to convey to me the commitment of his Government to back my initiative for an initial period of three months from 1 September to 30 November – on the understanding that its support would then have to be reviewed in the light of progress achieved, and the outcome of the October Elections.

The Ambassador informed me that in the course of a private discussion with Dr van der Merwe, he had received further confirmation of the South African Government's support for my initiative. The Minister had once again urged the Swiss Government to provide the required support. Van der Merwe had also sought to explain the delays which had occurred as 'unfortunate but politically unavoidable'.

Minister van der Merwe would be departing for his official visit to Switzerland the next day. The Ambassador anticipated that Mr Brunner might also seek confirmation from him of the Government's seriousness and commitment to a negotiation process, particularly as they were now involved in underwriting its cost. Mr Brunner would also be concerned to get some sense of a possible time frame. The Ambassador expressed himself personally 'unsurprised' by the Government's apparent lack of concern about time. He speculated that it could take as long as a year before leader-to-leader meetings could be achieved.

I learnt from the Ambassador that the present State Secretary, Mr Edouard Brunner, would be taking up appointment as the Swiss Ambassador in Washington from the end of February. This was no doubt one of the reasons contributing to his anxiety about a short-term time frame. The next State Secretary would be the currently serving Ambassador in Washington. He had stirred up some controversy by stating that his primary objective in his new position would be to promote Swiss commercial interests abroad. This vision had not met with universal acclaim. Mr Quinche confirmed that these changes would not affect the Swiss Government's backing for my initiative. There had also been changes in the Foreign Ministry. Ambassador Quinche predicted that the newly appointed Member of the Federal Council (Bundesrat), with responsibility for Political (Foreign) Affairs, Mr René Felber, who represented the Social Democratic Party (SPS) in the Government, would certainly be supportive of this initiative.

Our periodic discussions had come to include a review of major political events and issues upon which the Ambassador would no doubt report to Berne. On this occasion, we talked about the continuing speculation concerning the release of Nelson Mandela; the inconclusive negotiations for a complete withdrawal of Cuban forces from Angola; the ongoing Municipal Election campaigns; the Government's legislative proposals to 'streamline' the Group Areas Act; the bitter polemic between the State President ('the outstretched hand') and Dr Andries Treurnicht; the witch hunt being conducted by F W de Klerk, then Minister of National Education, into reported contacts between the ANC and the Crown Prince of rugby, Dr

Louis Luyt; and the President's forays into the African Continent.

We agreed to meet again before the end of the month, by which time the Ambassador hoped to be able to give me some feedback on Dr van der Merwe's visit to Switzerland. I asked if he could also try to ascertain the outcome of discussions which I understood to have taken place between the ANC and the Swiss Government, following my suggestion to Thabo Mbeki.

Accordingly, we resumed our discussion ten days later on Friday 30 September over dinner at Rozenfontein restaurant in Cape Town. Though the cuisine was excellent, it was a particularly poor venue for a confidential discussion. We were virtually the only patrons that night, and were afflicted by the cavernous acoustics, and the relentless attentions of over-zealous under-employed waiters, intent upon establishing our every need, and confirming our continued satisfaction, at four-minute intervals.

Mr Quinche had just received a lengthy written report from the Foreign Office in Berne. It dealt in detail with two significant meetings – the first between State Secretary Brunner and the Head of the ANC's Department of International Affairs, Johnny Makatini. The second meeting had taken place at Ministerial level between new Swiss Foreign Minister René Felber and Dr Stoffel van der Merwe. In both instances, despite my earlier cautions, they had apparently engaged in substantive discussions, covering important and sensitive issues affecting a future negotiation process. I was concerned that Stoffel should not have felt himself pressured by the Swiss, whose envisaged role was understood to be strictly non-partisan; and in the case of Mr Makatini, that the Swiss should not have inadvertently embarrassed the ANC leadership by engaging in a substantive discussion of a very sensitive issue with a relatively junior representative.

According to the Ambassador's description, the discussion with Johnny Makatini had gone well, and had covered a broad range of issues, affecting the relationship between the ANC and the Swiss Government, including what was termed the 'Rosenthal Initiative'. Makatini had stressed that it was up to the South African Government to create conditions conducive to negotiations, and he had indicated that the release of Nelson Mandela would be seen as an essential first step. Noting the Government's frequently stated pre-condition, that he first renounce violence, Mr Brunner had suggested a possible way past this impasse – namely, that the Government might release Mandela 'on humanitarian grounds' to recuperate in a Swiss sanatorium, as a prelude to his release in South Africa.

Makatini had made it clear that he had no authority to discuss any such proposal, which would have to be taken up with the leadership in Lusaka. However, he had no doubt that the ANC would try to be flexible and pragmatic. Mr Brunner urged that both parties (Government and the ANC) should consider the potential value of an initial secret meeting, to explore their respective positions, to search for common ground, and to commence to establish an agenda for future dialogue. Depending on the success of such initial meeting, substantive discussions could begin at a later stage on a pre-agreed basis.

Mr Brunner had commented that Makatini seemed quite interested in this scenario, and had accepted the concept of initial 'talks about talks'. However, it seemed that he had not been fully briefed in regard to the 'Rosenthal initiative'. He had asked Mr Brunner to explain how it had commenced; which parties would be entitled to participate; and what might be the context and agenda for the initial meetings. Mr Brunner stressed that one should refrain from prescribing who might or might not participate in future negotiations, and said that the context and agenda would have to be determined by the parties themselves, through bilateral discussions. He had used words to the effect that: 'When people actually sit down, they're doomed to succeed!'

Makatini had been informed of the imminent visit to Switzerland of Stoffel van der Merwe, and Mr Brunner said that he was hoping to have a similar conversation with him on this occasion. He believed it was vital that the parties begin to talk and communicate with each other, because only in this manner would it be possible to establish the necessary trust and confidence. Makatini had also raised the matter of Swiss trade and financial relations with South Africa. He saw sanctions as necessary to pressure the South African Government to come to the negotiation table. Mr Brunner responded that statistics showed that the activities of Swiss banks in South Africa had been considerably reduced. The Government preferred to leave such matters to the banks themselves to regulate.

They had formed a favourable impression of Johnny Makatini, regarding him as 'reasonable' and 'flexible'. (Dr Slabbert later told me jokingly that the Swiss were particularly impressed with Makatini because he spoke fluent French!) Mr Brunner raised the possibility of further contact after Dr van der Merwe's visit, in case something significant should emerge from their discussions. It was hoped that after the elections real progress might be made in pursuing the concept of 'talks about talks'. Hopefully, it would then be possible to discuss a time and venue for an initial meeting.

At their separate meeting, Foreign Minister Felber had told Dr van der Merwe that he saw their discussion in the context of on-going contacts with various parties involved in the South African situation. He expressed his own and the Swiss Government's appreciation for the fact that steps were being taken towards exploring the possibility of negotiations. He saw it as significant that the initiative was 'completely South African'. He was happy to confirm the Swiss Government's agreement to provide support for my initiative, and reassured Van der Merwe of their understanding of the need for absolute confidentiality. In due course, the Swiss Government might be willing to provide not only financial assistance, but also technical and physical resources which might be required for a successful process.

Minister Felber had gone on to suggest to Van der Merwe a possible way forward, involving an initial phase in which there would be secret contacts, evolving into a more substantive 'open' phase. He had said the Swiss Government would wish to re-examine its own role at the end of the year, to consider whether it was justified in continuing its support and involvement. It was therefore important that some progress be achieved during this initial period. Van der Merwe had evidently responded that when the initiative commenced, a somewhat different situation existed from that which now prevailed. In the interim, the ANC had chosen to intensify its campaign of violence, and this now constituted a considerable obstacle to any negotiation process. Moreover, the impending Local Authority elections had created a political context in which it was extremely difficult to pursue such a sensitive matter. He said the ANC apparently hoped by its campaign of violence to disrupt the elections, and thereby inhibit the development of a democratic system. This could result in the 'Rosenthal initiative' being deferred or even aborted. He hoped after the elections, an atmosphere more conducive to this process might be established.

Van der Merwe had stressed that the process needed to be seen in a long-term context, and that one had to allow for reasonable time – and be prepared for disappointments and delays. Although he was personally ready to go ahead, his Ministry had experienced problems in securing the necessary agreement to proceed with my initiative. Minister Felber had expressed understanding that little could be achieved before the elections, and believed that this would probably also be understood by the ANC. The ANC saw the time-frame as increasingly 'tight', and spoke of pressures from its younger members for more drastic action.

Van der Merwe had reportedly responded that the Government wished to facilitate a genuine democratic process, but this could not be achieved overnight. There were already a number of tangible results to show for its reformist intentions. He said the Government was anxious to establish a system which could enable blacks to participate in genuine negotiations. He recognised that no such process could be effective unless all parties participated. For this reason, the Government could not compromise on the issue of intimidation and violence. Surveys showed that 80 per cent of Blacks wanted peace and democracy. It was unfortunate that the ANC and the UDF were engaged in widespread intimidation aimed at preventing people from freely expressing their will through the ballot box. No democracy could be established in such an atmosphere. He had said that although the Government had undergone radical change, the ANC still seemed locked into the past, and saw no practical alternative to its policy of violence. The ANC looked for 'quick results'. It therefore played 'the card of power'. Van der Merwe commented that the Government could also play that game. However, what it really wanted was 'the game of democracy'.

Minister Felber commented that the Swiss Government recognised efforts being made towards the establishment of a change process. It was also appreciative of some of the results already obtained. The Swiss believed that whites had a right to a place in the sun, but equally that the ANC had a right to exist in its own country, and to conduct normal peaceful political activity. Having had discussions with both parties, he sensed their objectives were not very different, nor were they incapable of reconciliation. He was of the view that the ANC did not wish to destroy the South African economy; nor could everyone in the ANC be dismissed as a Marxist. People in the ANC had to realise that they could not achieve power overnight through force. Blacks were looking for a promise of change to come, even if it took time to achieve.

Van der Merwe had suggested that the Swiss should take care to establish what kind of people they were dealing with. The Government's plans for change were detailed and well known. Hitherto neither the ANC nor the UDF had responded to the Government's ideas. Thus, the Government had made a number of suggestions, including the National Statutory Council, which was intended as a forum in which all groups could be represented. But the Government did not want to be prescriptive. The composition and even the name of this body was open to discussion. He had stated that this body 'could even include people like Nelson Mandela and Thabo Mbeki'. Its purpose would be to search for a constitutional solution. Already the Government had plans to integrate blacks at local authority level. Similar steps were being taken to bring blacks into Government at other levels.

Foreign Minister Felber had interjected at one stage that one could hardly conduct meaningful negotiations with leaders who were still in prison. He had said that the creation of martyrs did not promote the search for peaceful solutions. Dr van der Merwe had replied that the banning of the ANC went back to the '60s, but that it should be appreciated that President Botha was a very different man from Dr Verwoerd. The present Government wanted everyone to participate in negotiations, including the ANC. It also wanted to be able to free Nelson Mandela. This could only be achieved if the ANC renounced violence. He had added that it would not have necessarily been expected of Mr Mandela that he renounce violence publicly.

Minister Felber had pointed out that the ANC could hardly be expected to renounce violence at this early stage, particularly as it represented 'one of the few real weapons it has in its hands'. Dr van der Merwe reportedly 'exploded', stating that this was a total misunderstanding of the situation. According to the Ambassador, the meeting then proceeded very badly. Dr van der Merwe's reaction was described as 'highly emotional'. Minister Felber had sought to explain that he did not seek to justify violence, but believed it was a reality one had to recognise.

At one stage, Van der Merwe had confronted Felber with having encouraged Swiss banks to support sanctions. He pointed out that South Africa was a proud nation, and would not allow itself to be 'blackmailed'. In fact, it would not allow itself to be in any way deflected from what it believed to be right. According to Van der Merwe, South Africa didn't need outside help to solve its problems. What it did need was time and tolerance. It was fully capable of helping itself. Minister Felber sought to explain that the remarks attributed to him had been spoken in a different context, and were not correctly quoted. He had not urged companies to divest, but had advised them to consider what their response should be to the present situation.

The Swiss were pleased with the outcome of their discussion with Mr Makatini, but had felt less certain about their meeting with Dr van der Merwe. Expressing his personal opinion, the Ambassador said that this was not entirely unexpected to him. He had been in this country long enough to realise that peacemaking would be a difficult and delicate process. He found the impatience and optimism of Mr Felber and Mr Brunner somewhat unrealistic, particularly as regards a time-scale. However, he believed there might be a little more time than was at one stage foreseen.

18

'Meddling in our affairs'

On 28 September 1988, P W Botha celebrated the tenth anniversary of his accession to power, initially as Prime Minister, and subsequently as State President. He marked the occasion with a self-eulogy, in which he noted 'the great success' that had been achieved. No matter that the country was racked by violence; its economy in tatters; its currency debased; its policies morally bankrupt; a society permeated by informers and spies, in which information was managed, manufactured and manipulated by the Government; nor that the current State of Emergency was the fourth since Botha came to power. By his judgment, it was a great success.

The President's perspective from the window of his Tuynhuys office was expressed in these terms: 'It is true that bombs explode in South Africa now and again, but they also explode in Britain and France and in many other countries ... Most people in South Africa are free. Only people who transgress and break the law are not free.' There was no mention or recognition of the tens of thousands then held in detention without trial, nor that South Africa had become a country in which the holding of a forbidden political belief constituted a crime; nor that such laws were regarded elsewhere in the world as totalitarian and undemocratic. A great success?

An *Argus* editorial marked the occasion, by recalling how President Botha's tenure had begun with so much hope and promise, including 'the scrapping of some of apartheid's most vulgar instruments ... but partly through lack of proper appreciation of the magnitude of what he was up against, he failed at the most vital moments to grasp the nettle, and to see his reforms through'. The writer still nurtured the hope – which I fervently shared – that 'with the right will, he can still go down in history as the man who finally changed the course of this country for the better'.

In dealing with his vision for future constitutional development, the President made one particular comment that gave me reason to pause. He said: 'I reject the attempt by some people to call in support from outside South Africa to help with their political aims in South Africa.' I wondered whether this sentiment had any relevance to the role assumed by the Swiss Government, and the help they had agreed to offer. Events were soon to provide me with the answer.

The unexpected catalyst was the death on 3 October of one of Botha's rare foreign admirers, controversial right-wing leader, Franz-Josef Strauss, Minister President of Bavaria, who had visited South Africa only a few months earlier, and had congratulated the President on his achievements. The two Bothas – P W and Foreign Minister, Pik – travelled together to Germany to pay posthumous homage at the State funeral in Munich. En route they visited Switzerland, where they conferred with Swiss bankers in Zurich, and had meetings with the Swiss Foreign Minister and State Secretary in Berne.

The first indication I had that something had gone awry, was a cluster of 'extremely urgent' messages waiting for me when I arrived at my office early on the Monday morning, 17 October. Apparently Stoffel van der Merwe had been desperately trying to contact me. He had telephoned my office and home repeatedly over the past hour. Hilary said he sounded very agitated, and asked that I telephone him the very moment I came in. He had said it was of the utmost urgency. The dawn cracks later in my home than it does in some others, and I reached the office only at about 9.15 a.m.

'Where *on earth* have you been?' asked his distraught secretary accusingly, when I called her back. 'We've been looking for you everywhere. Now it's too late!'

'Too late for what?' I asked innocently.

'I don't know what's going on,' she said, 'but the Minister is very upset. He's been trying to get hold of you since early this morning. Now he's with the State President. He said he had to speak to you first. But he's had to leave – he's already on his way!'

I was both mystified and apprehensive. What could possibly have gone wrong? My first thought was that perhaps the secrecy of the initiative had been 'blown'. This had always been a risk, and with only ten days to go before the Elections, the timing could hardly have been worse. The other possibility was that perhaps 'they' were having second thoughts about my plan to visit Lusaka in two days' time. I had informed Stoffel of this intended visit, in case there was a document which he could entrust with me to be delivered. His overall response had been positive. He was pleased to learn I was going to be in touch with the ANC again, and had undertaken to give urgent attention to the matter of a message.

Just before lunch, Stoffel telephoned again. I had had almost four hours of suspense. His voice was sepulchral and hardly recognisable.

'I have some very bad news for you,' he said.

'The State President returned last night from Switzerland. He has instructed me that the whole thing must be called off.'

'What on earth has happened?'

'I think it's better we discuss it together,' he replied. 'How soon can you come to Pretoria?'

I cancelled all appointments, including a scheduled court appearance on behalf of Jenny Schreiner, and was in Pretoria the following day. Weekly Cabinet meetings took place every Tuesday, and we were therefore unable to meet until 5 p.m.

When I arrived, Stoffel's personal secretary, Petra van Niekerk, came out to greet me. 'What have you done?' she said, 'I don't know what's going on. My boss looks terrible!'

Indeed he did. His eyes were dark and bloodshot. It looked like a death in the family. As soon as I arrived, he took me straight into his office and said we'd better come straight to the point.

Early on Monday morning he was summoned to the Union Buildings, 'like a schoolboy to the headmaster's office'. The President was in a total rage. He had only just arrived back from Switzerland. It was the very first thing he did. Everything else was cancelled. Their meeting had lasted most of the morning. Stoffel said he had never experienced anything like it – Mr P W Botha's unbridled fury. It was the worst tongue-lashing of his life.

'It's all the fault of your Swiss friends', he explained. They had apparently embarrassed the State President. In the course of a meeting, the Swiss Foreign Minister had called the State President aside, and had said to him – in front of South Africa's Foreign Minister, Pik Botha – 'Why is the Rosenthal Initiative moving along so slowly?'

Stoffel commented: 'Imagine confronting a man like P W Botha that way? He was completely taken aback. What did Mr Felber expect? I've never seen the President so angry.'

He viewed the situation as so serious that it was likely to spell the end of his political career. He added philosophically that he had always known that if things went wrong, he would have to take the rap. I understood this was now happening. He said manfully that he had to take the blame for not having kept Mr Botha fully informed about how far the initiative had already progressed. In particular, he said, the State President had not been advised of my meetings with the ANC. I listened to his apologia with some scepticism. Was he telling me the truth, or was he 'taking the rap', as he was required to do?

It was not difficult to imagine the scene. Despite all the meticulous precautions of the past twelve months to conceal the President's personal involvement with this most delicate matter, he was being directly confronted by the Swiss Foreign Minister, just days before the crucial local authority elections. And, to make matters worse, this indelicacy had happened within earshot of South Africa's Foreign Minister, Pik Botha, who might not have been privy to this highly sensitive arrangement involving another Government. The Swiss had repeatedly commented, that Pik Botha didn't seem to be aware of this matter. If this were true, it would imply a truly amazing situation. A foreign Government had been approached for assistance, which it had agreed to give – without the Foreign Minister being involved or informed, but with the implicit support of the State President! Small wonder that Mr Felber's question had unleashed P W Botha's legendary rage.

Later in our discussion Stoffel referred to his own visit to Switzerland, which we had not previously discussed. He recalled that he too had been questioned by the Swiss Foreign Minister about this initiative, and had been asked to explain why he was unwilling to meet Thabo Mbeki. He tried to explain the delicacy of the matter, particularly in the light of the forthcoming elections, and the recent ANC bombing of civilian targets. The Swiss Foreign Minister had then pressed him for some kind of a timetable. Stoffel said he regarded this as highly intrusive and unacceptable. Their discussion had then become 'quite heated'. Although he had been back some weeks, unfortunately he had not yet been able to report to the State President on his visit to Switzerland. They had been planning to meet shortly, but then the President and the Foreign Minister went 'on a breeze to Europe'.

He was obviously in a terrible state, and leaving aside my own shock and disappointment, I began to feel quite sorry for him. With the recklessness of a condemned man, Van der Merwe began to talk about his personal disappointment with the Government's conduct of its reform process. He spoke of continual vacillation and failure to implement programmes which had been discussed and agreed. He said that over the next weeks he would have to take stock and make some far-reaching decisions about his own future. He expressed regret and embarrassment about the repetitive delays in implementing my initiative, which he protested had been due to his inability to get 'the necessary authority to proceed'.

I asked what he now expected me to do, in the light of the fact that I had cut loose from my legal practice and would now have to consider my own future. He looked dismayed, no doubt anticipating my claim for financial damages. I decided that he deserved some comfort. 'You owe me nothing,' I assured him. 'Not a brass farthing. I chose to do this, and it was at my own risk.' He looked greatly relieved. 'And another thing', I added, 'I will not be giving any interviews to the *Sunday Times!*'

A preposterous situation had arisen. In absolute good faith, and with the implicit, if not explicit, approval of the State President, I had approached the ANC regarding the possibility of a substantive negotiation process. This was without doubt the most critical matter on South Africa's political agenda. An important foreign Government had been approached for assistance, and had agreed to the request. Already there were the makings of some tentative understandings. Expectations had been created. If the initiative was now summarily terminated, this could have unpredictable ramifications, not only affecting future attempts to initiate a similar process, but also in relation to the ANC's attitude to its armed struggle, and its view of the deviousness of the South African regime. It would furthermore have a very negative impact upon South Africa's important economic relationship with Switzerland.

I asked Van der Merwe whether I had understood him correctly to mean that over a period of a year he had communicated *nothing* to the State President? To this, he replied equivocally, 'He knew of your existence, and of our discussions; but he didn't know that you had already met the ANC.' As an afterthought, he added, 'He also didn't know about my discussions with the Swiss Ambassador.' I pointed out that if these facts came to be disputed, it would be rather difficult to convince others of the ignorance of the State President. The ANC had been made aware of my communications with the State President. There was far too much circumstantial evidence of his knowledge. It would be known that the initiative had been launched in response to a personal letter addressed to the State President, and there had been other correspondence exchanged with him. When he had referred to a need to consult with 'certain unnamed persons', I had understood him to be referring also to the State President. Was this not correct? He did not admit or deny. At the time he had been a Deputy Minister in the Office of the State President. I asked how he could expect to be believed, if he was going to say that over a period of a year he had been acting in a matter of such huge importance, entirely on his own initiative, and had not even reported on the outcome of these overtures?

As I thought about the situation, I became increasingly alarmed at the implications, and my responsibility for the consequences which could follow. I was already packed and booked to leave for Lusaka the next day. Arrangements had been made more than two weeks before. As usual, it had proved incredibly difficult to penetrate the recalcitrance of the Zambian telephone exchange, and the insensitivity of the ANC's Lusaka switchboard. No, I could not leave a message. No, I could not give my phone number. No, I could not send them a telex. No, they had no idea where Mr Mbeki was, nor when he would be back, nor did they know whether he had received my earlier messages. 'He's very busy,' I was assured. According to my notes, 'Richard Frankfurt' had phoned Lusaka on 15 separate occasions over a period of 3 days! I couldn't help wondering what might have happened had it been a matter of life and death – on the other hand, maybe it was.

I sat there trying to grapple with the reality. How was I to explain this situation to the ANC, and to the Swiss?

'What do you now expect me to do?' I asked Stoffel. 'I surely can't just say to them that the State President is feeling angry, and has called off all negotiations with the ANC! It sounds lunatic. D'you wish me to go to the ANC and slam the door? If so, I want written instructions. Who knows what the consequences might be?'

He looked pitiful and baffled. After a while, he said he really didn't know how to answer me. Perhaps I should just go and tell them the truth.

'That's fine', I said, 'but tell me, what is the truth?'

He replied, 'The Swiss Government tried to meddle in our affairs, and therefore the initiative has been closed down.'

Apart from this being a gross misrepresentation of the reality, I was not about to defame the very people who had been generously willing to help us. Even if Botha was justified in his irritation with the Swiss Foreign Minister, this didn't seem like an adequate reason for aborting the opportunity of threading lines of dialogue across the divide. I feared that a summary and capricious closure of the initiative would vindicate the hawks, and discredit the conciliators within the ANC. The eventual result might be an intensification of armed hostilities, and the loss of an historic opportunity to achieve a negotiated peace.

It seemed almost incredible that no one was taking responsibility for the consequences of what I was being asked to do. Apart from the internal political ramifications, if I simply went and slammed the door in Lusaka, one of the ANC's options might be to call in the media – and spill the beans! I didn't think they would do that, but it was at least a possibility. Moreover, no one appeared to have given consideration to the possible reaction of the Swiss. I was sure they would not break the confidence of the parties, but they had other options too, particularly if it became apparent that the ANC was prepared to engage in dialogue but the Government was not.

Stoffel said he really didn't know what to suggest. Probably I would have to make up my own mind what to say. I told him that for me to decide on my own such a matter would be highly irresponsible. We were dealing with very serious issues, and it was not just a question of what I personally thought about it. If I was to convey a message of the nature discussed, then I wanted a written instruction, preferably from the President himself. Stoffel said perhaps he should speak to the Swiss. I said he was welcome to do so, but I would in any event need to explain to them what had happened. He said that presumably the State President would already have conveyed his feelings to the Swiss Foreign Minister, and this should therefore come as no surprise to them. He was quite unable to go back to Mr Botha and seek advice. 'Maybe', he speculated, 'you should try to get in touch with Mr Botha yourself.' He doubted I would succeed.

I then asked whose advice the State President might be expected to take in this situation. He replied, 'Well certainly not mine. Perhaps you should go and discuss the matter with someone like Niel Barnard of the National Intelligence Service. I could arrange for you to meet him.' The enigmatic Dr Barnard was known to preside over a highly professional espionage organisation with virtually unlimited powers and resources. He was one of the most influential – and feared – members of the informal inner Cabinet, the State Security Council, and was a key figure in devising and implementing the National Security Management System. However, of more importance at this moment was that he was a close confidant and adviser to the State President.

'Surely I must see the President, not Dr Barnard?' I ventured. Van der Merwe agreed, but urged that I first speak with Barnard. He said he was intimately involved in all dealings with the ANC, and was someone who had influence with the President. I expressed misgivings about my having anything to do with the intelligence community, adding, 'I am not going to become a spy!' Stoffel appeared embarrassed at the inference. He said he hadn't meant to imply that the N I S itself would become involved, but that Dr Barnard was very influential with the State President.

I said it would be absolutely tragic if the present opportunity to initiate a peace process were lost as a result of an intemperate reaction to a third-party indiscretion. In my opinion, there existed a genuine and substantial opportunity that agreement could be reached regarding the principle of a process leading to negotiations. Van der Merwe said he also believed this was possible. 'Perhaps', he said, 'one should regard this as just a temporary reversal.' He was personally convinced that negotiations would eventually take place, but much depended on the outcome of the forthcoming elections.

We then returned to the pressing topic of my visit to Lusaka the following morning. It was already late in the day. There was clearly no way a meeting could be arranged with Botha or Barnard that evening. Moreover, it was clear that Van der Merwe was not going to be of any help in advising me what to do next. I said I needed time to think, and would let him know in due course what I decided.

As I departed, he said, 'Thank you for everything you've done'; to which I could only respond, 'As yet, I haven't been able to do anything!'

The inscrutable Dr Barnard

By the time I arrived back at my hotel, it was almost 9 p.m. It seemed as though the whole impossible dream lay in tatters, the work of the past year was wasted, my legal career destroyed – all on account of a single indiscretion. It was quite unbelievable, and it had happened at the very moment when it had all begun to seem possible. After a while, I phoned Hilary, who had been anxiously awaiting my call. We spoke for a long time. She was, as always, calm, reassuring, and philosophical. We retraced the steps of the past year, and talked about our children and the future. Perhaps this meant Canada after all? Caroline and Jonathan had borne the secret and strain of our lives with a strength and maturity far beyond their years. In a few weeks Caroline would write her B.Sc. final examinations, and Jonathan would write Matric.

However, the immediate issue was, whether or not to travel to Lusaka in the morning. I had a booking and an airticket. It had been arranged with some difficulty. What should I tell the ANC? I decided that I couldn't simply announce that the initiative had been summarily terminated, without giving an explanation and an account of these events, preferably with an assurance about the Government's intention to pursue negotiations at another time and in another way. Until I had been able to communicate with the President, I had no mandate to convey any such message. I knew that I would be incapable of engaging the ANC in a vacuous discussion, without reference to this event. Needless to say, I didn't get much sleep that night. By the small hours, it had become clear that I had to cancel the trip.

The sun rises early in Zambia, and for once the telephone system was cooperative. I spoke to Tom Sebina at the ANC head office, and asked him to let Thabo Mbeki know that I had been forced at the last moment to cancel our meeting. I explained, 'There have been certain important developments, which I need to clarify before coming to see him.' I would explain later. In the meanwhile, I apologised for any inconvenience this had caused. I would get in touch again as soon as possible.

A little later in the morning, I telephoned Stoffel van der Merwe. He still sounded stricken and mortified. He thanked me for letting him know what

I had decided, and said he thought I had made the right decision. I said it was now up to him to ensure that I met Niel Barnard as soon as possible. He said he was on his way to a Cabinet meeting, but promised to speak to Barnard later in the day, as soon as he became free.

Feeling in dire need of some calm objectivity, I telephoned Van Zyl Slabbert, and asked if we could get together urgently. He put aside other plans, and we met at his office in the Wits Business School. I suggested we go and have coffee at a nearby restaurant, because I wished to have a discussion 'without Niel Barnard listening!' He condoned my paranoia, and agreed that his office was not the most secure venue.

Van Zyl's comment was: 'Well, it's like the nightmare come true.' He agreed with my decision to postpone visiting Lusaka, but felt I had to meet the ANC as soon as the waters had cleared a little. In the meanwhile, he counselled that our concern should be to contain the damage, and give the ANC some reassurance that all was not lost. He would be seeing Thabo Mbeki within a few weeks, and would confirm my continuing commitment to the concept.

He confessed that it seemed quite extraordinary that the Swiss Foreign Minister could have raised the matter with the State President in the manner described. If so, P W's explosion was entirely predictable – particularly with Pik Botha listening in. We agreed that I would now need to report to the Swiss, but that the first priority should be to meet with Niel Barnard. It remained to be seen what might come of such meeting. It was true, said Van Zyl, that Barnard had a 'direct line' to the President, and that he was a very influential figure. 'But don't forget, he's also a player,' he warned. 'He's got his own agenda, and ambitions.' He wondered whether Barnard had known about the initiative.

Concerning Stoffel, he said: 'The man is finished. He'll be seen to have bungled. P W doesn't forgive fools.' One of the things that had always troubled him, was how much Stoffel was reporting to the State President. One might never know the answer to that. 'This is the big game,' he reminded me. 'There are a number of would-be players – and Niel Barnard is only one of them. You'd better watch your back!'

With little over a week to go before election day, the situation posed huge risks for the National Party – and for the State President. Already the succession was being openly debated, and there were signs of a looming leadership battle. Though Botha might believe he was immortal, said Van Zyl, there was an amazing climate of disloyalty developing. Pik Botha regarded himself as the front-runner, and was working hard to consolidate support. It had been reported in the media that he had let it be known at a cocktail party in Paris that he was being considered to take over Constitutional Affairs from Chris

Heunis. This had been promptly denied but rumours had persisted, and had not endeared two of the principal contenders for the leadership to one another. Van Zyl thought there was even the possibility of a further split in the Party, but he didn't see Stoffel as the catalyst. 'He's too small a player,' he judged.

There was something else he had wanted to talk to me about. Recently, he'd had 'a most extraordinary meeting' with Professor Willie Esterhuyse of Stellenbosh University. 'D'you know Willie?' he asked tentatively. It transpired that Willie had spoken to Van Zyl 'in the strictest confidence' about his own activities, and had told him that 'information had come his way' about another initiative involving a certain Richard Rosenthal. Willie had asked Van Zyl whether he knew me, and whether he knew anything about it? Van Zyl said he was rather taken aback, having been sworn to secrecy by me as well as by Willie! He replied along the lines that he knew me, but had only a vague idea of what he was referring to.

I explained to Van Zyl the circumstances in which this information had come Willie's way. He and Van Zyl had discussed the extraordinary coincidence of two parallel but similar initiatives being pursued by different parties, at the same time, with neither being aware of the other. This had led them to speculate whether P W Botha was playing a sly game, or whether perhaps he had been unaware of my initiative. Willie confirmed to Van Zyl that in his case, he was reporting directly to the State President. They concluded that it would be difficult for P W to deny the existence of either initiative! The possibility existed that Botha's Cabinet and close advisers were not in the picture.

When I got back to my hotel, I rang Willie and said I would like to meet him again, and we arranged a meeting a few days hence. I also tried to make contact with the Swiss State Secretary, but he was away until the following day. The Ambassador was also away, and I left messages.

The following day, Thursday 20 October, I became increasingly concerned that I had received no word back from Stoffel. I rang his office and left a number of messages, none of which were returned. I then decided that this simply could not be left in abeyance, and I decided to try to make direct contact with the enigmatic Dr Barnard. This was easier said than done. How did one telephone the country's principal spymaster? Referring to the local telephone directory, I discovered that the National Intelligence Service had a listed phone number, but no address! I left an urgent message for Dr Barnard to ring me.

By the following day I had still heard nothing from either Van der Merwe or Barnard. I was unable to explain to their respective telephonists what it was about, and so left further messages. Later in the day, Stoffel called back, very apologetic, still sounding like death itself. He said that unfortunately he had not yet been able to speak to Niel Barnard, but would keep trying. Like me, he had left several messages.

I then had a conversation with the Swiss Ambassador in Pretoria, and told him in broad outline of these developments. He seemed absolutely astonished. As yet, he had received no report of these matters from Berne, but would make contact with them immediately. The following day, Friday 21 October, he called again and confirmed the broad outline of my report. He didn't yet have details, but sincerely hoped the utterances of his Foreign Minister had not fatally wounded the project. 'He's a new Minister,' he pleaded, 'a Socialist, and by reputation, very outspoken.'

Late in the day, I received a phone call from Mr Brunner in Berne. He had received a brief report from the Ambassador regarding our discussion, and was equally distressed to hear of these developments. He had not been personally present when the conversation between the Foreign Minister and Mr Botha had occurred, but had learnt from someone else that there had been a brief private conversation, which had lasted no more than a few minutes. He said it had initially appeared as if the State President had not understood what Foreign Minister Felber was talking about. The parties should be assured that a matter of this nature would ordinarily be handled by professional diplomats like himself, and not by the Minister, who was a political appointee.

Mr Brunner confirmed that since we had last spoken, he had again met with the ANC representative in Europe, Johnny Makatini – in fact, just three days ago. He was well satisfied with their discussion, and as far as the ANC was concerned, 'It seems your initiative is certainly working.' He had concluded that there was acceptance in principle of the need for 'talks about talks', and that the ANC, for its part, was open to the possibility of an initial meeting in Switzerland, or elsewhere if preferred. He had learnt that Mr Makatini had been involved in the recent Harare talks, which had given rise to the possibility of some relaxation of the ban on South Africa's international sporting ties. Mr Makatini had pointed out that such conciliatory moves created problems not only for the South African Government, but also for the ANC. The Anti-Apartheid Movement, for example, was adamantly opposed to any relaxation or rapprochement, and felt strongly that the sports boycott had to be rigorously maintained. The ANC had to deal with such differences of opinion.

Mr Brunner believed that the South African Government should have ample evidence of Switzerland's sympathetic consideration of its problems, and of its wish to play a constructive role. They also had understanding for the complexity of the issues. During his separate discussions with the South

African State President and Foreign Minister, he had compared the situation with that of Russia prior to the Gorbachev era. They had also talked of the possibility of Nelson Mandela's release, comparing his situation with that of Sakharov, the imprisoned Soviet physicist. The State President had not seemed to dismiss the idea out of hand, but was not prepared to give any undertakings. Mr Brunner felt their discussions had gone off 'reasonably well'. He was sure they could not feel that he was 'anti-South African!'

Mr Brunner agreed that it was entirely appropriate that I now seek an urgent meeting with the State President to clarify the future of this initiative. He hoped the present problem would prove no more than a temporary obstacle, and that the initiative might go ahead, as it had begun to appear that it really had some potential. We agreed upon the need to review the situation again after next week's elections.

By Friday morning, I still had no word from Van der Merwe or Barnard. I left them further messages. I then travelled out to Stellenbosch for a lunch with Willie Esterhuyse, who was obviously discomforted by my having learnt of his discussion with Slabbert. He explained that he had deemed it necessary to verify my credibility and background. Unfortunately most confidants also have confidants. By way of mitigation, Willie said that he had also come to hear of my initiative through 'another source within the Intelligence Establishment'. He didn't identify this source. It was unclear to me whether Willie had already learnt about the events in Switzerland prior to our meeting. When I described what had occurred, he told me that he had also decided to abort his participation in an IDASA consultation due to take place in Munich the following weekend. On the other hand, he would still participate in another seminar arranged at a different venue, a few weeks hence.

Willie contrasted the way each of us had been working, and extolled the virtues of working within a group, rather than as an individual. He had been acting in consultation with an ad hoc group, which included Professor Sampie Terblanche, and W A de Klerk (brother of F W), 'all under the guise of attending seminars'. All the parties, including the ANC, understood that their real purpose in attending was the private discussions which took place simultaneously with but separately from the official sessions. There was still need for some areas of secrecy, for example he had not told the other members of his group of his conversations with the State President, 'although perhaps they could draw inferences'.

Willie felt that it was a pity that our respective initiatives could not be drawn together. He felt they should be co-ordinated to avoid duplication and confusion. It should not be too difficult to include me in his group. On the other hand, he wouldn't like to 'contaminate' my credibility by association – to which I responded that after the latest events, perhaps the reverse might also be a concern. He was obviously exercised by my linkage to the Swiss Government, and intimated that his own funding came from 'a non-Governmental source', which he preferred not to identify, save to state that it was 'an overseas company having only marginal links with South Africa'. He seemed greatly surprised that I should have invested my own money in this initiative.

After I had finished describing the events of the past week, Willie said he had always wondered whether Stoffel was operating in a vacuum, and whether he was reporting fully to the State President. It now appeared that his misgivings had been well founded. At the same time, he recognised that 'a certain momentum has been created', and he believed that nothing should be done to damage these possibilities. I assured him – as I had repeatedly assured Stoffel – that I would do nothing to jeopardise these prospects. I considered myself bound by an undertaking of confidentiality. He agreed that the untimely revelation of these initiatives carried momentous implications, just days before the elections. He was in a similar situation, in that he would be bound to 'take the rap', if his activities became known. The only beneficiaries of an exposé would be the Conservative Party, who opposed the principle of negotiations.

I asked his advice in the light of what had now occurred. He said Stoffel's suggestion of a meeting with Barnard was a good one. When I explained my difficulty in contacting him, Willie said this should be no problem, and he would be willing to assist me in arranging such a meeting. I thanked him, but said I would prefer to keep our activities entirely separate, and deal with the matter myself.

A weekend passed, with still no indication whether or when I might be able to meet the inscrutable Dr Barnard. On Monday 24 October, I left further messages. Stoffel called me back just before 5 p.m., and apologised profusely for the delays. He said that he had now got an appointment with Barnard for precisely this time, but 'it had to be deferred until lunch tomorrow'. He would revert to me immediately after they had discussed the matter.

Earlier in the day, Ambassador Quinche also called to ascertain what was happening, and to ask 'whether the negative reaction of the President was directed against the concept itself, or against Swiss involvement'. I said I knew no more than I had already told him, and was still trying to clarify the situation for myself, thus far to no avail.

The long-awaited local authority elections finally took place on Wednesday 26 October. Although the CP made gains in the Transvaal and Orange Free State, the much feared landslide to the Right failed to materialise. Instead, the really significant result was the substantial stayaway and refusal to participate of the black community. Whilst the Government – through its Minister of Information, Stoffel van der Merwe – trumpeted that there had been a 23 per cent poll, in fact only 1,5 million black South Africans were even registered as voters, making the nominal turnout a minuscule proportion of the estimated 26 million black South Africans living outside the homelands. Thus, an 11 per cent poll in Soweto really represented a mere 2,8 per cent of the adult population in that area. A motion rejecting the election results was passed in the General Assembly of the United Nations (146 - 0), Great Britain and the United States abstaining.

On the day following the elections, I again telephoned Van der Merwe's office. We spoke briefly, and he indicated that he had been completely absorbed by the election campaign, which had now mercifully come to an end. In fact, he said, he only had one hour's sleep the previous night. He was sorry that as a result, there had been a further delay in his meeting Niel Barnard, but he undertook to take steps to ensure that it now happened soon. I said it was essential that I clarify the situation, and that I needed to report to the ANC and the Swiss Government with the minimum of delay.

At approximately 12.30 p.m. I telephoned the N I S yet again, and asked to speak to Dr Barnard. As usual, the telephonist said he was not available, but she would give him a message. I pointed out that I had now left several messages, and I really needed to speak to him. The matter was urgent and important. She said a message to this effect would be passed on to him. 'If necessary' he would return my call.

To my enormous relief, some time during the afternoon of Thursday 27 October I finally heard from the N I S. It had taken ten days since my meeting with Van der Merwe, and seven days since the first urgent message I had left for Dr Barnard. However, the call was from someone who called himself 'Mike Kuhn'. He said Dr Barnard had asked him to contact me. He had 'in any event' been trying to locate my telephone number! Admittedly, it was unlisted, but it seemed a little lame that the National Intelligence Service, with its access to 'all the king's horses and all the king's men', could not have dealt with so trivial an obstacle.

Mike Kuhn said that Dr Barnard wished him to meet me, and he therefore proposed coming to Cape Town for that purpose. The following day, Friday 28 October, he called again to confirm that he was booked on flight SA 315, departing Johannesburg on Monday 31 October, and would arrive in Cape Town at 12.50 p.m. We agreed to meet opposite the Avis Car Hire counter. 'How will I recognise you?' I asked. He replied that he was 'approximately 1,78 metres long'. I confessed to being a little longer – and bald to boot. He said he was *not* bald!

20

The N I S and a hotel bedroom

Who was this man who called himself 'Mike Kuhn', and reminded me that it would be a criminal offence to divulge his real identity. Apart from his 'length', the only thing I knew about him was his clandestine profession – he was a professional spy. After we had talked for some four hours, I had learnt only three other things about him – that he was married; had been born in Bloemfontein; and was the father of two children – of whom one, like my son Jonathan, was about to write Matric.

I confess to having felt more than a little nervous meeting him – not entirely without good cause. Under Niel Barnard's direction the N I S had gained a formidable reputation for efficiency and ruthlessness. Although its ostensible function was no more than information-gathering, in fact it played a Machiavellian role in the Government of P W Botha, largely unseen and choosing to be feared rather than loved. Through its hegemony over the State Security Council, and the National Security Management System, it was able to exercise a pervasive influence over decisions at all levels of government. The particular focus at this time was to neutralise 'the enemy' – principally, the ANC – but it also focused its sometimes lethal attention upon perceived fellow-travellers, both inside and outside the country. It had a licence to operate without legal accountability, and to engage in all manner of what were euphemistically termed 'dirty tricks'. It saw itself as promoting lofty State purposes, and made no apology for serving the interests of the State President and the National Party.

For a number of reasons, I believed myself to be particularly vulnerable at this time. This arose from the fact that I was not only 'consorting with the enemy', but was the only first-hand witness to flagrant political duplicity, concerning the issue of negotiations with the ANC. Those who had the temerity to advocate dialogue and negotiations were being subjected to a torrent of calumny and abuse; yet Willie Esterhuyse and I were authorised to explore that very option. This deception had continued throughout the recent election campaign, with the connivance at least of the State President. Was it not a function of the N I S to protect the State President's credibility?

Despite these daunting premonitions, 'Mike Kuhn' came off the midday plane looking reassuringly ordinary, in fact almost indistinguishable from scores of other peripatetic businessmen hustling through the airport, bearing their trademark toolbox, the sleek brown briefcase. His manner was friendly and direct, and we were immediately on first-name terms. He apologised that Dr Barnard had been unable to come personally, but assured me that he would be reporting directly to him. We went to a nearby restaurant in Pinelands, where I had reserved a table – in the farthest corner. He told me that he was booked to return to Pretoria on a flight departing at 5 p.m. that same afternoon. With limited time, we got down to business immediately.

Despite the omniscience of the N I S, we colluded in the rather quaint pretence that Mike Kuhn knew nothing about me, so I gave him an account of who I was, of what I had been doing, and of what had led me to launch this initiative. I described the sequence of events, commencing with my letter to the President, and culminating in Botha's démarche with the Swiss Foreign Minister. As the story unfolded, and despite his professional inscrutability, Mike Kuhn began to look increasingly astonished at the ramifications of what I was describing. Eyeing his brown briefcase, I assumed I was being recorded and took care to give him as full and accurate an account as possible.

What seemed particularly to amaze him was the degree of secrecy that I had been able to preserve, and – perhaps to his embarrassment and/or admiration – the extent to which this had all occurred without the participation or knowledge of the N I S, whose task it was to know everything about everyone involved with such matters. After lunch we visited my unmarked office-flat in Higgovale, from which I had discreetly operated for some time, and he seemed even more amazed. 'When you come to Pretoria,' he said, 'I'd like you to come and give my people a lecture on how to conduct a clandestine operation!' I didn't altogether appreciate this intended compliment. However, one thing would now be certain, whatever the position in the past – in the future, I would not be unobserved. Henceforth I would mistrust the sanctity of my mailbox, telephone, office, car, and even on occasion, my home ... and some very strange things did happen.

I told Mike Kuhn that my greatest concern at this particular juncture was to ensure that the State President was made fully aware of the facts, in order that a valuable, possibly a unique, opportunity should not be lost. I needed to be assured that the President appreciated the consequences of summarily aborting the initiative. I drew the analogy of an 'illegitimate' child – in whatever circumstances it had been conceived, the initiative was now a reality that had to be reckoned with.

Of particular interest to Mike Kuhn was of course the personal involvement of the State President, and the link to the Swiss Government. He seemed immediately to appreciate the combustible potential of this information, though he was careful to withhold his own views and opinions. He gave the impression of a clinician systematically gathering facts, to be subsequently regurgitated for the benefit of Niel Barnard. From time to time, he would repeat something I had said, ensuring that he had understood correctly – or perhaps, that it had been heard (and recorded?). Clearly, he grasped the sensitivity of the matter, and the danger it now posed, if maladroitly handled. He said he would report immediately to Dr Barnard, who would report to the President.

I pointed out that I could only presume the terms of the original mandate the State President had given Dr van der Merwe, and the degree to which he had been kept abreast of developments. Whatever the truth, the initiative could not be simply wished away. There was now an opportunity, and the issues were far too important to be placed in jeopardy by any possible indiscretion or impropriety on the part of the Swiss Foreign Minister. If Mr Botha no longer had confidence in Van der Merwe, I needed access to Mr Botha himself, or to someone who enjoyed his confidence. Perhaps Dr Barnard was such a person?

Mike Kuhn asked many seemingly innocuous questions, but one in particular, which made my thinning hair stand on end. He asked abruptly, 'Are you a Jew?' I wondered what on earth that had to do with the matter we were discussing.

Another topic he raised was whether there could be potential in the idea of an 'internal dialogue'. I said that if this was seen as a substitute for top-level leader-to-leader negotiations, or as a means of exploiting supposed differences between the internal and external wings of the ANC, it would not only fail but probably discredit the entire process. I made it clear that I was unavailable to assist in any such alternative strategy.

Towards the end of our lunch, Mike Kuhn asked whether I would be willing to prepare a written report describing the initiative – including copies of letters and documents – so that he could be sure the matter was accurately placed before the 'political people', who would make the decisions. He contrasted the role of the N I S in gathering and interpreting information with that of the politicians who took decisions, and also with that of the security forces which undertook actions, and had what he described as a 'rather negative role'.

At some stage he said he would like to be able to talk about my impressions of particular individuals I had met in the ANC. I told him bluntly that I was not available as a source of intelligence information. My role was that of an uncompromised intermediary, acting with the full knowledge and consent of both parties. I would not abuse that trust. He said he understood my position.

Mike Kuhn hoped that 'something positive' might yet come of my initiative, and agreed that it was important that it be fully and accurately reported to the President. I said my further involvement should not depend upon the political future of Stoffel van der Merwe. He appeared to have fallen from grace with the President, which meant that my 'channel' was no longer functioning. Did he have any suggestions? He rather skilfully evaded this question, and suggested that when I next saw Dr van der Merwe – and he was in favour of my continuing to see him – I should discuss this problem.

When it came to the mundane detail of paying for lunch, Mike Kuhn made a spirited attempt to appropriate the bill. I declined his munificence, despite his vain protest, 'Surely this is an opportunity for you to get back some of what you've spent?' I said my 'virginity' was too precious to be compromised at this stage.

I returned him to the airport at about 4.30 p.m. He confirmed that the matter would be dealt with most urgently, and that I might expect to hear from him again within the week.

I spent the ensuing days preparing a detailed written report, which I decided to address directly to the State President. There were several reasons – one of which was to reaffirm that my actions had resulted from Mr Botha's personal response to my original offer, and further to ensure the accuracy of any report he might receive – and to try to prevent any possible 'gloss' by the N I S, who were not disinterested rapporteurs, and had their own ambitions as Slabbert had warned.

After two days of silence, I telephoned Kuhn and Van der Merwe again. Both were 'out', and I left messages, which they returned the following day. Mike Kuhn said he had reported fully on our discussion, and 'they' were now anxious to meet again soon and resume our discussion. I confirmed that a formal Report as had been suggested by him was now ready for the State President, and he proposed that we meet the next day, Friday 4 November – in Cape Town or Pretoria, as I preferred.

After deciding that Pretoria would be the better venue, Mike Kuhn said he would make the necessary bookings, and take care of my costs. Once again I declined his offer, reminding him that it was an important principle that I looked after my own costs. He was quite insistent, arguing that coming to Pretoria saved them the costs of travelling in the opposite direction. However, he lost this debate.

'We'll meet you at Jan Smuts airport,' he volunteered, but once again I refused, saying that I would prefer to hire my own car. 'Where are your offices?' I asked, with pristine innocence. 'I think we'll meet at the Holiday

Inn,' he replied. This seemed a curious arrangement, and I said, 'Surely it would be easier if I come straight to your offices?' But he wasn't about to tell me where 'they' had their offices. 'We'll probably go to a flat or somewhere to have our discussion,' he said. I was mystified. We agreed to meet in the foyer of the Arcadia Holiday Inn, Pretoria, at 1 p.m.

We spoke again later in the day, and I confirmed my air bookings. During the afternoon I had two further calls from Mike Kuhn – he wished to confirm yet again the time and venue of our meeting; and then, he wished to confirm that it would be all right if he was accompanied by one of his colleagues? For no particular reason, I began to feel uneasy. I decided that a few basic precautions were appropriate, and made an appointment with the Swiss Ambassador.

I also decided it was time I spoke with Stoffel again to tell him what was happening. His personal assistant Riaan Smit returned my call at 4 p.m. to say that his Minister would not be available for a meeting owing to 'commitments in his constituency'. He suggested we meet the following week. This didn't seem good enough, and I asked to be transferred to the Minister. When Stoffel came on the line he sounded exceedingly sombre. I told him that as a result of his suggestion, I had sought a meeting with Niel Barnard, but had thus far succeeded only in meeting one of his officials. I had been requested to prepare a written Memorandum, and I planned to hand this over in Pretoria tomorrow. As it obviously concerned him, I would have preferred to have his comment on the draft, but there didn't seem to be time. He would very much like to see the document, and asked that I leave a copy with his secretary, Caro Hoon. 'Please make sure you put it in a double-sealed envelope,' he advised. He would explain to her that it should be locked in his overnight safe. I asked how he was feeling, to which he replied, 'All right, I suppose – in the circumstances.'

Next I spoke to Ambassador Quinche, explaining that I would be in Pretoria the following day, and would very much like to see him, if possible during the course of the morning. 'If I don't arrive,' I said, 'please make a few enquiries what happened to me.' He laughed and said, 'I hope that won't be necessary.'

Upon arrival in Pretoria, I proceeded straight to the Embassy, convinced that I was being followed. Indeed, I had been uncomfortable about the person sitting next to me on the plane, who seemed unduly interested in what I was reading. The Ambassador received me immediately. We had not met for five weeks, and he was concerned to be briefed on the latest developments. He had not yet been advised of my latest telephone discussions with Mr Brunner in Berne. He wished to know whether I had succeeded in arranging a meeting with the State President? I explained that Stoffel van der Merwe was no longer persona grata in the President's office, and that I was therefore attempting to secure a meeting with the President, through Dr Niel Barnard of the N I S. This was in fact the reason I was now in Pretoria. I told the Ambassador that I had been requested to prepare a Memorandum describing the initiative, and this document would be handed over at our meeting. I proposed he should also have a copy for his government. The document should be treated extremely carefully as it contained sensitive information. It was addressed to the State President, and I would be delivering a copy to him only later in the day, to motivate my request for a meeting.

This led to a further discussion about the encounter between his Foreign Minister and the President. He emphasised that in their view the meeting had seemed to go off reasonably well. They were therefore surprised to learn of the President's adverse reaction. I pointed out the obvious – that Botha was naturally sensitive about what he might see as 'foreign interference in our domestic affairs'. His government would resist and resent any attempt to manipulate the handling of such a sensitive matter. This had been recognised and discussed between us right at the outset. It was fundamental that the Swiss should not attempt to control the process. They were entitled to information, but this did not imply a right to confront the President.

Ambassador Quinche seemed shocked to hear of Dr van der Merwe's suggestion that I should inform his government and the ANC that the initiative had been halted on the grounds of what he termed 'Swiss meddling'. He had no information to corroborate this description of the event. The Ambassador wondered whether the South African Government realised that the manner in which they were handling this matter could have an effect upon its relationship with Switzerland. He believed his country was important to the South African Government, not only because of its banking arrangements, but also because thus far Switzerland had stood aside from trade and financial sanctions. He sincerely hoped the present problems would be resolved, and some benefit might emerge.

According to reports he had received, it had appeared initially that neither South Africa's President nor its Foreign Minister had understood what Minister Felber was talking about. This had caused his colleagues to wonder whether this was fact or fiction. I replied that I had no way of knowing, but it would be almost unbelievable if the State President had been completely ignorant of the matter. I recalled Van der Merwe's warning that their knowledge and support might be denied, if this became necessary. Realising that my own credibility was also likely to be on the line, I asked once again, whether at his separate meetings with Minister van der Merwe, he had obtained a clear and unambiguous assurance that the Government approved the initiative and the principle of Swiss financing. 'Yes,' he replied.

Before I left, I told Ambassador Quinche that in meeting with 'the little grey men from the N I S', I felt vulnerable, having regard to the contents of the documents I was about to deliver, and their import. I hoped I was not being melodramatic, but again asked that if anything untoward happened, would he please make enquiries. I also confirmed our earlier arrangement that Hilary should contact him 'if a problem arose'. He said he would do what he could in the circumstances.

I then made my way to the Holiday Inn, arriving half an hour earlier than arranged. It was 12.30 p.m., and I sat down at a coffee table in the first-floor foyer facing the Reception desk, and pretended to be calm and preoccupied. At precisely 1 p.m. the lift doors opened, and out came Mike Kuhn. He led the way back to the lift, and then pressed the UP rather than the DOWN button. I pointed out his error. He smiled, and said there didn't seem any point going elsewhere, so they'd booked a room in the hotel where we could have our meeting!

I was absolutely shocked. Pretoria was home base for the N I S. However, instead of using their own offices and meeting-places, they had incurred the trouble and expense of reserving a hotel bedroom for our meeting! It seemed incredible. Then a terrifying thought occurred to me. In most spy novels I had ever read, the 'hit' was made in a hotel bedroom, the culprits were never traced, and it was rumoured that 'the room had been booked under an assumed name for purposes of a sexual liaison'.

My heart was thumping as I followed Mike Kuhn down the sixth-floor corridor. I had a terrible feeling that I might be walking straight into a trap. Noting my discomfort, he said they had asked for a suite, but there had only been a single bedroom available. 'I hope you don't mind?' he added. He said it was a bit cramped, but they'd managed to get an extra chair from Room Service, and we shouldn't be too uncomfortable. Then he stopped and knocked at a door, and it was immediately opened by an extremely forbidding-looking character. My heart stopped.

'Let me introduce you to my colleague, Koos Kruger,' he said.

We shook hands, and I looked around. There was a tight cluster of chairs awkwardly placed around a small coffee table next to the window. For the rest, it looked no different from any of the rooms I had occupied in this hotel over the years. Koos Kruger suggested I sit in the middle. I guessed that was where the camera was focused. For a manic instant, I thought I would be contra-suggestible, and sit on one of the other chairs, but it was no time to be devious. Then I had a brain-wave.

'If you will forgive me, I have to make a couple of phone calls,' I said. My purpose was to let someone know where I was, and to let Messrs Kruger and Kuhn know that they should take good care. So I proceeded firstly to telephone the State President's office and said that I was at the Holiday Inn, and had a letter to deliver to the President. I asked when their office would be closing that afternoon? (The President was apparently in Durban, and would be returning later in the day.) Then I telephoned Dr van der Merwe's office and told his secretary, Caro Hoon, that I was at the Holiday Inn, with a letter for Dr van der Merwe, which I would be delivering during the course of the afternoon. She promised to wait until it arrived. Then I told Kuhn and Kruger that I had just come from the Swiss Ambassador, and 'of course' had mentioned that we would be meeting here at the Holiday Inn. I hoped that was in order?

Sandwiches and coffee were then ordered, and we sat down, a *ménage-à-trois*. Mike Kuhn thanked me for coming to Pretoria. He said they really wanted to do something about my costs. I shook my head. They wanted to know how much I had spent and was I out of pocket? I said it really wasn't relevant. Most of my expenses had been covered by the Swiss, and I was happy to carry any balance. I was determined to remain financially independent of the parties. They continued to argue about this, asking what difference it would make. The issue seemed unduly important to them. I had saved them not one but two airfares, they said. The Government would like to see that I was not financially prejudiced. I assured them this was the least of my worries. Repeatedly they came back to the subject. Eventually, Koos Kruger said if I didn't want to accept cash, he might send me 'a small gift'. He said I couldn't stop him giving me a present of a box of whisky, for example. I replied that there was really no point, because I would simply return it. Hoping to bring this digression to an end, I said 'as a special concession' I would allow them to pay for the sandwiches laid out before us. It must therefore be acknowledged that I did receive from the N I S several lousy sandwiches and a pot of coffee.

Coming to what I assumed to have been the purpose of our meeting, I confirmed that my Memorandum was available and I was ready to hand them a copy. I had also arranged for Dr van der Merwe to receive a copy, as this seemed appropriate. Moreover, as the purpose was to motivate for my meeting the State President, I would be delivering him a separate copy later in the day. They agreed this was all very proper.

In describing my role, I said that one was accustomed, as a lawyer, to put aside personal opinions and preferences, and to adopt an attitude of what I termed 'professional schizophrenia'. This phrase appealed to Koos Kruger, who interposed, 'That's why lawyers make such good agents!' I blanched. 'I don't suppose either of you are lawyers?' I enquired. They smiled wanly. Mr Kruger indicated that he'd done some legal studies whilst in the Police, before he was seconded to the N I S. *En passant*, and for good measure, I reminded them that I was not to be used as one of their sources or agents. Koos Kruger smiled mischievously. 'Why not?' he asked. Well, I'm just a simple fellow,' I said, 'and not very good at telling lies.' 'No problem,' said Koos, 'I'd be happy to teach you!' I was sure he would. We all laughed – in a manner of speaking.

Mike Kuhn confirmed that following our earlier meeting, he had reported fully to Dr Barnard, who had then had a meeting with Dr Van der Merwe. They imagined that certain decisions would be taken by the 'political people', once their report was completed. I mentioned that Dr van der Merwe was sounding very stressed, and asked facetiously, 'Is Stoffel nog in die stof?' ('Is Stoffel still in the dog-box?') 'Not necessarily,' was the reply.

I said I was anxious to get back to the ANC as soon as possible, and would obviously tell them of my having had these meetings with the N I S. They prevaricated, and asked why this would be necessary. I replied that the crux of my role was complete openness with both parties, and that if I did not tell them this, I would be in breach of trust. That was the only basis on which I could continue. They argued that if I succeeded in meeting the State President, then their meeting with me would have become 'insignificant'.

We proceeded to discuss the general ambit of the document I was handing them, and various aspects of the initiative. I stressed once again the possible consequences of 'the door being slammed'. The process had created a valuable opportunity, and this should not be wasted, I argued. But time was a critical factor, and I was bound to report to the ANC soon. They asked about the various persons I had met in Lusaka, and particularly whether Oliver Tambo had been involved. When I mentioned the name of Anthony Mongalo, Mr Kruger commented that he was a personal assistant to Mr Tambo, which indicated that he must be involved. They were also keen to know more about the meetings between the Swiss and Mr Makatini.

They sought my views about how the process might be developed, and I referred them to the reply given in the document itself – namely, that I was reluctant to put myself in the position of a protagonist or antagonist of any particular method or strategy. A great deal had to be done in devising a suitable methodology, if there was to be a real prospect of success.

At 3.30 p.m. our meeting came to an end. I bade them farewell, with some considerable relief, and left them with an account to settle for sandwiches, coffee, and a hotel bedroom. Mike Kuhn offered to accompany me to the Reception desk, where we borrowed some glue and sealed two large envelopes, which I then delivered to the State President and Dr van der Merwe.

21

Waiting upon the President

I returned to Johannesburg with a sense of relief at having finally communicated a full and detailed description of the initiative direct to the State President.

The covering letter which I had delivered to the Union Buildings was marked 'Personal & Confidential', and it read:

Dear Mr President

AN INDEPENDENT NEGOTIATION INITIATIVE: RICHARD ROSENTHAL

Pursuant to recent discussions which I have had with the Minister of Information, Dr Stoffel van der Merwe, and Senior Officers of the National Intelligence Service, I have prepared at their request, a Memorandum with annexures recording the origin and development of a Negotiation Initiative with which I have been concerned for more than a year, and which commenced with a letter addressed to you on 23rd September 1987.

In view of the extreme sensitivity and importance of these matters, I have deemed it appropriate to forward you personally a copy of this Memo-randum, which has this day been delivered to the National Intelligence Service and Dr S. van der Merwe, in which I have also requested the privilege of a personal interview with you in order to make personal representations to you concerning the possible implications of any future course of action.

Suffice it to say that I am tremendously concerned to preserve the confidentiality of the initiative and the strategic opportunity which I believe may presently exist. I realise that it is also of the greatest importance to ensure, as I specifically proposed in my original letter to you, that any steps taken have your personal concurrence.

In the circumstances I would greatly value the opportunity to consult with you at your very earliest convenience regarding the situation which presently subsists.

Yours sincerely
Richard Rosenthal

Accompanying this letter was a document with Annexures entitled 'Background Documentation Concerning an Independent Negotiation Initiative', which comprised a 63-page bundle. In an introductory section it explained its purpose as being to provide 'a record of the origin and development of an independent negotiation initiative ... with the intention of facilitating the commencement of a substantive negotiation process ...' The initiative itself was explained in these terms:

> The fundamental concept underlying the initiative is the belief that a delicately-managed and highly discreet process of unofficial contacts between representatives of the Government and certain radical political groupings, including the African National Congress, may be able to contribute by way of an exploratory process, to the fulfilment of certain preconditions essential to the commencement of a successful negotiation process.
>
> Accordingly, the essential character of the initiative is that it should be undertaken:
>
> 1 with the full knowledge and consent – at least implied – of the principal constituent parties;
>
> 2 by South Africans acting independently of foreign manipulation or interference;
>
> 3 financed by a mutually-acceptable and disinterested third party;
>
> 4 on a basis of absolute confidentiality, and initial 'deniability';
>
> 5 without preconditions or prescriptive assumptions concerning the nature of the process or the ultimate 'product' thereof.

The document recorded the progression of events, including:

• Twelve successive meetings with Dr van der Merwe over the preceding year;

• The reciprocal approvals, by Dr van der Merwe on behalf of the South African Government on 7 April 1988, and by Mr Thabo Mbeki on behalf of the African National Congress on 14 July 1988, in respect of:

1 the principle of a negotiation initiative;

2 the principle of myself as an intermediary;

3 the principle of funding by the Swiss Government.

• The approach to the Swiss Government, and its eventual agreement to underwrite the costs of the initiative – 'with the knowledge and approval of both Dr van der Merwe and the representatives of the African National Congress';

• The proposal by the Swiss to 'host' an initial meeting during Dr van der Merwe's recent visit to Switzerland;

• The ANC's requirement of 'some initial indication of seriousness of intent' by the South African Government;

• Dr van der Merwe's proposal regarding the delivery of a document outlining the Government's goals and parameters in future negotiations;

• Dr van der Merwe's request that the initiative be abruptly terminated, following the State President's meeting with the Swiss Foreign Minister.

The Report concluded:

In summary, it will be apparent that over a period of twelve months since the despatch of Mr Rosenthal's original communication to the State President (23rd September 1987), significant steps have been taken to create an opportunity for initiating some limited exchange of ideas between the South African Government and the African National Congress.

From the outset, the process has been undertaken on a base of absolute confidentiality – a requirement of both parties. Although the element of 'deniability' has been expressly preserved – and still exists – there can be no doubt that an expectation has been raised and a certain momentum established.

Although it would be theoretically possible at this stage or at any later time to terminate or 'disown' the process, the opportunity cost of closing the door must be carefully weighed, as it would unquestionably have profound implications upon a number of important issues, including:

1 It would tend to confirm scepticism and discredit any similar overtures in the future.

2 It would tend to undermine the rationale and status of those who favour a negotiated approach, to the advantage of 'hawks' on either side who doubt the relevance of a negotiation process, and favour what one side terms 'the armed struggle' and what the other terms 'a military or managed security response'.

3 It could affect future leadership choices, once again tending to reinforce the succession claims of the 'hardliners' to the detriment of the 'conciliators'!

4 It could have international ramifications, by signalling a negative message with reference to a negotiation process, and thereby detrimentally affecting South Africa's relationship not only with Switzerland (which is directly involved with this initiative), but also conceivably with other countries such as Britain, the United States, West Germany and Japan, who are obviously anxious to encourage the commencement of a negotiation process and who could view this development as retrogressive.

In the circumstances, whatever deficiencies of communication may have been identified during the initial stages of the process, I believe it is of the utmost importance that the initiative be not summarily terminated; but rather that very serious consideration be given to advancing the process under appropriate conditions (including secrecy and 'deniability'), in order that the maximum possible advantage be gained from the existence of this 'window of opportunity'.

It is appreciated that the most meticulous and delicate handling will be necessary in respect of any further steps, and it is of equal importance that not too much time or momentum be lost in the process of review and consideration.

I have been invited to suggest ideas and possible future scenarios, and it would be less than frank to acknowledge that I do have some thoughts in this regard. However, my attitude to this request has been clearly stated in my letter to Dr S. van der Merwe of 15th March 1988, as follows:

'With reference to your suggestion that I commit to paper some "ideas" as to future steps, I am hesitant to accede to such request at this stage, as it seems on reflection to be inappropriate and even presumptuous for me to suggest objectives or a particular modus operandi. If I can be helpful then it would seem to me that my role is likely to be that of an intermediary and whilst I am certainly willing to share my thoughts in the matter, perhaps it is preferable that I withhold personal opinions in order that I can avoid becoming perceived as either the proponent or the opponent of any particular formula.

'Suffice it to say that I am available to play any role of integrity in the evolution of a constructive process directed to the achievement of a negotiated future for our country.

'To this end, and with the greatest respect, I request the privilege of a personal meeting with the State President, and/ or with such other person/s as may be deputed by him for this purpose.'

It was the end of a tumultuous day, and I needed to talk to a friend. It was already late on a Friday afternoon, and most people would have made their arrangements for the evening. However, the prospect of spending the evening alone at the Sunnyside Park Hotel was mortifying, and I imposed again on the long-suffering Arthur Chaskalson. I reached him as he was about to leave his office at the LRC. Stoically, he agreed to defer their family gathering so that we could spend time together.

Arthur listened to my rather breathless account of the day's events, and agreed that the situation held some peril for me. I was somewhat shaken by his comment: 'This could become even bigger than the Information scandal!'

He felt one needed to be prepared for various possible contingencies, and suggested that I try to anticipate my response to at least three scenarios: first, the President agreeing to meet me; second, the President refusing to meet me; and third, the President deciding to disown the process and to deny all knowledge of it. We discussed each in turn, and how best to respond.

My immediate fear was that – under the guise of the Emergency Regulations – it might be decided to detain me, as had been the fate of many others at this time, including at least two of my contacts, Advocate Dullah Omar and editor Rashied Seria. It would have been a simple way of removing any threat I might pose. Arthur asked what he should do in such an event, and we talked about the possibility of a Supreme Court application. I decided to duplicate various notes and memos, and to leave Hilary with an Affidavit and a Power of Attorney 'just in case'. We also agreed that the Swiss Embassy would be an ideal repository for copies of my documents. If review proceedings were instituted, the basis would have to be an abuse of a quasi-judicial discretion for a political purpose. Arthur recommended that I discuss these possibilities with Hilary 'not to create unnecessary panic', but so that she would know what to do, and where to find my papers.

I began to think of all sorts of ways in which they might seek to discredit me. The N I S was adept at manufacturing information. One presumed that the security establishment would be loyal to the State President, but within the ranks of the Police and the Military there was strong support for the Conservative Party. I thought about my meeting with two of their agents at the Holiday Inn; and about my application to emigrate to Canada. Arthur sought to reassure me that victimisation was most unlikely, particularly in the light of the Swiss involvement. In the last resort, the Swiss were my best protection. The Government would realise that any arbitrary attempt at silencing me could have other consequences. The fact remained that the initiative held some menace, not only for Stoffel van der Merwe but also for the State President and the National Party.

We speculated whether these events could have had any bearing upon the precipitate sidelining of two senior officials in the Department of Constitutional Development – Chief Director of Constitutional Planning, Dr Fanie Cloete, and Chief Departmental negotiator, Mr Cobus Jordaan. It had been reported that they had visited Lusaka, held talks with the ANC, and had since been placed on compulsory leave, with the withdrawal of their security clearances. Heunis's involvement in this exploit was unclear. The Afrikaans newspaper *Rapport* referred to these punitive steps as having originated 'on high', which was regarded as code for the State President. The *Cape Times* referred to 'the two key negotiators having been knifed', and predicted: 'Future talks between the government and blacks in South Africa could now be burdened by the impression that they are controlled or at least sanctioned by the security bosses.'

It had also been reported by the political correspondent to the *Argus* newspapers, that 'The Government is considering a ban on publicity flowing from contacts between South Africans and the ANC – along the lines of similar legislation introduced in Britain to starve the IRA of publicity.' I had wondered whether a device of this nature might be employed as a means of preventing my initiative being reported in the media. The article went further to speculate that: 'Government sources have also indicated that consideration is being given to legislating against contacts with the ANC.' It sounded ominous.

I sought Arthur's view as to my responsibility in relation to the hiatus in communications with Lusaka. He pointed out that the ANC might in fact be less concerned than I imagined. In recent days, there had been renewed speculation about the imminent release of Nelson Mandela, and a suggestion that this might be timed to coincide with the impending visit of Britain's Foreign Secretary, Linda Chalker. Various Embassies had expected the release to occur on November 14, but despite denials from the Mandela family and attorney Ismail Ayob, it was now believed the most likely date would be early December. In the circumstances, Arthur felt that ironically the ANC might interpret a last-minute deferral of my visit to Lusaka 'in the light of important developments', as possibly a positive signal!

Back in Cape Town, I had little choice but to await the President's reply. Weeks passed, and I busied myself with office minutiae, and continued 'tending my roses', both literally and metaphorically. Meanwhile it was reported from Zurich that Foreign Minister René Felber, 'in a highly unusual move', had requested Swiss banks to furnish their Foreign Office with general information regarding their financial relationship with the South African Government. He had apparently made it clear that he believed it would be prudent for banks to initiate some dialogue with South Africa's black politicians, in the expectation of a future black government.

On 16 November I also met Van Zyl again. He had just returned from a further IDASA-sponsored event, at Leverkusen near Keulen in West Germany, convened under the auspices of the Friedrich-Naumann Foundation. Van Zyl said that these latest discussions had been greatly enriched by the presence of a delegation from the Soviet Union, and their interactions with some of the ANC delegates, including Joe Slovo and Thabo Mbeki. There had been a growing realisation that the dramatic changes in the Soviet Union held particular relevance to the South African situation. Already it had become apparent that progress in the Angola peace talks was in large measure due to the positive influence of the Soviet Union upon its Cuban surrogates. Perestroika held out certain perils for the ANC, which could no longer assume unqualified support from the Soviet Union. Increasingly, Russia was becoming concerned about its economic interests, rather than ideological ambitions. This might result in a reluctance to support regional conflicts and liberation movements. In the long term, this could favour a negotiation process in South Africa.

Die Burger, which could generally be relied upon to reflect Nationalist thinking, berated the IDASA event as: 'Another futile discussion with the ANC'. 'What naiveté', it adjudged Alex Boraine's view that the meeting had contributed to the process of creating a climate conducive to a new democracy in South Africa. The *Argus* also tended to trivialise the event by reporting as newsworthy that Joe Slovo, SA Communist Party leader, had been found by the delegates to be not 'some kind of ogre' as generally expected, but, 'pragmatic, sensible, and ... even charming'. It left me pondering the meaning of 'naiveté', the term used by rugby luminary, Professor Fritz Eloff to describe attempts by the SA Rugby Board to negotiate its way out of international isolation.

Van Zyl confirmed that whilst in Europe he had spoken to Thabo Mbeki about the problems besetting my initiative. He had not detailed the nature of these problems, save to indicate that the status of 'my Government contact' was in issue. He had given Mbeki the assurance that, despite these present difficulties, I remained committed to the initiative, and would be in contact again as soon as this seemed appropriate. Van Zyl gained the impression that the ANC regarded what I had been doing as potentially useful, and he concluded that the initiative could still have a future if the present difficulties were resolved. He speculated that there might even be some beneficial outcome, particularly if I ceased to be restricted to Stoffel as my sole Government contact. This had always seemed to him its principal vulnerability.

Political fortunes waxed and waned. At this stage, Stoffel seemed to have suffered a serious setback, but one couldn't discount the possibility that his star might rise again. P W's loves and hates were fickle. The political standing of some Ministers seemed to ebb and flow like the tide. After a period of relegation, F W de Klerk seemed once again to be in the ascendant, whereas Pik Botha and Chris Heunis were currently out of favour. Van Zyl said he doubted there was reason to fear that my conveying a negative message could provoke a violent response from the ANC. It was involved in this struggle over 'the long haul'. One adverse event was unlikely to have a dramatic impact. However, it was essential that I continued to play open cards with both sides, and he urged that I should contact Thabo Mbeki before too long. It was my responsibility to convey these events and communications as they occurred, he said, adding, 'To some extent you have them over a barrel.' He was concerned that the Government might hold out the promise of future prospects, whilst doing little or nothing. I assured him that neither I nor the Swiss were willing to be consciously manipulated in this manner.

Van Zyl drew my attention to a document issued recently by the ANC regarding its own view of negotiations, in which it committed itself to 'no secret negotiations'. (This was highlighted in black type.) We talked about how the ANC might distinguish these exploratory contacts from actual negotiations. No doubt it could argue that these discussions were no more than 'talks about talks'. Van Zyl said that, despite the Government's bluster and threats, there was a growing stream of people wishing to talk to the ANC, including many prominent Afrikaners. The procession of sporting bodies to Lusaka continued unabated, the latest being the South African Soccer Federation, and a politically improbable organisation known as the Federation of SA Amateur Body Builders! The fact was, said Van Zyl, that the Government had lost control over this issue, and its advice was being widely disregarded.

Van Zyl said he had asked Mbeki's views whether Willie Esterhuyse and I should consider 'merging' our activities? He had pointed to the anomaly of two similar co-existent initiatives, and the resultant possibility of confusion. Their discussion had been inconclusive, but Van Zyl urged that I maintain contact with Willie, and let him know about these developments.

In fact, I was to meet Willie at his home in Stellenbosch one Sunday evening shortly thereafter. We spent a few hours reviewing the status of our respective activities. Willie confessed that he too had been at a loss to understand the present situation. He said that during recent weeks he had been unable to gain access to the State President, and wondered whether this had any significance. In the past, he had been given ready access. Perhaps, he speculated, P W wished to keep himself at a distance from the polemic surrounding the issue of negotiations – and hence his use of surrogates like ourselves. He also referred to the necessity to preserve presidential 'deniability'.

Willie said he expected little progress in the immediate future. The President might make some announcements in his New Year's message, including perhaps something about the release of Nelson Mandela, and a long-term intention to initiate 'the National Indaba'. However, he didn't anticipate the release of Mandela until at least February/March, although there might be some interim arrangement involving his living in a warder's house within the prison compound. (Once again, Willie's prophetic instincts or privileged sources proved remarkably accurate.)

Willie obviously had contacts and sources of information that were inaccessible to me. Sometimes I gained the impression that what I was telling him about my initiative he already knew. He said, for example, that no one wanted to take responsibility for giving me a clear and definite reply. He also suggested that the State President had been 'shielded' from the facts. He said he had received independent corroboration of Stoffel's present woes. Stoffel had been P W's political protégé, but these events had put his future in jeopardy. Although Stoffel was a member of the State Security Council, he had not reported on his activities in relation to my initiative. Stoffel had received 'a real roasting' from the President, and had emerged from a three-hour meeting looking 'completely beaten'.

In his view, it was extremely unlikely that any significant moves could be expected from the Government in the immediate future. Willie suggested we might meet again about two weeks hence. Perhaps, he suggested, one had to think about some of the other ideas we had discussed at an earlier stage. For example, he would like to be involved in efforts to promote a broader 'South African Consultation' – maybe under the auspices of the Swiss or the EEC. Something of this nature had been attempted at Wilton House in Britain. Useful discussions had taken place, although the ANC had not been present, owing to an issue involving the participation of certain Government representatives.

However, the relationship between myself and Willie had become somewhat ambiguous. For the past few months, since disclosing my activities to him, I had continued to share confidences with him. I gained the impression that he was being more selective about what he shared with me. I realised that his proximity to the State President, his membership of the Broederbond, his status as an elder of the Dutch Reformed Church, and his venerated position as political philosopher and National Party guru, meant that he was part of the privileged Afrikaner information-loop. I preferred to think of our activities as complementary rather than competitive. We were both involved in trying to open lines of communication between the Government and the ANC. However, I suspected that my problems were being transmuted into his opportunities. Indeed, unbeknown to me, Willie had assumed another role, which I would only discover years later, when that part of the story came to be told.

In the meanwhile, I continued to await the President's reply. On Friday 11 November I met Ambassador Quinche again in Pretoria. He was anxious to know of any further developments. Since our last meeting, he had studied my Memorandum to the State President, and told me that he felt that it was comprehensive, although there were a few matters which he felt could also have been mentioned. He stressed that although the Swiss Government required some financial accountability, it did not wish to be seen as trying to manage or control the initiative. He saw some parallels in the role Switzerland had been able to play in relation to peace talks between Morocco and Algeria. Switzerland had hosted that conference, but had not participated in the proceedings, except for helping to communicate some sensitive messages.

The Ambassador was concerned about the issue of confidentiality. He was not entirely comfortable with my having quoted State Secretary Brunner, in relation to comments made about the Swiss Foreign Minister – ie: that he was a 'political' appointee, and that a delicate matter of this nature should be handled by the State Secretary. He said, 'That might be true, but I don't know what Minister Felber may feel about that being actually stated.' He said that perhaps it was all to the good, as it could only serve to underline the extreme delicacy of this matter. Concerning my reference to detailed notes of meetings, he asked with a nervous smile whether I had also made notes of my meetings with him? I confirmed that I had indeed!

We also spoke about possible next steps, in the event that a favourable response was received from Botha. I suggested it might be desirable in that event to undertake some scenario planning, to identify and explore the various options. The Ambassador mentioned that he had recently given a talk on the Swiss Constitution to an IDASA gathering in Port Elizabeth, which had been quite well received. However, he had been taken aback by some comments from the floor, which had been highly critical of his country for pursuing its economic self-interest in the South African situation.

As usual, our discussions ranged over a number of topical issues which had a contextual bearing upon the situation. Of particular significance at this time were the pressures building up in the economy, with soaring interest rates, a virtually non-existent growth rate, plunging foreign exchange reserves (now representing less than one and a half months' import cover), and a further depreciation of the Rand to a level of 2,5 to the dollar, as compared with parity a mere four years before. The economy was also facing the imminent necessity to make initial capital repayments in terms of the Swiss-brokered Leutweiler debt-rescheduling agreement.

On the positive side, the latest news from Geneva, where the Angolan peace talks had resumed, was encouraging. On 16 November it was announced that a draft treaty had been initialled by representatives of South Africa, Cuba, and Angola. This treaty would be formally adopted by the South African Government a week later, bringing to an end 73 years of South Africa's hegemony over Namibia, and the prospect of peace in Angola after 23 years civil war. The South African negotiators had received acclamation for their skill and pragmatism, and this novel spirit of international approval was further enhanced two days later when the President announced that he had decided to reprieve the death sentences passed on the Sharpeville Six. *The Times* of London commented that it was 'evidence not only of a new political wisdom in Pretoria, but of that even rarer quality, compassion'.

However, this atmosphere of hopefulness was abruptly extinguished by an event which took place near the State Theatre in Pretoria, on 15 November. A 23-year-old ex-policeman, and member of the AWB, Barend Hendrik Strydom, describing himself as leader of 'Die Wit Wolwe' (the 'White Wolves'), methodically gunned down at random black pedestrians on the streets of the capital city, killing 6 and wounding 17. This unprece-dented display of racial hatred sent shock-waves throughout the length and breadth of South Africa. It seemed like the beginning of the apocalyptic horror we had all feared, a racial holocaust. History will record that, despite incredible provocation, blacks curbed their anger. Newspapers were filled with horrific pictures of bleeding victims and a smiling gunman. Court-appointed psychiatrists later pronounced him sane, having no regrets, and being proud of what he had done. It is surely one of the most remarkable acts of generosity that Barend Hendrik Strydom should today walk free in the new democratic South Africa, having been pardoned for an act deemed to have been committed with 'a political motive'. Indeed, he has now published his memoirs, in which he explains: 'Die slag van Strijdomplein is nie gedryf deur haat vir die vyand nie, maar deur liefde vir die eie. Laat ons in die uur van beslissing mekaar se hande vat, mekaar se kant kies, en bymekaar staan as God se volk . . .'*

Immediately following this news, I decided to wait no longer. Two weeks had passed since my letter to the State President. On the morning of 16 November, I telephoned Mr Botha's office and spoke to Ian Putter, his Administrative Secretary. He confirmed that my letter and the accompanying Memorandum had been received and studied by the State President. A reply was in the post.

---

* The massacre of Strijdom Square was not motivated by hate for the enemy, but by love for the own. Let us take one another's hands in this hour of decision and stand together as God's nation.

22

Taking the President's advice

A few days later a letter from the President arrived (see next page). I read the letter several times, and found myself again trying to dissect the syntax, and discern subtleties in a letter of just three sentences. Though reassuringly friendly, it was completely ambiguous. Two things seemed clear – the President wished to maintain his distance from the coalface; and he wished Stoffel van der Merwe and the N I S to continue as my points of contact. I pondered the significance of the phrase '*pursue* the matter'? It certainly didn't imply on the face of it that the initiative was already dead and buried; nor did it convey, as I had feared, that I was persona non grata. Arguably, it could even mean that under appropriate circumstances the initiative might be pursued. Or was I just being 'stellenbosched' – marginalised without an explicit rebuff? Despite my best efforts to establish a line to the President, I remained reliant upon his reluctant surrogates. At least there could no longer be any doubt that the President was fully informed.

My next step was to get in touch again with Stoffel and the N I S. I telephoned both their offices, and left messages. Later in the day, I had a return call from Stoffel's secretary, Petra van Niekerk, who informed me that her Minister wished to meet me over the weekend at his official residence 'Uitzicht', on the Groote Schuur Estate. We agreed upon 6 p.m. that Saturday afternoon. A little later Mike Kuhn returned my call, and we too discussed the need for a meeting. He suggested two days hence, over breakfast at the Holiday Inn – evidently his favourite venue!

Happily, on this occasion, we did not have to secrete ourselves in a sixth-floor bedroom, but met brazenly in the restaurant, with Mr Kruger also in attendance. Before I had time to raise the issue of the President's letter, Mike Kuhn informed me that Niel Barnard had given instructions that the N I S was to have nothing further to do with this matter! In Barnard's view, it was a 'political initiative' involving Stoffel van der Merwe only. It was apparent that Messrs Kuhn & Kruger knew nothing about the President's letter. My memorandum had been carefully studied, they assured me, and had led to discussions taking place between Drs Barnard and Van der Merwe. Kuhn said he understood there had also been discussions involving Van der

B.9/1

Union Buildings
Pretoria

11 November 1988

Mr R Rosenthal
P O Box 3800
CAPE TOWN
8000

Dear Mr Rosenthal

The State President has received your letter of the 3rd instant
and appreciates your sending him the memorandum which was
enclosed.

It is unfortunately not possible for the President to grant you
an interview due to his hectic program and he suggests that you
pursue the matter with Dr Stoffel van der Merwe and the offices
of National Intelligence Service.

The President nevertheless appreciates your writing to him in
this regard, but trusts that you will appreciate his situation.

With kind regards

ADMINISTRATIVE SECRETARY
/ss

Merwe and the State President. In the result – as they understood the position – it had been decided that the initiative should in fact proceed, but without their involvement. Accordingly, they wished me well; expressed regret that they would not be further involved; and said that I should feel free to contact them if there was anything they could do to help.

The impression conveyed was entirely positive. They hoped that the present hiatus would be no more than 'a temporary set-back'. Along with their appreciation, I was once again offered the metaphorical 'box of whisky', which was once again ritually declined. As an afterthought, I said there was perhaps one situation in which I might need their assistance – I was concerned that at some stage the Security Police might tumble to what I was about, and if so, it might prove difficult to allay their curiosity. Kuhn said should this happen I could certainly contact them. I also raised a concern about my travel documents, and asked if there was any way they could assist me with another passport, particularly if I needed to travel to countries in Africa where a South African passport was unwelcome. They said that a second passport could be organised, but perhaps a better solution might be for the Swiss to give me a travel document known as a '*Laissez-Passer*', which would serve a similar purpose.

As usual, we discussed some topical news, including the saga of *Wit Wolf* Barend Strydom. They were working on the matter, and mentioned his parents' right-wing background and links to the AWB. They also asked a few 'fishing' questions – for example: whether I would be attending a meeting that evening at Louis Luyt's home to discuss the formation of a new combined Opposition Party? I assured them that I had received no invitation. They were also curious about Slabbert's relationship with Alex Boraine: was there any personal animosity between them? Another question: had I seen a report in *Beeld* about someone in the Department of Foreign Affairs wishing to attend the recent IDASA conference in Germany? Did I know who this person might be? At some stage I had to remind them that I was not a source of information.

After a high-cholesterol breakfast, I made my way to the Pretoria Supreme Court, where Justice K van Dijkhorst was busy reading extracts from his 1500-page judgment at the end of the marathon Delmas trial, in which Arthur Chaskalson and George Bizos had been involved. The courtroom was already crowded to overflowing. I came across US Ambassador Edward Perkins trying unsuccessfully to penetrate the portals of justice. I spoke to a police constable who arranged for the Ambassador to be admitted through a side-door. Inside the court, I was greeted by Archbishop Tutu, who asked, 'How are you getting along with your wonderful plans?' It was the first time we'd spoken for more than a year. I smiled inscrutably.

The judge found the crime of Treason to have been proved against all but 3 of the 19 accused, and pronounced that, 'For practical purposes, the Government is at war with the ANC. In the circumstances, the intent of the UDF was no less hostile than one would find in time of war, in the case of a treasonable act.' He said further that 'Since its launch the UDF has consistently popularised the ANC, and fomented distrust and even hatred of the Government and its organisations among the black population.' The convictions were later set aside on appeal, owing to the fact that the trial judge had irregularly dismissed one of his assessors.

The following day I met Stoffel van der Merwe. It was our fourteenth meeting, and the first to take place outside the environment of his office. The atmosphere was informal with Stoffel in jeans and an open-necked shirt. Mrs van der Merwe made us a pot of tea, and children wandered in and out. We discussed family affairs; how children coped differently with the stress of exams; and the merits and demerits of boarding schools. Stoffel spoke repeatedly of his exhaustion and what a difficult year this had been. He sometimes felt as though he was 'holding on by his teeth' until the family was able to go away for their year-end holidays at Stilbaai.

I told Stoffel that I had received another letter from the State President. He looked surprised. I then read it to him, and he looked even more surprised. He asked if he could have a copy, which I found somewhat ironic. He told me that for more than two weeks he had been trying to set up a meeting with the President, but to no avail. He couldn't even get an appointment. He found the President's letter to me completely baffling, and didn't know what to make of it. The President hadn't communicated with him at all since their fateful meeting four weeks ago. He thought he might try to get some explanation from the person who'd signed the letter. He wasn't sure whether the letter should be seen as positive, or merely non-committal. He made no bones about his own frustrations and disillusionment with the current situation, raising the possibility that he might resign. He would take this question away with him on holiday. It would be unwise to try to make this kind of decision 'at the end of a week, or at this time of the year'. Stoffel looked like a man overwhelmed by pressures, and quite close to the edge.

He asked what had finally transpired between me and the N I S – I thought I could discern a measure of anxiety. Maybe I was not the only person who felt apprehensive about dealing with Dr Barnard? Stoffel said he too had been unable to set up a further discussion with him. He was mystified by the message conveyed through Mike Kuhn – that this was 'a political initiative', and that the N I S was to have no part in it.

I pleaded for an end to the Government's vacillation and delay. He said he was in sympathy with my feelings, but from time to time in a process it was necessary for there to be periods of no movement and no communication. He pointed out that such periods had occurred periodically between the Soviet Union and the United States. This hadn't precluded the conclusion of arms limitation treaties when the time was ripe. 'Can you imagine what might have happened to a Minister in Mrs Thatcher's Cabinet, if he had tried to engage the IRA in dialogue without her approval?' I put it to him that some situations required just that kind of independent courage. He replied that 'in certain circumstances' he would be willing to take risks with his political future – for example, if he believed the result might be a shift in the ANC's position on violence. He had already had the equivalent of three careers, and leaving politics at this stage would frankly be a relief.

I asked once again whether he could suggest any persons other than himself with whom I could discuss these matters, to which he replied that there were only the State President and Niel Barnard. The pressures on his own time were such that he had not even been able to study my Memorandum properly. In due course, he might try to draft a response to the ANC, and outline some future possibilities. At this stage however, he was unable to attempt such a task. 'I'm simply exhausted,' he pleaded.

He acknowledged that due to the intrusion of other issues, reform and negotiations hadn't been receiving proper time and attention. He had also been distracted by some ongoing scandals involving his Department, including its financing of a film called 'Escape to Freedom', and a commissioned 'peace song' which had been the subject of much media ridicule. Some people were unwilling to recognise any good the Government did, he complained. In his view, the recent elections had done little more than confirm the results of the previous General Election. In some respects the result had been encouraging to the National Party, particularly as the Conservatives had failed to realise their electoral aspirations, and the ANC's efforts to disrupt the elections had also failed. However, ten candidates had been killed, and there was now a campaign to disrupt the newly elected black Councils. In one instance, a complete Council had resigned through what he termed 'lack of nerve'.

For the time being, the main focus was the economic situation. Without foreign aid and investment the country would be unable to afford any reform programme. A special meeting of the Cabinet and the State Security Council was to be held later in the month to start addressing the reform agenda once again. After that, things might become clearer – in particular, whether the process could be speeded up, or whether it had to be slowed down. At this stage, he wouldn't like to try to predict the prospects for negotiations. I raised the perennial issue of Nelson Mandela's release, and he replied that it was unlikely to take place until the following year. 'If properly handled,' he agreed, 'it could open up new possibilities.'

At this stage Mrs van der Merwe came in to remind us that they were going out to dinner. It was approaching 7.30 p.m. I went home feeling utterly frustrated. The Government seemed paralysed through lack of direction, courage, imagination, and energy. The State President had referred me to Stoffel van der Merwe and Niel Barnard, but neither was able or willing to deal effectively with the matter. Something had to be done to bring matters to a head.

I sat down that evening and wrote a letter to the Ambassador forwarding him a copy of the State President's letter, and advising that my latest meeting with Dr van der Merwe, 'unfortunately has not removed the ambiguity about the long-term future of this initiative. Consequently, I am obliged to make further enquiries ...'

Before making any moves, I took counsel again from the small circle of friends with whom I had consulted over the year – Arthur Chaskalson, Van Zyl Slabbert, and Willie Esterhuyse. To each I explained the situation, and sought his perspective and advice. No one knew the answer. I was gradually coming to the conclusion that either I would have to acquiesce in the present standstill or I would need to act decisively to bring matters to a head, and precipitate a decision. Wearying of the uncertainty, I now favoured the latter course.

One Sunday evening, over dinner at his home in Stellenbosch, Willie Esterhuyse warned me, 'The climate has taken a turn for the worse.' He had just returned from what he described as 'a very discouraging meeting in Pretoria'. The President seemed to be withdrawing from personal involvement with reform issues. Even Willie was experiencing difficulty in gaining access to him. It was impossible to know whether this was deliberate, or the result of other competing pressures. As concerning my own initiative, Willie said he didn't know what to suggest. And this brought us to the problem of Niel Barnard. He had persistently refused to meet me, and had now also withdrawn his lieutenants. I asked Willie's interpretation of his impervious attitude. Willie said that my initiative had become a 'prickly pear' and nobody wanted to touch it. Dr Barnard had decided that it was 'Stoffel's problem'.

But Willie knew a good deal more than he was choosing to tell me. According to Allister Sparks's account in *Tomorrow Is Another Country*, Willie had by this time declined an invitation to visit the ANC in Lusaka, after having been warned by Botha that he and another invitee, Professor Sampie Terreblanche, should not 'go and talk to murderers'. Esterhuyse was then approached by none other than Niel Barnard himself, who propositioned Willie on the basis that the Government needed 'an informal contact' with the ANC. Willie recounts that he was asked whether he would be willing to report to Barnard on discussions with the ANC. This referred to a series of meetings commencing in November 1987, involving ANC and Afrikaner leaders, funded and hosted by Consgold Chairman Rudolph Agnew. Sparks comments, 'Esterhuyse was hesitant about acting as an intelligence agent – literally acting like a spy – but at the same time could see the value of making a link between the ANC and someone so close to the President. He told Barnard he would do so, provided he could tell Thabo Mbeki and Jacob Zuma, the key ANC figures, about it.' Sparks relates that Willie squared from the beginning with Thabo Mbeki, who understood that Willie was talking to Barnard, who was talking to Botha. However, it seems that Willie didn't square with Terreblanche, or for that matter anyone else. He certainly didn't square with me.

In due course it would be revealed that Dr Niel Barnard had yet another agenda at this time, of which I was blissfully unaware. In his autobiography, *Long Walk to Freedom*, Mandela records that since May 1988 – at the time when I was first meeting with Thabo Mbeki in Frankfurt – a Special Committee of which Barnard was a member had begun meeting with him regularly at Pollsmoor Prison, as part of a plan to broaden discussions that had taken place informally between Mandela and Minister of Prisons Kobie Coetsee, following Mandela's proposal for talks. This contact group also included another N I S operative, one Mike Louw, and I wondered whether by any chance he was some relation of Mike Kuhn!

Some years later, Barnard gave an illuminating interview to Alf Ries, political editor of *Die Burger*, in which he described himself and the N I S as the correct channel for sensitive communications with the ANC. 'N I het oor die jare sterk standpunt ingeneem dat hy self met die ANC moes kontak maak. .... Ons standpunt was dat N I die aanvanklike kontak moes maak, sodat die pad oopgemaak kon word.'*

In these circumstances, and with the benefit of hindsight, it is hardly surprising that Willie Esterhuyse was opaque, and that Niel Barnard was inaccessible and incensed that he had not been consulted earlier. I believe that Barnard had discovered about my initiative only when I chose to approach him. His annoyance and embarrassment had probably turned into a competitive hostility. As he saw the position, they were the professionals, and I was a civilian interloper. He would be opposed to Government using some neo-Jewish liberal lawyer as an intermediary in this most sensitive

---

* N I had over the years strongly held the view that it must itself make contact with the ANC. Our opinion was that N I must make the initial contact so that the way could be opened.'

matter. What made matters worse, this 'third party' was now the custodian of highly sensitive information, potentially damaging to the National Party and the President.

On Thursday 24 November it was announced by Minister Kobie Coetsee – another contender for the role of interlocutor – that Mandela would not be returning to Pollsmoor Prison after his discharge from Constantiaberg Clinic. This was seen as part of an orchestrated plan to effect a phased release. The announcement read: 'In view of the particular circumstances of the case, including possible threats to his safety from different quarters, it has been decided that when the time arrives he will be transferred to suitable, comfortable and secure living accommodation, where he will be able to receive members of his family more freely and on a continual basis.'

The following day I received a telephone call from Ambassador Quinche, who said he had received an important message from the Swiss Foreign Office, which he needed to convey to me as soon as possible. We arranged to meet in Pretoria on Monday.

In preparation for this meeting, I tried again, but still unsuccessfully, to contact the dramatis personae. After several abortive attempts, I finally spoke to Mike Kuhn late on the afternoon of Friday 25 November. I told him that I was now completely at a loss. The State President had told me by letter 'to pursue the matter' in consultation with the N I S, and Dr van der Merwe. Dr Barnard was unwilling to meet me, and Dr van der Merwe was unable to be helpful. What on earth was I now to do? Mike Kuhn agreed I had a problem!

I said I was calling him again despite his earlier advice to the contrary, because it seemed absolutely essential that I discuss the matter with 'someone who has the ear of the old man'. Despite his declared preference, I believed it was appropriate for Dr Barnard to meet me, as the President had specifically suggested. In the circumstances, I asked that he communicate my request once more to his boss. He said this would be 'rather difficult', and suggested instead that I write another letter to the State President. Had it not concerned a matter of such momentous importance, the situation would have been almost comic. The Head of State had issued a pronouncement *ex cathedra*, but was being obdurately resisted by the head of his Intelligence Service, and a member of his Cabinet. Mike Kuhn said that in my letter to Mr Botha I should indicate my sense of frustration. I responded that another communication to the President might be offensive, particularly in view of his explicit wish to remain at a distance from the initiative. Eventually Mike Kuhn said he would see what he could do, and it was agreed that I would contact him when I reached Pretoria at lunchtime on Monday.

My attempts to communicate with Stoffel van der Merwe were equally frustrating. On Thursday 24 November I telephoned his office, to be advised that he was 'in his constituency', and would not be returning until the following day. His assistant, Riaan Smit, undertook to have him ring me in the morning. When the call failed to materialise, I telephoned again and was now advised by Mr Smit that the Minister was 'busy in a meeting'. He would try to get him to phone me before lunch, because after that 'We will all be at our Christmas Party!' When there was still no call, I phoned again, to be advised that the Minister had 'just left'. It was suggested that I contact him at his Cape Town home on Saturday afternoon.

Despite my reluctance to disturb the family sanctum, I did ring him, apologising for the necessity to do so. I explained that I would be meeting the Swiss Ambassador on Monday morning, and I needed to know whether he had been able to clarify Mr Botha's intention? He said unfortunately he had still not been able to contact the State President. He undertook to try to ascertain the position early on Monday morning, when he would be at a meeting 'in the vicinity of the President's office'. If the opportunity arose, he promised, he would try to get me some information. I was to ring him when I got to Pretoria. He still sounded dark and sepulchral, and said he was totally exhausted. I suggested as it was a Saturday afternoon that we might go for a walk on the mountain. He said it would probably be a very sensible idea, but he had work to do.

Upon arrival in Pretoria I telephoned Stoffel as arranged, but as expected he was once more unavailable. I told his secretary that I now needed to speak to him very urgently, and after having me hold on for a moment, she returned with a message to the effect that he had not yet succeeded in getting clarification of the President's letter, because of other pressing matters. Also from the Holiday Inn, I contacted Mike Kuhn, and we had a somewhat hasty half-hour meeting after lunch, before he rushed off to another appointment.

He asked whether I had remembered to bring him a copy of the President's letter, which I then handed him. I could not help marvelling at the amazing situation that the country's National Intelligence Service was unable to obtain from the source a copy of the State President's letter involving their own role in this matter. Mike Kuhn said he had not yet spoken to Dr Barnard about my further request for a meeting. I said it was vital and urgent that we meet, and that further discussions with Dr van der Merwe really served no purpose. Mike Kuhn said he would do his best, and agreed to revert to me the following day between 3 and 5 p.m. at the Johannesburg Towers Hotel.

True to his word, he telephoned at 3.20 p.m., and advised that he had now spoken to his boss along the lines we had discussed. 'Unfortunately due to the nature of the matter, it is not possible for us to be further involved with this matter in any way.' Accordingly, Dr Barnard would not agree to meet me. Mike Kuhn said he was sorry. There was nothing further he could do. When I asked what he thought I should now do, he said very reasonably, that it was hardly appropriate for him to advise me. 'Perhaps you should write another letter to the State President,' he suggested. It seemed that I had no alternative but to continue working with Dr van der Merwe. He said I could contact him again when I was next in Pretoria.

My appointment with His Excellency the Swiss Ambassador was for 11 a.m., Monday 28 November. He read from a telex message just received from Berne. It was in French, and I made notes of his ad hoc translation:

> Having given careful consideration to the documentation addressed by Mr Rosenthal to the State President, and on the basis of their discussions with Mr P W Botha and Mr Pik Botha earlier in the year, after assessing also the separate talks held with representatives of the ANC, the Swiss Government is convinced that there exists a real and present opportunity, allowing for the essential goodwill which exists on both sides, to organise in Switzerland at an early date an informal meeting of a preliminary nature, without excessive formality and without preconditions. (That is, 'talks about talks'.)
>
> It is proposed that such a meeting be attended by suitable representatives appointed by the State President on the one hand, and by the ANC on the other.
>
> The relevant date and place for a meeting would obviously need to be agreed between the two parties; but it was the preference of the Swiss Government that such meeting be scheduled before the end of December 1988, which it believed would be the best timing to take advantage of the favourable conditions which now existed.
>
> The Swiss Government would cover all costs involved, including travelling, hotel, food and accommodation.
>
> The Ambassador was requested to convey this message to Mr Rosenthal, and to ask that he transmit the same to President Botha and to his contacts in Lusaka, as soon as possible.
>
> The Swiss request a report as to the contacts made, and the response given, as soon as possible after the message has been delivered.

This was precisely the kind of next step I had in mind. However, it was crucial – particularly in the light of the earlier debacle – that the process be handled with the utmost care and discretion. There needed to be full appreciation by the Swiss of the delicacy of the process. I therefore suggested that, before any formal messages were conveyed, we have a full discussion to ensure that our ideas were in accord. I therefore proposed a meeting in Switzerland as soon as possible, and hoped that both State Secretary Mr Brunner and the Foreign Minister, Mr Felber, would be able to attend.

We went on to discuss the issue of timing. Whilst it was clearly urgent that we act before any window of opportunity was closed, the Ambassador felt there might not be full appreciation in Switzerland of the fact that December in South Africa was not a good time to try to do business with the Government. Like August in Switzerland, it was the time of summer holidays.

The Ambasssador pointed out the significance his Government attached to this initiative, and their confidence in my role. He said it was very unusual for a third party such as myself to be entrusted with a message of this nature, as between governments. The normal diplomatic procedure would have been to use their Ambassador to convey a communication through official channels.

There was no doubt in my mind that the Swiss proposal was a high-risk move, which in some way or another would bring matters to a head. As a government-to-government communication, it could not be ignored. I was apprehensive that it might once more be seen as 'the Swiss trying to meddle in our affairs', and in that event, might lead to another Presidential explosion. At the same time, the current enigmatic situation was becoming intolerable, and it was entirely reasonable that the Swiss should insist that the parties clarify their intentions.

Immediately following my meeting with the Ambassador, I contacted Arthur Chaskalson and, despite his preoccupation with the Delmas trial, we were able to meet briefly at the end of the day. He appreciated the risks, and was very supportive and reassuring. He found it particularly incredible that Stoffel had still not read my Memorandum to the President. 'It seems', he commented, 'as though they want the initiative to go ahead, but no one wants to take responsibility for it.'

Three days later I received confirmation through the Ambassador of a meeting to take place in Berne at 10 a.m. on Wednesday 7 December at the Bundeshauswes. There was more than a whisper of excitement.

Just before leaving for Switzerland, I telephoned Dr van der Merwe – in case there had been any significant developments. I told him that I was about to depart overseas for discussions with the Swiss, and that I might also decide to meet 'our friends in Lusaka'. In the circumstances, I asked whether there was anything he would like me to convey? He said I should try to convey 'a message of cautious optimism, without arousing undue hopes'. He realised this would be difficult to convey. I could not help commenting that, without some basis for my optimism, it might also be meaningless.

He said he was on the point of leaving for his annual holiday at Stilbaai. Although he had to go to Pretoria during the next week, he didn't expect to be back in harness until 3 January, and possibly only 9 January. The latest Cabinet Meeting had been largely taken up with matters involving the Budget, which forecast a rather bleak situation. He had been unable to raise this particular matter, as tempers had become a bit frayed towards the end. Accordingly, he had nothing further to report, save to say that he viewed the situation 'in a slightly more favourable light' than a few weeks back. He felt there was some reason for optimism, but confessed, 'I am by nature an optimist.'

I wished him a good holiday, and promised that I would disturb him only if something really urgent and important arose. He said that his holiday house didn't have a telephone, but if necessary he could be contacted by telegram, care of the S A Police Station at Stilbaai.

23

Talks about talks about talks

My Swissair flight miraculously arrived in Geneva one minute early after a 6 000-mile journey across the continent of Africa, despite a go-slow in Nairobi which caused a two-hour delay. Mindful of the Swiss chronometric obsession, I plotted my one-mile journey from the Berner Palace Hotel to the Swiss Government offices with meticulous care, to ensure that I arrived neither early nor late – but to no avail. I arrived as planned, but at the wrong building, and the wrong entrance. A guard suggested helpfully that I should come back another day, as Parliament was not in session! I scurried off, and arrived ten minutes late. No doubt inured to such foreign shortcomings my hosts forgave my sins, and I was warmly welcomed in from the snowy streets of Berne.

Mr Edouard Brunner, the State Secretary in the Federal Department of Foreign Affairs, informed me that he and his colleagues had set aside the entire day for our discussions. He said they regarded this initiative as being of the greatest importance, and had arranged for the participation of a small group of officials, who would be able to contribute and carry the matter forward. I was introduced to Ambassador Alfred Ruegg, who headed what is described as 'Political Division 2', denoting the entire Southern Hemisphere! He was assisted by a bespectacled deputy, Christian Blickenstorfer, and a bearded Francis Gruber, who had special responsibility for the Southern Africa desk. Also present was the Foreign Minister's personal representative, Pierre Combernous, who had previously been involved with the recent successful Namibian talks in Geneva, and who proved particularly well informed. It was his role to ensure that Foreign Minister Felber was kept informed of these discussions.

Mr Brunner explained that he would have to absent himself briefly later in the day, as he was simultaneously involved with the arrangements for an extraordinary meeting of the United Nations due to take place in Geneva a few days hence, following the United States's refusal to grant a visitor's visa to the PLO's Yasser Arafat. I was also reminded that Mr Brunner would be departing for Washington in the near future, to take up his appointment as Ambassador, and accordingly the attendance of the others was necessary to ensure continuity.

After some introductory comments, I was invited to share my thoughts about recent developments in South Africa. I made some general observations about the overall political context, noting that the National Party seemed relatively satisfied with its performance in the recent local authority elections. However, it now faced the prospect of a General Election during the latter half of next year. I feared this might inhibit bold initiatives, as the Government remained fearful of issues which could be exploited by its right-wing adversaries. I also noted a number of positive developments which could be indicative of the Government's wish to project a more reformist image – including, the last-minute reprieve of the Sharpeville Six; progress in implementation of the Angola/Namibia accord; and the release of two further long-serving political prisoners – PAC leader Zephania Mothopeng, and the sick and ageing Harry Gwala of the ANC. Serendipitously, news arrived during the course of the day, that Nelson Mandela had been transferred from Constantiaberg Clinic to a house within the confines of Victor Verster Prison, near Paarl.

However, there was little progress to report on the Government's plans for 'reform', but rather a seeming dearth of courage or creative ideas. Increasingly desperate attempts were being made to suppress ongoing protests, but the popular momentum had not been stalled. The internal situation was increasingly out of control, and the Government found itself unable to govern without a permanent State of Emergency. The former monolithic unity of the National Party was coming under stress, as speculation mounted about the possible retirement of P W Botha. There had been a few early salvos in the scramble between aspirant successors. Under challenge from the Conservative Party and various Afrikaner separatist groups, the National Party seemed uncertain whether to move to the right or the left.

We then discussed the virtual paralysis that had overtaken my initiative, as a result of the diplomatic debacle two months earlier. Apart from my written Memorandum to the President, I had been unable to communicate with him directly, and his deputed surrogates were reluctant or impotent. As a result, the initiative was now stalled, and neither Van der Merwe nor Barnard was able or willing to take responsibility, each preferring to defer to the other. The President's letter was puzzling. It could imply qualified approval, but we were left speculating about the meaning of Botha's monosyllabic communication, and his sphinx-like thought processes.

The Swiss listened attentively to my rather pessimistic overview. We agreed that there were now basically three alternatives. Firstly, there was what I termed 'Micawberism', that is, waiting for something to happen, and abiding the outcome of future events. Secondly, there was the option of actively using the time created by the present hiatus to undertake consultation and research in order to identify options and develop a future agenda. Neither of these possibilities seemed to have great appeal to the Swiss, who were anxious to become more proactive – but not to appear intrusive.

Finally, there was the option which they themselves now mooted – namely, to launch a carefully devised positive intervention, such as a specific invitation to the parties to participate in 'talks about talks'. I favoured this latter course, although it was obviously fraught with peril. However, one would have to consider various factors, including the specific timing of such invitation, it being just three weeks to Christmas and the most difficult time of the year to elicit any action from a Government on holiday. One would obviously also have to take great care to avoid the impression of 'interference'. The personal approval of the State President was seen as absolutely critical. It was suggested that we prepare for the possibility of a negative response, and consider alternative ideas in such circumstances. I responded that I didn't think we should 'do too much cooking, until we know the ingredients and the recipe, and are assured at least that the guests will arrive'.

Would the initiative be at an end, if the proposal was rejected? The Swiss felt one couldn't predetermine such a decision until the specific responses had been evaluated. However, the initiative could not be indefinitely prolonged, if there was no discernible progress. This fact needed to be communicated to the parties. I had in mind the possibility at some stage, of a broadly based 'constitutional colloquium', which would represent a gathering of minds, without dignifying the event as formal negotiations. Apart from the internal constituencies, one might seek the participation of other interested parties, including the frontline states, and South Africa's important trading partners; and perhaps grant 'observer' status to a few international organisations, such as the OAU, the UN, and the EEC. I believed there was merit in broadening the context.

We also discussed the supportive role which could be played by parties such as the United Kingdom and Soviet Union. The Swiss believed the advent of Perestroika had meant that the Russians were now able to play an important role in the Namibian/Angola negotiations, and they were evidencing a constructive pragmatism in other conflict situations, including Afghanistan. The Swiss had good access to the Soviets, and were willing to intercede with them, if deemed appropriate. I learnt that in recent Angolan negotiations, the Swiss had been able to play a low-profile role, with the approval of the Soviets. Apparently, a recent 'brainstorming session' had taken place between the ANC and the Soviet Union, at which the ANC was urged to adopt a more flexible approach to issues such as the economy of a future liberated South Africa. The Swiss believed the Soviet Union could exercise a positive influence on the ANC's negotiation stance.

I asked their view whether Margaret Thatcher's Government, or that of newly elected US President George Bush, might be able to influence the Botha Government in a similar way? The UK and US leaders shared a similar attitude to negotiating under threat of violence. The Swiss felt the inclusion of another party such as the United Kingdom or the United States at this stage would be counterproductive. The United States, represented by Chester Crocker, was playing a substantive role in the Angola/Namibia talks, where the US had a direct involvement as UNITA's major supplier. In the case of the United Kingdom, there was a linkage based upon a measure of historical complicity in the South African situation, and its recent involvement with the abortive Commonwealth initiative – the Eminent Persons' Group. There was a risk that their further involvement in this initiative might be perceived as a continuation of such earlier efforts. Moreover, the Swiss were cautious about the possibility of some sort of 'competition' developing amongst those wishing to promote a South African peace process.

Mr Brunner saw a useful analogy in the situation presently pertaining in the Middle East. He pointed out that at this very time, Yasser Arafat was meeting with American Jews in Stockholm. 'This is exactly the opposite of what we are trying to achieve,' he observed. 'It's a big media event, and not much else.' What the Swiss hoped to achieve, by contrast, was a discreet meeting of the principals themselves, without attendant media publicity. 'Imagine how much more significant it would be if Arafat was meeting with the Jews of Israel,' he said. I suggested that perhaps a better analogy would be a meeting between the IRA and British Government. There were similarities between our Government's refusal to meet the ANC, and Margaret Thatcher's refusal to meet the IRA, until each had forsworn violence. Mr Brunner felt there was a big difference. 'The IRA is a minority terrorist organisation. It doesn't claim to represent the majority; whereas the ANC can legitimately claim to represent the majority. It has even more diplomatic missions than the South African Government, and has attained an international status almost equivalent to that of the PLO.'

In an exclusive interview with the editor of *Beeld*, Mrs Thatcher had been quoted a few days earlier as holding a similar view. She said, 'South Africa and Northern Ireland can in no way be compared. There is no apartheid in Northern Ireland. There it is a case of people who have the vote, but don't want to accept the result of an election, and now turn to terrorism.' It was her standpoint that the way must be opened up for negotiations between all parties, in the context of a cessation of violence by all sides. Once the process of dialogue had been accepted, violence had to be relinquished.

I asked about the enquiry addressed by the Swiss Foreign Minister to

Swiss banks concerning their financial involvement in South Africa. Did this herald some more proactive role on the part of the Swiss banking system? I was told that the Ministerial enquiry was directed simply at establishing facts and information. By long tradition, the Swiss banking system was fiercely independent of any attempt by its Government to influence business decisions. It would not lightly countenance political intrusion in its lending practices. I suggested that, at some future stage, one might consider ways and means whereby South Africa could be rewarded for progress towards reforms. They stressed that my initiative was not known to the banking sector, but obviously they would favour a more constructive political climate, which would be conducive to their ability to do business. Perhaps the highwater mark of their benediction might be a statement to the effect that the banks were 'attentive' to developments taking place in South Africa. Apparently, Swiss banks were now having some regular contact with the ANC, and were particularly concerned about ideas affecting the future economy. I was reminded of the caveat of my Swiss friend Professor Markus Barth, who said to me, 'Don't imagine that the banking system takes advice from the Government. They have a single guiding star – whether they can make money!'

We adjourned to a nearby restaurant for lunch, and then resumed and continued throughout a snowy afternoon until about 6 p.m. I caused some mirth in describing my abortive attempt to bring floral comfort to old Professor Barth, whom I had visited the previous day at a Basle clinic, where he was recovering from a heart attack. I had been congratulating myself on having found what I assumed to have been the perfect gift for him – a large bouquet of South African proteas, which I bought from a station florist at a prodigious cost in Rand terms. To my disappointment, and despite the parlous state of his health, Markus rose from his pillow and chastened me on the grounds, 'We don't buy those flowers, because we support a boycott of South African goods!' I hadn't realised that a bouquet could be politically incorrect.

During the afternoon session, our discussion focused upon the next steps, and the practical arrangements that would be involved. Firstly, we agreed that the time had arrived to test the commitment of both the ANC and the South African Government towards the concept of a negotiation process. The Swiss felt that the timing could be propitious in the light of the good-will and flexibility they had discerned in their meetings with Mr Makatini, and also in their brief encounter with Mr P W Botha. They furnished me with a copy of the formal Declaration by the Swiss Parliament on 22 September 1986, concerning 'The promoting of dialogue between the parties in South Africa'. They advised that this remained the basis of Swiss foreign policy, and was consistent with their present involvement.

They stressed that in their meeting with State President Botha, he had been left in no doubt as to the importance the Swiss Government attached to this initiative. Despite his subsequent reported exasperation with Dr van der Merwe, they felt their meeting with the President had gone off 'reasonably well'. For this reason, they were surprised to learn of his adverse reaction, which certainly didn't conform to their impression, nor to the tone of subsequent communications. His attitude had been basically positive. They had been struck by his unchallenged authority. 'He was clearly the boss.' By contrast, they had been rather troubled by the attitude of Foreign Minister Pik Botha, whom they described as 'a bit nervous and tense'. They said, 'One may disagree with what the President says, but at least one can understand his opinion.' They had also been impressed with Neil van Heerden, Director General of Foreign Affairs, and said they would have welcomed his participation in this project. I shared this view, but we unfortunately did not have the prerogative to choose the President's men.

The discussion also touched upon the role of other liberation movements in a future negotiation process. It would be essential that they also become involved at an appropriate stage. This led to a discussion of the relative strengths of AZAPO and the PAC, and the difficulty of determining popular support in the absence of a free political process. The Swiss were also concerned about the implications of being in contact only with the ANC leadership outside the country, thereby excluding those within the country. They reported that Mr Makatini had not excluded the possibility of 'enlarging the context', but it was agreed that this should not be done at the outset.

They had been saddened to learn of the recent death of Johnny Makatini. This was all the more regrettable as they had found him pragmatic and flexible. By contrast, their discussions with Van der Merwe had been less satisfactory. They found him rather wordy and difficult to understand. He seemed 'more of an academic than a politician' – many words; not enough action. He seemed to lack the necessary authority and status to launch this process in an effective manner, and had not proved 'a satisfactory channel of communication'. They wanted to know, 'What is really his representative capacity?' They would clearly have preferred the involvement of someone with more authority and influence. Even in his talks with the Swiss Foreign Minister, Van der Merwe had remained wary and defensive, and unwilling to 'put his cards on the table'. Under these circumstances, it seemed essential that any invitation should be directed personally to the State President. Hopefully, this might in the future create an opportunity for the involvement of other persons.

Ultimately, it was agreed that a formal offer should be extended on behalf of the Swiss Government to both the ANC and the South African Government. Each would be invited to nominate one or more persons to participate in an initial exploratory discussion to take place somewhere in Switzerland, if possible before the end of January, under guaranteed conditions of security and secrecy. The Swiss urged that the meeting take place as soon as possible, to take advantage of the relatively favourable climate which now prevailed. It was self-evident that the opportunity could be lost through delay and the intervention of inauspicious events. The invitation would indicate a proposed date and venue, and perhaps also a time for acceptance – mid-January was mentioned as a possibility. I proposed that the invitation be couched in terms that were as specific as possible – 'in order to compel a response'. The terms must obviously avoid any suggestion of 'interference', but must be substantive, and deserving of the most serious consideration.

The Swiss urged that the participants be encouraged not to set pre-conditions, and that the meeting should take place with a minimum of formality, preferably without a pre-negotiated agenda. They would provide a venue, guarantee security, and assure the parties of confidentiality. Their role would be facilitative. They would not become involved in substantive discussions, nor even in developing an agenda, or defining the process – unless of course the parties specifically requested that assistance.

The initial meetings should be characterised as 'talks about talks', and not substantive negotiations. It was noted that the ANC had stipulated a principle of 'no secret negotiations', but in discussion with Mr Makatini they had had the impression that an exploratory meeting of the nature envisaged could be accommodated in terms of that policy, as not being substantive. On the other hand, the South African Government had repeatedly expressed itself unwilling to meet, let alone to negotiate, with so-called 'terrorists', until they had abandoned violence as a means of achieving their political ends. These fixed positions needed delicate handling.

We anticipated that there was unlikely to be outright rejection by either party, but rather qualified or conditional responses. One would then need to evaluate such qualifications and conditions. If responses were entirely negative, then the viability of the initiative might have to be reconsidered. The Swiss urged that this invitation should be conveyed personally to the State President as a matter of urgency. They believed Botha had three possible responses: he could sanction the initiative; or he could repudiate it; or – and this seemed the most likely – he could prevaricate, temporise, and neither accept nor reject it.

It was their view that these initial contacts could take place at whatever level seemed appropriate to the parties themselves. They could, for example, start at a lower than Ministerial level of representation. If such tentative contacts deadlocked, then the Swiss might be able to assist by holding separate discussions with each party. It would certainly be preferable to encourage direct party-to-party talks, but one should not exclude 'proximity talks'. There was no doubt that secrecy could be maintained, provided both parties accepted that this was desirable. In due course, there would need to be discussion about the conditions under which the parties might meet again. In the Swiss experience, it was essential to handle this delicate initial phase with the utmost sensitivity, as the most serious errors often occurred at the outset of a process of this nature.

As to the mechanics of delivering the invitation, they had considered several possibilities, including a direct communication to be delivered through their Ambassador; alternatively, a joint approach involving both myself and their Ambassador; or a letter of proposal by the Swiss Government addressed to me in the first instance. The Ambassador would be in a position, if approached, to corroborate the contents of any communication I might address to the South African Government. They had decided that I would be the preferred channel, and they now sought my advice as to how best this should be handled.

I proposed that, as the first step, I should proceed to Lusaka, and present the proposal for consideration by the ANC. Thereafter – and hopefully armed with their initial response – I should then seek a meeting with President Botha. I had in mind that it would be far more difficult for Mr Botha to dismiss an invitation from the Swiss Government, if it had already been accepted by the ANC.

Before concluding, we discussed various practical matters, including their problem with reconciling the need for secrecy and the constitutional requirement of accountability to the Swiss Parliament. This was a delicate matter, for which there were few precedents, although some method had been devised to deal with a discreet role they had played in relation to the Afghanistan situation. We also discussed my difficulty in travelling through Africa on a South African passport, whilst maintaining the confidentiality of my mission. I mentioned my inability to route my journeys through Nairobi. They were prepared to give this matter some thought, but felt that a 'Laissez-Passer' would not really be adequate. It was arranged that certain documentation which I had brought with me to Switzerland for purposes of this meeting should be returned through their diplomatic bag, to avoid customs inspection in Zambia or South Africa. The Swiss wished me good luck, and assured me of their moral and practical support.

By the time I left the Foreign Office, it had already grown dark. I walked back to the hotel along snow-covered pavements, feeling incredibly excited.

Fifteen months had passed since I delivered my first letter to the State President. What an incredibly difficult journey it had been. One hardly dared to imagine the possibilities that could now open up.

24

High Noon in Lusaka

First thing next morning I called ANC headquarters in Cha Cha Cha Road, Lusaka, and explained to the efficient Tom Sebina my need to see Thabo Mbeki as a matter of urgency. He was apparently away at the time, but later in the day the arrangements were confirmed. On Friday night, I flew Zambia Airways to Lusaka via London, arriving early on the morning of Saturday 10 December. Once again I travelled without visa, and once again I declined to discuss with a desk clerk at Heathrow 'the nature of my business'. She handed me the now familiar 'Form of Disclaimer', which I happily signed.

Thabo was at the airport to meet me on the early morning flight, and with the aid of an ANC official nicknamed 'Squash' who was on airport duty, I was hustled through Immigration and Customs, and driven by Thabo himself to the Intercontinental Hotel. The drive from the airport gave us the first opportunity for some preliminary discussion about the reason I had come to Lusaka. Thabo said that he wished to involve certain other colleagues, but that a funeral that afternoon meant that the meeting would need to be delayed a few hours. I was told that the funeral was for the latest victim of a car bomb assassination, undoubtedly the work of South African agents. As I climbed into his car, I thought of Albie Sachs opening his car door, and was again conscious of the fact that there were certain physical risks involved in this venture.

Shortly after 4 p.m. Thabo arrived to collect me from the hotel, and we drove to his modest duplex on the outskirts of the city. On the way, we picked up Anthony Mongalo and were joined later by Jacob Zuma, whom I had not met before. We entered through large steel gates which were opened by a guard, and Thabo led us through an attractive garden into his house, where he served us all with drinks.

This was our first meeting since the precipitate cancellation of my aborted visit in October, and I felt they were now entitled to an explanation of what had happened to cause its abrupt cancellation. I recounted the events surrounding the ill-fated meeting between State President Botha and Swiss Foreign Minister Felber; the resultant directive that Van der Merwe was to close down the initiative; my subsequent letter and memorandum to the

President; his obtuse reply; my abortive attempts to meet Niel Barnard; and my several inconclusive meetings with his proxies, Kuhn and Kruger.

I gave them an outline of the review which had just taken place in Berne, and informed them that the Swiss believed this was an opportune moment to attempt to bring about an initial meeting between the Government and the ANC. In reply to a question, I said that this view was based upon their interpretation of the current political climate. The Swiss had stressed the critical importance of timing, and believed that a meeting should take place as soon as possible, with a minimum of formality, and preferably without a predetermined agenda. I also made it clear that the Swiss proposal had not yet been conveyed to Pretoria, but that I would be seeking an urgent meeting with the State President for this purpose.

Thabo Mbeki responded by carefully retracing the sequence of events thus far, noting that the ANC had already given its response to the concept of a meeting. They had received no reply to either of their requests – for some practical indication of seriousness of intent, and for reassurance about the significance of the agenda to be discussed at any such meeting. He confirmed that the late Mr Makatini had met the Swiss State Secretary on more than one occasion, and had reported to the ANC on their discussions. Thabo himself had telephoned State Secretary Brunner, although they had not yet met. Accordingly, they had some understanding of the sequence of the events I had just described, and of the views of the Swiss Government. Makatini had also noted Brunner's belief that 'the other side' could be ready for a meeting. He understood that the Swiss involvement was envisaged at the level of making practical arrangements, and guaranteeing the secrecy and security of a venue.

Thabo said that the Swiss had evidently expected some progress to be made during Van der Merwe's visit in September, and for this reason a second meeting with Makatini had been scheduled immediately following his visit. This second meeting had in fact taken place, but had been rather unproductive. However, the Swiss had assured Makatini that the initiative should be viewed as 'serious and substantial'. He was given to understand that the State President had confirmed the possibility of a meeting, but that this couldn't take place before the October Elections. Five months had now elapsed, and some progress should have been made by this time. When last we met in July he had communicated those two fundamental questions, to which they still awaited a reply.

Mbeki said they would like clarification whether their impression had been correct, that there existed some kind of preliminary understanding between the Swiss and Van der Merwe concerning the possibility of a future meeting, which might have been confirmed during his visit to Switzerland?

I said I had no knowledge of any such arrangement. He said it was curious that the Swiss seemed so confident and optimistic about the likelihood of such meeting. 'Do they know something we don't know?' he asked. He continued: 'When one looks at the situation dispassionately, what is there really to justify their optimism, or to encourage the ANC to go to a meeting?'

He would be very surprised if it were true that the Swiss Foreign Minister had confronted P W Botha with the accusation of delaying tactics. Given what one knew of his personality, such an allegation could be expected to provoke a strong negative reaction. Concerning Botha's indignation, he said their understanding had been that this may have been caused by the fact that Pik Botha had overheard the conversation, and may not have been previously aware of these overtures.

In reality, he said, the ANC found no evidence of a 'change of heart' on the part of the South African Government. Such decisions and actions as the Swiss described as 'positive' – the reprieve of the Sharpeville Six; progress in the Namibian negotiations; and the release of a few political prisoners – were really acts of political expediency and a response to military pressures. For example, the regime was trying to extract some moral gain from the fact of its weakened military position in Angola. The President was trying to advance his credibility in Africa by seeking undeserved credit for having called for a ceasefire. In reality, they were trying to make a virtue of the necessity of having to pull their troops out of Angola. The fact was that the SADF had suffered significant battlefield reverses, and it had become neces- sary to rescue men and material, and save themselves from the indignity of a forced retreat, or face casualties on a scale that would be 'politically unac- ceptable'.

'P W Botha is a wily old fox,' Thabo continued. He felt the Swiss might be misinterpreting the situation. The Government was trying to convince the world that the situation was undergoing fundamental social and polit- ical change; that it was sincere in its declared commitment to reform; and that it was dedicated to the task of promoting regional peace rather than destabilisation. The President's attempts to engage African leaders in dialogue – the so-called 'Afrika Politik' – had been relatively successful, making it necessary for the OAU to intervene and prevent President Mobutu's proposed State visit to Pretoria. 'The fact is that Botha has to be prepared to lose,' he said, 'nothing less.' He drew the analogy of Hitler's last days, and the choice of the Nazi leaders to die rather than surrender, even when defeat was inevitable. It took a pragmatist like Admiral Doenitz to sign the final Act of Surrender on behalf of an already defeated country.

Similarly, the ANC believed that the reprieve of the Sharpeville Six was, in reality, not an act of compassion, but a response to international pressure, and particularly the threat by the West German Government to impose sanctions if the executions took place. Likewise, the release of two sick old prisoners was not an act of mercy, but an act of expediency – 'They didn't want the deaths of two old men on their hands,' he said. Concerning developments affecting Comrade Nelson Mandela, the ANC viewed this in a similar light. The Government was responding to his recent illness ('which incidentally was a poor reflection on conditions in South African prisons!'), and to pressures brought to bear by the Broederbond and Afrikaner and business interests. What Botha was really trying to do was 'to buy time through a staged release, or through putting out rumours of an impending release, in the hope that this might be sufficient'. In the circumstances, he felt the Swiss could be reading the situation incorrectly, and their optimism might be tinged by 'wishful thinking'.

This led to a discussion of the current political situation. Quoting Stoffel van der Merwe, I said the National Party insisted on its commitment to reform, and stressed the political costs it had borne as a result of reforms and changes already implemented – as evidenced by the right-wing split and the formation of the Conservative Party. Mbeki responded that even the split in the National Party was not really a cost 'deliberately incurred', but simply the unavoidable result of pressures building up within the system. Zuma intervened to say, 'I don't think Mr Botha ever sat down and worked out a logical plan for the future – he seems to react to pressures and events as they occur. The National Party seems bankrupt of new ideas. It has no real game plan.'

We talked about the horrifying events involving Barend Strydom. Newspapers had described him as 'having gone berserk'. Thabo said these reports were incorrect. He had not 'gone berserk'. He explained: He was a policeman, and had been 'programmed' to kill blacks. All he did wrong on this occasion was to kill without instructions, or in the context of an 'unrest situation'. Strydom was a 'political monster'. The recent events in Brakpan could also be seen as the work of such monsters. They were the children of apartheid, and in the future we faced the difficulty of how to change their programming. Thabo pointed out that the situation prompted 'an anti-White reaction', but the ANC had resolutely fought against this tendency, even within its own ranks. It had insisted that the struggle was not against whites as such, but against the apartheid system.

Responding further to the claim that the Nationalist Government had suffered high political cost as a result of its modest reforms, he said it could also be said of the ANC that it too had suffered high political cost as a result of its insistence upon a non-racial struggle. Just as the Nationalists could point to the existence of the Conservative Party, the ANC could point to the existence of the PAC and AZAPO. Young people in particular were becoming impatient with ANC policy in this regard, adding, 'We also have a need to confront our own "political monsters". If one doesn't effectively deal with them, then, like Dr Faustus, one day the devil comes to collect his due.' We were going to have to find a way to cope with these 'monsters' in the future.

Thabo continued: 'If only P W realised it, he has an opportunity no other South African leader ever had – to actually solve the problem. However, it requires that he rise above the level of politician, and start acting like a statesman.' I asked why he regarded the present situation as unique, and he said it was because of 'the chemistry in the situation'. One of the things Botha needed to do, was 'lift the iron curtain, and allow untrue stories about the ANC to be corrected'. The horror stories about the ANC represented them as 'monsters'. There was a deliberate distortion of the public perception of the ANC. 'If Botha lifts the iron curtain, there would be surprise about some of the things said by Oliver Tambo, which would give a very different impression of the man.' He drew attention to the Government's prohibition on his father speaking in public, and suggested this too was because the Government had been upset by his initial statements. Nelson Mandela was being kept behind bars 'not so much because the Government fears his unreasonableness, but because they fear his reasonableness'. He said it was strange how Afrikaners sometimes seemed shocked when they met the ANC. 'They expect monsters, and they find themselves talking to human beings!'

He reiterated, 'P W has a real opportunity. For the first time, Afrikaners realise that change is coming. Previously, they were too intimidated and too politically cohesive. Now university people, intellectuals, businessmen, even rugby players, are showing independence and making their own political decisions.' Across the globe, old conflicts were being addressed and new solutions were being found. 'Tragically, South Africans are left behind, trapped in their own history, locked into an old problem.'

As to whether I should try to gain access to Mandela, or speak to the ANC leadership inside the country, Mbeki said this was not essential; implying as before that there were other means of communication. It had been anticipated that the establishment would try to create division between the internal and external wings. They expected Mandela's release to be tied to a Government demand that the ANC commit itself to participate in a negotiation process. As far as the improvement of his prison conditions was concerned, this didn't affect the basic fact: 'He remains a political prisoner. The whole process is a sham. Winnie is right to insist that her visits be confined to the prescribed forty minutes.' He said it was not important that I meet Mandela at this stage, but it might be important if his father could be given access.

Mbeki commented also on the pressures being exerted on both sides by the international community. Neither side could lightly risk being seen as having obstructed the peace process – which was one of the reasons the Swiss proposal had to be taken seriously. He would have been concerned if the Swiss had concluded that an opportunity for a meeting had arisen, but that it was the ANC that was unwilling to participate. A message of this kind could also be damaging to the international standing of the ANC. I pointed out that these factors were similar for both sides, and this had been one of the reasons I had launched the initiative.

Discussion ensued regarding the summary document I had prepared for the State President. They too now wanted a copy. I said I needed to think about this, because the document had formed an attachment to a letter to the President, marked 'Personal and Confidential'. I didn't want to be accused of having breached an implied undertaking of confidentiality. Mbeki responded that there also had to be equivalence to ensure that neither side was given information not available to the other. I understood this concern, and tried to assure him that the document contained no more than a factual account of the events, coupled with a strong plea that the initiative be not terminated. My commitment was to serve the process as an honest, open, and even-handed channel. It could happen from time to time that, as an intermediary, I might receive confidences that I was not free to share.

Referring again to the issue of confidentiality, Mbeki re-affirmed the ANC's commitment to honouring its pledge of secrecy – provided the other side similarly kept to its promises. It was partly for this reason that the matter was being dealt with by a very small group at the present stage. I was assured that the ANC would meticulously honour its undertakings, although it had no confidence the Government would do the same.

After about five hours of intense discussion, the meeting terminated at roughly 9 p.m. We had both made copious notes during the evening. I asked whether it would not be a good idea if I tried to prepare some kind of minute of our discussion, but they demurred. Mbeki read from his notes and accurately summarised our discussion. He then said that they would convene an urgent meeting of the ANC Executive to consider the matter the following morning. He hoped to be able to convey some initial response to me before the afternoon flight back to Johannesburg.

After breakfast the following morning, I waited for our meeting to resume. This had been originally arranged for 11 a.m. However, it was almost 12.30 before Mbeki, Zuma and Mongalo finally arrived, and rescued me from Zambian television. I was becoming a little anxious because of the imminent departure of my flight to Johannesburg. They apologised for being late, but explained that the meeting had taken far longer than expected. The atmosphere was good-humoured and congenial. I told them that their television was almost as bad as ours – I had just been watching a women's programme in which the presenter had announced that the next speaker would be talking about 'tits and bits'! Jacob Zuma ordered a Coke, and the rest of us indulged in Chivas Regal. It emerged that Coke was less available in Zambia than good whisky. I chided Messrs Zuma and Mbeki on their 'capitalist bourgeois tastes'. Thabo laughingly responded that if I achieved no more than getting the Swiss to buy them some drinks, this in itself should be seen as an achievement!

Coming to the business of the meeting, Mbeki commenced by stating, 'We seem to be really no further than we were in July.' The argument of the Swiss concerning a possible 'change of heart' on the part of the South African Government seemed flawed, for the reasons mentioned yesterday – 'unless of course they know something we don't know'. As far as they were concerned, nothing significant had changed. The kind of assurances the ANC had already mentioned, they still required – in other words, some positive substantive action as a clear signal on the part of the Government, and some indication of the issues to be discussed.

In the absence of replies to these questions, it was not possible for the ANC simply to say, 'OK, we're ready for a meeting.' I asked, precisely what message they wished me to convey to the Government. Thabo replied: 'Tell Botha, that you have seen the ANC and the Swiss; and that it is your own view that a meeting is possible. However, from the ANC's standpoint it is essential that they first receive a reasonable response to their queries communicated as far back as July.' If the Government had placed me in a position to hand them a document indicating negotiating parameters – as had evidently been considered – 'at least you would then have been able to answer one of our questions. Therefore, it is not possible for you at this stage to say to Botha simply the ANC is willing to meet.' The ANC was concerned to secure the release not only of Nelson Mandela, but also of all other political prisoners. It was not concerned with 'reforming' apartheid, but bringing it to an end. 'We are not interested in gamesmanship. Our answer to any proposal for negotiations will be the same: "What do you want to negotiate about?" '

Zuma added, 'In our view, things don't seem to have moved at all. We have no reason to trust the good faith of the Government. With us, they don't have a reputation for honest dealing, and we have no basis for trusting them. Until there are grounds for trust, it will be difficult for us to overcome our lack of confidence.'

We talked of the Commonwealth EPG initiative. Mbeki recalled how in

April 1986 the Group had come to Lusaka on the final leg of its journey. They had conveyed their ideas for a negotiating concept, which had been presented to the Pretoria regime nine weeks before. However, the EPG now wanted the ANC to respond 'virtually immediately'. He said, 'We had to tell them that was impossible. We needed at least ten days to consider the matter; and this was in fact modest in view of the time given to the other side.' However, he pointed out, the proposals had not been rejected out of hand. Unlike the South African Government, the ANC took decisions in a democratic manner. This was part of the reason why time was required to consider such important matters. By contrast, 'the Botha regime' was largely 'a one-man show'. Mbeki commented, 'Botha can say anything he likes, and doesn't need to consult anyone.' The incident involving the Swiss Foreign Minister was a good example of how the State President acted unilaterally in summarily aborting the whole process, without even consulting his Cabinet. All it took was for him to lose his temper.

When the EPG returned to South Africa, they had reported to Botha that the ANC had not rejected the proposals out of hand, but was considering the proposals in a constructive manner. What then happened is a matter of historical record. The State Security Council had second thoughts, and decided to 'spin the process out'. Mbeki said there had been 'quite a detailed proposal' under consideration, but it had been 'shot down' – literally. Within days, the SADF bombed targets in Zimbabwe, Botswana and Zambia. Inevitably, the whole thing then collapsed. 'They deliberately killed it,' he said.

As a result of this kind of behaviour, they were extremely sceptical as to the true intentions of South Africa in Namibia. The present hiatus in those discussions could be just a 'hiccup'. 'But we would not be surprised if they decide to abort the whole Namibia thing, because they like playing a time-wasting game.' At Brazzaville the obstacle had evidently been the Government's insistence upon SADF officers being quartered with Cuban troops – so they could observe and monitor the Cuban withdrawal. Naturally, this had been unacceptable. The South Africans should have been willing to leave any monitoring to the United Nations.

With reference to their two unanswered questions, I suggested that perhaps the first purpose of an initial meeting might be to obtain those answers. 'Perhaps one should not insist upon prior answers.' Mbeki replied that it was most important that the ANC remained logical and consistent. These questions had been asked a long time back, and they must insist upon receiving answers. They were not unreasonable questions. They had first to convince themselves of the Government's bona fides and seriousness of intent. They were concerned that there might be an attempt simply to prolong the process, through using the possibility of negotiations as 'mere window dressing', and thereby earn approval from the world community, and the Swiss banks in particular. On the basis of past experience, there was 'deep-seated mistrust of the regime'. They cited as an example, the publication by Prime Minister B J Vorster of confidential correspondence he had exchanged with Zambian President Kaunda. This incident had caused much embarrassment to Kenneth Kaunda, and had set back the communication process. Again, on the occasion of Govan Mbeki's release, they felt there had been a breach of trust involving an understanding that there would be prior notice to the ANC.

I asked that they try to give me some constructive message for the State President. I needed to justify my request for a personal meeting with him. Their reply was: 'The Swiss have given you the knocker. Go and use it. Knock at P W's door.' They suggested I try to assure the President that the Swiss did not want to 'meddle' in South Africa's internal affairs, but believed sincerely that a favourable climate for dialogue might exist. I should inform Botha that I had met with the ANC; that I had been well received; and that negotiations were certainly 'on the cards', despite doubts about the bona fides of the South African Government. 'Say to him that the ANC did not chase you away, but was anxious that the same kind of thing shouldn't happen to them as happened to Kenneth Kaunda – in other words, that confidences should not be broken.' They repeatedly stressed that under no circumstances would they be the first to break confidentiality. 'The issues confronting us are far too serious for any kind of opportunism or attempt to gain short-term propaganda advantage. We are dealing with the future of our country.'

Mbeki mentioned that even Danie Craven had commended the ANC for keeping its promise about confidentiality, and contrasted this with the South African Government's exposé of discussions that had involved the SA Rugby Union. They believed this had come about through Louis Luyt's disillusionment with the Government's intransigence. Luyt had apparently prepared a memorandum in which he had noted the ANC's 'willingness to consider a cessation of hostilities', under appropriate conditions. He had handed this to Pik Botha with a request that he pass it on to the State President. When nothing had happened, he decided to involve another rugby heavyweight, Jan Pickard. Pickard had been given a copy of Luyt's memorandum – at a rugby match at Newlands! – and this he had handed to the State President's secretary, Jannie Roux. Someone had then decided to sabotage the issue, by leaking these facts to ultra-conservative OFS rugby chief, Steve Strydom. After that, it had all become 'a media event'.

Time ran out and we drove to the airport, where we continued talking in a small huddle in the VIP lounge. There were a few last-minute exchanges, clarifying issues previously discussed.

Referring to our earlier discussion about the memorandum I had prepared for the State President, I told them that I had thought about the problem, and was prepared to create another document, which would contain the same or similar information. Someone said, 'If you do this kind of thing, you're going to have to develop the characteristics of a Henry Kissinger.' I responded, 'Well, that's going to be difficult. I'm not even good-looking.' 'Never mind,' came the reply, 'Kissinger was also ugly like you!'

I raised again the possibility of a role for certain other governments who might be able to bring influence to bear on the Botha regime, and I mentioned Margaret Thatcher, in particular. Mr Mbeki replied that he didn't favour my involving the British at this stage. He agreed with the Swiss view that broadening participation could provoke an unhelpful competitive element.

I also mentioned my accidental 'discovery' of Willie Esterhuyse. They looked surprised. I asked, whether it might be a good idea, if he and I were to get a little closer? Thabo replied that this would not necessarily be a good idea. They saw Willie's function as completely different from my own. He was really gathering information and conveying it to the other side.

Just before leaving, I ran through a summary of our discussions, to ensure that I had correctly understood their message – in particular, that although sceptical of the Government's bona fides, they would be prepared to consider some kind of meeting, described as 'talks about talks', as suggested by the Swiss, which could take place even before the end of January, provided satisfactory responses were received to the two issues they had first raised with me almost five months before.

Three hours later I was back in Johannesburg, anxious to see P W Botha as soon as possible.

25

Knocking at PW's door

I was up early the following morning, my first port of call being the Swiss Ambassador, who agreed to see me at once. Stoffel van der Merwe was however unavailable and reluctant. He was about to leave on holiday. I stressed that there had been certain developments which were of great importance, and I needed to see him urgently. In fact, I believed I needed to see the State President in this regard. This was intended to arouse Stoffel, and it had the desired effect. He finally agreed that we should meet at his official residence in Cape Town on Wednesday 14 December.

At the Swiss Embassy in Pretoria I was greeted by a very animated Mr Quinche. He had received a full account of our discussions in Berne, and now sat with pen poised to hear what had happened in Lusaka. 'What was Mr Brunner's mood?' he asked. I said he had seemed optimistic but impatient. The Ambassador was worried about the time factor. Perhaps Mr Brunner was in too much of a hurry. He would soon be leaving for Washington. 'After all', he reminded me, 'this is Africa!'

When I had related to him the conditioned response of the ANC, he commented that this seemed 'very negative'. I disagreed, and pointed out that we were still at a very early stage, and the ANC's response was not unexpected. It would be quite unrealistic to expect either party to open its arms to the other at the first opportunity.

How was I going to pursue the matter with P W Botha, he asked? Van der Merwe surely couldn't be the channel, and Barnard was unavailable. I had been thinking about this over the past twenty-four hours, and had decided to address the President directly by means of another urgent personal letter. There seemed no better way of ensuring that he received my message in the precise terms intended. It couldn't be entrusted to an interlocutor. The Ambassador agreed. However, he feared Botha's reaction was likely to be one of anger at another case of 'Swiss meddling'. I said the real art of the letter would be to convey to Botha the reality of an opportunity, without provoking his rage. 'Botha hates pressure,' warned Quinche. He thought it might help that the message came through me rather than himself. Time would tell.

Once again, we discussed the vital importance of maintaining confidentiality at this stage. The more time that passed, the more people that knew, the greater the risk of unintended disclosure. When I suggested that I might fax him a copy of my letter to the President, he replied that this would not be sufficiently secure. In any event, the Swiss Embassy had not yet been equipped with a fax machine! He would be reporting our discussion this morning by cipher telex to Berne.

Back in Cape Town, I spent virtually the entire next day drafting a momentous letter to the State President. It had to be near-perfect. As Slabbert had frequently warned me, I would have only one chance. It had to avoid the Scylla of his mercurial anger, and the Charybdis of his end-of-year ennui. It had also to convey urgency, but not pressure. It had to be firm, but respectful; explicit, but not prescriptive; comprehensive, but not prolix. This was finally the best I could devise:

PERSONAL & CONFIDENTIAL

Mr P.W. Botha
State President
Union Buildings
PRETORIA   14 December 1988
URGENT

Dear Mr President

I very much regret the necessity to write to you personally once again, particularly in the light of your tremendously heavy programme, and the understandable difficulty of contending with major issues at this time of the year. Nevertheless, during the past few days there have been certain major developments affecting the initiative with which I have been concerned, which I believe may be of such significance as to warrant your urgent personal consideration, even at this most awkward time.

Following receipt of your letter to me of 11th November, I have as suggested by you held further discussions with Dr Stoffel van der Merwe and officers of the National Intelligence Service, as a result of which it has seemed appropriate that I should pursue my initial exploratory discussions with the African National Congress, and the Swiss Government. Accordingly, separate meetings have taken place over the past week in Lusaka and Berne on the basis of reciprocal undertakings of utmost confidentiality, involving in both instances, very senior representatives – Mr Thabo Mbeki, Mr Anthony Mongalo and Mr Jacob Xuma, members of the Executive Committee of the African National Congress; and on behalf of the Swiss Government, Secretary of State Mr Edouard Brunner, Ambassador Mr Alfred Ruegg, Head of Political Division 2, his Deputy Mr Christian Blickenstorfer, and Mr Pierre Combernous, Secretary to the Foreign Minister.

Arising from these confidential discussions, it has become clear that a unique opportunity may presently exist to bring about an initial secret meeting between representatives of the Government and of the African National Congress, to take place in Switzerland without preconditions or excessive formality, and against reciprocal undertakings of confidentiality. The purpose of such meeting would seem to be to explore the feasibility and the conditions under which further substantive discussions might take place: in other words, 'talks about talks'.

Whilst it would be premature to anticipate the probable success or failure of any such exploratory meeting, I believe that the risks involved would be amply justified against the landmark possibility of initiating a process of communication which could ultimately lead to a consensual negotiated future for our country. I have no doubt that the political courage thus manifested – irrespective of the success or failure of the attempt – would be widely applauded, and evoke enormous goodwill from the vast majority of all groups within our population. Following upon the success of the Namibian/Angola negotiations, it would be viewed as an historic act of statesmanship.

It is the opinion of the Swiss Government, that recent initiatives by your Government – and in particular the substantial progress achieved in resolving both the Angola conflict and the impasse on implementation of UN Resolution 435; as well as the reprieve of the Sharpeville Six; and the release of certain longserving political prisoners – have succeeded in creating an unprecedented opportunity and climate conducive to the commencement of a negotiation process. The Swiss are anxious to assist in any way possible, and to play a discreet and helpful role in facilitating dialogue between representatives of the different groups, whilst avoiding interference in South Africa's internal political affairs. This facilitative role would be in conformity with the long-established Swiss tradition of neutrality, and its official policy on South Africa, as set forth in paragraph 6 of the Resolution of the Swiss Parliament dated 22nd September 1986.

Accordingly, the Swiss Government has authorised me to convey its willingness – if acceptable to the parties – to provide a venue in Switzerland for a secret meeting to take place if possible before the end of January 1989. In order that the requisite arrangements can be made and with a view to securing absolute confidentiality, the Swiss have requested that the parties' response be communicated to them if at all possible, by Monday 16th January 1989.

The African National Congress through its representatives, duly authorised by a special meeting of the Executive, has indicated to me its unequivocal assurance that it would respect a reciprocal undertaking of confidentiality. Whilst its official policy disavows any process of 'secret negotiations', it would view an initial exploratory meeting of this nature (implying 'talks about talks') as falling outside the ambit of this principle. However, the African National Congress's willingness to participate would presuppose a satisfactory response to two questions which they have posed – being the same questions posed and communicated through me to Dr Stoffel van der Merwe as far back as July of this year.

These questions are as follows :

1. The African National Congress requests the South African Government to provide some 'indication of seriousness of intent' :

> Despite my enquiry, they have declined to be prescriptive as to what they would regard as appropriate. In brief, they seek some substantive signal to authenticate the bona fides of any intended process. They are clearly anxious to avoid being drawn into a meeting which in their view was no more than 'cosmetic or propagandist'.

2. The African National Congress requests some indication as to the agenda for any such meeting :

> I have stressed that the essential character of an exploratory meeting would be that it take place without fixed agenda or excessive formality. However, their concern once again is to avoid inadvertently becoming involved in discussions which, in their judgment, were irrelevant or trivial.

I have expended much effort in attempting to avoid any attempt to impose pre-conditions for such an initial meeting. Thus I have emphasised that the statement of conditions for future negotiations, having already received the attention of the parties, should if possible be avoided, but that the further clarification and restatement of such conditions could well constitute part of the business of such preliminary meeting itself. The African National Congress has assured me that, provided it receives a reasonable response to the two issues posed above, it will not seek to 'pre-negotiate' conditions or 'posture' in an attempt to achieve initial gains ahead of such meeting. Whilst recognising the measure of fundamental difference, it will approach the suggested meeting in complete good faith, having regard to the long-term future of our country as a whole. It has stated, 'The issues confronting us are far too serious for any kind of opportunism or attempt to gain a short-term propaganda advantage'.

In this letter I have sought, to the best of my ability, to set forth the circumstances and background to the proposal. However, it is not possible to convey by letter a full account of these events, without unduly burdening an already lengthy letter. The Swiss have urged that in these circumstances I should again request, with all due deference, the privilege of a meeting, and I do so with a sense of urgency and responsibility for the delicate role which I have sought to play.

In conclusion, may I once again reiterate my undertaking of confidentiality, and my commitment to do whatever lies within my power to advance the cause of peace and justice in our beloved country. I wish you and your family a very happy Christmas and a New Year of hope and reconciliation.

Yours sincerely,
Richard Rosenthal

When the letter was finally settled and signed, I telephoned the President's office, and left messages for secretary, Ian Putter. They were never returned. Thus, just after lunch, I walked down to Tuynhuys, and personally delivered the letter. I then went to the Swiss Consulate, where Mr Saxod was waiting. He had no idea what was afoot, but had instructions what to do with an envelope that I would hand him. In fact, there were two double-sealed envelopes addressed respectively to Ambassador Quinche in Pretoria, and to State Secretary Edouard Brunner in Berne. The following day, Mr Quinche called to confirm that both letters had been safely received, and that Mr Brunner's copy would leave that evening under courier in the diplomatic bag. There was nothing left to do, but wait – breathlessly.

We had woken that Wednesday morning, 14 December, to a headline, reading: 'It's agreed: Freedom for Namibia, Cubans to go.' My immediate thought was that the timing of my letter might be absolutely perfect. After a protracted stop-start process, the South African, Cuban and Angolan negotiators had finally agreed at Brazzaville to end the war, involving a withdrawal of all foreign troops, an exchange of prisoners, and the implementation of UN Resolution 435 leading to Namibian independence. Foreign Minister Pik Botha was quoted: 'We want to be accepted by our African brothers. We need each other.' The *Financial Times* of London foresaw this accord as leading to a negotiated framework for reconciliation between whites and blacks in South Africa, facilitated by the new spirit of cooperation between Washington and Moscow. It was a rare moment of euphoria.

Earlier that morning, I had gone out to 'Uitsig' on the Groote Schuur Estate, and met for one and a half hours with Stoffel Van der Merwe, who was busy packing his bags for the family holiday at Stilbaai. Understandably, he seemed less than overjoyed to see me. By the time he knew what had transpired, he looked even less gratified. When I told him that I had decided to address the State President directly, he showed great concern and said hastily, 'Please don't mention that I've met you since November.' I pointed out that this was precisely what the State President's letter recommended that we do. I could see no reason for diffidence. In any event, our discussions had yielded no decisions or actions whatsoever.

I asked whether he had made any progress in clarifying the State President's letter to me of 11 November. He said the right opportunity had just not arisen. I asked whether his 'political scars' were beginning to heal, and he replied that only time would tell. He said the past year had left him feeling totally exhausted, and he was sleeping no more than a few hours a night. It had been like this for six to eight weeks. He seemed deeply depressed. I said I had brought him a book to read on holiday – Mikhail

Gorbachev's *Perestroika*, which I hoped would serve as 'mind food'. I had also brought him some 'soul food', which I hoped he would also find helpful. It was a book by Rabbi Harold Kushner, called *When Bad Things Happen to Good People*. I felt he might identify with the title? As a Dopper, he might also be interested to read what a Jew had to say about the Book of Job!

Concerning the substance and urgency of my message, he said, 'Again I'm going to have to be a bit negative.' To expect some kind of decision before the end of January was totally unrealistic. The political process did not get going again until after the holidays – around 16 January. He would be attending a meeting of the State Security Council on 20 December, and would be in Cape Town briefly on 2–4 January, but he would only really return to his desk on the 20th. The major priority would then be the forthcoming session of Parliament, and the President's opening speech. It sounded like *déjà vu*. He added that the week of 9 to 16 January was largely taken up with the annual southward migration of the Pretoria bureaucracy. As far as he knew, the State President had in any event already left for his holiday house at the Wilderness. Traditionally, he would only return after his birthday on 12 January.

For these reasons, Stoffel was very doubtful that any significant discussion could take place before the second week of February. The parties must realise that the Government had other urgent commitments. Whilst he agreed one should not lose an opportunity through delay, this matter was far too important to be dealt with hurriedly. It needed careful analysis and planning. 'These are life and death issues for us,' he said. 'The Swiss need to remember how long it took them to devise their Constitution. You should tell them that we also hope to achieve a Constitution that will last as long as theirs!' He drew attention to the time it had taken to launch the disarmament talks, and the SALT and Vietnam negotiations. 'One is not talking of days or even weeks. They will have to bear with us a little bit on this.' His approach was to spend effort at this stage 'getting the machinery ready, so that we are ready when the opportunity arises. ''n Boer moet wag totdat die vrug ryp is om te druk.' ('A farmer must wait until the fruit is ripe for the picking.')

He undertook that as soon as the correct opportunity arose he would use his best efforts to ensure a favourable outcome, but it must be understood that he no longer had a special brief in this matter. He would have to wait for an opportunity to arise in Cabinet discussions. 'You see, I can't simply go to the State President and say, "I want to meet with the ANC." Botha would blow his top!' He thought the opportunity could arise during the latter half of January. 'But, it mustn't be rushed,' he insisted. He needed to bide his time, and would be ready to 'grab the opportunity' when it arose. 'We mustn't fall into the trap of trying to make instant coffee. We are living in Africa, not Switzerland!'

Concerning the attitude of the ANC, as reported by me, he took issue with the suggestion that the Namibian/Angola accord had anything to do with reverses on the battlefield, or that the other developments were the result of international pressures. But he agreed with the ANC that the Swiss were misinterpreting events if they saw reason for optimism in these developments. 'All right, to a limited extent. Yes. In other words, if there were a Conservative Party Government in power, some of these things wouldn't have happened. To that extent.'

He didn't see why the ANC should look for further evidence of the Government's seriousness of intent. There were plenty of decisions and actions which provided ample evidence of the Government's sincerity. 'Of course, it may be necessary for us to re-emphasise, and even reformulate some of these matters.' There was a possibility that he might in due course produce a paper not specifically addressed to the ANC, which would deal with some issues, including 'the seriousness of the Government's commitment to reform'.

As far as the subject matter of a future meeting was concerned, he stated, 'Of course we're not going to ask them to discuss Bantustans. If that was the agenda, I wouldn't expect the ANC to take part. The most significant item on an agenda would be the future agenda. It's important we don't go with a set of proposals for this or that. One must try to explore various ideas and possibilities; the emphasis being on *explore*. Concerning a meeting in the near future, I'm a bit pessimistic. The Swiss must not become impatient. We're not trying to pull off some propaganda coup. You don't build prefabs if you want to stay a long time.'

I mentioned that the Swiss believed their meeting with President Botha had not gone as badly as he had given me to understand. I wondered whether, as they had suggested, the difficulty might not have arisen in translation, but Stoffel disagreed. However, he did ask whether there was present at my meetings a certain bearded interpreter from whom he sensed a degree of hostility. He understood enough French to be sure that any 'misunderstanding' had nothing to do with the quality of translation. He believed Foreign Minister Felber spoke English quite well, but preferred to use his own first language, hence the need for a translator. In fact, said Stoffel with a chuckle, on any future occasion he might 'return the compliment' – by speaking Afrikaans, and taking his translator!

Before leaving, I spoke about the necessity for decisions and actions. It was not just a question of the Swiss becoming impatient. After fifteen months, I too had become impatient. Perhaps, I suggested, there was good reason for impatience? Stoffel reproved me gently, 'Part of the make-up of a good facilitator is patience.'

I wished him well on his holiday, and returned to my office, hoping for an early reply from the State President.

I must ask you to desist

When I opened my mail on Monday morning following the long weekend, my heart missed a beat. There was an official-looking envelope date-marked Pretoria, which I hastily opened (see next page).

Two months had passed since the start of my futile attempt to communicate with Dr Niel Barnard. The 'very interesting document' to which he referred was my Memorandum to the State President, of which a copy had been handed to his aides seven weeks before. I had long since given up hope of hearing from him. He had chosen to contract out of the duet to which he had been assigned by the President. After so much ambiguity, here at least was a letter which, whatever its shortcomings, was quite clear and unambiguous. I was to 'desist', and put my faith in 'the judgment and capabilities' of the 'official instances' – strange phrases! Indeed, what cause had I to presume the existence of such esoteric faculties? It was the lack of such faith that had eventually given rise to my initiative.

Nonetheless, Barnard's letter presented me with a great dilemma. Unbeknown to him, matters had already progressed far beyond the situation described in my Memorandum to the President. Moreover, Barnard's letter bore no reference to the watershed proposal of the Swiss Government, which now lay presumably unopened on the desk of the State President – and the ANC was already on record as having given its qualified acceptance. The letter had somehow meandered for two weeks between Pretoria and Cape Town, competing no doubt with the annual deluge of Christmas cards. It bore the date 6 December, a day I had spent in Berne consulting with the Swiss.

Having regard to Barnard's awesome capabilities, his request that I 'desist' could not lightly be ignored. It had the unmistakable undertones of a directive. I was taken aback by its bluntness, seen against the background of his Olympian inaccessibility, and his unwillingness to accommodate any discussion about the matter. Who were these 'relevant official instances'? My first thought was – as Slabbert and Esterhuyse had suggested – that this might be a euphemism for none other than Niel Barnard himself? Did a mere Cabinet Minister like Stoffel not qualify as an 'official instance'? Was Barnard

Nasionale Intelligensiediens
Die Direkteur-generaal

Tel. 322-8133

National Intelligence Service
The Director-General

Privaatsak
Private Bag X87
PRETORIA
0001

CONFIDENTIAL

NI/DG/13/1/13/2

6 *December 1988*

Mr R Rosenthal
P O Box 3800
CAPE TOWN
8000

Dear mr Rosenthal

I studied the very interesting document you sent me and have taken note of the State President's letter to you, dated 11 November 1988.

While I appreciate your concern as well as your efforts regarding a most delicate issue, I must ask you to desist from further action and to trust the judgement and capabilities of the relevant official instances.

Yours sincerely

DIRECTOR–GENERAL
(L D BARNARD)

CONFIDENTIAL

telling me in effect that Stoffel lacked the necessary 'judgment and capabilities'? I couldn't believe that Barnard's five-line letter was my valedictory, after the time, effort, risk, and cost I had invested in the initiative. The President had been personally consulted at the outset of the venture. It was he who had referred me to Van der Merwe, and subsequently to Barnard. What if they disagreed? Obviously, they were not communicating. The situation seemed quite incredible. I suppose this *was* illustrative of how South Africa was being governed towards the end of the Botha era.

At that stage I was unaware of the personal ambitions and professional prerogatives assumed by Niel Barnard. Three years later in February 1992, he briefly lifted the veil of inscrutability to source a series of articles which appeared in *Die Burger*, under the byline of its political editor, Alf Ries. These articles made it clear, as I had suspected, that Barnard saw himself as the 'relevant official instance', to whose judgment and capabilities I was being 'asked' to defer. The Barnard revelations appeared under a headline reading: 'N I wou sonder middelman na ANC gaan.' (N I wanted to go to the ANC without an intermediary.) That said it all.

'Ons uitgangspunt was dat, anders as in Suidwes of in Rhodesië, daar nie middelmanne moes wees om ons bymekaar uit te bring nie. N I het oor die jare sterk standpunt ingeneem dat hy self met die ANC moes kontak maak. Want die oomblik as daar 'n middelman is, wil hy ook iets uit die ding kry. Buitendien regeer akademici en sakelui nie die land nie. N I het geglo dat hy dit kon doen omdat hy kon optree sonder dat iemand daarvan geweet het. Ons standpunt was dat N I die aanvanklike kontak moes maak sodat die pad oopgemaak kon word. Dan kon dit aan die politici en die departemente oorhandig word wat daarmee gemoeid was.'*

When I read this, I began to understand Barnard's impermeability, and his sense of panic at having been bypassed and superseded. In other words he saw this as an N I S prerogative, and my initiative had pre-empted him. No wonder he wished me to 'desist' and place my faith in 'the relevant official instances'. My independent contacts with the external leadership of the ANC held out implications that I had not foreseen. Not only did it create the possibility of a two-track process, with the likelihood of dissonance between the internal Mandela dialogue on the one hand and my proposed 'external'

---

* Our starting point was that unlike in South West Africa or Rhodesia there should not be intermediaries to bring us together. Over the years N I took the firm position that it had to make contact with the ANC itself because as soon as there's an intermediary he will also want to derive something from it. Moreover academics and businessmen do not govern the country. N I believed that it could do it because it could act without anybody else knowing. Our position was that N I had to make the initial contact so that the way could be opened. Then it could be handed over to the politicians and the state departments who were involved.

dialogue on the other. It also unwittingly posed a threat to the 'negotiations monopoly' which Barnard and the N I S sought to claim and assert.

Clearly, it was Barnard's intent to seek to exploit the physical separation of the internal and external wings of the ANC, and to further fragment 'the enemy' by physically separating Mandela from his longtime prison colleagues. In his revealing memoir, Barnard acknowledges the desirability of having two separate channels of communication: 'Ons benadering was dat ons die inisiatief die hele tyd moes behou. Ons wou die groep in die buiteland inbind in 'n eerste gesprek voordat mnr. Mandela vrygelaat is.'*

In his own account of the genesis of the negotiation process, Barnard implies that the policy initiative came from himself. Without acknowledging Mandela as the author of the proposal for talks, he describes how he obtained Botha's approval for exploratory discussions by a four-man committee, whilst Mandela remained captive at Pollsmoor and Victor Verster prisons. The first of these committee discussions, he tells us, took place in May 1988 – when I was simultaneously meeting for the first time with Thabo Mbeki in Germany, and eight months after my original proposal to the State President.

In fact, long before my own efforts, Nelson Mandela had taken the first crucial steps that would ultimately lead to a negotiated settlement. In his personal chronicle, *Long Walk to Freedom*, Mandela describes how shortly before his admission to the Volkshospitaal for prostate surgery in November 1985, he wrote a letter to Police Minister Kobie Coetsee pressing him for a meeting to discuss the possibility of talks between the ANC and the Government. Though Coetsee did not respond directly, he visited his prisoner in hospital, and Mandela interpreted this as 'an olive branch'. Upon his return to Pollsmoor, Mandela was transferred to separate quarters – on instructions from Pretoria. He saw this as an opportunity to initiate in-depth discussions, and explains: 'I had concluded that the time had come when the struggle could best be pushed forward through negotiations. If we did not start a dialogue soon, both sides would soon be plunged into a dark night of oppression, violence and war. My solitude would give me an opportunity to take the first steps in that direction, without the kind of scrutiny that would destroy such efforts.'

Mandela was faced with a dilemma similar to that which had troubled me at the outset of this initiative – namely, whether, and if so how, to engage both the 'internal' and 'external' leadership of the ANC, as a banned organisation. I had concluded that it would be impracticable for me to engage the

---

* Our approach was that we had to keep the initiative the whole time. We wanted to involve the group overseas in an initial discussion before Mr Mandela was released.

internal leadership, who could not be safely identified, and who were almost certainly under Barnard's vigilant scrutiny. Mandela similarly decided that, despite the momentous nature of the issue, it would be impracticable for him to engage either the Lusaka leadership or even his own prison colleagues. He explains: 'I chose to tell no one what I was about to do. Not my colleagues upstairs, nor those in Lusaka. The ANC is a collective, but the Government had made collectivity in this case impossible.' His personal initiative was not without misgivings or qualms. 'A decision to talk to the Government was of such importance that it should only have been made in Lusaka. But I felt that the process needed to begin, and I had neither the time nor the means to communicate fully with Oliver. Someone from our side needed to take the first step ...'

Incredibly, despite several reminders from Mandela, he received no response from Minister Kobie Coetsee, and it was not until the Eminent Persons' Group arrived in February 1986 that he was finally able to renew his efforts to initiate a process of dialogue. In June of that year – after the EPG mediation attempts had collapsed – Mandela wrote a further letter to Coetsee via the Head of Prisons, Brigadier Johan Willemse. This resulted in a series of meetings, after Coetsee had obtained Botha's authority to explore the situation. Allister Sparks records: 'He instructed Coetsee to probe Mandela more closely and report back to him, *but not to breathe a word to other Cabinet members*, for Botha was still terrified of word leaking out that his Government was meeting with the ANC.'

But it was not only Botha who felt threatened by these secret talks. The Lusaka leadership had heard rumours – probably through conversation with Mandela's itinerant lawyers – and was deeply concerned. Mandela relates that towards the end of 1987 – when I was awaiting Botha's response to my original letter – Oliver Tambo smuggled a note to Mandela, using one of his lawyers as a courier, in which he referred to the reports of secret talks, and asked what Mandela was discussing? 'Oliver could not have believed I was selling out, but he might have thought I was making an error of judgment. In fact, the tenor of his note suggested that. I replied to Oliver in a very terse letter saying that I was talking to the Government about one thing, and one thing only: a meeting between the National Executive of the ANC and the South African Government. I would not spell out the details, for I could not trust the confidentiality of the communication. I simply said the time had come for such talks and that I would not compromise the organisation in any way.'

I too had heard rumours, but had no certain information or knowledge of the Mandela–Coetsee dialogue. I am certain that neither Mandela nor Coetsee was aware that I was raising the same issues at the same time with the external leadership. From the astonished reaction of the N I S, it was apparent that even the supposedly omniscient Niel Barnard was blithely ignorant of the 'Rosenthal initiative' until I chose to approach him in October 1988. Stoffel van der Merwe was also being kept at a distance, notwithstanding that he sat on the State Security Council. He had complained to me that 'the people handling Mandela are keeping their cards close to their chests'! Even the 'president-in-waiting', F W de Klerk, was apparently unaware of the facts. As Allister Sparks records: 'It was not until late 1988 that he (De Klerk) became aware of the secret negotiations with Mandela. They had been taking place with Mandela for nearly four years, but without his knowledge.' Only P W Botha knew it all – a fox or croco-dile indeed!

However, all this information lay in the future. I was faced with the urgent necessity to respond to Barnard's fiat. It was a few days to Christmas. The ANC in Lusaka and the Swiss in Berne were awaiting Botha's response to the invitation to initial talks. Barnard's letter cut right across these momentous possibilities. The President and Stoffel were on holiday. 'The processes of Government had wound down,' in Stoffel's quaint phrase. I faced, alone, the baffling conundrum of what to do. Frankly, I was scared.

After giving the matter twenty-four hours' thought, on the morning of Tuesday 20 December I telephoned Barnard's office in Pretoria, only to learn that he too was on holiday! His personal assistant, a Mr Louwrens, told me that he was not expected back until 9 January. In fact, it would seem that Botha, Barnard and Van der Merwe had all interrupted their family holidays that day, and were attending a meeting of the State Security Council in Cape Town. Louwrens undertook to give Barnard an urgent message that I was very anxious to speak to him as a matter of urgency. But he never contacted me, and finally after the Christmas–New Year holidays I reconciled myself to the inevitable, and made arrangements to go away with my own family for a much-needed two-week break at Nature's Valley – just a few miles up the coast from P W Botha's Wilderness retreat.

Before departing, I made certain that the respective offices of Botha, Van der Merwe, and Barnard, all knew how to contact me. On 4 January I made a final series of telephone calls, during which the President's secretary, Ian Putter, assured me that the President would not be back 'vir 'n geruime tyd' ('for quite a while'), and Stoffel bemoaned the fact that he had been compelled to abort his short holiday. I asked him whether there had been any developments? 'No developments, thank goodness!' he replied. He hoped something tangible might be attempted in the foreseeable future. I dropped a note to the Swiss Ambassador – who was also on holiday in Switzerland, and reported, '... that a reply to my letter of 14 December is most unlikely to be available prior to my return on 19 January ... In the circumstances there would appear to be no option but to await developments, and I shall naturally liaise with you in Cape Town immediately upon my return ...'

For two weeks, we swam and baked in the sun, and went for long walks along the wild coast of Nature's Valley. It was a chance to rediscover ourselves as human beings, reintegrate as a family, and prepare for the daunting challenges of the year ahead. I tried not to think about the future, and took particular care to avoid newspapers, radio and television. Occasionally, I would spare a thought for P W Botha, as I did on his birthday, Thursday 12 January; and I imagined him returning to Groote Schuur over the following weekend.

With time for reflection, I read books and wrote in my Journal:

Thursday, 12 January 1989

A week has passed during which I have done my best 'not to think of an elephant'. This is meant to be a holiday, but 'the elephant' is very difficult not to think of.

I feel baffled and lost – and afraid. The experience of this initiative, of dismembering my career, of departing the firm, of becoming reclusive and opaque, and bearing a huge secret for more than a year, has left me feeling alienated from a normal life. It has been wonderful to be an ordinary family again. Hilary and the children have been magnificent, but this whole experience has exacted a cost from us all.

Saturday, 14 January 1989

I have a 'scare' that one day, when the story of this experience is told, people may look at me and at what I tried to do, and say with justification, How on earth did you imagine that you were competent to undertake this thing on your own, single-handed? It's ridiculous! Naive!

Today, I read Sheldon Kopp:

'Perhaps it demands such a Holy Fool as Don Quixote to take the evil of the world seriously enough, and to imagine himself sufficiently adequate to be willing to dedicate his life to improving the suffering lot of others.

'I wish to point out that in a world in which true madness masquerades as sanity, creative struggles against the ongoing myths will seem eccentric, and will be labelled as "crazy" by the challenged establishment in power.'

On Wednesday 18 January, we packed up our holiday house, and set off on the eight-hour journey home. We reluctantly said goodbye to the peace and tranquillity of Nature's Valley, and began to think about what lay ahead. Jonathan would be starting medicine at the University of Cape Town. Caroline had just graduated as an environmental biologist, and would be turning 21 in February. As we drove through the seaside village of The Wilderness, I looked across the lagoon at Botha's holiday home, 'Die Anker', and imagined him returning to Cape Town over the previous weekend. He would have been away from his office for four weeks. I imagined him attending to the accumulated urgent business of the Executive President on Monday, his first day back in office. I imagined him opening his 'Personal and Confidential' mail on Tuesday – that was yesterday! I could not guess what his reaction would be. In a sense he was cornered.

At a filling-station in Albertinia, I bought my first newspaper in a fortnight – and was absolutely staggered by the headline: **P W BOTHA HAS A STROKE!**

27

No personal malevolence

The timing seemed absolutely incredible. I stood in the Albertinia Café, rooted to the ground, reading the story again and again, trying to absorb its implications. I stared at the pictures of the President being wheeled into 2 Military Hospital, Wynberg, and read medical comments on the prospects for his recovery. Chris Heunis had been sworn in as Acting President. After a few moments, I returned to the car, and shared the news with the family. Then an apocalyptic thought occurred to me – Botha's stroke had occurred during the course of the previous morning, Tuesday 17 January! That was precisely when I had imagined him opening my letter. Could it have caused the stroke? Had he read the letter, and become enraged?

When we got home, there were more shocks in store. Arthur and Lorraine Chaskalson had spent their holiday at our home in Constantia whilst we were away at Nature's Valley. They left us a letter, which reported a mysterious burglary at our little garden cottage. Seemingly, nothing was missing, though the cottage had been expertly broken into, and all drawers and cupboards searched. Arthur reported that our tenant, a young woman, whom we knew as Wendy Adams, had not been seen for several weeks. The burglary had been reported to the police by our vigilant gardener, and we were requested to telephone the police as soon as we returned. We had not finished unpacking the car when the phone rang and the police asked if they could come at once and make another inspection of the cottage. I was amazed by their zeal in this small matter, having had previous experience of their benign indifference. They said they wished to come as soon as possible, and would like to take some photographs and fingerprints. They were insistent that I should be there. The fact that Wendy Adams was still away, and that as far as we knew nothing was nothing missing, didn't seem to deter them. They asked pointedly whether we had heard from our tenant, and I explained that we had only just returned moments before.

Next day, our neighbours must have been amazed to witness the arrival in our little country lane of half-a-dozen police cars, parked at a short distance from our house. At the appointed time, roughly a dozen men – several armed with automatic weapons and accompanied by sniffer dogs –

made their dramatic appearance. In charge was a certain Captain (later Colonel) Liebenberg, of whose formidable reputation I had heard, and whom I knew as the Commanding Officer of the Police Anti-Terrorism Unit. He had been involved in the operations which resulted in the arrest of my client Jenny Schreiner, and her leader Tony Yengeni. It was evident that this was no ordinary burglary. My first thought was whether this could be 'a set-up' to implicate me? Was this the work of Niel Barnard? It would certainly be an effective way of discrediting my bona fides and impartiality as an intermediary.

I tried to affect an air of innocence, although I was extremely frightened. Every corner of the cottage was meticulously searched; sniffer dogs rooted around amongst the vegetables; and two men with metal-detectors and spades probed the ground. A photographer took pictures, and fingerprint experts were also at work. I could only guess what they were really pursuing. If 'Wendy Adams' was not as innocent as I had supposed, how was I going to be believed? How could I explain the synchronicity of my parallel involvement with the trial of Jenny Schreiner? If this was not a 'set-up', it was such an incredible coincidence as to be almost inevitably disbelieved. Their suspicions regarding my playing a double role would be compounded by the fact that I was involved with this improbable personal initiative regarding negotiations with the ANC. The pieces would all fall into place. They would also know of my long-standing involvement with various 'radical' organisations. It felt Kafkaesque. Who knows, there might in fact be some link between my client Jenny Schreiner and my tenant 'Wendy Adams'.

Wendy had responded to our advertisement of a 'cottage to let', last November. The previous tenant had screened a dozen applicants. I had interviewed only his short list, and had chosen a rather anxious woman, heavily pregnant, who said she was 'desperate to find a home in which to have a baby'. She said her name was 'Wendy Adams', and that she was a teacher recently arrived from the Transvaal. I remembered that I was concerned that she had no call-back number, which she explained on the basis that she had only just arrived. She said our cottage was exactly the kind of place she had been looking for – above all, it was quiet and secluded! She seemed entirely believable and was happy to sign the lease immediately, and pay two months' rent in advance – in cash! Thinking back, I recalled that she had seemed to stumble once or twice when asked about her husband. She said he was also a teacher; that his name was Joseph; and that he would be joining her in a few weeks.

Eventually, after several hours, the police contingent departed. They asked for a statement which I said I would prefer to draft. They also left me with several telephone numbers, which I was to call if 'Ms Adams' should return – including that of Captain Liebenberg, and a Detective Warrant Officer Nortje.

Not long after they left, the phone rang, and a man who said I didn't know him asked if he could see me as a matter of urgency. He declined to say who he was or what it was about. I was inured to such veiled communications, having acted for persons under surveillance or threat for a long time, and therefore did not pursue a line of questions which he was obviously evading. He repeated that he needed to meet me as soon as possible, and that we couldn't talk on the phone. Though worried about this statement which had probably been recorded on my own phone, I agreed to meet him the following day, but insisted that it should take place at my former law office.

Next day a young man came to see me, dressed in jersey and jeans, looking very tense and anxious. I took him into the boardroom, thinking it might be a safer milieu. He said he had heard I was a lawyer who could be trusted. He was therefore taking a risk in speaking to me frankly. He had come on behalf of my tenant, 'whom you know as Wendy Adams'. She was in great danger, he explained, and needed my help! He said Wendy ('but that isn't her real name'), would not be coming back to the cottage. She was actually in hiding, and wanted to apologise for the trouble she had caused us. I was completely nonplussed. How did I know whether he was genuine, or part of an elaborate 'set-up'. Had the police been to the cottage, he wanted to know. I hesitated before replying, not wishing to be recorded, and then nodded. There were certain items 'Wendy' needed me to remove from the cottage - and it was very urgent. It wouldn't be safe for anyone else to go, he insisted. Was I willing to help? I blanched. 'She really needs your help.' 'What d'you want me remove?' I asked. He said the main thing was a baby's cradle! There were also 'a few other things'.

If it was a scheme to incriminate me, then any attempt on my part to remove evidence could render me culpable as an accessory, subject to all the formidable penalties of the main offence – which was presumably terrorism or treason. On the other hand, if I declined to help, and she was in fact an ANC or MK operative, then my refusal might reflect adversely upon me in my other role. It was 'Catch 22'. The request might be genuine, but it might just as easily be a trap. If he was an emissary of Dr Niel Barnard, then whatever I was saying to him would now be recorded. There was no possibility of winks and nudges; nor could I think of any other way in which he could authenticate himself to me.

Eventually, I opted to make the simplest of statements, indicating that I would have liked to help 'Wendy', but I had no idea who he was, or who she was. Although I felt sorry for her, I was afraid I just couldn't help. He looked genuinely baffled, and then departed hastily. He said he might contact me again. I asked him please not to do that, adding, 'I am also involved with certain things you know nothing about, and your contacting me could place those matters in jeopardy.' He looked understandably mystified. Such were the times.

In their parting note Arthur and Lorraine Chaskalson had written: 'Some days before the burglary, an adult European male of indeterminate age, black hair, and a curiously insistent manner, who was in the company of a black labrador, and had a cloth bag (woven) strung around his shoulder, questioned me about a woman who was living in a cottage in a house whose number he did not know. I said that I had seen a woman in the cottage of the house, but I did not know her name. He questioned me closely about this, saying the person he was looking for was pregnant. He was unhappy with my replies, walked to the cottage with his labrador, and I did not see him again. I do not know whether there was any connection between this and the subsequent disturbances, but I mention it for what it was worth.'

Not wishing to frighten the family, I decided initially to keep this to myself. But when I got home that night, Hilary said that she was worried about a car hidden in the bushes opposite our cottage. It had been parked there all day, and there were two men sitting in it. She'd noticed it when she left for work in the morning, and they were still there in the late afternoon when she got home. It seemed they were watching the cottage. This was pretty scary. I decided nonchalantly to take the dog for a walk in that direction. Sure enough, there were two very tough-looking characters in plain clothes, sitting cramped in the front seats of a small car, silently smoking. I nodded as I passed by. Later that night they were still there. I could see the glow from their cigarettes across the river.

After dinner, Hilary handed me a note that she needed to talk but was afraid to do so. We were used to a suspect telephone, but had begun to think that our house might also be bugged. So we turned up the TV volume, and spoke to each other in whispers. I told her that I would not be surprised if they raided our house that evening. Hilary was afraid they were going to detain me. If this happened, what was she to do? We went over the details again, and I made sure she had various telephone numbers. I didn't tell her at the time of my anonymous visitor, nor of my fear that those men in the car were actually waiting to see whether I attempted to remove certain items from the cottage, as had been requested. My nightmare was that if 'Wendy' returned, or anyone else attempted to enter the cottage, they might open up with automatic weapons. It had happened before. That would be one way of terminating the initiative! Before going to bed, I went through our house and bookcases and removed various items which were banned or possibly incriminating, and hid them in a plastic bag under the trees in the garden. It was a warm summer's night, but I lay in bed shivering from fear. I hadn't done that since I was a very young child.

Throughout that weekend, the twenty-four-hour surveillance continued. We tried to behave as normally as possible, but confined our conversation to things we were happy to share with whoever might be listening. Trying to behave as normally as possible, I even went down to the cottage and watered the garden – albeit with some trepidation. I couldn't help wondering whether the cottage itself had been wired. It was not uncommon for 'suspected terrorists' to be shot, allegedly attempting to escape. Late on Saturday afternoon, I went for another walk past the parked car. This time there were two different men sitting there, pretending to ignore me. I knocked at the window and asked: 'Are you from the police?' They looked at each other, and nodded. When I asked what they were doing, they said there had been some burglaries in the area! 'It must be rather boring sitting here,' I said solicitously. They nodded, but they were not great conversationalists.

On Sunday afternoon, Hilary made an uncharacteristic suggestion that we go for a drive! She wanted to talk, and I had to caution her not to regard the car as safe. In the end, we walked along Muizenberg beach, but the strain was beginning to tell. There seemed little we could do to relieve the tension. Hil said she'd had a nightmare about 'Wendy' being killed in our garden. I tried to 'reassure' her by mentioning that I had been in touch with one of Wendy's friends, who had told me that she would not be coming back. However, we would need to behave as though we didn't know this. Hilary felt anything but reassured. 'What are we going to do about her belongings?' she asked. I explained that we would have to pretend that we were expecting her back. Only when her rent fell in arrear – in two months' time – could we think about reletting the cottage. We would have to go through the motions of issuing a summons, getting a Court Judgment, and formally 'evicting' her, even though we knew it was really a charade. Wendy had pre-paid two months' rent!

That night we had dinner with Arthur Chaskalson at the Vineyard Hotel, and were able to share with him the continuing saga of 'Wendy Adams'. I also showed him the correspondence received from Niel Barnard. Arthur was as calm and unflappable as ever, though conceding that the situation was quite alarming. He agreed that Barnard's letter had to be taken very seriously, although it was apparently not the answer from P W Botha himself. The 73-year-old President remained shielded from public view, recovering from what was officially described as 'a mild stroke'. It was obvious that the duration and gravity of Botha's illness would be decisive not only for my initiative, but also for the prospect of a change of leadership in the National Party.

There is nothing to worry about,' said Acting State President, Chris Heunis. 'We will continue within the parameters and policy guidelines laid down by the State President.' However, the pro-National Party newspaper *Beeld* appeared not to be listening. It caused a near-sensation by daring some audible introspection. 'Are talks between the Government and an African National Congress delegation under the leadership of a free Nelson Mandela really so unthinkable?' it asked rhetorically. Answering its own question, it suggested: '... we should begin to think of giving the ANC a chance to show whether they are serious when they say they want a political solution.' There were also early rumblings of a battle for the succession in which Heunis clearly saw himself as the front-runner. The official version was that the President was making a better-than-expected recovery, and in the sanctimonious words of Heunis, 'It would be distasteful if Mr Botha's illness was to be used as an opportunity to look for his successor.'

However, KwaZulu Chief Minister and Inkatha President, Mangosuthu Buthelezi had no such qualms. He made his own views known in a statement issued from Ulundi: 'In anybody's language, a stroke is a signal of the coming of a rest that is well deserved ... Mr Botha has served South Africa as he best knew how, and nobody should begrudge him the rest which should now follow ... We just have to believe that history is working for the benefit of all South Africans. History will always move the undesirable out of our midst ... and direct us to (our) destiny.'

We shared with Arthur the strain of trying to live a normal life under the gaze of two armed men sitting in a car parked opposite our house, presumably waiting to pounce. Both our children were in the process of leaving home and establishing their separate lives. One half of me wanted them to leave and get out of the way of this nightmare; the other half was heartbroken at the prospect of their departure. Hil asked whether we should not begin to think in terms of the initiative being at an end? Arthur thought for a while before replying. At the outset, he had been highly sceptical, he said, but had been surprised how far the initiative had actually progressed. He remained 'cautiously sceptical', but felt it was too early to abandon it. We talked about a recent statement of the National Executive of the ANC, which had affirmed that it was 'ready and willing to enter into genuine negotiations', provided the objective was 'a united non-racial democracy', and provided it was not called upon unilaterally to renounce violence. 'Any cessation of hostilities would have to be negotiated,' it stated. Personally, Arthur doubted that the National Party was ready for negotiations. 'But I could be wrong.' We discussed a recent article in *Beeld*, and another by Mark Swilling which had appeared in the *Weekly Mail* under the title 'Quietly thinking the Unthinkable', which suggested that the Government was cautiously nudging towards a dialogue with the ANC.

After this meeting, I decided to try once more to communicate with the ephemeral Niel Barnard, who appeared to be the effective nightwatchman in the absence of the President. I drafted him a letter in which I referred to 'a number of very significant developments since the date of the report to which you refer'. Not knowing whether he was in fact aware of my latest letter to the President, I urged that, 'it is of utmost importance that you be fully informed regarding these latest developments at the earliest opportunity. It seems appropriate in view of the sensitivity of these matters that I should report to you personally, and accordingly request the privilege of an urgent meeting at a time and venue suitable to yourself.'

However this letter was never despatched, for it was superseded before posting by another registered letter from Dr Barnard (see next page).

When a man of Barnard's daunting capabilities gratuitously disavows 'any personal malevolence towards you', one sits bolt upright. I regarded the letter as extremely disturbing. It evidenced a belief that in pursuing what he termed 'your inopportune initiative', I was deliberately defying his advice, misrepresenting the facts, and worse still, 'conniving' with a foreign power. I had no doubt that the letter was intended to convey the most serious possible warning. Indeed the undertone of the letter, which even Barnard regretted, seemed to indicate a degree of menace. Curiously, the signature clause was quite dissonant – 'Respectfully yours'. What on earth did that denote? His prior letter to me had concluded, 'Sincerely yours' – I assumed that this was simply a typing glitch, transposing a phrase that might have been intended for Barnard's correspondence with the State President?

After reading the letter several times, I felt really anxious. I had no illusions about the kind of political philosophy – and theology – which justified the use of violence against wrong-thinking individuals. Niel Barnard's beliefs were manifest in his essay entitled 'Theoretical Reconnaissance in International Relations'. He had written: 'In world politics fragmented by sin, the sword must always be applied justifiably for the punishment of evil. The attitude that the Christian may never take up the sword and must suffer for injustice is dangerous cowardice. The Government receives the sword from the hand of God to guarantee inter-state stability and provide justice in a crooked and twisted generation.' These were chilling words.

As I drove home, I was more than ever conscious of 'the sword' held by the two men watching our house, day and night. They had been there for more than a week.

Nasionale Intelligensiediens
Die Direkteur-generaal

Tel. 322-8133

National Intelligence Service
The Director-General

Privaatsak
Private Bag X87
PRETORIA
0001

CONFIDENTIAL

NI/DG/13/1/13/2   *19 January 1989*

Mr R Rosenthal
P O Box 3800
CAPE TOWN
8000

Sir

The State President has referred your letter of December 14, 1988, to me.

In my letter, dated 6 December 1988, I specifically but politely asked you to desist from any further moves. In spite of this you persisted in your inopportune initiative, and even mentioned talks with members of my Service as motivation for doing so!

You leave me no alternative but to react very bluntly: The issue involved is of such a delicate and complex nature that the Government will certainly not pursue it through third parties, least of all with the connivance of a foreign power. I am afraid that you are only succeeding in complicating the very process you are evidently in favour of.

I regret the tone of this letter. Please accept my assurances that it is not the result of any personal malevolence towards you or, indeed, of a jaundiced approach to the important issue concerned.

Respectfully yours

DIRECTOR GENERAL

CONFIDENTIAL

The following day, January 24, I sent a reply to Barnard, marked '*Personal and Confidential*':

Dear Dr Barnard,

Your letter of 19th January 1989 reached me yesterday afternoon upon my return to office after a period of two weeks' leave. In fact, I was about to despatch my reply to your earlier letter of 6th December 1988, but this has been largely superseded by your latest letter.

It is of the utmost importance that I correct a serious misconception which is apparent from your latest letter. I refer in particular to the fact that you have characterised my most recent actions as persistence 'in spite of' the contents of your letter of 6th December. This is not correct. Your letter dated 6th December and postmarked 'Pretoria 7th December 1988', was received by me on the morning of Monday 19th December. At that stage I had already returned from my journey to Berne and Lusaka (3rd–11th December), and had already reported on these developments, both verbally and in writing to Dr Stoffel van der Merwe, and to the State President by letter written and delivered on 14th December. Indeed the only reason I had not also been in contact with your office at that stage, was the advice which had been conveyed to me by members of your Service (Mike Kuhn and Koos Kruger) at our meeting on 18th November, that because my work was viewed as 'a political initiative', it was deemed inappropriate for your Service to have further contact with me in this regard.

In the circumstances I trust you will understand the reason for my omission to communicate further with you regarding subsequent developments in this matter as they evolved.

Far from ignoring your letter of 6th December, may I assure you that I have taken careful note of your advice. No further steps whatsoever have been taken by me since receipt of your letter on 19th December. In fact, when I realised the apparent contradiction between your advice to me and developments which had already taken place, I immediately attempted to contact you personally by telephone on 20th December. Mr Louwrens of your Pretoria office informed me that you had already departed on leave and were not expected back until approximately 9th January. I emphasised the urgency and importance of my communicating with you, and he undertook to try to contact you in Cape Town where you were apparently meeting on that day. In the result, I received no further message.

I have set out these events in some detail in order to dispel any possible interpretation that I may have either ignored your letter of 6th December, or proceeded without the utmost care and circumspection as befits a matter of this complexity and importance.

I assume the facts of this matter are sufficiently clear from the documentation in your possession, but if necessary, I am available to amplify any aspect which may require clarification. Suffice it to say, that at the outset - in my original letter to the State President of 23rd September 1987 - I made an offer of my personal assistance, if this would be considered helpful 'in the delicate initial stages of the preparatory work leading to the establishment of a successful negotiating process'. This offer was made 'in the utmost good faith and in the hope that it could prove to be of assistance'. I believe that I have acted scrupulously in terms of this undertaking.

There is one crucial matter upon which I need your guidance. A secret but nonetheless formal invitation by the Swiss Government has been extended to our own Government and to the African National Congress. The African National Congress has posed certain questions in this regard. In order to bring the process to an immediate end, in terms of your advice, I urgently need some guidance as to the manner in which this can best be achieved, and in particular the nature of the message to be conveyed to each of the parties. I am extremely anxious at this delicate stage to do nothing which could in any way embarrass the parties, or jeopardise the possibility or success of a future process. In view of the sensitivity of the matter, I would greatly value the opportunity to meet and consult in this regard at your very earliest convenience.

Yours sincerely
Richard Rosenthal

The day after this letter was despatched, it was reported that Botha had been discharged from hospital and had returned to his official residence, 'Westbrook', to continue his convalescence. Barnard's letter clearly implied that the President had read my letter prior to his stroke. This was also borne out by a subsequent letter received from Botha's secretary (see next page):

From Lusaka came word that ANC President, Oliver Tambo, flanked by the ubiquitous Revd Jesse Jackson, had declared 1989 'The Year of Mass Action for People's Power'. Speaking at the organisation's 77th birthday celebrations, he had emphasised the importance of enlisting international support, stating: 'It is of the greatest importance that the biggest possible campaigns should be launched in the major Western countries to oblige their governments to impose further and more meaningful economic sanctions ... ' However, in the same month it was reported that a consortium of Swiss banks had granted the South African Government a new R100m 'rollover' loan.

Despite the fact that Van der Merwe had been sidelined, I was anxious to have his views, and after several attempts to make contact we made an appointment for the morning of Saturday 28 January, when we met at his office in Stalplein House, Cape Town. It was our first meeting in more than

I.2

Tuynhuys
Kaapstad

24 January 1989

Mr R Rosenthal
P O Box 3800
CAPE TOWN
8000

Dear Mr Rosenthal

I confirm receipt of your letter dated December 14, 1988. As instructed by the State President, I have referred it to the Director General of the National Intelligence Service.

With kind regards

ADMINISTRATIVE SECRETARY

a month. Stoffel seemed invigorated by his recent vacation, but bemoaned the fact that, after only a few weeks back in harness, he was already feeling 'exhausted'. He needed another holiday, he said. Apart from the extra burdens arising from the illness of the State President, he had been dealing with a number of corruption scandals, one of which would lead to the resignation of Cabinet Minister Pietie du Plessis, and another the political demise of Nationalist Member of Parliament Peet de Pontes.

Stoffel raised the matter of 'that very tough letter you have received from Niel Barnard'. For once, he had received a copy. I showed him my reply, which he read carefully, and then commented, 'It's an excellent letter. You've dealt with the matter very well.' In his view these difficulties had their origin in the 'unfortunate discussion' between the State President and the Swiss Foreign Minister. This had caused a complete change of attitude. The matter had been taken entirely out of his hands. He felt disappointed, but there was nothing he could do about it.

This led to our discussing once again how the initiative had commenced, and I asked that he confirm once again that the President had given him authority to pursue the initiative. He said that was quite correct. It had been handled on the authority of the President. 'But that authority was given quite a long time back.' I asked him whether the State Security Council had been involved, and he shook his head. The initiative had not formed part of its agenda, nor had any other Cabinet minister been involved. At one stage, he had felt optimistic, expecting that we could make real progress after the October Elections. Unfortunately, this had never materialised.

Concerning my abortive attempts to meet Barnard, Stoffel said: 'He's deliberately avoiding you. I can't tell him how to conduct his affairs.' I said I found Barnard's attitude extraordinary, because the judgments and decisions he was required to make would involve an understanding of what I had been involved with. Van der Merwe said he agreed, and that he was also 'a bit mystified' why Barnard seemed so reluctant to meet me. He said he might try once more to persuade him to meet me – if only to consider the nature of the messages which had now to be conveyed to the ANC, and the Swiss Government. However, Barnard had been completely adamant about terminating my involvement. Stoffel didn't expect an opportunity to discuss the matter with Barnard until the State Security Council met again in ten days' time.

I thought it unwise to complicate matters with Stoffel further by giving him an account of the unfolding drama of 'Wendy Adams'. On the other hand, circumstances could arise in which I needed his help. Accordingly, and without giving him details, I mentioned certain alarming occurrences involving a tenant in our cottage, which could give rise to quite serious misunderstandings as to my independence and good faith. Stoffel said that if a problem arose I could contact him.

The President was apparently making a good recovery, but Stoffel said it was too early to know whether he would be able to resume the leadership. This could also have a bearing on the prospects for my initiative. I told him that my immediate concern was the message to be conveyed to the ANC and the Swiss. I hadn't communicated with either for some time, hoping that the situation might first clarify. I reminded him that the ANC were still waiting for a reply to the issues they had raised; and that the involvement of the Swiss involved a generous contribution towards the costs I had incurred – following his personal request and assurance to Ambassador Quinche. Stoffel looked somewhat pained. He was aware of the situation, he assured me, but really had no suggestion to offer. All he could do was promise to try to persuade Niel Barnard to meet me.

He asked, what were my plans for the future? The situation had not yet crystallised, I said, and at this stage I really had no idea what the future held for me. Stoffel seemed embarrassed and concerned. I had in all respects kept my word, he said. He'd not at any time felt misquoted or misrepresented, and was generally satisfied with the accuracy of my reports.

A few days later, I wrote Stoffel another reminder concerning his promise to speak to Niel Barnard, 'to try to facilitate an early meeting ... to review the present situation, and decide upon appropriate practical steps in relation to this initiative. You will understand my extreme concern to clarify the nature of "the message" to be delivered to the various interested parties, not to mention the necessity to clarify my own situation. In the circumstances, I would be very grateful if this matter could receive your most urgent attention.' However, Stoffel's efforts were in vain, and Barnard persisted in his refusal to meet me. He was adamantly opposed to any involvement of facilitators, other than himself. In his *Burger* memoire, Barnard explains his attitude which caused him to oppose the Dakar conference (at which his eyes and ears were Willie Esterhuyse) and all other attempts at opening up an unofficial dialogue: 'Ons was nooit gekant daarteen en het ook nie gedink dat ons 'n aantwoord vir die land se probleme sonder die ANC sou kon kry nie. Maar ons wou nie toelaat dat groepe en regerings van buite as fasiliteerders vir die gesprek optree nie.'*

He and his Committee of four were now meeting regularly with Nelson Mandela at his new abode in a warder's house at Victor Verster Prison, trying

---

* 'We were never against it and we never thought that we would be able to solve the country's problems without the ANC. But we did not want to allow outside parties or governments to act as facilitators for the discussion.

to ascertain as Barnard put it 'how Mr Mandela's mind works'. Mandela described Barnard as 'exceedingly bright, a man of controlled intelligence and self-discipline'. He adds, 'although they were all sophisticated Afrikaners, and far more open-minded than nearly all their brethren, they were the victims of so much propaganda that it was necessary to straighten them out about certain facts. Even Dr Barnard had received most of his information from police and intelligence files, which were in the main inaccurate and sullied by the prejudices of the men who had gathered them.'

But 'the times they were a-changin' '. From January 1989, the prison authorities began to allow Mandela 'rudimentary communications' with his comrades at Pollsmoor and Robben Island, and also with the ANC in Lusaka. In reality, the journey towards negotiations had begun.

28

Connivance with a foreign power

Parliament reconvened at the beginning of February, and Botha lost no time in dispelling premature rumours of his political demise. In characteristic style, he issued an imperial fiat, without consulting his party or Cabinet, in which he declared that he was resigning as leader of the National Party, but would retain the office of Executive State President. This self-architectured political dichotomy was quite unprecedented, but Botha argued that it would enable the Presidency to become 'a unifying force in our country'. Within twenty-four hours, the National Party caucus had met and, despite Botha's preference for any of the alternative candidates, Pik Botha, Chris Heunis, or Barend du Plessis, it was Frederick W de Klerk that was elected by the Party as its new leader, albeit by the narrowest of margins – a mere 8 votes. Six months later, Botha would resign after a bruising battle with his successor, and a humiliating confrontation with his Cabinet colleagues. Within twelve months, De Klerk would release Nelson Mandela, unban the ANC, and formally initiate a process leading to negotiations.

In his opening address to the new Parliament, Acting President Heunis proffered his ritual 'high esteem' and 'compassion' for President Botha, and made a few pontifical observations of his own. 'Reason is replacing emotionalism,' he declared. 'Impatience with time-wasting on senseless infighting is increasing ... all communities are growing tired of leaders who delay the negotiation process for petty political reasons.' Heunis said that much had been achieved under Botha's leadership, 'quietly, though with dedication and purpose'. With stoic faith in his own doomed progeny, the still-born National Council, Heunis stated, 'This Government refuses to grant legitimacy to the perpetrators of violence by negotiating with them on constitutional development.' Paradoxically, he affirmed: 'The Government remains committed to the viewpoint that solutions can only be achieved through a process of negotiation ...'

The *Argus* commented: 'In spite of Government disapproval, dialogue with the African National Congress continues to flourish ... it is naive and idle to expect the ANC to make a unilateral capitulation to the Government's demands while it remains banned and is denied access to the political life of the country. It is equally naive to expect the ANC and its popular support inside the country to simply disappear.' Even *Rapport*, long regarded as the guardian of political orthodoxy, published an article by Piet Muller, suggesting that the Government might one day discover that by continuing to ignore the ANC, 'it had in fact accorded the organisation an exceptionally high stature'; and if it didn't soon propose an alternative vision for the future, the ANC's stature would continue to grow.

Whilst these internecine dramas played themselves out, the Government found itself virtually paralysed, and incapable of initiating or responding to negotiation initiatives. Its de facto immobility was recognised by the ANC in Lusaka, and the Swiss in Berne. Nonetheless, I felt it appropriate at this stage to prepare a formal record of the current status of my initiative, in the hope that further steps might become possible once the wrangling was over. Accordingly, I spent the first week of February drafting a 'Status Report', of which I delivered a copy to Ambassador Quinche on Thursday 9 February.

The Ambassador did not take kindly to Barnard's reference to 'the connivance of a foreign power', which seemed to him a rather strange and ungrateful way to characterise his Government's unsolicited supportive role. It was particularly inappropriate, if regard were had to the circumstances in which the Swiss had first become involved, with the 'connivance' (if that was the correct term) of Stoffel van der Merwe, who had been delegated to the task by the State President himself. The Ambassador also expressed surprise at Barnard's 'completely negative attitude'. He speculated – correctly as it transpired – that the N I S supremo probably wanted a primary role for himself in this matter of negotiations.

My Report concluded with the following paragraphs:

It will be apparent that a critical stage has been reached in which the future and continuance of the initiative is now at issue.

A great deal has been achieved in that, by implication, the African National Congress has probably accepted the principle of direct negotiations, commencing with an initial secret meeting to discuss agenda+s and future process ('talks about talks'). Moreover, the African National Congress has appeared to signal its willingness to consider incremental confidence-building measures, possibly including a suspension of violence, if the South African Government is willing to reciprocate. The good offices of myself as an interme-diary, and the assistance of the Swiss Government have likewise been accepted in principle, and despite the lapse of time and intervening circumstances, confidentiality has been maintained and respected by all parties.

However, the attitude of the South African Government seems

ambiguous. Whereas the initiative commenced with a personal letter to the State President, from whom subsequent correspondence has been received indicating his awareness of the matter, it now seems that his delegation to Dr Stoffel van der Merwe has been withdrawn. The latter has confirmed that I have honoured my undertakings to him, have demonstrated the ability to execute this delicate mandate, and have accurately reported upon events and his involvement with this matter. In the circumstances it is difficult to understand the tenor of the correspondence received from Dr Barnard, who appears to impute the unwanted interference of myself as a 'third party', and what he terms 'connivance with a foreign power'.

It has been my longstanding concern to have a personal meeting with the State President and/or Dr Barnard, but despite all endeavours this has not been achieved. Indeed it is still uncertain whether Mr P.W. Botha will recover sufficiently from his illness to take up the reins of office again. In the meanwhile, uncertainty prevails as to the future leadership of the country, and the prospects for reform and negotiation. What is certain is that a General Election will have to take place within a year, and this could quite possibly occur in the short-term. In the light of this reality, the Government's apparent stalling in the matter of opening up a dialogue may be more comprehensible.

In the result, I have sought – but still await – the South African Government's guidance as to what message it would like me to convey to the African National Congress and to the Swiss Government. At the very outset, I made it clear that my assistance was available if it was acceptable to BOTH parties. Whatever the outcome, it has been my prime concern to do nothing which could directly or indirectly exacerbate an already delicate situation. At the same time I am committed to maintain my pledge of confidentiality. In the ensuing days, I shall be seeking the advice of various confidential consultants, and would welcome any guidance you may consider appropriate.

This meeting was my first opportunity to tell the Ambassador about the continuing saga of 'Wendy Adams'. The police were still mounting a day-and-night watch on our property, and I explained my apprehension that the whole episode might have been 'manufactured' for some ulterior purpose – perhaps, to discredit or even eliminate me. Quinche said that if I was arrested or detained, Hilary should let him know, and he would see whether there was anything he could do to assist. Not for the first or last time, I felt extraordinarily grateful for his friendship and for the support of the Swiss

Government. Following this meeting, there were two further developments in the 'Wendy Adams' situation. On 11 February, the Security Police telephoned and said they would like to visit the cottage again. They arrived almost at once, and removed two items, for which they insisted upon giving me a written receipt, which refered to:

'1. Two metal plates (one has a No. 11 written on it). And 2. One "safety" belt (black). (found in red plastic bag with screws and pieces of wood inside).'

I realised that these were precisely the items I had been asked by Wendy Adams's emissary to remove! The metal plates were hidden in the folds of a baby's cradle, and apparently contained encryption codes. The other items were identified as having been attached to a case of munitions. I was left reeling at the thought of what might have happened if I had done Wendy the kindness requested. Immediately following this visit, I had a further call from her mysterious emissary, despite my earlier request that he not contact me again. Somehow he had located my private office number, and insisted that it was 'absolutely essential that we meet'. When he arrived at my office, he wanted to know whether the cottage was still being watched, and repeated that 'Wendy' would not be coming back. She wished me to give her belongings to our gardener, Albert. I knew the Security Police had a detailed inventory of the cottage, and told him that it would be perilous to do what he was requesting. Was this man for real, or an *agent provocateur*? I didn't know. On his departure, I told him that I hoped we wouldn't have the pleasure of meeting again!

During the week that followed, I sought out Van Zyl, Arthur, and Willie once again. I described to each of them the present baffling situation, and asked their advice. Van Zyl was surprised at the dismissive tone of Barnard's letters. He agreed that I should persist in my efforts to meet him, and try to pre-empt any antagonistic actions. He saw De Klerk's emergence as leader of the National Party as a hopeful portent. He also suggested that I might think about speaking to Prof. J P de Lange, head of the Broederbond, who Van Zyl felt could play a constructive role.

Arthur likewise viewed the imminent end of the Botha era as propitious for change. He was encouraged by De Klerk's initial pragmatism in releasing several detainees who had been on hunger strike, and also by the tone of his recent public utterances. Despite Barnard's negative attitude, Arthur believed something of value could have been achieved. One couldn't discount the possibility that my role might be revived under a new President. However, for the time being, the hiatus was likely to continue until the leadership issue had been resolved, and possibly until after the next General Election. Arthur saw no purpose in trying to force progress at this stage.

Willie seemed curiously unsurprised by the correspondence I had received from Niel Barnard. He said the future of his own contact role was also in the balance. Wishing to make common cause, I asked whether he would like to take a look at some of my notes and minutes, in which each step of my initiative had been meticulously recorded. To my surprise, Willie demurred, saying he didn't want to 'compromise' himself in any way. I didn't understand that he needed to keep me at some distance for another reason, if he was to retain the patronage of Niel Barnard. Indeed, not realising the nature of their relationship, I asked Willie if he could possibly assist me in arranging a meeting with Barnard. Willie looked somewhat pained, and said he would need to think about that before giving me an answer. He would let me know in a few days once he'd made up his mind. He did acknowledge that he knew Barnard 'quite well', and was in 'fairly regular contact' with him. I had no idea that he was actually working for Barnard and the N I S, though he did mention on this occasion that he would be giving a lecture to N I S officers the following week – on the improbable subject of Antonio Gramsci! Apparently, Barnard wished to educate his operatives in the deep mysteries of socialist political philosophy. Willie also viewed the change in party command as conducive to progress in reform being made. He described De Klerk as 'a pragmatist rather than an idealist', but warned that 'die ou krokodil' could still return! Willie did not have long to ponder my request, because the following day a further letter from Barnard arrived (see next page).

There was nothing further to be said. In Barnard's commanding view, the eighteen months spent in pursuing this initiative amounted to no more that an ill-advised frolic of my own. It was obviously of no consequence to him, that the initial concept and each subsequent step had been undertaken with the State President's approval, whether express or implied. With hindsight, Barnard's attitude becomes a little more intelligible, in that he and the N I S had become involved, albeit belatedly, with the same issue – and hence his reference to 'but one of several' initiatives. If, as he suggested, 'a disorderly situation' had arisen, it was surely no fault of my own. Nor had I need of his solicitous hope that I would find it possible, as he put it, to 'extricate' myself from 'undue embarrassment'.

My personal feelings of disappointment, and the objective merits of the issue were now irrelevant. Upon receiving Barnard's letter, I tried to make contact with the ANC in Lusaka, and left several messages for Thabo Mbeki to call me. Ultimately, we spoke on Monday 6 March. 'How's the year progressing for you?' he asked cheerily. 'Each day brings new surprises,' I answered, 'and they're not all good ones!' I told him of the advice received from Barnard that my initiative was to be summarily terminated. However,

NI/DG/13/1/13/2 *17* February 1989

Mr R Rosenthal
P.O.Box 3800
CAPE TOWN
8000

Dear mr Rosenthal

Your letter of 24 January 1989 was received with thanks.

Despite your meticulous explanation regarding misunderstandings, the fact remains that you are pursing a course which has already created expectations which you cannot fulfil. In the process, a situation has come about in which the Government is under pressure to undertake commitments not in sequence with its own program.

The involvement of mediators, and even a foreign power, in any event predestines a clash of interests and in procedures. Furthermore your initiative is but one of several and merely adds to a disorderly situation.

This very important and sensitive issue is therefore best left to official instances, who will act when it is opportune to do so. You are at liberty to notify both parties accordingly, assuring your Swiss contacts that the sincerity of their offer is appreciated. I sincerely hope that you will thus be able to extricate yourself without undue embarrassment.

With regard to your request for a personal meeting, I regretfully have to inform you that I cannot accede to it. You must accept that I am fully familiar with the theme in question and that I will in any case, in accordance with the codes of my responsibility, not be able to pursue the subject with you in any more detail. It is surely better to avoid a situation that can serve no purpose other than to create mutual discomfort.

Yours sincerely

....
DIRECTOR GENERAL
(L D BARNARD)

the battle for control of the National Party was not yet over, and the situation could change again. At this stage, there seemed no option but to await developments. We discussed the possibility of an early meeting. He would be away for ten days, and so we agreed to meet in Lusaka on Sunday 19 March.

Next I spoke with Ambassador Quinche, and informed him of these developments. We arranged to meet at the Embassy in Cape Town on Wednesday 1 March, when I gave him copies of the Barnard correspondence, which he described as 'not too unfriendly'. He speculated that perhaps the Government was 'clearing the decks' for a more significant step. One thing was clear – they didn't want assistance from third parties.

The Ambassador said that in present circumstances his Government could no longer underwrite my efforts, as their assistance was on the basis that it was acceptable to both sides. In his view it was regrettable that the initiative had been aborted at this particular stage, but he believed it could have served a valuable purpose. I should let him know about any further developments. 'If we can possibly save this thing, we must do so,' he said. The Ambassador commented that it was impossible to predict several present imponderables. Only last week he'd reported to Berne that rumour had it that Botha would not be returning to office at all. Present indications were exactly to the opposite effect.

I expressed my appreciation for his Government's assistance and for his personal friendship and concern. We discussed the need for maintaining confidentiality, in the interests of both parties. If these contacts were to be publicly divulged, the Swiss Government would have to admit its role, but would stress that it had become involved upon invitation, and only after it had obtained the prior agreement of both sides. I assured him that I would not be the source of any 'leak'. 'One day you must write a book!' he said with a grin. 'It'll read like a novel.'

That evening F W De Klerk delivered an important speech in the little town of Nigel. He declared, 'The time for the Great Indaba has arrived.' However, the attitude of the recuperating President was still definitive. Contrary to expectation, he flew to Cape Town the following day, and declared that he would be resuming his office after the Easter weekend. Newspapers commented on the bizarre circumstance that in matters of policy, the leader of the National Party could be overruled by the State President. In an editorial published on 28 February, the *Cape Times* made its own views clear: 'The Government cannot continue in a state of suspended animation. Mr Botha should accept that the time has come to hand over power. It is time to go in dignity.'

Six weeks had passed since my last contact with Stoffel, who was engrossed – if not enmeshed – in the unfolding drama involving F W de Klerk and P W Botha. At a news briefing, following the first week of the session, he was quoted as saying: 'A new constitution needs to be negotiated and the Head of State needs to be redefined.' I was not at all sure what that meant. Echoing a sentiment first expressed a few years earlier by Foreign Minister Pik Botha – which at the time earned him a Presidential reprimand – Stoffel predicted that in a future political dispensation 'it would not matter whether the President was black or white'. H e boldly proclaimed that the colour or origin of a particular incumbent would cease to be important, but then he diluted this vaulting vision by adding, 'especially when it comes to the more symbolic positions'.

On Wednesday 15 February, Stoffel's secretary Petra van Niekerk called to say she had been requested to give me a message. 'The Minister doesn't have time to meet you at this stage, but he has discussed the question of your meeting with the other person involved, who will contact you if he feels a meeting is necessary'! When I tried to contact Stoffel again on Tuesday 28 February, Petra once more demurred because her Minister was 'in Parliament, and very busy'. The following day her assistant Cecilia Schoeman told me that he had cancelled all appointments to go to the dentist, which seemed like a particularly good idea! Later Petra called again to say it would be impossible for him to speak to me, even on the telephone, 'until we come back from somewhere'! Finally, I spoke to Stoffel on Saturday 4 March. It was a brief conversation during which we agreed upon a date for a further meeting. He said he had been sent a copy of Barnard's latest letter to me. 'These are interesting days,' he said wryly. I could not but agree.

If making an appointment with Stoffel was difficult, making it happen was even worse. Three hours before our scheduled meeting Ms Schoeman telephoned to say it had to be postponed. A special caucus meeting had been arranged at short notice, she explained, 'to consider the position of Mr Botha'. Our meeting was then re-scheduled to 6 p.m. on Monday 13 March, but this too had to be postponed, and later it was cancelled, 'due to the events you've read about in the newspapers'. Petra van Niekerk explained that she'd been instructed to cancel all his appointments. As the drama continued, Petra said she was at a loss to know what to do 'because of the number of appointments I've had to cancel'. She too had been unable to speak to him for several days, but she promised to revert to me as soon as possible.

Willie Esterhuyse also called me on Monday 13 March to say that he had been feeling a bit guilty about not having contacted me earlier. In fact, he had tried to call from London, but without success. He had now spoken to the 'individual whom we mentioned in our last discussion', but his response had been, 'The best advice you can give him is to close down his initiative!'

A week later Willie came to see me at my office. He had just returned from a conference at Wilton Park in England, which had included several Soviet and British academics, and a few other key figures such as Dr Chester Crocker, US Assistant Secretary of State, and the principal architect of the Namibian settlement. Amongst those also attending had been Broederbond chief Prof. de Lange, and two Nationalist Members of Parliament. It was significant, said Willie, that the Soviets favoured a negotiated solution in South Africa, and were urging the ANC along those lines. However, Willie was despondent about the leadership impasse. He had deliberately refrained from contacting either P W or F W during the past few weeks, as he didn't wish to be seen as supporting either faction. In his view, the entire political process was at a crossroads. It was extremely unlikely that any progress could be made until the leadership issue was resolved. Moreover, he didn't expect it to be resolved easily or happily. In his words, 'If you want to kill a crocodile, you've got to be a crocodile; and I'm not sure F W is a crocodile!'

Willie said the President was in a particularly assertive mood – hence his decision to anticipate his return to Parliament on Budget Day, prior to the Easter Recess. I told him that I might have stumbled upon the real reason for his unexpected move – Section 10(3) of the South African Constitution Act, 1983, stipulated that if the incapacity of a President persisted beyond 60 days, he ceased to be entitled to name his surrogate; and the Speaker in liaison with the Chief Justice had to convene an Electoral College to elect the Acting State President. This would no doubt result in De Klerk replacing Heunis! I had counted the days since his stroke, and it seemed 56 days would have passed if the President returned on Budget Day, but the critical 60-day period would have expired if he waited until after Easter.

P W was a crocodile, indeed. Willie reiterated that one should never underestimate the man. His past record indicated that he wouldn't hesitate to use his powers under the Constitution. Willie drew attention to a curious use of words Botha had employed in a recent television address to the nation. He had said that it should be remembered that he was 'the custodian of the Great Seal of the Republic'. No one was quite sure what he was talking about, but Willie believed he was reminding his adversaries that he held powers which he would not hesitate to use, if he deemed them necessary. I said I also discerned a studied choice of words when Botha replied to a media question as to what he would do if the Caucus chose someone other than himself as State President? His response had been carefully phrased: 'I hope I will then have the honour of formally handing over the Great Seal to a chosen successor, who will pledge to uphold the constitution.' Did this imply that he might not have such honour, or that his successor might not give such pledge? The President concluded with these unctuous words: 'I don't believe in usurping the Lord's work ahead of time!'

I was scheduled to meet Thabo Mbeki a week later, and decided first to keep my promise to visit his father before our next meeting. Govan Mbeki was restricted to New Brighton, Port Elizabeth. I asked Advocate Fikile Bam to help me with the arrangements for a meeting on Thursday 16 March. When I arrived at his home, Mr Mbeki Snr suggested we go to a neighbouring house, where 'it would be easier for us to talk'. He was obviously frustrated by the continuing restriction order, and the fact that he could not address meetings or be quoted by the media. His initial press conference had been a fiasco. Now he was afraid that if he chose to ignore these restrictions, it might prejudice the chance of release for others.

He had been made aware of the general nature of what I was involved with, and asked that I give him an account of the present status of the matter. When I had finished, he commented that he thought I had done 'something good'. No matter what happened, I could have planted a seed and raised the possibility of a dialogue. This was important, but it would be understandable if the Government now decided to handle the matter itself without involving third parties.

He was well informed about the current situation, and an astute observer of human nature. He wanted to know my understanding of De Klerk's statement that the time had arrived for the Great Indaba? He also referred to a statement of Acting President Chris Heunis, in opening the KwaZulu Legislative Assembly (which Govan Mbeki referred to humorously as 'that Zulu contraption'). Heunis said that the only thing now preventing the participation of the ANC at the negotiation table was its refusal to abandon violence. Mbeki noted that even the Afrikaans churches were beginning to make a positive contribution to the debate. Prof. Johan Heyns, Moderator of the Nederduitse Gereformeerde Kerk, who was later assassinated, was quoted as having criticised the Government for having demanded that the ANC be the first to forswear violence, before it entered negotiations. Heyns referred to this as 'an ethical problem', because an end to violence should be seen as an outcome rather than as a precondition for negotiations. In Mbeki's view, these were unprecedented developments and might signal a climate more conducive to the possibility of a dialogue. He said the ANC favoured negotiations, subject to what he termed 'those very reasonable conditions set out by Lusaka'.

I told him that I had been advised by Lusaka not to try to meet Nelson Mandela myself, but rather to try to facilitate a meeting between himself and Mandela. He confirmed that he had sought permission for them to meet again last year, but this had been refused. Their last discussion had taken place just prior to his release. They were permitted an hour to talk. He had been brought to Pollsmoor from Robben Island by helicopter. With very limited time, they had discussed the role the Rivonia trialists might try to play in the future and it was agreed that they would try to facilitate negotiations, and bringing the two sides together. However, their discussion had been brief, and took place in the presence of someone he assumed was Director-General of Prisons.

After two hours, I left to catch a return flight. He thanked me for having come to visit him, and I promised to take greetings to Thabo, in Lusaka. Owing to his own imprisonment and his sons' exile, the family had not been able to meet for a long time. In fact, he had last seen Thabo when he was about 20 years old, and his other son when he was 12. Recently, they had spoken on a phone call from Washington. He had been given pictures of his sons, but had needed to stare at them for a while before he could make up his mind which was which!

I had been expecting a car to take me back to the airport. Parked outside Mr Mbeki's house when I emerged was a smart car with two young men chatting inside. I went up to them and asked whether they were waiting for me? 'Yes!', they replied enthusiastically. As I got into their car, I repeated the question and they explained they were salesmen working for Sanlam! I hastily retreated, and wondered whether they were also working for Niel Barnard, and had been eavesdropping our conversation.

A telex from ANC Headquarters in Lusaka awaited my return to Cape Town:

NO: 4055   17.03.89   11:10
TO: RICHARD ROSENTHAL
FR: DIP/TOM SEBINA

PLEASE PASS ON THE FOLLOWING MESSAGE TO MR R. ROSEN-THAL:
YR VISA TO ENTER ZAMBIA WILL BE ISSUED TO U ON ARRIVAL AT LSK INTERNATIONAL AIRPORT. YOU WILL BE MET AND ASSISTED. HOTEL BOOKINGS HAVE BEEN CONFIRMED.

REGARDS.

29

I think I can hear the sea!

I met Stoffel two days before my departure for Lusaka, and he seemed surprisingly upbeat. He expected that it would still take several weeks before the leadership issue was resolved, but present indications were that F W de Klerk would emerge as the next President, and this, he believed, was likely to lead to a new era of constitutional negotiations. He felt more confident and hopeful about the future than he had for a very long time.

I asked what message he wished me to convey to the ANC at this stage; and he replied that I should try to reassure them that the latest events around the leadership issue should be seen as 'extremely positive'. They should not be discouraged by the 'negative correspondence' I had received from Niel Barnard. If the leadership was conferred on De Klerk, there was a good prospect that negotiations would become the first priority. Indications were that a formula acceptable to all could be found, and that it would not involve 'too much loss of face for P W Botha'.

Stoffel said that he was able to make this prediction, because 'as a fellow Dopper' he felt much greater empathy with F W than he'd ever felt with P W. The Doppers were 'something of a subculture', he said, and F W epitomised some of their best qualities, including rigorous intellectual honesty. They were not afraid to ask fundamental questions, theological or political, and would tend to go back to first principles, and follow through logically on the consequences. As a result, he had less difficulty understanding F W's thought processes than those of P W. 'P W Botha is not a man with strong intellectual processes,' he said, 'although he has a fine political instinct. On the other hand, F W always relies, like a good Dopper, upon analytical thinking and logical deduction.' Doppers had been the first amongst the Afrikaans churches to recognise the absence of any scriptural foundation for apartheid. Their landmark statement *Woord en Daad*, had set them apart from other Afrikaans churches. They maintained separate congregations for different race groups, but envisaged a 'single combined synod, irrespective of race'.

He mentioned several factors which had contributed to his sense of optimism. For example, at the recent Wilton Park conference, evidence had emerged of a fundamental shift in Soviet policy. The Soviet Union, which had played such a crucial role in the Angola–Namibia negotiations, was urging the ANC to adopt negotiations as the most appropriate means to end apartheid. According to the official Soviet news agency Tass, the ANC had held talks in Moscow with the Soviet leadership just the previous weekend. In a report headlined 'Moscow snubs ANC in shift on Pretoria', *The Times* of London had claimed that a rift had developed between ANC President Oliver Tambo and his Soviet counterparts, concerning the role of 'the armed struggle'. Subsequently, the ANC had held a strategic review summit in Norway, under the chairmanship of Secretary-General Alfred Nzo. ANC spokesperson Frene Ginwala had conceded, on a BBC programme the day before, that the ANC was under heavy pressure to abandon the armed struggle and enter into peace talks. She said it was prepared to enter such talks, but that the onus rested on the Government to create 'a climate for peace'. She vehemently denied the existence of a rift as reported in *The Times*, and insisted that 'there was [Soviet] support for the struggle in all its forms, including armed struggle'.

I asked why there had been a widely held perception that De Klerk was the more '*verkramp*' of the Presidential candidates? Stoffel replied that this too was because of his intellectual honesty. Frequently De Klerk found himself questioning the improvised reforms emanating from Chris Heunis's department – principally because they were not coherent and largely cosmetic. De Klerk would oppose such measures, because he was unconvinced that they were more than expedient manipulations of principle. These interventions created the opportunity for people to see him as *verkramp*. In the caucus, he often played the role of Devil's Advocate, 'unmasking half-baked reform proposals'. Another factor had been that, as Transvaal leader of the National Party, he had borne the brunt of the Conservative threat to the Party. What could not be denied was that F W had committed himself over the past weeks to substantial reform, and a process of constitutional negotiations. Stoffel believed this must be accepted at face value and was very significant.

He spoke about 'a recent inner conversation of important Afrikaners of *verligte* disposition' – which I assumed to be a circumlocution for a Broederbond cabal – at which De Klerk had given his analysis of the alternatives now facing the country. He said there were four options:

1. To capitulate to the dominant black majority (the 'Liberal option').

2. To 'dig in'; resist demands for power-sharing, and do whatever might be necessary to maintain white domination (the 'Masada option').

3. To make adaptations and adjustments to the Constitution, whilst maintaining white control through 'indirect means' (the 'Heunis option').

4. To confront the necessity for fundamental constitutional change, recognising democratic principles, but negotiating to prevent the domination or subordination of any group (the 'Negotiations option').

De Klerk had concluded: 'Personally, I've made up my mind. I've come to terms with the consequences. I've taken the leap.' This had evidently made a great impression.

To my considerable surprise Stoffel predicted that, 'provided one or two things could first be sorted out', it might become possible for my initiative to be carried forward at long last. He apologised for having successively postponed our meeting, but it had served the purpose of enabling various factors to clarify. 'I hope I'm not becoming the victim of my own optimism,' he said, 'but I believe we are closer to the target than we've ever been before.' Everything would depend on the leadership issue being satisfactorily resolved, without too much delay, and without too much damage to the Party. Time was of the essence. If things took too long, it would undermine the authority presently enjoyed by F W. He could only play the envisaged role if he continued to project an image of steadfast determination. He said there was a mood in the caucus that 'Enough time has already been wasted, and we must now get something going.' De Klerk had correctly interpreted this mood, and had consolidated his position virtually beyond challenge. His recent utterances had naturally pleased the *verligtes*, but he also had loyal backing from conservative elements in the Party. There was 'only a small faction' that remained loyal to P W, and they were becoming increasingly muted.

Turning to my visit to Lusaka in two days' time, he said it could be helpful if the ANC were to make some sort of statement, along the lines that they had taken note of recent utterances of F W de Klerk, and were 'ready to review the situation in the light of any significant developments that might occur'. He hoped that the advent of a new leader of the National Party might encourage the ANC also to make adjustments to its previously held positions. In particular, the ANC needed to understand that it would be impossible for the South African Government to enter negotiations 'under the threat of violence'. 'One cannot create a democracy at the point of a gun,' he said.

Stoffel believed that the time had come for a positive move from the ANC – such as a clear statement to the effect that the ANC was ready to reconsider its attitude to the armed struggle, in the light of statements made by the new leadership. However, he cautioned, they had to be careful not to embarrass De Klerk. He was sure a formula could be found to convey a constructive message, without appearing to interfere in the National Party's decisions. With reference to future Swiss Government assistance, Stoffel said that I should convey to them that he remained positive about the future of the initiative, and would urge that it not be terminated, pending developments which could be anticipated 'over the next few months'.

I asked what I should do if I received a message from the ANC during my visit, particularly as I was unable to communicate with either the President or Niel Barnard? Stoffel agreed this was a problem. He found himself in an invidious position, because he remained 'out on a limb – no longer holding a brief in the matter'. Nonetheless, he said, if there was a message to be conveyed, I should contact him, and he would see that it was passed on.

I left him with a 'Van der Merwe story', lifted from the *Cape Times* a few days earlier: Van der Merwe and two co-conspirators were sentenced to death, and given the choice of the electric chair, a shotgun, or the guillotine. The first man said he wanted the guillotine. By some miracle the blade missed, and he was set free. Seeing what happened, the second man also chose the guillotine. Again the blade missed, and he too was set free. Then it was Van der Merwe's turn. He said, 'I prefer the shotgun.' Asked why, Van der Merwe explained, 'It is because the guillotine doesn't work!' 'Yes,' said Stoffel van der Merwe with feeling.

On 7 March the country passed an ignominious milestone – the State of Emergency, first imposed on 12 June 1986, was 1 000 days old. Asked to comment, Adriaan Vlok, Minister of Law and Order, said that the State of Emergency was still 'very necessary', because the revolutionary climate remained 'unacceptably high'. The voice from the Wilderness, P W Botha, was quoted in an interview published in Nasionale Pers newspapers, as saying: 'Every day I get evidence of goodwill, and there are literally thousands of letters of support from the population, which are overwhelming. This makes me realise my responsibility more deeply, and I will continue in humility to carry out my daily task.' The President's imperviousness to adverse public sentiment was well depicted by a newspaper cartoon which portrayed him standing on a balcony overlooking a great crowd. An aide says: 'It's the People, Sire. They've come to say Goodbye!' 'Goodbye?' replies the President. 'I wonder where they're going ...'

I arrived in Lusaka in the early evening of Monday 20 March, and was met by Anthony Mongalo and a young East Berliner, who took me directly to the Intercontinental Hotel, where a suite and conference room had been reserved. They told me that Thabo Mbeki had not yet returned from the ANC strategy conference in Oslo, and our meeting would have to be deferred until he arrived back the following day.

Ultimately we got together in my hotel at 5 p.m. on Tuesday afternoon. The meeting continued for about four hours. Only Thabo Mbeki and Anthony Mongalo were present, as Jacob Zuma was still out of the country.

As promised, I gave them a document entitled 'Report on the Development of an Independent Initiative', in which I had chronicled the genesis and evolution of this initiative, with copies of all relevant correspondence, including the latest letters from Niel Barnard. This document closely paralleled the earlier 'confidential' Report which I had forwarded to the State President. It concluded with these comments:

At the time of this report (15th March 1989), great uncertainty prevails as to the outcome of an impending clash between Mr PW Botha and Mr FW de Klerk regarding the future leadership of the country. It is reported that Mr de Klerk is insistent upon being accorded not merely the political leadership of the National Party, to which he has acceded through the resignation of President Botha, but also the executive power of the State Presidency. It is reported that the incumbent State President is reluctant to relinquish the reins of office, despite a substantial consensus to this effect within his own party and Parliamentary Caucus.

On 1st March 1989, Mr FW de Klerk called for a 'Great Indaba'. He said the present state of affairs in South Africa could not continue. 'We must start talking earnestly with one another now ... the time for the Great Indaba has arrived.' He envisaged constitutional negotiations – without preconditions – for all those who strive for peaceful solutions. It is difficult to ignore the relevance of these and similar utterances in relation to what lies at the heart of this initiative. Similarly the Dutch Reformed Church (NGK), through its Moderator, Professor Johan Heyns, has expressed itself troubled by the 'ethical' implications of the Government's refusal to entertain talks with the African National Congress, before it has renounced force as a means of achieving its political objectives.

Minister Chris Heunis, in addressing the KwaZulu Legislative Assembly, stated that if the African National Congress wish to act in South Africa's national interest, it can best do so 'by abandoning violence and declaring itself in favour of the peaceful process of political negotiations together with other political leaders in South Africa'.

Attempts to meet with Dr van der Merwe over these past days have been unsuccessful – in fact a meeting has been scheduled five times – and then postponed at the last moment. His office has counselled that a meeting should be postponed as long as possible, not only to accommodate his personal involvement with these events, but in order that the present ambiguity should hopefully be resolved. It is therefore inferred that the outcome of the leadership issue may have an influence upon the future of this initiative.

It would seem that a political atmosphere is being created which anticipates the commencement of a substantive negotiation process. What mechanisms, structure, and procedures the Government has in mind remain in doubt. In particular, it remains to be seen whether the National Statutory Council will be the forum of choice, and whether that forum, modified if necessary, would be acceptable to the other parties. It is understandable in these circumstances that the Government might seek to terminate or at least consolidate under its own direct management and control, any 'independent' initiative. In this context, Dr Barnard's characterisation of 'a disorderly situation' becomes significant.

In the circumstance, the future of the initiative remains problematical. The Swiss involvement has thus far been conditional upon the agreement of both parties. Mr Rosenthal's role has similarly been envisaged as that of a direct but unofficial intermediary operating with the approval of both parties and on a basis of mutual confidentiality.

Mbeki responded with an insightful analysis of the political situation as viewed from the ANC perspective. He speculated that the leadership struggle could have arisen not so much because of Botha's illness as because of his autocratic style and the tensions which this had engendered within his own Cabinet. He said with a chuckle that some of the good wishes for Mr Botha's speedy recovery were a little suspect – his well-wishers had included Winnie Mandela and Kenneth Kaunda. P W Botha found himself largely 'marginalised'. The only real issues now were the time and manner of his departure. The continued dominance of the 'securocrats' might also become an issue. He wondered whether Botha might also be defying calls for his resignation because of his unhappiness with the Party's choice of De Klerk as the new leader.

The ANC was following events closely, and had noted reports emanating from London that a new Eminent Persons' Group, with American participation, was being considered. Following talks with South Africa's Foreign Minister, Pik Botha, the British Prime Minister, Margaret Thatcher, had told the British Parliament that she was optimistic that Mandela would soon be released, and that this would 'change the atmosphere completely', and make possible the commencement of meaningful talks between the Government and black communities. There seemed to be a deliberate attempt to create the expectation of some forward movement in negotiations. In the ANC's view this could be genuine, or it might just be a smoke-screen or an attempt to manipulate the situation, by cultivating issues and unrealistic expectations in the ranks of the ANC.

Some relevant feedback had also come from the Soviet Union. Two weeks before, whilst in Moscow, Oliver Tambo had been informed of a discussion between the South African and Soviet representatives on the Namibia–Angola Monitoring Commission. Glenn Babb from South Africa had spoken of certain imminent developments in the short-term, including the release of Nelson Mandela and other long-serving political prisoners; the lifting of the State of Emergency; and the appointment of a Cabinet Minister with special responsibility for pursuing negotiations. He said the Soviets were also urging the ANC to 'give the South African Government a chance to prove its bona fides'. However, media speculation that the ANC was under pressure from the Soviets to suspend the armed struggle was not correct.

The N I S had played an important role in the Namibian negotiations and was basically loyal to P W Botha. Botha had used them before in sensitive situations as his 'trusted political arm', particularly where the loyalty or judgment of his own Cabinet members might be in doubt. Mbeki saw a tension developing between those he termed 'the strategists' (men like Barnard of the N I S, Van Heerden of Foreign Affairs, and General Geldenhuys of the SADF), and others whom he termed 'the tacticians', including Magnus Malan and some of the top brass in the Police who handled the day-to-day security situation. He felt the 'tacticians' were opposing negotiations, whereas the 'strategists', particularly following their Namibian success, were intent upon replicating the process of negotiation to include the whole of Southern Africa.

It seemed that the monolithic unity of Afrikanerdom was beginning to crumble. The ANC witnessed a continual stream of disaffected visitors wishing to engage them in dialogue. The latest arrivals would be a group of twenty Stellenbosch University students, who were due the next day. They had gone ahead with their visit in spite of opposition from their Rector, and from the political and cultural establishment. It was significant that they had resisted these pressures, stating that 'The arrangements were already too far advanced to call the thing off.' When it had become clear they were not going to be intimidated, efforts had been made to dilute the significance of their visit by proposals for an alternative venue, and a suggestion that they also try to meet Zambian and Namibian students.

Another example of the crumbling of mute conformity amongst Afrikaners was the emerging role of theologian Prof. Johan Heyns, who had spoken of an 'ethical problem' in the Government's insistence upon not talking to the ANC before it had abandoned violence. Puffing away on his pipe, Thabo recalled how he had first read Heyns's statement whilst sitting at the back of Kaunda's private plane – to which, he had been banished because of KK's intolerance for smokers! He was very happy with this arrangement, he said with a chuckle, because it gave him the opportunity to catch up on his reading – and also to 'smoke like a chimney'.

He then predicted how politics might evolve under a new democratic dispensation, maintaining that there should no longer be a place for political groupings based on colour. 'Group Rights' he described as 'an exclusive of Afrikaner politicians'. Every racial group contained a diversity of political opinions. Within the ANC, for example, there were whites who had risked and sacrificed their lives for the struggle. 'There have also been some black traitors, and some white martyrs.' If the political process was opened up, and banned parties were free to function, 'people of all races would come together, and realise that the future of South Africa was better represented by Nelson Mandela than by P W Botha'. When I suggested that such a scenario was unlikely on 'Day One', he countered that it didn't have to wait for 'Day Ten'. 'Perhaps "Day Three?",' I replied.

Thabo recalled how, at a press conference in Ghana, following the first Dakar consultation, he found himself having to defend the credibility of white delegates to media representatives who were sceptical of their sincerity. He said the media were surprised at this display of unity between South Africans, black and white. He went on to say, 'You see this sort of thing needs to happen not just in Ghana, but also in South Africa.' 'One day we may need whites to defend us, so that together we can deal with some of the fears of the past, and start to rebuild the country.'

One of the recent visitors to Lusaka had been Sam Motsuenyane, President of the black business organisation, NAFCOC, who had told them a personal story, which Thabo now repeated. Sam had related how one day he found himself stranded on a country road with a flat tyre. With some trepidation, he braved the farm dogs and approached a nearby farmhouse for help. Though continuing to address Sam as 'kaffir', the farmer went to a great deal of trouble to help him, and actually gave him a spare tyre. Sam thanked him for his generosity, and said he was surprised that an Afrikaner would go to such trouble to help 'a simple kaffir boy like me'. The farmer told him how one day he too had been stuck on a road in Swaziland. Many people – 'even whites!' – had ignored his requests for help. Finally, an Indian couple had come to his aid. When they said goodbye, the farmer said he would like to pay something for their trouble. They'd replied that they didn't need any payment, 'but, next time you come across someone stranded on the road, please help that person – no matter what colour they are. That's how you can repay me.'

After our first session, I had a late visit from Tom Sebina, who called at the hotel, because 'after speaking to you so many times on the telephone, I wanted to put a face to the voice'. As so often happened when talking to exiled South Africans, we got to talking about 'home'. He was hungry for news, and wanted to hear about the changes which had taken place in the years he had been in exile. I was moved by his obvious love for the country, and his longing to return.

The following morning, Thabo Mbeki came to my hotel on his own, and later drove me to the airport for my return flight to Johannesburg. We talked about the document I had handed him the previous evening, which he had by this time read. He said he found the document very interesting and useful. It was clear that Barnard was in charge, and believed that this matter was best handled by himself as 'the official instance'. It was also clear that they wished to exclude foreign powers and third-party intermediaries. Barnard seemed to believe this initiative could undermine their own plans. Mbeki said that although they were aware of discussions involving Nelson Mandela, he had no idea what Barnard was talking about when he referred to 'a number of other initiatives'. As far as the ANC was concerned, this was the only initiative of its kind, and was quite distinct from contacts with people such as Willie Esterhuyse.

He noted Stoffel's confidence that De Klerk would emerge as the new President, and that a substantive negotiation initiative might follow. However, one had to deal with the situation as it presently existed. In other words: Botha was still the President; Barnard was in effective control; and the official attitude was that my initiative should be terminated. That was the reality. Van der Merwe had conceded that he had no further mandate. Accordingly, there was no choice but to accept this situation, although one could not exclude the possibility of future change. He therefore suggested that, if possible, I should continue to hold myself available – in case Van der Merwe's prognosis proved correct. One would have to be patient, and just wait to see how things developed.

They noted the special interest of the N I S in the concept of negotiations. Members of an Indian delegation which had recently visited Lusaka, told them that upon their return to South Africa, they had been closely questioned by the N I S, as to whether the ANC might be in favout of negotiations? He believed the N I S had been a little late in 'getting in on the act', but was now anxious to 'catch up' – and of course overtake all others. He didn't think they were opposed to the principle of negotiations, but wanted to establish and control their own process. They certainly didn't wish to find themselves co-opted into someone else's initiative. 'They want their own show,' he observed. 'On the other hand, Van der Merwe and De Klerk would probably prefer this to be handled by politicians, rather than by bureaucrats.' The issue was no longer whether there would be a process, but rather, 'What kind of process will there be, and who will control it?'

Concerning Stoffel's suggestion of a statement which they might issue in order to be helpful, his initial feeling was that the suggestion was not unreasonable. In due course, the ANC might consider some statement along these lines. It would make sense to speak positively about certain developments, but the ANC had to be careful not to be seen trying to influence the leadership struggle. Mbeki noted that despite Van der Merwe having no formal mandate, 'he's still playing a role which you're still assisting. The Swiss should realise that there is a reason why Van der Merwe continues to speak to you, and we would therefore encourage you to continue talking to him.'

Anticipating that we were unlikely to meet again in the near future, I decided to broach a subject which had not been previously discussed between us, though it was in fact the pivotal issue, at least insofar as the South African Government was concerned. I asked whether there was a possibility that the ANC might be prepared to suspend hostilities unilaterally, and to demand a reciprocal response from the South African Government within a time limit, or 'window of opportunity'? For example, the ANC might set a period such as 100 days within which it would require a substantive response. Such a move would create enormous pressure on the Government to reciprocate. It would also give the ANC the 'moral high ground' amongst the international community. Surely, nothing would be lost, I argued, and a great deal might be gained?

Thabo seemed interested in this hypothetical proposition, but immediately pointed out the practical, political and strategic difficulties in the way of such a temporary ceasefire. The ANC would need to be very careful that it carried all its constituencies. Unless such a decision was carefully managed, it could lead to further alienation of the radical youth, who were already calling for an escalation of the armed struggle. If the ANC lost control of these young people, 'then a very ugly situation could develop'. In Natal, for example, they'd been involved in a protracted struggle with Inkatha, and were not ready to initiate peace talks, which could easily be interpreted as surrender.

To embark upon something such as I was suggesting would require that the ANC was 'reasonably certain' of a reciprocal move by the Botha regime. 'We would have to be sure of at least a 50 per cent chance that it would produce a result. Otherwise, if it was made to appear as some kind of gimmick, we would have done ourselves real damage.' One had always to be aware that the Government, through its agents, could themselves set off bombs, and claim that the ANC had broken its word, or had lost control over its own cadres. There had been incidents like this in the past, involving bombs and casualties, which had nothing to do with MK, though the ANC had of course been blamed. Such a move could also be manipulated to try to provoke division amongst the leadership. In a situation where the

Government had the predominant capacity for using force, it was surely logical that any such pre-emptive move should come from their side?

Before departing, I asked what he thought I might do in the interim, assuming the initiative was merely suspended, and not finally terminated. I floated various ideas, but Thabo was anxious I should not do anything to prejudice my perceived neutrality and availability as an intermediary – in case at some future date, this might become useful. However, he agreed it made no sense for me to maintain a special, dedicated office, 'in the hope that Stoffel may drop one or two pearls every six months'. If Stoffel's prognosis was correct, then we might be approaching a situation when a channel of this kind could again become useful. However, it was also possible that De Klerk might come to the same conclusion as Barnard – namely, that the process should be carried forward without intermediaries.

We also talked about the need for preserving confidentiality – both as to the fact of the initiative having taken place, and as to the nature of exchanges which had occurred. He gave me the assurance that confidentiality would not be breached by the ANC. Only a small number of people were aware of these facts.

Before leaving, I gave Thabo a small stone I had brought back from our holiday at Nature's Valley. He turned it over, examining it carefully. 'It's a small piece of the country', I said. 'Later, you'll come home and claim the rest of it.' He put it to his ear, and said, 'I think I can hear the sea!'

Thursday 23 March 1989

I am home again. It's the end of an incredible journey.

Somehow, the whole saga of these last two years seems to have come to an end in this moment. Perhaps I expected (and hoped?) that the ANC would urge me to continue, in spite of everything … but they didn't. They've accepted the reality – Botha on the skids; Barnard in control; Stoffel an enigma. For the time being at least, the initiative is at an end – though in Thabo's words, 'The situation is never static.'

These have been the most difficult years of my life. I did what I did, because – like the 'Holy Fool' – I believed it was needed, and I imagined that I could contribute something useful. It was sometimes scary, often lonely, occasionally wonderful.

There's still a very long way to go. Other roles will emerge, but for the time being mine at least is finished.

'It helps, I think, to consider ourselves on a very long journey. The main thing is to keep to the path, to endure, to help each other when we stumble or tire, to weep, but to press on.' – M C Richards

30

The prodigal returns

Over the ensuing months, I sought to resume the semblance of a normal life, and to re-establish friendships which had been sorely neglected over the past two years. I felt like Ulysses returning home after a long journey, and finding that the world which he knew had changed – or possibly, that I myself had changed? The difficulties of returning were compounded by my inability to talk about 'the journey'. I discovered that people were still wondering why I had left in the first place and now, of course, they would wonder why I had returned? Bound by my pledge of secrecy, I resorted to facetious explanations which served only to compound the mystery – 'I retired, but now I've retired from retirement!' To my surprise – and great disappointment – I discovered it was no longer feasible for me to return to my erstwhile law firm as I had intended and hoped. Confronted with the necessity to generate an independent source of income, and to conserve my substantially eroded savings, I decided to establish a separate law practice that would specialise in what was generically described as 'the law relating to NGOs, development, and the change process'.

Officially the initiative was at an end, but I continued to follow the dramatic events of the ensuing years with close attention, lest circumstances should change and the need for an intermediary again arise. Periodically, I would make contact with Thabo Mbeki and Stoffel van der Merwe as they had suggested, and I continued to meet from time to time those with whom I had been consulting over the years.

* * * * * *

Thus, on 1 April I met Stoffel van der Merwe once more at his Ministerial office in Cape Town. It was our 17th meeting during a period of as many months. My primary purpose was to pass on to him the substance of my last conversation with Thabo Mbeki, and to feed into 'the system' our dialogue about the hypothetical possibility of the ANC's initiating a suspension of the armed struggle – to give Government a chance to respond. Stoffel said this was important information, and he promised to pass it on to 'the relevant parties'. I told him that in my assessment, the ANC remained willing to participate in genuine substantive negotiations, and was still prepared to accept my role as an intermediary, if this was deemed appropriate. I also confirmed that I had passed on his own message about the potential value of some positive statement from the ANC about recent developments, and reported their tentative response.

Stoffel said that certain initiatives were under way concerning Nelson Mandela, and that 'some progress can be expected soon'; though he remained vague as to precisely what was under consideration. He didn't tell me however – and possibly didn't know at the time – that a few days prior to our meeting, Mandela had forwarded Botha an historic 11-page Memorandum, in which he had proposed a meeting between the Government and the ANC 'as a first step towards a negotiated settlement on the country's future'. Mandela had called for a two-stage process, commencing with an initial meeting to consider reciprocal steps needed to create a climate for negotiations. Allister Sparks has commented: 'Here, for the first time since Verwoerd spurned Mandela's letter asking for a National Convention 28 years before, was a concrete offer to negotiate a peaceful settlement of South Africa's bitter conflict, reversing the organisation's commitment to the revolutionary overthrow of white minority rule. A week later, Mandela received word that Botha was ready to meet him.'

Stoffel contended that there was already clear evidence of a new dispensation. He pointed to the successive releases of longtime detainees, and to the fact that the Emergency Regulations were no longer being rigorously enforced. However, 'previous bad experience had made Government anxious about lifting the State of Emergency in one single step'. When questioned about the unbanning of the ANC, Stoffel replied, 'That is more difficult. We have problems with that proposition at the present time.' He also mentioned that the appointment of a Minister with special responsibility for negotiations, an idea which I had suggested some time ago, was currently under active consideration.

I informed Stoffel that the ANC had been interested in the reasons for his optimism about the likely outcome of the leadership struggle – to which Stoffel responded that he remained optimistic that a compromise solution was going to be worked out with P W Botha – in fact, he said, 'It's all but agreed.' However, this was likely to lead to an early General Election, which regrettably meant that the country would be faced with another period of political paralysis. However, he believed that once these processes had been worked through, the initiative could again play an important role.

Accordingly, Stoffel proposed that I try to remain available, for the resumption of this work later in the year. Obviously, he could give me no guarantees, but in his view it was a reasonable speculation, 'certainly a risk worth taking'. I pointed out that my ability to take such risks had financial implications. The Swiss Government could no longer sustain its assistance beyond the end of the current month. Stoffel responded that he was reasonably confident that progress might become possible in the near future, and suggested a six-month waiting period.

Towards the end of May, during the course of yet another discussion with Stoffel, I learned to my dismay that he had not yet discussed my initiative, as promised, with the 'President-in-waiting', F W de Klerk; nor had he even passed on what he himself characterised as important information. I was frankly astonished, and said, 'If you were looking for a starting point, there it was!' Stoffel admitted this was so, but in his view they weren't yet ready, and nothing substantial could be attempted until after the elections. It was my impression that he was either unable or unwilling to beard the lion/crocodile, and thereby risk further Presidential displeasure, particularly in the run-up to the crucial forthcoming elections.

******

During these months, De Klerk made a number of enigmatic but encouraging statements in which he referred to the present state of affairs in the country as being 'untenable', and predicted that 'matters will have to change drastically and speedily'. An announcement also came of an early meeting in the United Kingdom between De Klerk and Prime Minister Margaret Thatcher. I decided the time had come to make contact direct, and wrote De Klerk a personal letter:

PERSONAL & CONFIDENTIAL   9th June 1989

Mr F.W. de Klerk
Minister of National Education
Private Bag 616
PRETORIA
0001
URGENT

Dear Mr de Klerk,

re: Negotiation Process – African National Congress (ANC)

Although fully cognisant of the extreme pressures upon your time, I am compelled

to write to you as a matter of urgency, concerning certain confidences and commu-
nications with which I have been entrusted by the African National Congress, and
which have a direct and substantive bearing upon the possibilities of a future nego-
tiation process.

As you may be aware, over the past 18 months, acting in close liaison with Dr
Stoffel van der Merwe and with the mutually-approved assistance of the Swiss
Government, I have been involved on a fulltime basis in a highly discreet process
of establishing secret contacts with top echelons of the ANC, with a view to facili-
tating the commencement of an eventual and substantive negotiation process,
thereby bringing to an end the 'armed struggle' of the ANC, and contributing to
the commencement of a process of national reconciliation.

In the result, a small Executive Committee of the ANC has been constituted to
deal with this very delicate issue, and they have imparted to me certain informa-
tion which they wish that I should convey to the South African Government on a
basis of absolute confidentiality.

In the circumstances, it would seem to be of the utmost importance and urgency,
that I be afforded the privilege of a personal meeting with you at your very earliest
convenience, and if possible prior to your forthcoming meeting with the British
Prime Minister.

I would naturally be available at any time and venue convenient to yourself.

Yours sincerely,
Richard Rosenthal

cc Dr Stoffel van der Merwe

A month passed without so much as an acknowledgment, let alone a
reply. This was only somewhat surprising in view of his hectic programme,
and the high drama playing itself out around the Presidency, and the forthcoming elections. On 12 July, in response to several telephone enquiries, De
Klerk's secretary Hennen van Wyk called me to confirm that my letter had
been received, but that Mr de Klerk was not yet in a position to respond, 'as
he wishes first to consult with his colleagues'. Soon after the famous
Botha–Mandela teaparty, which took place on 5 July (for which Niel Barnard
was the 'Impresario'), I decided to write De Klerk a second letter:

Dear Mr de Klerk

re: Negotiation Process – African National Congress (ANC)
I refer to my earlier letter of 9th June (erroneously dated 9th May), to which as
yet I have received no reply. In view of the extreme sensitivity and importance of

the matters referred to, I have become increasingly concerned by my inability to convey to you the information with which I have been entrusted, despite the elapse of a period of some 8 weeks.

I have some idea of the pressures and responsibilities with which you must presently be contending, compounded by the election process. I am therefore extremely diffident to reiterate my earlier request for an urgent meeting at this time. However the significance of certain recent events, their potential impact upon the prospects for a future negotiation process, and the need to maintain top-level informal contacts already established, lead me to believe that it is of great importance and urgency that I should be able to convey to you personally the nature and substance of certain informal communications with which I have been entrusted by the ANC.

In the circumstances, I would greatly value the opportunity of even a brief meeting at your very earliest convenience.

Yours faithfully

Richard Rosenthal

No reply to either of these letters was ever received.

******

On 30 July, I read with some astonishment a report from London of a BBC 'Newsnight' interview with Stoffel van der Merwe, in which he was quoted as saying: 'The ANC's commitment to the armed struggle disqualified it from joining "peace-loving people" around the Government's negotiating table.' The report went on: '... [Van der Merwe] dismissed the 120 liberal South Africans now in Lusaka for talks with the ANC, as just doing what was the "in-thing". It was now fashionable, he said, to be able to say you had been to Lusaka to meet the ANC, "like driving a Mercedes or having a swimming pool" ... Asked if the South African Government would negotiate with the ANC, Dr van der Merwe said the Government wanted to talk to "people with a genuine commitment to peace ... and I don't think the ANC qualifies on that score." Questioned whether there could be any settlement without the ANC, he said the Government did not consider the organisation's support within South Africa "all that strong ... the ANC may be one of the stronger (groups), but it is not representative of all black South Africans." Of the white liberals now in Lusaka, he said: "One always gets a fashion, a vogue, the thing to do. This seems to be the in-thing to do." He said the Government was no longer talking about races but about cultural groups.

Free settlement areas would allow blacks more freedom to choose where they lived.'

I spoke to Stoffel on the telephone on Friday 18 August following a number of dramatic developments, including Botha's embittered resignation four days earlier, and the resultant accession of De Klerk as Acting State President. I told him that although I was prepared to abide my agreement to 'mark time' until after the elections, this was proving difficult and frustrating. Was there anything further he could say at this stage to clarify my situation?

Stoffel replied that he had been giving the matter a good deal of thought, and was acutely aware of my awkward situation. Unfortunately, with the election campaign now in full swing, things were 'absolutely hectic', and it wasn't possible to do more than speculate about the course of events once the election was out of the way. He could only give me his 'best guess'. It was his feeling that things would not happen immediately after the election. There was likely to be 'an initial period of consolidation', during which they would be finding their feet. The 'aspect' with which I was concerned would constitute more of a second phase. 'On that front also,' he said, 'I don't expect any immediate developments. Things are more likely to happen a bit later on. The first priority will be to consolidate the internal situation. It's going to take a few months before we're ready to move on that level. Probably we'll wait until sometime next year. That's the best I can tell you.'

I mentioned my surprise that both my letters to De Klerk were unanswered and unacknowledged two months after despatch. How was I to interpret this silence? Did it imply 'No'? Stoffel said as far as he was aware this wasn't the right interpretation. The truth was Mr de Klerk was 'completely inundated', and hadn't been able to give the matter proper attention.

After more than 22 meetings during the period of the initiative, our encounters now gradually petered out. It seemed that despite his positive feeling of affinity and empathy for De Klerk, Stoffel didn't enjoy the same degree of patronage or confidence from the new President as he had during the hey-days of P W Botha. In due course, he resigned both his Cabinet position and his Parliamentary seat, and became fulltime Secretary-General of the National Party. After a time, we lost contact altogether, though I wrote to him when his wife died tragically during November 1992.

One day in early 1997, I was picking my way across the airport tarmac to collect a hire car at Johannesburg International Airport. Hastening in the opposite direction came a man pushing a barrow overflowing with computer components. As he approached, I recognised that familiar 'Cliff Barnes' grin. It was of course Stoffel. It had been almost seven years since we'd last met. We shook hands like old comrades in arms. 'What are you doing nowadays?' I asked. He said – as I might reasonably have inferred from the circumstantial evidence – that he was now involved in a computer business. I reminded him of his promise to let me know one day 'what really happened', and we agreed to get together again soon.

A couple of months later, on Thursday 3 April, we sat down to lunch at a small restaurant in Pretoria. Stoffel expressed a preference for a corner table, and we decided that it would be a good idea to keep an eye on the door! He confided that the *maître* was an old acquaintance of his, a onetime N I S operative, who had 'taken the package' and opened a restaurant. He now attended conscientiously to our gastronomic needs. I suggested that Stoffel check out the plant next to our table, 'in case it was infested with some other kind of bug than aphid!'

We quickly slipped back into our familiar conversational mode, with Stoffel delivering yet another learned exposition on the unremembered merits of 'separate development', and the all too familiar depravities of 'apartheid'. He saw Verwoerd as having been in reality a 'liberal', but time and opportunity had been squandered and his dream had become impossible of fulfilment. Other historic opportunities had also been lost – like the chance to negotiate with Chief Albert Luthuli, 'before the ANC came under the influence of international communism'. Although it was recognised that National Party policies had lost their moral foundation, the difficulty had been that it was impossible to abandon the system until an alternative was available to take its place.

He believed that the main problem in carrying out my initiative had been the element of competitiveness which had crept in, particularly in relation to moves being handled by Niel Barnard and others. Surprising as it might seem, motives like 'territorial jealousy' had played their part. The other problem had been Botha's failing health. Stoffel believed that Botha had actually suffered his first stroke a year before the illness that brought his Presidency to an end. His earlier illness had been kept a secret, and was known only to his close family. With hindsight, it had probably affected his capacity, which was in any event becoming somewhat suspect owing to advancing age and diminishing faculties. Stoffel recalled that sometimes Botha had given the impression of agreeing with proposals, but later had contradicted himself by agreeing to diametrically contrary proposals. Such unpredictability had been a reality entirely at odds with his public image. He recalled the late Mrs Botha having once said: 'My husband made two errors. The first was to have a stroke; but the second was not to die from that stroke!'

Stoffel said his own political career had come to an end not so much as a result of the fallout from my initiative, as because he had suffered 'complete burnout'. He had gone through a very dark period, which led to a need to withdraw from active politics for a while. Ironically, by the time he had withdrawn, he was already 'over the worst'.

I had the impression of a man who had finally come to terms with the tragedy of his wife's death, and other disappointments. He was sad he had not had the opportunity to participate in the final negotiations, because he believed he could have played some role. Nevertheless, he consoled himself with the thought that at certain important stages he had been able to make some contribution which had helped to lay the foundations for the eventual process. I assumed that I was, at least in part, responsible for Stoffel's having had that opportunity.

******

Following the General Election which took place on 6 September, I once again telephoned the office of the State President, and spoke with De Klerk's secretary, Hennen van Wyk. He confirmed that he had seen my latest (second) letter, though he had not had sight of the first, 'which the State President has kept to himself'. He said the matter was 'obviously very interesting and important'. He hoped Mr de Klerk would give him some instruction about the matter soon, but so far he'd only said that he was aware of the issue, and would deal with it in due course.

A week later, I made another attempt to communicate with the new administration, and on 25 September sent a personal letter to the newly appointed Minister of Constitutional Development, Dr Gerrit Viljoen, proposing a meeting 'to communicate to the South African Government accurately and in detail the nature and substance of certain indepth discussions held with the ANC, which have direct and substantive relevance to the inception and prospects of a negotiation process, as envisaged by the State President'.

Once again silence ensued, until eventually a secretary, Mr Volschenk, telephoned to advise that Dr Viljoen would like to meet me at his office in Sunnyside, Pretoria, at 3 p.m. on Friday 24 November – almost two months after the date of my letter. However, three weeks later, on Monday 13 November, Volschenk telephoned again to say he was sorry but Dr Viljoen had now instructed him to cancel our meeting, because 'something had cropped up'.

Eventually I received a letter from Viljoen dated 27 November in which he said 'Your interest in this matter is appreciated. It is, however, not considered expedient to involve you as an intermediary between the interested parties as you have suggested.'

On two further occasions – 21 March 1990 and 20 May 1991 – when the protracted negotiations had either been suspended or had become dead-locked, I wrote again to Viljoen, renewing my offer. His replies were friendly but inconclusive. In a letter dated 9 May 1990, he stated: 'I would like to assure you that I accept your bona fides and integrity and also your patrio-tism inspiring the efforts you have taken to promote contact between the South African Government and the ANC. I trust you will share our satisfac-tion about the fact that direct negotiations have now commenced. It would, therefore, appear that the need of a confidential intermediary is to be seen in a new context. I have, however, noted the points made in your letter and I shall keep in mind your availability, should occasion arise to make use of it.'

A year later, in a letter dated 24 May 1991, he assured me: 'In spite of the differences between the Government and the ANC, the channels of commu-nication are open and functioning on a regular basis. There is really no need for "independent channels" at this stage. Your continued interest in this matter is appreciated.'

******

In 1989, Ambassador Quinche met me on Wednesday 29 March, when he confirmed that the Swiss Government's assistance would terminate at the end of the month. He had received confirmation of a new posting to Israel which would commence at the end of June Thus he would be leaving this country shortly. His stay had been longer than the usual diplomatic term – partly as a result of my initiative. Israel would be a completely new chal-lenge. 'From the frying pan into the fire?' I suggested. 'Yes,' he replied, 'and from one Promised Land to another!'

Shortly before his departure, he invited me again to the Embassy to receive a letter he had been asked to deliver (see next page).

*****

Govan Mbeki wrote to me a few days later:

Dear Mr Rosenthal

Recent pronouncements by some Cabinet Ministers have set me thinking as to what to make of them. Mr Heunis makes a Statement in Parliament, which is regarded by many people as a departure from the well beaten path. Within a day

The Ambassador of Switzerland

Cape Town, May 3, 1989

Dr. Richard ROSENTHAL
P.O.Box　3800
<u>CAPE TOWN</u>
<u>8000</u>

Dear Dr. Rosenthal,

During the last twelve months you have been committed to an
initiative the aim of which was to try to bring about some sort of
dialogue between the government of South Africa and the ANC. You even
left your business in order to be completely free for the task you
had initiated yourself.

I would like to convey to you the highest appreciation of the Swiss
government and authorities who supported your initiative, for all
your efforts and commitments during this undertaking. You went out of
your way to endeavour to organise the mentioned dialogue.
Unfortunately it had to be suspended. Yet you have doubtlessly paved
the way, whatever should happen in the future, for a better
understanding.

The Swiss authorities consider that this initiative is only
provisionally suspended and not ended. They will be pleased to
consider the resuming of this process if new and more favourable
circumstances arise.

May I add on my behalf that I have also very much appreciated the
opportunity to be in touch with you on all the numerous occasions
that the events gave us to consider the developments of your
initiative. As I am going to leave this country soon, I would like to
extend to you my best wishes for the future. The doors of this
Embassy will not be closed with my departure and you will always have
the possibility to approach either my assistant, Mr. Georges Martin,
or my successor, Ambassador Blaise Schenk, after his arrival.

Yours sincerely,

Jean　O. Quinche

or two he resigns his seat in the Cabinet and declares he is pulling out of active politics. What does it all mean? The President to be has also been making noises that indicate vaguely his Party is considering some moves away from the Constitution they had only drawn but a few years back; and in addition he is seeking to talk to the Leaders that have been thrown up by the policies of his Party and Government. What does this mean?

I would be pleased to hear your views on the current happenings.

Regards
Yours sincerely
Govan Mbeki

Following this correspondence, we met surreptitiously on Monday 5 June, at Counsel's Chambers in Cape Town, and had a two-hour discussion. Mrs Farieda Omar arranged to transport Mr Mbeki Snr to this rendezvous, and deflected the inevitable police 'tail' which accompanied him, by remaining in her car throughout our meeting. Mr Mbeki commented on the beautiful winter's day: 'I know this Cape winter all too well, having spent more of my life here than I would have chosen. Robben Island is very cold and windy – and there's no heating!'

We didn't meet again for almost six years. But one day on a flight from Port Elizabeth to Cape Town, I found myself sitting next to a dignified old gentleman, who greeted me with great bonhomie and warmth. We discussed the strange circumstances of our earlier encounters. He was now 83 years old, and had been appointed Deputy President of the Senate. He said he was writing a history of the struggle, and encouraged me also to set down the story of some of the things I had been involved with over these climactic years. We talked about his son Thabo who was now Deputy President, and he expressed tremendous pride in his achievements. 'But whenever I disagree with him,' he added with a chuckle, 'I just hand him over to his mother!'

******

Following my initial approach to Willie Esterhuyse during September 1988, he and I remained in fairly regular contact, which involved five meetings and more than a dozen phone conversations. Initially, it appeared as though we might even merge our separate activities, or at least collaborate closely. We did share some confidences and spoke about mutual experiences in pursuing our respective missions, and our reciprocal dealings with the Botha Government and ANC leadership. However, in time I sensed a measure of 'reserve' on Willie's side, which I attributed to our different backgrounds, language, and beliefs; but it was only much later that I discovered another reason.

During September 1987 – at the very time I was writing my first letter to President Botha – Willie was being propositioned by Niel Barnard to undertake a delicate mission on behalf of the N I S, which according to Allister Sparks's account would involve his becoming 'an informal contact with the ANC', with their knowledge and forewarning. This meant that Willie was not only reporting to Botha as he had told me, but also to Barnard and the N I S, which he did not tell me. Perhaps Barnard's refusal to meet me had something to do with the fact that he had already met me, as it were, through Willie!

Thus in November 1987, at the time of my first meeting with Stoffel, Willie was one of a group of twenty Afrikaner leaders who met secretly with Aziz Pahad, Harold Wolpe ('the devil incarnate'), Jacob Zuma and others, at a picturesque little riverside hotel in Henley-on-Thames, England. It was the first of a series of 12 meetings which took place over the ensuing years – the last of which occurred during May 1990, a few months after De Klerk's historic 2 February speech. It was another example of Botha's multi-track strategy.

Allister Sparks comments: 'The meetings were considered top secret. President Botha had denounced any talks with the ANC, and so members of his government could not be seen engaging in them. That is why Barnard had to set up an indirect line of contact. And as far as the participants were concerned, the Old Crocodile knew nothing of them. "If P.W. Botha were to hear about what we are doing," wrote Wiempie de Klerk in his personal diary, "he would smash us into oblivion." Yet P W did know, because Barnard was keeping him informed. It was an elaborate exercise to have contact without running the political risk. If the meetings were found out, they could all be blamed on renegade individuals.'

With hindsight, perhaps I should have been a little more suspicious. Certainly Willie left several clues. On 24 November he told me he was going overseas and was anticipating 'a further meeting with our friends'. We met on the Sunday evening before his departure, and in the course of our discussion, Willie mentioned that his travelling and out-of-pocket expenses were being paid for 'from a private company'. If not an N I S 'front' enterprise, this could have been a reference to Consolidated Gold, which had agreed to fund and host a series of meetings involving the ANC and Afrikaner leadership.

But it was in relation to my attempts to communicate with Niel Barnard that our dealings became most seriously skewed. When I confided in Willie and sought his help, he gave me advice that I should accept the inevitable –

namely, my initiative was at an end. On a few occasions – as on 21 February 1989 – he asked for time to consider my requests for assistance, and I imagine he may have sought Barnard's guidance before responding. This he actually admitted in a conversation we had on 13 March 1989, when he referred to the need to await a response for two or three days, having 'spoken with a certain individual'. Of course, his subsequent message to me that 'The best advice you can give him is that his initiative should be closed down,' did not convey the fact that, with Barnard's patronage, Willie would henceforth assume the role I had been trying to play.

On 17 March 1989, shortly before my final meeting with the ANC, Willie referred to having discussed matters with 'the number two person in the N I S', whom he identified as Mike Kuhn. As a result of these discussions, he believed the principal difficulty in the way of my further involvement was the role of the Swiss Government, even though this had been discussed and approved by Stoffel. Willie explained that if Barnard were to meet me now 'this might imply some measure of tacit recognition'. The reality was that they were not prepared to cooperate or communicate with the ANC or any of their surrogates – or even a messenger acting on their behalf. He then added significantly, 'This doesn't preclude contacts at a lower level,' adding that they were keen to obtain information at IDASA-type conferences. This was of course Willie's forté.

Later in that momentous year, 1989, Willie's role became pivotal. He was chosen by Niel Barnard to convey a proposal for the first formal meeting between the N I S and the ANC in exile. According to Barnard, as quoted by Sparks, Nelson Mandela was not informed of this approach, despite their continuing dialogue with him. Barnard characterised this as the only act of deception in their relationship with Mandela, who had been concerned to discourage any parallel dialogue with the ANC in exile, for fear that an attempt would be made to drive a wedge between himself and the exiled leadership.

On Monday 15 May, Willie telephoned to say that unfortunately he had to cancel our dinner date for the following Thursday, 'because I have to go somewhere else'! It transpires that Willie went to London, where he met Thabo Mbeki, and secured agreement for the first ANC–N I S meeting. Sparks relates that 'Esterhuyse told Mbeki to expect a telephone call from an N I S agent named Maritz Spaarwater – who would announce himself as John Campbell. The purpose of the call would be to set up a meeting some-where in Switzerland. They called it "Operation Flair", and the arrangements were made over the next 3 months by covert phone calls between "John Campbell" and "John and Jack Simelane" – code names for Thabo Mbeki and Jacob Zuma.'

Ironically, they chose Switzerland as the most suitable venue, and on 12 September – one month after De Klerk's accession – a meeting involving Thabo Mbeki and Jacob Zuma on the one side, and 'Michael James' (alias Mike Louw, alias Mike Kuhn), and 'Jacobus Maritz' (alias Maritz Spaarwater *et al.*) on the other side, took place at the Palace Hotel, Lucerne. Sparks explains: 'They had chosen Switzerland for the rendezvous because it and Britain were the only European countries that did not require South Africans to have entry visas, and they felt they would be less conspicuous in Switzerland. ... There would be little sympathy for them if they were caught violating Swiss law again. In addition to which, they had to take care not to be spotted by agents of the US Central Intelligence Agency, or the British, French, or German Intelligence services, which would have delighted in exposing a secret South African meeting with the ANC ... When Louw and Spaarwater flew home the next morning, they had a clear message to deliver to their new Acting President: the ANC was willing to negotiate.'

This meeting in Switzerland had a sequel five months later. On 6 February 1990, a second meeting took place, just four days after De Klerk's watershed speech to Parliament. Sparks records: 'The meeting ended with a security scare for the N I S men. "We became aware that we were under surveillance," says Spaarwater. "I'm pretty sure it was the Swiss. And we were there on false documentation, false passports and cover names, which of course constitutes a criminal offence. So we decided to get out in a hurry."'

Perhaps the Swiss were not quite as ignorant or naive as they supposed? In any event, a third meeting took place one month later in Berne, where they stayed at the same hotel, the Bellevue Palace, at which I had stayed some 14 months earlier. Barnard is quoted by Sparks as saying: 'We can laugh about it today, but for us to go and see the ANC in Europe was a hell of a thing ... We had to prevent the KGB and CIA and other intelligence services from finding out. It was a very sensitive operation.' These clandestine meetings would be the precursors to formal meetings between the ANC and the Government, which commenced on 2–4 May 1990 with the initial historic encounter that took place on the Groote Schuur Estate.

******

Despite my persistent and abortive efforts, I never met Niel Barnard, until one night in November 1993 at the World Trade Centre, Kempton Park. It occurred during the closing stages of the Multi-Party Negotiation Process. I was busy helping myself to the coleslaw when I recognised him just ahead of me in the queue, engaging generously with the beetroot. At last, I thought, I have him cornered, this elusive eminence who had resolutely contrived not to meet me. It seemed a marvellous irony of time and place – South Africa's spy chief, finally trapped in a salad queue. I thought it wise to confirm my guess before accosting him, and asked State Law Adviser Johan Bruwer, who stood immediately behind me, whether I was correct. He nodded. 'That's great,' I said, 'I've been wanting to speak to him for quite a long time.'

Johan looked dubious. 'Why would you want to speak to him?' he asked pointedly. 'D'you want to be a spy?'

Putting down my plate, I tapped him on the shoulder. 'Dr Barnard, I presume?' He seemed unaccustomed to being casually accosted. I introduced myself, and he looked suitably astounded.

'D'you remember who I am?' I asked innocently.

'Of course,' he replied, with that stony expression which seemed the hallmark of the pictures I'd seen of him.

'I've been trying to meet you for nearly five years,' I said.

'What are you doing here?' he asked, as though entitled to some kind of explanation for my inopportune manifestation, even though without the connivance of a foreign power.

I might have asked him the same, had I not already known that after twelve years as Botha's Head of National Intelligence, he had recently metamorphosed to become deputy Director-General in the Department of Constitutional Affairs in F W de Klerk's administration. I told him that I too was involved in the Multi-Party Negotiating Process, although in a more humble capacity than his own. 'In what capacity?' he asked incredulously. I told him that I was Convenor of the Technical Committee appointed by the Negotiating Council to draft the new Electoral Laws. Barnard had the look of a man who felt he should have been told this, and perhaps wished that he'd had the opportunity to prevent it. We smiled genially at each other, and agreed it was high time we met.

'Why don't we make a date?' I suggested.

'I'd rather get in touch with you later,' he replied frostily. Of course, this also never came to pass.

When I reached our dinner table, fellow Committee members, Dr Frene Ginwala (now Speaker of Parliament) and Professor (now Judge) Dennis Davis, looked a little curious. Johan Bruwer didn't waste time with pleasantries. 'Did he give you a job?' he wanted to know.

******

One day I had an unexpected visit from a young blonde woman who arrived at our home, introducing herself as Shirley Gunn. When we had last met towards the end of 1988, she had been heavily pregnant, and her name had been 'Wendy Adams'. Now she came with her three-year-old son Haroun – named after an early martyr, an Imam, who died at the hands of the Security Police in 1969, after allegedly falling down some stairs. She came to thank me for what I *had* done – or perhaps, more accurately, for what I had not done. In fact, one of the things I *had* done, unbeknown to her, was to remove surreptitiously a Certificate evidencing a marriage 'duly performed in strict accordance with Moslem Rites'. The only unusual thing about this Marriage Certificate was that although signed by the Imam, it was blank as to the names of husband and wife, and as to the date of the ceremony, and the name of the Mosque!

I explained a little of what I had been doing during those years, and how I had eventually been compelled to go through the charade of obtaining an eviction order from the Wynberg Magistrates Court, on the grounds of her non-payment of rent – in order that I could remove her belongings and relet the cottage, and not broadcast the fact that I knew she wasn't coming back. After some months on the run, and after her baby had been born, Shirley Gunn was captured by the Security Police on a farm in the Karoo, and was held and interrogated for 112 days. Despite solitary confinement and torture, including the sadistically calculated separation of her from her child, she never 'broke' and was never charged.

However, Law and Order Minister Adriaan Vlok stood up in Parliament and accused Ms Gunn during the time of her detention, of having been responsible for the 1988 bombing of Khotso House, the headquarters of the SA Council of Churches, which had resulted in eighteen people being seriously injured, and more than one million Rands' damage. Ten years later, Vlok appeared before the Truth and Reconciliation Commission to seek amnesty and to acknowledge that he had lied to Parliament, and that the command to destroy Khotso House had come from himself; had been executed by the Security Police; and had originated with the State President! This version was later corroborated by several other Police amnesty applicants, including Commissioner of Police General Johann van der Merwe, and the infamous Eugene de Kock of Vlakplaas fame, who admitted to carrying out the deed. De Kock testified as a convicted murderer in the service of the Botha Government, for which he was sentenced to imprisonment for 212 years. P W Botha steadfastly refuses to give evidence about these matters, despite a subpoena, and despite the institution of contempt proceedings.

Shirley Gunn's (Wendy Adams's) own appearance before the TRC was vividly described in an article by Dr Steven Robins of the Department of

Anthropology and Sociology (UWC). It reads:

'Her testimony contained an emotionally charged and unforgiving account of how Security Police interrogators accused her of being an irresponsible mother by getting involved in radical politics that had landed her child in prison with her.

'Ms Gunn also spoke of her bouts of depression that began in detention, and her feelings of being left behind while many of her more ambitious and career-orientated comrades had moved on to high positions in Parliament and in the Government. She left a powerful impression on those present at this TRC hearing.'

The next time I heard Ms Gunn speak was a year later in January 1997, at a TRC panel discussion at the University of Cape Town. She challenged the religious rhetoric of reconciliation of the TRC, and questioned whether the poor were in the same position as President Mandela to forgive: 'Thank God, we have Mandela as President, but we must recognise that it is easier for Mandela to forgive. What about the millions of unemployed black South Africans living in the shacks who are still unemployed? Must they also forgive and forget, when nothing has changed for them?'

****

On the night of Wednesday 17 November 1993, when the momentous deal was finally sealed, Hilary and I took part in that historic gathering at the World Trade Centre in Kempton Park, and witnessed the miracle birth of the new South Africa in the small hours of that unforgettable morning. Exhausted and exhilarated, we listened insatiably to the deluge of 22 speeches, and we watched in awe the signing of the package of agreements, to which I had contributed as a legal draftsman over the past seven months. It was a deeply emotional occasion.

It had been an endless day, and several hours after midnight we remembered that we had had little or nothing to eat or drink. Hilary made an abortive attempt to quench her thirst from a partly consumed tin of soda water which Mac Maharaj had infiltrated into the Council Chamber. Her intended theft was theatrically discovered, as she choked on the unexpected contents of Mac's tin of 'soda water', which had been surreptitiously filled with whisky! Thus exposed, the author of the ANC's secret Vula strategy, laughed and offered her another sip. Eventually, despite our wish to miss not a word, we slipped away for a few moments into the adjacent bar.

'Le Club', as it is prosaically named, can surely never have hosted such an extraordinary company of tearful and ecstatic tipplers as gathered there that night. Like the adjacent café, where I had encountered Niel Barnard in the salad queue the previous evening, the bar is located in the frigid bowels of a former caravan factory, which in its latest incarnation is grandiloquently styled The World Trade Centre. This improbable and draughty venue, like the stable of Bethlehem, was the cradle to a miracle birth. For the first time 'in our short lives' (as Mr Mandela put it), we had all become proud South Africans.

Despite the fact that it was well past 3 in the morning, no one seemed interested in sleep. Roelf Meyer and Cyril Ramaphosa did a rousing quick-step together. I found myself drinking with erstwhile terrorists, securocrats, fascists, communists, and even plain simple liberals like myself. It was a night to remember. In Allister Sparks's memorable phrase, 'Tomorrow was another country.'

In the midst of all this revelry, as the speeches droned on, the familiar figure of Thabo Mbeki appeared in the doorway. We hadn't met for a long time. It was yet another synchronous event. He saw me standing at the bar counter, and came across to shake my hand and greet me.

'You were involved right at the beginning,' he said.

'I've often wondered what it all meant; whether it was worthwhile?' I asked.

'It was certainly not wasted,' he replied. He told me that the so-called 'Rosenthal initiative' had been raised at the start of the process in 1990. However, the Government's negotiators – and in particular, Niel Barnard – had said they didn't wish to entrust the process to that channel. 'But it played a role,' he added. 'Now you need to write the story.'

* * * * * *

Letter to a Swiss friend, Professor Markus Barth:

Election Day, 27 April 1994

Dear Markus,

I wanted to write to you today, because it is of course a momentous moment, marking the start of the first democratic elections in our history; but also because it marks the end of a stage in the journey on which you have accompanied us these past difficult years. Our phone has kept ringing most of the day. There have been calls from New Zealand, Canada, the United States, Britain, Australia, Switzerland, and Germany. Many calls have come from the diaspora of ex-South Africans, who lost hope, and went in search of another home all over the world. As you know, you played an important role in keeping me here and keeping me faithful – and for that I shall always thank you.

What joy there is in the return of the prodigal nation! (And I do remember your caveat about there being not one, but two prodigal sons!) Newly born – we are the youngest of the world's democracies – trembling, fragile, vulnerable, but growing stronger, and braver; and preparing for a new tomorrow. I woke this morning with the praise song of E E Cummings in my mind : 'We thank thee Lord for most this amazing day!'

This is indeed the day we have worked and prayed and dreamed and hoped for these long dark years; a day of wonder and miracles. What a rare privilege it is to be not only the witness but, in some small measure, also a player in this amazing drama. As of midnight last night, we have a new Constitution; a Bill of justiciable Human Rights; a Constitutional Court to enforce those rights; a new flag; and the most sublime of all national anthems. Soon we will have our first non-racial multi-party Government, and a new President, this strange black Moses who emerged from the shadows of a prison cell to lead us to the Promised Land, along the path of forgiveness and reconciliation. The sun has set on centuries of injustice, and there is hope for a new dawn.

We have just come back from a tour of the voting centres, and could not find anywhere that the queue involved less than 3 or 4 hours waiting – in pouring rain, here in the Cape; and in blistering heat elsewhere – so we decided to postpone our vote awhile, hoping that the human tide would abate. People are amazingly patient and good-humoured, but there is absolutely no way that those who have waited all their lives for this, are going to miss their date with destiny. It is truly an amazing spectacle. As there has been no precedent or experience, it was inevitable that there would be administrative snarl-ups, and of course that has happened. The latest news has it that there has been a gross underestimate of the number of people eligible and wishing to vote. (Perhaps, says the Commission, the Census figures were wrong? Perhaps, we think, [more sinister] the distribution has been tampered with?) Anyway, the fact is that they have run out of voting papers and ultra-violet marking ink, and I know not what else. So at noon today, in the midst of voting, the printing presses started up again, and they are rushing 10 million more papers, which will be helicoptered to 10 000 polling stations all across the country. Meanwhile, people stand waiting patiently in queues. My tender-hearted daughter Caroline has been handing out coffee and plastic bags (in lieu of raincoats) to total strangers waiting in the queue near her house.

There has surely never been an election like this one? An election without a voters' roll. Old men with University degrees voting for the first time in their lives. More than 60% of the electorate functionally illiterate. And one of the rarest of all political spectacles – a privileged and still powerful oligarchy, pressured but not finally coerced, choosing to negotiate and vote itself out of power. Despite months of planning, the whole thing has an almost surreal quality of 'ad hoc-ism'. Just two days before voting, Parliament reconvened to make some last-minute adjustments to the Constitution and to the Electoral Act (which I helped to draft!), to secure the participation of Gatsha Buthelezi's Inkatha Freedom Party! This has necessitated 25 million stickers being affixed to 25 million ballot papers in the last hours before voting started. And of course, they have now run out of stickers! Only a few hours ago, it was decided that tomorrow will also be a public holiday, like today! Now I hear the Electoral Commission is studying 'my Act', to see if it is legally possible to extend voting time by hours, or even days!

But no matter. The miracle is happening, even if it is less than perfect. By some incredible grace and bounty, we have been spared the agonising road that leads through revolution to civil war. I looked at those queues today in absolute amazement; conglomerations of all sorts of people stretching in long lines from block to block; from every walk of life, rich and poor, the employed and the unemployed, the homeless, workers and bosses, people of all colours and without distinction, sharing for the first time one common identity and purpose, serendipitously scrambled together in the queue, waiting hour after hour, in the heat and the cold, across the length and breadth of the country. We've never seen the likes of it. There was laughter and also tears – and I suspect, looking into some of those faces, a profound sense of anger.

'What did it feel like to vote?', Archbishop Desmond Tutu was asked by some smart-arse reporter. 'It felt like falling in love!' he replied ...

Historical postscript

The years that followed my initiative have become the very substance of history – a chronicle about the making of a modern miracle – the birth of a united, democratic, non-racial, non-sexist, South Africa, through free, fair and peaceful elections, involving for the first time all South Africans, irrespective of race, class or ethnic origin. It is one of those epic stories involving courage, statesmanship, imagination, generosity, endurance, brilliance, and the rest – all the ingredients of a fairy tale – and ultimately, the triumph of negotiations over conflict. Those of us who witnessed these incredible events experienced a sense of wonder, as though something amazing was happening in our midst.

****

P W Botha resigned his office as State President on 14 August 1989, six months after relinquishing the leadership of the National Party, following his stroke and hospital-isation. In an address to the nation on national TV, he bitterly accused his Cabinet Ministers of ignoring him, and of requiring that he tell lies about his state of health. He said that the last straw had been Mr de Klerk's planned visit to Lusaka, to meet Zambian President Kenneth Kaunda, without obtaining his 'presidential impri-matur'. His address concluded: 'I consequently have no choice other than to announce my resignation.'

The preceding months had been characterised by tortuous wrangling between the embattled State President and his Cabinet and Caucus. On 9 March, the Caucus had sent him a message suggesting his resignation. He reserved his decision until a month later, when on 6 April he said he would in fact resign, but only after the next General Election, of which he had not yet determined the date. In various statements and actions, he sought to supersede his successor, including a clandestine teaparty at Tuynhuys on 5 July, to which he had invited his prisoner, Nelson Mandela. De Klerk, who had evidently not been consulted about this extraordinary overture, was clearly taken aback, but commented magnanimously: 'It is the State President's prerogative to meet whom he wishes, and I abide by his decisions on such matters.' Van Zyl Slabbert was less charitable, and said that Botha was trying to make it as difficult as possible for De Klerk to run his own election campaign. 'It's part of the sulking bull syndrome,' he opined.

Five members of Botha's Cabinet retired successively during the first months of the year, the most senior of whom was Chris Heunis, who had acted as State

President during Botha's convalescence, and who was generally regarded as 'reformist', although the author of the National Party's failed constitutional 'gimmickry'.

An early General Election was forced upon the country by the Coloured Labour Party refusing to agree to a National Party proposal that the life of Parliament be prolonged beyond its normal five-year term. Its recalcitrance was seen as a calcu-lated rejoinder to the National Party's earlier refusal to accede to its demand that the Group Areas Act be repealed.

Towards the end of June, the National Party under F W de Klerk launched its election campaign with a five-year 'Action Plan', which presaged constitutional negotiations, and a new dispensation in which all races would be accorded a vote at national level. However, the Party stoically retained its adherence to the orthodox doctrines of 'own affairs' and 'group identities', and made a convoluted statement about alleviating discrimination through improving separate amenities, but opening them to all race groups 'in an orderly fashion' where this was 'practical'.

In the General Election which followed on 6 September, the National Party suffered unprecedented attrition both to the left and to the right, involving the loss of 27 seats – 16 going to the Conservative Party, and 11 to the newly constellated Democratic Party. It only narrowly avoided a 'hung' Parliament.

On 20 September 1989, F W de Klerk was sworn in as new State President. He dedicated himself to reform and renewal, and held out the vision of 'a South Africa which had rid itself of the antagonisms of the past', a country 'free of domination or oppression in whatever form'. De Klerk appointed former academic, Dr Gerrit Viljoen, to succeed Heunis as Minister of Constitutional Development. Dr Stoffel van der Merwe was assigned the portfolio of Education and Development Aid.

One of the most significant early decisions of the new President occurred on 28 November, when De Klerk announced that the sinister National Security Management System would be dismantled, and the State Security Council 'reduced' to the status of a Cabinet committee. This spelt impending doom to the hegemony of the so-called 'securocrats' – Military, Police and Intelligence officers, like Dr Niel Barnard, who had exercised extraordinary policy-making and executive powers during the suzerainty of President Botha.

Five months after taking office, on 2 February 1990, President de Klerk stunned the world by announcing the simultaneous unbanning of the ANC, the PAC, the SA Communist Party and other restricted organisations; the release of all political detainees and prisoners, including Nelson Mandela; the right of return for political exiles; the suspension of executions pending a review of the death penalty; and the scrapping of the Separate Amenities Act. De Klerk set the new direction of the polit-ical compass by declaring: 'The time for negotiations has arrived.' Thabo Mbeki responded that the speech went 'a very long way' towards meeting the ANC's demands that political conditions be created for everybody to participate in a peaceful political process.

On 11 February, Nelson Mandela walked through the gates of Victor Verster prison, a free man, having served 27 years' imprisonment. A few hours later, from the balcony of the City Hall, Cape Town, he addressed a quarter of a million people, and hundreds of millions of others around the world. In ringing tones, he declared: 'We have waited too long for our freedom. We can wait no longer. Now is the time to intensify the struggle on all fronts. To relax our efforts now would be a mistake which generations to come will not be able to forgive.' He continued: 'Our march to freedom is irreversible,' and he called for the creation of 'a climate conducive to a negotiated settlement ... so that there will no longer be the need for an armed struggle.' In his first public address, he referred to his pre-release prison talks with various securocrats, including Niel Barnard, Minister Kobie Coetsee and others. As if to emphasise his loyalty and commitment to the movement, he stressed: 'I have at no time entered into negotiations about the future of the country, except to insist on a meeting between the ANC and the Government.'

The first official talks between the Government and the ANC took place at Groote Schuur, Cape Town between 2–4 May 1990, following the granting of temporary indemnity to the returning negotiators. A month later the State of Emergency was lifted throughout the country, except in Natal and KwaZulu where the Inkatha–UDF war continued inexorably. A second round of talks took place in Pretoria on 7 August, as a result of which 'the Pretoria Minute' was signed, committing the ANC to the suspension of armed action, and the Government to procuring the phased release of political prisoners.

After a protracted period of disputation over the nature of the body which would negotiate and write the new Constitution, a compromise was found, in terms of which there would be a two-stage process, firstly involving an 'interim' Constitution to be negotiated by an all-party congress, and thereafter a 'final' Constitution to be negotiated by an elected Constituent Assembly. A few days before Christmas, on 21–22 December 1991, the initial negotiating forum, which was called the Convention for a Democratic South Africa (CODESA), gathered at the World Trade Centre, just outside Johannesburg. Two years had elapsed since the release of Nelson Mandela. At the conclusion of the proceedings, 228 delegates representing nineteen political parties pledged themselves in a solemn Declaration of Intent, to bring into being the new South Africa 'where the dignity, worth and rights of every South African are protected by law'.

Amidst great controversy, the last whites-only Referendum was held during March 1992, which by an impressive majority confirmed President de Klerk's mandate for reform and the negotiation of a new Constitution. Two months later, a further session of CODESA was convened – known as CODESA 2. However, to the dismay of the watching world, it failed, was dissolved, and never reconvened. Communication between the parties was initially severed, but later re-established during a perilous period of stand-off, through what became unofficially known as 'the Channel' – a personal relationship of trust between Roelf Meyer representing the National Party, and Cyril Ramaphosa representing the ANC–COSATU–SACP alliance.

Nine months after the failure of CODESA 2, a summit took place on 26 September 1992, when Mandela and De Klerk signed a Record of Understanding, in terms of which they agreed to resume multi-party negotiations. In the months that followed, two informal *'bosberaad'* meetings were held at a game resort in the north-eastern Transvaal. These unique encounters enabled the future negotiators to meet without media attention, to talk, play, and become acquainted with each other as ordinary human beings – and in the process to establish the personal 'chemistry' and shared commitment which made eventual compromise possible.

In March 1993 the resumption/commencement (it was never decided which term was correct) of Multi-Party Negotiations was agreed. The name of this new conclave was also never finally agreed, but it became known by default as the Multi-Party Negotiating Process. This process culminated eight months later in the Plenary Session of the Negotiating Forum, that started in the late hours of 17 November 1993, and continued until the light dawned on the morning of the following day. Though subsequent working sessions would flesh out the details, the miracle deal was done, and the first democratic, inclusive elections would take place, as originally scheduled, on 27 April 1994.

In his closing address to the Plenary Session, President F W de Klerk recalled: 'Three years and ten months ago we began an historical process. It was based on the proposition that we could, through peaceful negotiation, bridge the chasms which for so many years have divided our people.' He reminded those who were anxious about the future, that they should not forget 'how desperate our situation was four years ago ... how implacable the enmity was ... how seemingly hopeless the prospect of finding any peaceful way out ...' He predicted that future generations would look back to this event and say: 'Yes, it was on this day that we laid the foundation for a new South African nation. Yes, it was on this day that we created a basis for good hope, for this, and for future generations of our people.'

Nelson Mandela responded: 'We have reached the end of an era. We are at the beginning of a new era.' He also addressed those who felt themselves excluded, alienated and afraid of the future. 'To them we say: you have a place in our country. You have a right to raise your fears and your concerns. We, for our part, are committed to giving you the opportunity to bring forth those views so that they may be addressed within the framework of a democracy.' He concluded with this vision: 'Together, we can build a society free of violence. We can build a society grounded on friendship and our common humanity – a society founded on tolerance. That is the only road open to us. It is a road to a glorious future in this beautiful country of ours. Let us join hands and march into the future.'

Index